TWENTY-FIRST CENTURY MUSICALS

Twenty-First Century Musicals stakes a place for the musical in today's cinematic landscape, taking a look at leading contemporary shows from their stage origins to their big-screen adaptations.

Each chapter offers a new perspective on a single musical, challenging populist narratives and exploring underlying narratives and sub-texts in depth. Themes of national identity; race, class and gender; the 'voice' and 'singing live' on film; authenticity; camp sensibilities; and the celebration of failure are addressed in a series of questions including:

- How does the film adaptation provide a different viewing experience from the stage version?
- What themes are highlighted in the film adaptation?
- What does the new casting bring to the work?
- Do camera angles dictate a different reading from the stage version?
- What is lost/gained in the process of adaptation to film?

Re-interpreting the contemporary film musical as a compelling art form, *Twenty-First Century Musicals* is a must-read for any student or scholar keen to broaden their understanding of musical performance.

George Rodosthenous is Associate Professor in Theatre Directing at the School of Performance and Cultural Industries, University of Leeds, UK.

TWENTY-FIRST CENTURY MUSICALS

From Stage to Screen

Edited by
George Rodosthenous

Routledge
Taylor & Francis Group

LONDON AND NEW YORK

First published 2018
by Routledge
2 Park Square, Milton Park, Abingdon, Oxon OX14 4RN

and by Routledge
711 Third Avenue, New York, NY 10017

Routledge is an imprint of the Taylor & Francis Group, an informa business

British Library Cataloguing-in-Publication Data
A catalogue record for this book is available from the British Library

Library of Congress Cataloging-in-Publication Data
Names: Rodosthenous, George, 1973- author.
Title: Twenty-first century musicals : from stage to screen / George Rodosthenous.
Description: Abingdon, Oxon ; New York, NY : Routledge, 2017. | Includes bibliographical references.
Identifiers: LCCN 2017013965| ISBN 9781138648906 (hardback) | ISBN 9781138648890 (pbk.) | ISBN 9781315626123 (ebook)
Subjects: LCSH: Musicals--21st century--History and criticism.
Classification: LCC ML1706 .R63 2017 | DDC 782.1/4--dc23
LC record available at https://lccn.loc.gov/2017013965

ISBN: 978-1-138-64890-6 (hbk)
ISBN: 978-1-138-64889-0 (pbk)
ISBN: 978-1-315-62612-3 (ebk)

Typeset in Bembo
by Saxon Graphics Ltd, Derby

CONTENTS

FIGURES

CONTRIBUTORS

Sarah Browne is Head of Music and Principal Lecturer at the University of Wolverhampton. She has worked extensively as conductor, arranger and musical director. Her research interests include the politics of race and gender in musical theatre, American musical theatre of the 1960s, and stage-to-screen transitions of musicals. Previous work includes a number of papers and book chapters on British revivals of the American canon, the male gaze in film musicals, the music of *Hamilton*, and the musical *Hair*, which was the primary focus of Sarah's doctoral thesis.

Todd Decker is Professor of Music and Chair of the Music Department at Washington University. He has published four books on American popular music and media: *Hymns for the Fallen: Combat Movie Music and Sound after Vietnam* (California, 2017), *Who Should Sing Ol' Man River?: The Lives of an American Song* (Oxford, 2015), *Show Boat: Performing Race in an American Musical* (Oxford, 2013) and *Music Makes Me: Fred Astaire and Jazz* (California, 2011). Decker has lectured on the stage and screen musical at the Library of Congress and London's Victoria and Albert Museum. In autumn 2016 he was a visiting International Chair at Labex Arts-H2H, a humanities centre at Université Paris 8.

Robert Gordon is Professor of Theatre and Performance and Director of the Pinter Research Centre at Goldsmiths, University of London, where he established the first MA in Europe in Musical Theatre for writers and producers. His publications include *The Purpose of Playing* (2006), *Pinter's Theatre of Power* (2012), and *The Oxford Handbook of Sondheim Studies* (2014). An actor, director and playwright who has worked in South Africa, Ireland, USA, Italy, Czech Republic and the UK, he has recently completed the book for a children's musical and is co-author of *British Musical Theatre since 1950* (Bloomsbury, 2016) and *The Oxford Handbook of the British Musical* (OUP, 2016).

Olaf Jubin is Reader in Media Studies and Musical Theatre at Regent's University London and Associate Lecturer on the MA in Musical Theatre at Goldsmiths, University of London. He gained his PhD from the Ruhr-Universität Bochum, Germany and has written and co-edited several books on the mass media and musical theatre, including a study of the German dubbing and subtitling of Hollywood musicals and a comparative analysis of reviews of the musicals of Stephen Sondheim and Andrew Lloyd Webber. Among his recent publications as co-author and co-editor are *British Musical Theatre Since 1950* (Bloomsbury, 2016) and *The Oxford Handbook of the British Musical* (Oxford University Press, 2016).

Helen Deborah Lewis is an Assistant Professor in the Theater Division at The Boston Conservatory at Berklee in Boston, Massachusetts. Her research focuses on musical theatre, popular entertainment, queer theory and historiography, and gay urban culture. Recently she was a featured speaker on the pedagogy of drag history and performance at the Tedx-Berklee Conference in Valencia, Spain. Lewis holds a Ph.D. from Tufts University.

Linda Mokdad is an Assistant Professor of Film and English, and the Director of the Film Studies programme at St. Olaf College, Minnesota. She is co-editor of *The International Film Musical* (Edinburgh University Press, 2012) and is currently finishing a book on post-9/11 American cinema (under contract with Rutgers University Press). Her teaching and research topics are diverse, and include everything from classical Hollywood to world cinema.

Arthur Pritchard is a retired Senior Teaching Fellow in the School of Performance and Cultural Industries of the University of Leeds. He is co-founder with Mike Casey of Plain Quakers, a touring theatre company that explores themes of economic and social justice by re-telling historical Quaker stories from a contemporary perspective. He has co-written and performed *Nine Parts a Quaker* on Thomas Clarkson's work to end the slave trade; *On Human Folly* about the American anti-slavery campaigner John Woolman's 1772 visit to England; and *The Chocolate Paradox* about ethical issues in the sourcing of cocoa. The most recent project *For Conscience Sake* considers conscientious objection in The Great War beside present-day militarism in education. The company has given over 250 performances in the United Kingdom, Ireland, The Netherlands and France.

George Rodosthenous is Associate Professor in Theatre Directing at the School of Performance and Cultural Industries, University of Leeds. His research interests are the body in performance, refining improvisational techniques and compositional practices for performance, devising pieces with live musical soundscapes as interdisciplinary process, theatre directing, updating Greek tragedy and the British musical. He has edited the books *Theatre as Voyeurism: the Pleasures of Watching* (Palgrave), *Contemporary Approaches to Greek Tragedy:*

Auteurship and Directorial Visions (Bloomsbury Methuen Drama) and *The Disney Musical on Stage and Screen: Critical Approaches from* Snow White *to* Frozen (Bloomsbury Methuen Drama).

Mark Shields is a graduate of the University of Leeds (2011) and the Royal Central School of Speech and Drama (2016). His research interests include queer theory and actor training pedagogy, verbatim theatre techniques and practices, and research ethics. Mark has worked as an educator and activist with the HIV community for the past eleven years, holding positions at the Terrence Higgins Trust, the leading HIV and sexual health charity in the UK, and as a member of the AIDS Coalition To Unleash Power (ACT UP), London. Mark is currently a visiting lecturer at the Royal Central School of Speech and Drama.

Tim Stephenson is Senior Lecturer at the University of Leeds in Creative and Cultural Industries (Socio-political Analysis of the Performing Arts, Cultural Analysis of Musical Theatre and the Management of Performance). His career in higher education has encompassed the Universities of Westminster, Northumbria, Bretton Hall and Leeds, fulfilling various roles from Head of School, through Dean of Faculty, to Director of Teaching and Research. Tim trained initially as a professional musician (percussionist and composer) and maintains a musical career alongside research and teaching, which now focuses on the theory and practice of cultural management and the socio-political analysis of the performing arts, with a particular focus upon musicals and music theatre. Recently he has published on *Hair*, *Mary Poppins* and the work of Stephen Sondheim.

Jessica Sternfeld (Ph.D. Princeton 2002) specializes in the cultural work of stage, film, and TV musicals of the last fifty years. Her book *The Megamusical* (2006) explored the reception history of blockbusters of the 1980s. Her work appears in *The Cambridge Companion to the Musical*, *The Oxford Handbook of the American Musical*, *The Oxford Handbook of Music and Disability Studies*, and the journal *Studies in Musical Theatre*. She is co-editing, with Elizabeth Wollman, *The Routledge Companion to the Contemporary American Stage Musical*, the first interdisciplinary collection focusing on recent repertoire. She also has a book forthcoming that focuses on musicals and presentations of trauma. She is Associate Professor and Director of the BA in Music at Chapman University in Orange, California.

Dominic Symonds is Reader in Drama at the University of Lincoln, UK. He is joint editor of *Studies in Musical Theatre* and co-founder of the conference series 'Song, Stage and Screen'. From 2010–2014 he was co-convenor of the Music Theatre Working Group of the International Federation for Theatre Research. His monograph *We'll Have Manhattan: the Early Work of Rodgers and Hart* (2015) is part of OUP's 'Broadway Legacies' series; meanwhile, his book *Broadway Rhythm: Imaging the City in Song* is forthcoming with University of Michigan Press (2017).

Other publications include *The Legacy of Opera: Reading Music Theatre as Experience and Performance* (Rodopi, 2013), *Gestures of Music Theater: The Performativity of Song and Dance* (OUP, 2013), and *Studying Musical Theatre: Theory and Practice* (Palgrave Macmillan, 2014). He is also a co-editor of the book series Palgrave Studies in British Musical Theatre (Palgrave Macmillan) and Critical Perspectives in Musical Theatre (OUP).

Sarah Whitfield is a Senior Lecturer in Musical Theatre, practitioner and academic, and course leader for the MA in Musical Theatre at the University of Wolverhampton. She writes about musical theatre history with a particular focus on uncovering the work that women do, and reconsiderations of race, gender and sexuality in the genre. As a dramaturg she has collaborated and advised on a range of projects from site-specific immersive theatre to West End musicals. Her PhD thesis proposed a cultural materialist approach to revealing collaborative practices in musical theatre, with a focus on the projects that Kurt Weill became involved with after his exile to New York. She has published work on rethinking the labour of composition in musical theatre; Sondheim and contemporary music theatre; and on feminist readings of *Frozen*. She is editing a forthcoming collection *Re-framing the Musical: Race, Culture and Identity*, to be published by Palgrave Macmillan in 2018.

Julian Woolford is a British theatre director, playwright and lyricist, based in the UK and working internationally. He is currently the Head of Musical Theatre at Guildford School of Acting at the University of Surrey. Julian's plays and musicals have been produced in the UK, the USA, the Netherlands, New Zealand and Bermuda and he has directed productions in the West End, off-Broadway, Germany, Australia, Poland, Holland and Austria. In 2015 he became the first person to direct a commercial musical in Egypt when he staged *The Sound of Music* in a tent in the desert outside Cairo. Julian is the author of *How Musicals Work* (Nick Hern Books) and a forthcoming book in Routledge's The Fourth Wall Series on *The Sound of Music*.

Demetris Zavros is a Senior Lecturer in Drama and Course Leader of BA Acting at the University of Wolverhampton. He teaches across the BA Drama, BA Acting and the MA in Contemporary Theatre and Performance. Demetris is research group depute for CCHIP (Centre for Creativity, History and Identity in Performance). His research interests lie in the areas of contemporary theatre and performance praxis; postdramatic theatre; composed theatre and musical dramaturgies; and intermedial theatre practices and Practice-as-Research methodologies. Zavros has a special interest in verbatim (musical) theatre (aesthetics and politics) and is currently involved in a PaR project exploring intermediality and compositional practice in site-specific verbatim musical theatre for Pafos 2017 European Capital of Culture. He has published in the areas of composed theatre, Jan Fabre, postdramatic music theatre, and music-centric re-conceptualisations of myth in theatre and performance (through practice and publication). He is Associate Director of the theatre company Altitude North and has also worked as a freelance composer for the theatre internationally. In 2012 he received the Best Music Award for *Electra and Orestes: The Trial* (THOC).

ACKNOWLEDGMENTS

I would like to thank Ben Piggott at Routledge for his genuine interest in my research on Musical Theatre, Kate Edwards and the editorial team at Routledge for all their help and guidance towards the final steps of the publishing process.

I am grateful to all the contributors of the volume for their excellent contributions and working together to ensure the smooth publication of this volume. I also need to thank Dr Duška Radosavljević for her feedback on the initial proposal and constructive presence in everything I do.

Sincere thanks to the editors of *Studies in Musical Theatre*, Dr Dominic Symonds and Dr George Burrows; the members of the Music Theatre Working Group of the International Federation of Theatre Research for all their feedback, discussions and encouragement throughout the years; Arthur Pritchard for his guidance in the past fifteen years; Dr Tim Stephenson for our inspiring co-teaching on the 'Exploring the Musical' modules; Ms Susan Daniels, Professor Alice O'Grady, Dr Joslin McKinney, Professor Jonathan Pitches, Dr Scott Palmer, Dr Kara McKechnie, Dr Fiona Bannon, Dr Tony Gardner, Dr Philip Kiszely, Dr Ben Walmsley, Dr David Shearing, Dr Anna Fenemore, Steve Ansell and all my colleagues, technical and support staff, stage@leeds and students at the School of Performance and Cultural Industries for their support.

Additional thanks to Professor Barry Keith Grant, Professor Robert Gordon, Dr Olaf Jubin, Dr Demetris Zavros, Dr Angela Hadjipanteli, Georgea Solomontos, Varnavas Kyriazis, Stergios Mavrikis, Jordan James Taylor, Dave Wright, Kate Hughes, Kelli Zezulka, Michael Fentiman, Michalis Christodoulou, Dimitri Biniaris, Scott Harris, Todd Cijunelis, Joel Jenkins, Tom Colley, Rebecca Young, Patrick Bannon, Jon Dean, Sheila Howarth, Nikolai Foster, the West Yorkshire Playhouse, the cast and creative team of *Body Faded Blue* at the Theatrical Organization of Cyprus (THOC), and all the performers I worked with for helping me develop and shape my directorial practice in Musical Theatre. Special thanks to

Biddy Hayward and Mike Markiewicz at ArenaPAL for their tireless help regarding the photographic material and Ken Cerniglia at Disney Theatrical Group.

I would like to thank my sister Marina Rodosthenous and my brother Nektarios Rodosthenous for their continuous support of my work. And, finally, my mother Aphrodite and my late father Andreas who generously introduced me to the pleasures of musical theatre.

Dr George Rodosthenous

Associate Professor in Theatre Directing

FOREWORD

Barry Keith Grant

There may be fewer musicals today than in the past, but they are as important now as they have ever been. True, the golden ages of the Broadway stage musical and the Hollywood film musical may be gone. The great songwriters are no longer producing great tunes, and in the cinema Hollywood is producing fewer musicals than before, certainly fewer than during the classical era when the studios, as one historian of the genre has written, ground them out like sausages. During the period of the New Hollywood in the 1970s, with few exceptions male cinephile auteurs concentrated on the 'masculine' genres of the western, horror, and gangster and crime film while virtually ignoring the musical. It has never recovered its dominant place in the genre system since.

In today's uncertain and dangerous world, perhaps audiences find it more difficult to be charmed by song and dance. Yet musicals continue to loom large in the cultural landscape. Some, like *Mamma Mia!*, *The Phantom of the Opera* and *Beauty and the Beast*, for example, are now fully ensconced in popular culture, no longer merely theatrical productions but, as the hyperbolic publicity for blockbuster movies is fond of putting it, significant events. Musicals today, such as those mentioned above, often participate in, and are part of, larger cultural mega-texts: each belongs to a larger network generated by a cultural property comprised of multiple texts in a range of cultural forms, including various forms of print, recorded and live music, a panoply of merchandising possibilities and, of course, film adaptation.

For this reason musicals are at the centre of the evolving structures of cultural production, distribution and consumption within today's corporate and globalized cultural industries. As media corporations have merged in recent decades, franchise synergies have become an increasingly important and defining feature of the contemporary mediascape. Narratives, characters and concepts migrate across a range of media forms and platforms, and fans follow the developing 'universe' of properties while media producers gain increased brand awareness. Just as the stage musical and cinema are hybrid forms, a transmedia confluence of cultural forms, so film adaptations of stage musicals are by their nature an essential component of contemporary transmedia and convergence culture.

The musical should be of more interest to scholars than has been the case. While there has been a more or less steady trickle of work on the genre for decades, some contributing greatly to our understanding of its history and ideology and the workings of the genre system, the musical hasn't enjoyed nearly the same degree of attention as, say, westerns, science fiction or horror. When the musical film is discussed, scholars today sometime seem more interested in the cultural signification of sound design and the various levels of the soundtrack than in detailed explication of specific musicals and their life across media. Given the increasing transmediality of musicals in the twenty-first century, the musical film adaptation offers a potentially rich but thus far largely unexamined area of study.

George Rodosthenous' *Twenty-First Century Musicals: From Stage to Screen* is thus an especially timely and welcome book. The first scholarly collection to focus on film musicals adapted from the stage, the book brings together scholars with the kind of interdisciplinary knowledge required to understand musicals today. In these pages the authors discuss the most important musicals since the millennium. And in doing so, they reveal a keen understanding of multiple areas of cultural studies including, but not limited to, camp, popular music, gender studies, and adaptation theory. At the same time they make a major contribution by remaining sensitive to, and appreciative of, the particulars of both theatre and cinema as distinct and different expressive forms.

INTRODUCTION

George Rodosthenous

The key area of investigation of *Twenty-First Century Musicals: From Stage to Screen* is to understand the different ways that the film adaptations provide new contexts, layers and dimensions of meaning. The volume aims to revisit the genre by discussing fifteen case studies of film musicals from the early twenty-first century that have been adapted from the stage. How does each case study make the 'move' from a work of stage musical theatre to the medium of film? The authors provide detailed and extremely articulate critical analyses of the works, in juxtaposition with issues of drag, camp, race, identity and performativity, satire, irony and failure. Cari McDonnell's extensive survey, 'Genre Theory and the Film Musical' in the *Oxford Handbook of Film Music Studies* identifies some gaps in the study of the film musical and suggests that new academic writing should cover these unrepresented areas of 'style, structure, and specific musical makeup of performance', 'the relationship between character and star persona' and 'the genre's relationship with the popular music industry and the star system' (McDonnell 2014: 245). Through the range of case studies, this book aims to address other under-represented areas and also answer some of the questions raised above.

After *Dancer in the Dark* (2000) and *Moulin Rouge* (2001) the film musical changed for ever. In the former, the songs became the only moments of happiness in a sombre narrative that, despite paying homage to the classic *The Sound of Music*, usurped the traditional narrative formula, concluding in the gloomy Bjorkian despair of the execution of a coerced murderess. Along the way, its infamous director Lars von Trier broke nearly every single rule from the Dogme 95 Vows of Chastity. In *Moulin Rouge* we had the opposite: an excess of spectacle, innovative treatments of well-known songs ('Like a Virgin' by the Duke) and flirtations with Bollywood ('Hindi Sad Diamonds'). Its excesses redefined entertainment and star casting, and brought MTV and reality show TV culture to the forefront of the film musical. These novelties have affected the way musicals are created and experienced ever since.

The case studies offer narratives that develop our understanding of the traditional norms of film musicals, which stem from the Golden Age of the film musical and reach to the works produced at the end of the twentieth century. Barry Keith Grant, in the Foreword to this volume, reminds us that '[j]ust as the stage musical and cinema are hybrid forms, a transmedia confluence of cultural forms, so film adaptations of stage musicals are by nature an essential component of contemporary transmedia and convergence culture' (xvi). And it is this hybridity that essentially makes binary discussions ineffectual. In the film musicals produced since the beginning of the millennium, relationships no longer have to conform to the dual boy meets girl formula (Dyer 2002), and non-heteronormative narratives emerge (*Rent*) featuring characters who were originally marginalised (*Hedwig*). Impressive female personas achieve emancipation (*Chicago*) and liberated taverna-owners are having fun on Greek islands (*Mamma Mia!*), while original classics such as *Phantom of the Opera* and *Sweeney Todd* are reinvigorated through receiving the full post-millennial cinematic treatment. The aesthetic of the musical becomes heavily politicised (*Dreamgirls*) and important racial issues are no longer overlooked but explored in depth (*Hairspray*). The theme of disaster becomes a structural device to create new narratives in *Nine* and *The Producers*, and even if the end products of the film versions have themselves proved to be non-commercial successes, the formula of rags to riches is now challenged. The jukebox musical gains a new heightened role within the production of *The Jersey Boys*, while film companies such as Disney take risks by exploring dark, adult Sondheim works that were previously regarded as solely suitable for the stage (*Into the Woods*). Perceptions of time are also challenged in works such as *The Last Five Years*, where linear narratives are reversed and juxtaposed, while multiple adaptations of works such as *Annie* from TV to stage and film and then vice versa provide a platform for new, diverse readings. Finally, the twenty-first-century revolution abandons traditional melody completely and uses speech patterns and intonations to provide the vocal lines for new verbatim works such as *London Road*, where the lyrics, pitch and rhythm are constructed entirely from everyday spoken utterances.

These revolutions in narrative, sexual and racial politics, linear representation and thematic content give us the opportunity to see the musical in a different light. The structural revolutions (in the musical's form) are intimately connected to the thematic considerations and politics of musical theatre performance, including the politics of its reception. Mike Alfreds writes about the power of the theatre: 'During a performance, we are all growing old together, actors, audience – and characters. The transience of theatre is part of its uniqueness, its poignancy. As soon as it's happened, it's gone' (Alfreds 2007: 18). The 'transplantation' into the new medium inadvertently invites a discussion of the resulting aesthetics and audience reception, as well as politics. This is yet another gap in the literature that is expanded upon by the chapters of this book. The millennial generation has been raised on Disney musicals and *Glee*, so it comes as no surprise to anybody of that age group when people on screen suddenly burst out singing and dancing. Indeed, they expect characters to burst out singing and dancing, which contradicts

FIGURE 0.1 Catherine Zeta-Jones as Velma Kelly in *Chicago*.

Dyer's (1979) earlier writings about the ontology of the film musical (Dyer 2012). One cannot underestimate the effect of reality competition shows and the television series *Glee* (as well as *Smash*) and this revitalised, positive-effect attitude towards musicals. The shift is reflected in the attitudes towards works that are now designed for younger audiences (*Billy Elliot*, *Frozen*, *Matilda*, *The Lion King* and *Wicked*). In the same way, the presence of political statements is evidently more prominent. Musical theatre is not just mere entertainment – it never was. But when it deals with immigrants, deaths of prostitutes, AIDS, weight issues, racial issues and deformity, then it transforms into a powerful tool for political change.

Twenty-First Century Musicals: From Stage to Screen endeavours to provide multiple perspectives on key film musicals of the twenty-first century, to unlock hidden narratives and sub-texts that are evident in the film adaptations, to critique and expose the differences of the film adaptations in relation to the original stage works, and to offer new insights and contexts. All the authors were prompted to tackle the same research questions covering areas such as:

- How does the film adaptation provide a different viewing experience from the stage version?
- What themes are highlighted in the film adaptation?
- What does the new casting bring to the work?
- Do camera angles dictate a different reading from the stage version?
- What is lost/gained in the process of adaptation to film?

Contemporary trends in the film musical genre

Since the beginning of the century other works, such as *Newsies* (2011), *Frozen* (2013) and *Mrs Henderson Presents* (2015), have undergone a reverse process, making the transition from screen to the stage. New original film musicals such as *Moulin Rouge* and *Dancer in the Dark* are not included in this volume because they fall outside its scope. Other notable absences are *Les Misérables* (2012), the sensitive Scottish musical that received a filmic adaptation in *Sunshine on Leith* (2013), the eagerly awaited forthcoming *Wicked* (directed by Stephen Daldry) and *Miss Saigon* (directed by Danny Boyle); all will hopefully be included in a second volume covering work up to 2020. During the period discussed in this book there has also been a television adaptation of *South Pacific* (2001), headed by the feisty Glenn Close, and NBC's *The Sound of Music Live!* (2013), *Peter Pan Live!* (2014), *The Wiz Live!* (2015), *Hairspray Live!* (2016), and Fox's *Grease Live!* (2016). In addition, there has been a musical biopic of Cole Porter's life in which most of his songs get new, inventive orchestrations and are performed by a star-led cast in *De-Lovely* (2004).

Billy Elliot (2005) became a musical after being a successful film, and that is also the case with the folk musical *Once* (2006), which started as a low-budget film. The *High School Musical* TV musicals enjoyed huge financial success, and in 2007 Julie Taymor used a young, unknown cast and divided the critics in *Across the Universe*, perhaps the most successful attempt to create a jukebox film musical. She 'elevated the film "jukebox musical" genre into a panorama of filmic abundance through a barrage of visual surprises and inventions that characterize her own recklessly extravagant directorial style, thus inspiring the makers of the stage and television musicals of the future' (Rodosthenous 2014: 52). This also relates to the notion of 'ghosting' and how this has a very real impact on our perception of the 'real' in experiencing musical theatre (see Rodosthenous 2014). *Fame* received an

FIGURE 0.2 Ensemble cast in *Across the Universe* (2007).

Credit: Collection Christophel/ArenaPAL

unmemorable remake in 2009, and Cher starred in the song-packed *Burlesque* (2010), while *Walking on Sunshine* (2014) is a glaring example of a banal jukebox musical that was instantly forgettable.

In a detailed discussion of the Disney musical elsewhere,[1] I suggest that

> Disney has been around for over ninety years, so it is possible that some audiences associate watching a Disney musical with how they felt when they (or their parents, or grandparents, or great grandparents) first encountered the source material. This creates an invaluable dynamic: the nostalgia of reimagining one's childhood.
>
> (Rodosthenous 2017: 12)

Disney's live-action *Beauty and the Beast* (2017), directed by Bill Condon, will be followed by 22 more live-action movies of its animated classics.

With the regular production of 'filmed live versions' of musicals such as *Love Never Dies* (2010), *Billy Elliot* (2014), *Gypsy* (2015), *Miss Saigon* (2016) and Disney's *Newsies* (2017), the producers take on the 'challenge of translating stage to screen to create premium theatrical content'.[2] The filmed production of *Newsies* (see Figure 0.3) had an original three-day cinematic release, which took $3.47 million at the box office[3] and will be released digitally and on demand, thus providing a

FIGURE 0.3 The cast of Disney's *Newsies* from the filmed live version.

Photo © Disney

new digital form of engagement with the work. Steam Motion and Sound managed to deliver stage versions of musical theatre to its audience, shot and finished in 4K. Its co-founder Brett Sullivan reflects that

> [i]t's got to be filmic because it's going to be projected onto a big screen, but it also has to feel like live entertainment … Those two worlds can be hard to reconcile. Often in live cuts, the cameras are all at the back of the room and you feel removed from the action. We want to get close, so close that you can see into the eyes of the actors. When you see the eyes of actors on the screen, the story becomes much deeper.[4]

And as *The Stage* reviewer Mark Shenton remarks, the audiences get some additional bonus shots: 'Once or twice, we also get a view no theatre audience would get, as the camera observes the action from above.'[5]

A plethora of new film musicals is being prepared, or are rumoured to be in development for the immediate future, which proves that the revised interest in the film musical genre continues unabated. Film adaptations in progress include the musicals *Hello Again* (an adaptation of Michael John LaChiusa's musical based on Arthur Schnitzler's *La Ronde*), *Mamma Mia!: Here We Go Again!*, *West Side Story* (Steven Spielberg), *South Pacific* (Michael Mayer), *Oliver* (Toby Haynes), *Guys and Dolls* (Michael Grandage), Jason Robert Brown's *13*, plus *American Idiot*, *Beautiful: The Carole King Musical*, *Cats*, *Finding Neverland*, *Gypsy*, *In the Heights*, *Jekyll &*

Hyde, Joseph and the Amazing Technicolor Dreamcoat, Little Shop of Horrors, Lysistrata Jones, Matilda, Memphis, Pippin, Spring Awakening and *Sunset Boulevard*.[6]

In discussing the creative teams of the (film) musical, the contributors to this book expose the issue of gender inequality. Out of the fifteen case studies it becomes clear that the film musical world remains stubbornly patriarchal and male dominated, with only two film musicals being directed by women (interestingly, both of them are directed by the original stage director: Phyllida Lloyd for *Mamma Mia!* and Susan Stroman for *The Producers*). All the composers of the film musicals discussed here are male.[7] What is also noteworthy is the inclusion of British stage directors in the film musical-making canon. One of the most eagerly awaited new film musicals, *Wicked*, is directed by eminent British stage director Stephen Daldry. In addition, Michael Grandage, another celebrated British director, will be responsible for Disney's stage version of *Frozen*.

Celebrity casting has always been a major part of film musicals. There were some fortunate surprises in *Moulin Rouge*, with both Ewan McGregor and Nicole Kidman singing wonderfully – but this trend has led to some embarrassing moments in the recent history of the film musical. It must be really frustrating for triple threat actors to see major films being cast with celebrities who cannot sing, at least at the standard audiences are used to in stage productions of musicals. While the work's artistic integrity may have been slightly compromised, the decision will be justified by the box office benefits. Even so, die-hard fans of Russell Crowe walked out when they realised *Les Misérables* was not an action film but a musical. With *Nine*, not even the decision to cast seven female celebrities managed to save the film from being regarded as a financial and critical catastrophe.

Film musicals usually operate in linear time fashion, using flash-forwards/backs and (day-)dream sequences as a means to disrupt this conformity. While in *Merrily We Roll Along* the whole narrative is presented backwards, this is still an exception to the canon. Only a few other composers have experimented with non-linear and experimental time narratives, most notably found in concept musicals. *The Last Five Years* is a fine example of mixing the timescales of the two protagonists and presenting them in opposing time (Jason Robert Brown was inspired by his mentor's *Merrily We Roll Along*). This device gets an even more complex treatment in the film version, as discussed by Sarah Browne in Chapter 12.

Back in 1951, *Singin' in the Rain* exposed, and made comedy from, one of the film making techniques used extensively: dubbing the voice. And there are plenty of examples where the actual actor the audience sees on the screen is not the one whose voice the audience is actually hearing.[8] Tom Hooper's adaptation of *Les Misérables*, though, has brought a double revolution. The singing takes place live during the filming, so that moment is captured live. This process removes the divide between voice and image, 'severing the body from the voice' (Dyer 2012: 16), and provides new opportunities for discussion, evaluation and analysis.

Live singing was a common practice in some of the first movie musicals (*Love Me Tonight, The Gay Divorcee*), but the idea of capturing the image and the voice live still offers a closer, intensely intimate and perhaps more authentic single performance than the obvious attempt to lip-sync to an existing pre-recorded soundtrack. According to Mordden, it offers 'a solution to a problem almost as old as the talkie itself: how to project above all dramatic music when the actors aren't being musically dramatic during the actual shooting' (Mordden 2016: 223). Demetris Zavros discusses this further in his chapter on *London Road* and concludes that it tries to capture (but actually inescapably fails to capture) the 'reality of the moment' and its 'transient quality' by not resorting to the more 'traditional dubbing of the singing'. In addition, he comments on the fact that the ensemble numbers sung by the chorus are occasionally treated through rather intimate sound localisations (effectively, extreme sound 'close-ups' coupled with their visual counterparts) as we focus down to a particular performer's voice within the ensemble sound. This last technique produces 'an illusion of a (hyper) "realistic" approach and also acts as a faint reminder of performing these pieces live' (Zavros: 224).

The notion of 'faithfulness' in the adaptation, and the departure from it, can take different guises in the case of a cross-medial adaptation. But this is an essential part of the discussion in the book. Zavros is suggesting that the adaptation needs to use the new medium's aesthetics to get to the core of the politics of the original performance (and perhaps how this is not completely achieved in the case of *London Road*). What counts as 'failure' or 'success' in the adaptation is not exhausted at the box office. As film critic Andrew Lapin asserts,

> Musicals excite senses and erase distances, and audiences shouldn't need to be weeded out for them. The walkouts […] could be a blessing in disguise: They're an excellent opportunity to rid the landscape of such knee-jerk aversion to the form, and start critical dialogue about a place for musicals in today's cinematic ecosystem. Maybe a few walkouts are just what this genre needs to check in.
>
> (Lapin 2015)

Existing academic writing: identifying the gaps

Admittedly, academic writing about (film) musicals has gained momentum in recent years. Alongside the *Studies in Musical Theatre* journal, a number of new books and anthologies have been published addressing current issues in musical theatre. Previously, the study of the film musical paralleled film criticism of the 1980s and focused, as Altman stated, on auteurship, ideology, structuralism, ritual and technology (Altman 1981). More recently, the musical has been discussed in terms of film music analysis (Cochran 1990, Cook 1998), dual focus narrative (Altman 1987), theories of adaptation (Hutcheon 2006), the self-reflexivity of the musical (Feuer 1977, Altman 1987), gender (Dolan 1993, Fischer 2000, Wolf 2002, 2011), representation (Farmer 2000, Dyer 2002, 2012), narrative subtexts and performativity (Symonds and Taylor 2014), ideology (Feuer 1977), politics

(Siropoulos 2010), utopianism (Dyer 2002), cultural fusion and impact (Ladkin 2014), and globalisation of culture (Rebellato 2009). Hillier and Pye (2011: 3) confirm that '[n]egotiating the relationships between narrative and number and between various levels of artifice became second nature to the musical'. This has been the most constant framework that has utilised binary oppositions to conceptualise the aesthetics of musical theatre (narrative/number, reality/ imaginary, escapist/utopian space). It is important to distinguish between lyric and book time, and McMillin's *The Musical as Drama* study (2006) clarifies the distinction. In our current study, we also incorporate critical analyses that depart from and interrogate these models that have focused on the juxtaposition between binary oppositions/orders of time/performative layers/senses and sensibilities. On the performativity of music theatre, Symonds' and Taylor's volume *Gestures of Music Theater: The Performativity of Song and Dance* (2014) is another recent work that provides a focus to song and dance and how they contribute to performances beyond narrative.

Altman's seminal 1987 study divides the film musical genre into three types: the fairy tale musical, the show (backstage) musical and the folk musical. I would like to suggest some more categories, such as community musical, verbatim musical, biographical musical, the unhappy-ending musical and the musical celebrating failure. The contributors to the present anthology explore issues beyond the genre's 'vulnerability' (Dyer 2012: 2) or 'transcendence' (Altman 1987: 66–67) and allow for a critical analysis of the film musical's aesthetics, propensity to failure and intense interconnection with the original stage work's theatricality. Through the adaptation process the new work becomes an intertextual puzzle of forensically identifying the original material. Farmer separates the genre's individual qualities and notes the

> exceedingly complex signifying formations, made of literally thousands of texts and intertexts, including most obviously the films themselves and their myriad structural interrelations as well as the wide range of interreferential discourses that circulate around and help constitute genre films – advertisements, studio publicity, critical reviews popular and academic studies, fan discourses, and so on. This (over)abundant intertextuality means that the genres are sites of a radical semiotic polysemy, a plurality of meanings, replete with all the complexities, discrepancies, contradictions, and possibilities of variable interpretation that this entails.
>
> (Farmer 2000: 70)

In his essay *Entertainment and Utopia* (1977), Dyer encouraged us to view musicals through both representational and non-representational signs such as colour, texture, movement, rhythm, melody and camerawork. The critical analyses in this book will build upon Dyer's later work *In the Space of a Song* (2012) and Cohan (2002), as well as work by Altman (1987), Grant (2012), Kessler (2010) and Smith (2005). According to McDonnell,

> the musical narrative's structure attempts to resolve two diametrically opposed poles. These poles may be represented by the male and female numbers of a romantic couple (Schatz, Altman), work and entertainment (Altman; Feuer; Dyer), narrative and number (Dyer), performers and spectators (Feuer), of fantasy and reality (Feuer; Dyer).
>
> (McDonnell 2014: 249)

These concerns are applied to contemporary musicals and developed further, especially when they deviate from narrative structure and traditional musical theatre approaches to form (*The Last Five Years*, *London Road*, etc.).

> Film musicals typically present their song-and/or-dance numbers in an imaginary space, even if this space is ostensibly a real location, and contained within a narrative framework. While other genres may construct a space distinctly their own … only the musical depicts its space as charmed by the magic of performance, where anyone and everyone may burst into magnificent, breathtaking song and dance in order to give unhindered expression to their emotions.
>
> (Grant 2012: 1–2)

FIGURE 0.4 Anna Kendrick as Cinderella and Emily Blunt as Baker's Wife in *Into the Woods*.

Credit: Peter Mountain/Disney Enterprises/DR/Collection Christophel/ArenaPAL.

For Scott McMillin, the interruption of the narrative is akin to Greek tragedy and what he calls 'the second order of time, which interrupts book time in the form of songs and dances' (2006: 7).

Barrios celebrates the nature of musicals by asserting that they are 'balanced unsteadily between the sublime and the inane … They can indeed bring that joy, yet it is their fate and nature to be precarious, with vastly rewarding rhythms that are ceaselessly in danger of failure' (Barrios 2014: 4). And in Ethan Mordden's latest offering, *When Broadway Went to Hollywood*, the discussion of *Into the Woods* culminates in the statement that 'everyone we see is from the same time and place, with no intrusions from the modern world, in accordance with a newish rule in the filming of concept musicals: the meta-theatricality must be tamed. Or let's just say "naturalized"' (Mordden 2016: 227). Finally, the forthcoming *Contemporary Musical Film* will be the latest literature dealing with the genre's aesthetics through a range of conventional and unconventional works released since the turn of the millennium. What became evidently clear in our investigation is that there is no real overlap between film audiences and musical theatre audiences. This tome will cover the gaps in existing literature and provide a new way of thinking of film musicals as works of sincere and serious political complexity, beyond utopia and entertainment.

Structure of the book

The fifteen case studies are presented chronologically rather than thematically (except for *Sweeney Todd*, which is a joint discussion with *Into the Woods*), and this allows for an organic unfolding of the developments in the genre and its interconnections and intertextual references. In the fourteen chapters of this collection, each case study will address the processes of adaptation from stage to screen and focus on one or two specific aspects of the film musical version (critically analysing the differences from the original). The authors of these studies highlight how many of these works were financial, critical and artistic failures, and sometimes allude to the fact that they were 'too faithful' to the original stage version. The anthology wants to consider whether there are certain trends in this 'move' from one medium to another and to portray the directorial choices as catalysts for new meaning, including both semantic and affective layers. It is the specific relationship between the semantic and affective potential of the musical theatre aesthetic that affords it such a special political power. Byci (2002) attempts to unpick this by introducing the idea of 'musical sensibility', which connects to Langer's (1954) 'unconsummated symbol'.[9] The film medium, with its new set of aesthetic considerations, needs to always recalibrate that balance anew. And this is what this study investigates, through the multiple perspectives and approaches that characterise its case studies.

Dominic Symonds opens the volume with his examination of *Hedwig and the Angry Inch* in which he interrogates in-betweenness, gender and national identity, as well as the 'ambivalence that characterizes post-millennial identity' (19). He offers a rich contextualisation of drag in performance and links it to issues of transition, sincerity and pastiche, and integration and transformation. The extremely successful and Oscar-winning *Chicago* is the focus of Robert Gordon's contribution, in which he identifies the difficulties of transferring material from stage to screen. He analyses these in relation to the work's inherent vaudeville qualities and intense meta-theatricality, which involves satire, cynicism, trauma, distancing, and the real and imaginary worlds presented. Gordon positions the film musical as a gangster film and proposes that Roxie's escapist fantasy is more central than in the stage version and that the film's emphasis shifts away from satire. Jessica Sternfeld's discussion of *The Phantom of the Opera* gives us some great insights into the specific and explicit differences between the portrayal of the Phantom on stage and screen. In doing so, she introduces issues of disfigurement, 'expectations and stigmas about disability' (54) , the erasure of the Phantom's magical powers and the addition of a backstory, and supports these with detailed examples from the stage and screen versions. New York City and the history of AIDS form the backbone of Mark Shields' chapter on *Rent*, which traces how the audience's reception can be seen in a post 9/11 context. This rich contextualisation allows the reader to parallel the 'physical gentrification of New York City' with a 'gentrification of the mind' (70). Themes of personal experience, representation and nostalgia are juxtaposed with the film version, in which audiences' expectations are fulfilled but not transcended.

The fifth chapter is dedicated to *The Producers*, and Julian Woolford argues that part of the screen version's commercial and critical failure was due to its slavish faithfulness to the stage version. In this context, he considers the extended intertextual engagements with the original and how commercial success affects re-mediation. Woolford reads the work as a meta-musical comedy and links it to the aftershock of 9/11, suggesting that imaginative adaptations can perhaps be more successful in a highly commercialised business ecology. Todd Decker evaluates differences in the performance of gender, blackness and popular music in *Dreamgirls*. The focus of his argument is on dancing black masculinity and how this was toned down in the film version, as well as vocal contrasts that are lost in the film. He indicates that the film eliminated the sung dialogue and that the omission of the male dancing is linked to some of the casting decisions (Jamie Foxx), thus diminishing the power of the original stage work. Linda Mokdad continues with a chapter on music, sexuality and race in *Hairspray*. She bases her analysis on history and race, and how in the film the camp aesthetics 'do not fully sustain its irony or distance to history, privileging a conclusion that … diminishes a political critique of the form' (115). In examining the use of space in the musical she addresses issues of marginalisation, boundaries and parody.

Mamma Mia! is the first jukebox musical to be discussed here. Helen Lewis engages with notions of camp, kitsch and fluff and associates these with the film version. She compares the wedding scenes with those in another film (*Muriel's Wedding*) and offers a queer reading of the work by highlighting its camp potential. Thus, Lewis views the three principal female roles as camp because they can be read as 'surrogate drag queens' (130). *Nine* is the focus of investigation for Arthur

Pritchard, who takes a closer look at representations of women and how Fellini's *8½* was an important source of adaptation. Celebrity casting is another area of discussion here, as well as the disruption of dramatic narrative with the inclusion of dream sequences, backstage narratives and nostalgia. Pritchard ends his chapter with a consideration of artistic failure as a creative stimulus and suggests that the film embraces the 'vulnerability of failure' (146). Sarah Whitfield addresses representations of masculinity in the second jukebox musical of the volume, *Jersey Boys*, and explains that director Clint Eastwood (an icon of masculinity) actually removes the musical from the musical in an anti-theatrical way. The author questions the kind of masculinity presented in the film version of the musical in relation to the hegemonic masculinity of the band. She postulates that '[i]n attempting to minimise theatricality from a film adaptation of a musical, Eastwood reveals the fundamental workings of a jukebox musical' (160).

Moral disambiguation and rectitude are the main themes of Tim Stephenson's dual contribution that covers both *Into the Woods* and *Sweeney Todd*. In a critical way the author chronicles the journey of Sondheim's work from concept musicals to horror works and fairy tales and exposes the symmetries with *Into the Woods*. He reminds us that in the transition from stage to screen all the chorus sections in *Sweeney Todd* were lost. Stephenson aptly problematises Sondheim's changing position in the musical theatre canon and emphasises the composer's willingness to adapt in order to find 'an appropriate balance between the commercial necessities of the genre' (176). Sarah Browne, in the twelfth chapter, provides an analysis of *The Last Five Years* and its use of reverse chronology in its storytelling. The screen director's approach to the musical is considered in relation to the medium of film (its signifiers and contexts), modes of filmmaking, and how these decisions impact on the viewer. Browne observes that the film version brings 'new dimensions to the character of Cathy', and that this film version 'fills the gaps of the stage production' (191). In his evaluation of *Annie*, Olaf Jubin explains why some film musicals are bound to fail. He records how one of the most successful stage musicals failed to have a commercially successful screen adaptation (citing the 1982, 1999 and 2014 versions) and concentrates on issues of casting, creative teams, and the use of 'realism'. His critique is associated with consumerist and neoliberal trends, offering new contexts in viewing the work.

Demetris Zavros identifies *London Road* as a verbatim musical in which the re-composition of the everyday allows a new approach to musical theatre's relationship to the 'real'. In the final chapter of the anthology, the film adaptation of this extraordinary work is examined through the lenses of reality and construct, ghosting celebrity and cinematic tracing of the speech/song continuum, and the number and narrative context. Zavros stresses that there is no promise of utopia in the film version and that '[t]he ontology of the verbatim musical allows for a significant new reconceptualization of the possibilities engendered in the form, not only in terms of a shift in aesthetics, but also the resulting political engagement' (226).

In the twenty-first century, the film (movie) musical does not strictly adhere to the traditional canon. It deviates both thematically and structurally, providing new avenues and possibilities. There are, of course, overlaps with existing narratives, but the introduction of film musicals about (auto)biographical work (verbatim), the community (which goes beyond the traditional backstage chorus) and unhappy endings (intrinsically linked with failure) are now emerging as part of the genre. No other study addresses this 'move' in depth, and thus it is hoped that this edited collection will contribute significant findings to the genre of the contemporary film musical.

As Barry Keith Grant writes in his Foreword (xvi),

> The first scholarly collection to focus on film musicals adapted from the stage, the book brings together scholars with the kind of interdisciplinary knowledge required to understand musicals today. ... [T]hey reveal a keen understanding of multiple areas of cultural studies including, but not limited to, camp, popular music, gender studies, and adaptation theory. At the same time they make a major contribution by remaining sensitive to, and appreciative of, the particulars of both theatre and cinema as distinct and different expressive forms.

The book discusses how artistic choices are sometimes defined by commercial decisions that are an integral part of the creation and marketing of each work. The breadth of contributions covers the range of research interests of the authors but also maintains the common, unifying theme of adaptation as a multi-layered process seeking contemporary resonance.

Notes

1   This volume does not include a discussion of Disney's animated film musicals and their huge impact on children and their personal development. Regarding film musical animations and, specifically, the Disney musical, please see *The Disney Musical on Stage and Screen: Critical Approaches from* Snow White *to* Frozen (Rodosthenous 2017).

2   www.steammotionandsound.com/#about-section. Accessed 1 May 2017.

3   See www.playbill.com/article/the-filmed-production-of-newsies-will-be-released-digitally-and-on-demand. Accessed 1 May 2017.

4   www.broadcastbeat.com/sullivan-and-jacobsen-deliver-disneys-newsies-the-broadway-musical/. Accessed 1 May 2017.

5   www.thestage.co.uk/reviews/2017/film-review-disneys-newsies-broadway-musical/. Accessed 1 May 2017.

6   www.whatsonstage.com/london-theatre/news/13-musicals-set-for-movie-film-adaptations_42992.htmlandwww.playbill.com/article/schedule-of-upcoming-movie-musical-adaptations-com-216487.

7   Even though the volume discusses gender representations in detail and offers new insights into the character of the works themselves, there is still more work to be done in discussing the gender imbalance in the creative teams of musical theatre. Is it still a closed-shop only for men? Three of the films discussed are directed by Rob Marshall, who is also working on *Mary Poppins Returns* (2018).

8   See *West Side Story* and *The King and I* amongst others and the Marni Nixon example as well.

9   Thanks to Demetris Zavros for pointing this out in conversation.

Bibliography

Alfreds, Mike (2007). *Different Every Night: Freeing the Actor*. London: Nick Hern Books.

Altman, Rick (1987). *The American Film Musical*. Bloomington: Indiana University Press.

Altman, Rick (ed.) (1981). *Genre: The Musical*. London: Routledge.

Babington, B. and Evans, P.W. (1985). *Blue Skies and Silver Linings: Aspects of the Hollywood Musical*. Manchester: Manchester University Press.

Barrios, Richard (1995). *A Song in the Dark: The Birth of the Musical Film*. New York: Oxford University Press.

Barrios, Richard (2014). *Dangerous Rhythm: Why Movie Musicals Matter*. New York: Oxford University Press.

Carroll, Rachel (2009). *Adaptation in Contemporary Culture: Textual Infidelities*. London and New York: Continuum.

Carlson, Marvin (2003). *The Haunted Stage: The Theatre as Memory Machine*. Ann Arbor: University of Michigan Press.

Cochran, Alfred W. (1990). 'The Spear of Cephalus: Observations on Film Music Analysis.' *Indiana Theory Review* 11, pp. 65–80.

Cohan, Steven (ed.) (2001). *Hollywood Musicals: The Film Reader*. London: Routledge.

Cook, Nicholas (1998). *Analysing Musical Multimedia*. Oxford: Clarendon Press.

Creekmur, Corey K. and Mokdad, Linda Y. (eds) (2012). *The International Film Musical*. Edinburgh: Edinburgh University Press.

Dolan, Jill (1993). *Presence and Desire: Essays on Gender, Sexuality, Performance*. Ann Arbor: University of Michigan Press.

Donnelly, Kevin J. and Carroll, Beth (eds) (2017). *Contemporary Musical Film*. Edinburgh: Edinburgh University Press.

Dunne, Michael (2004). *American Film Musical Themes and Forms*. Jefferson: McFarland.

Dyer, Richard (1979). *Stars*. London: British Film Institute.

Dyer, Richard ([1992] 2002). *Only Entertainment*. London: Routledge.

Dyer, Richard (2012). *In The Space Of A Song: The Uses of Song in Film*. New York: Routledge.

Farmer, Brett, (2000). *Spectacular Passions: Cinema, Fantasy, Gay Male Spectatorships*. Durham, NC: Duke University Press.

Feuer, Jane (1977). 'The Self-reflective Musical and the Myth of Entertainment.' *Quarterly Review of Film Studies* 2(3), pp. 313–326.

Fischer, Agneta H. (ed.) (2000). *Gender and emotion: Social psychological perspectives*. Cambridge:

Gewirtzman, David (2017). 'Schedule of Upcoming Movie Musical Adaptations.' *Playbill*; www.playbill.com/article/schedule-of-upcoming-movie-musical-adaptations-com-216487. Accessed 13 March 2017.

Grant, Barry Keith (2012). *The Hollywood Film Musical*. New Approaches to Film Genre vol. 9. Oxford: John Wiley & Sons.

Grishakova, Marina and Ryan, Marie-Laure (eds) (2010). *Intermediality and Storytelling*. Boston: de Gruyter.

Hillier, Jim and Pye, Douglas (2011). *100 Film Musicals*. 1st edn. New York: Palgrave Macmillan.

Hutcheon, Linda (2006). *A Theory of Adaptation*. New York: Routledge.

Kessler, Kelly (2010). *Destabilizing the Hollywood Musical: Music, Masculinity and Mayhem*. Basingstoke: Palgrave Macmillan.

Kislan, Richard (1995). *The Musical: A Look at the American Musical Theater*. New York, London: Applause, p. 245.

Knapp, Raymond (2005). *The American Musical and the Formation of National Identity*. Princeton, Oxford: Princeton University Press.

Knapp, Raymond (2006). *The American Musical and the Performance of Personal Identity*. Princeton, Oxford: Princeton University Press.

Ladkin, Sam (2014). *AHRC Critical Review – Against Value in the Arts*. Sheffield: The University of Sheffield.

Langer, Susanne K. (1954) *Philosophy in a New Key*. New York: The New American Library, p. 195.

Lapin, Andrew (2015). '21st-century musicals still haven't found a way out of the woods.' *The Dissolve*, https://thedissolve.com/features/exposition/876-2014s-musicals-might-just-save-us-all/. Accessed 13 March 2017.

Marshall, B. and Stilwell, R. (eds) (2000). *Musicals: Hollywood and Beyond*. Exeter: Intellect.

McDonnell, Cari (2014). 'Genre Theory and the Film Musical.' In David Neumeyer (ed.), *The Oxford Handbook of Film Music Studies*. Oxford, New York: Oxford University Press.

McMillin, Scott (2006). *The Musical as Drama: A Study of the Principles and Conventions behind Musical Shows from Kern to Sondheim*. Princeton: Princeton University Press.

Mordden, Ethan (2004). *The Happiest Corpse I've Ever Seen: The Last 25 Years of the Broadway Musical*. New York: Palgrave Macmillan.

Mordden, Ethan (2013). *Anything Goes: A History of American Musical Theatre*. Oxford: Oxford University Press.

Mordden, Ethan (2016). *When Broadway Went to Hollywood*. Oxford: Oxford University Press.

Neale, Steve (2000). *Genre and Hollywood*. London: Routledge.

O'Hanlon, Dom (2017). 'La La Land – a Movie Musical for the Modern Age.' www.londontheatre.co.uk/theatre-news/west-end-features/la-la-land-a-movie-musical-for-the-modern-age. Accessed 13 March 2017.

Rebellato, D. (2009). *Theatre & Globalization*. Basingstoke: Palgrave Macmillan.

Rodosthenous, George (2014). 'Relocating the Song: Julie Taymor's Jukebox Musical, *Across the Universe* (2007).' In D. Symonds and M. Taylor (eds), *Gestures of Music Theater: The Performativity of Song and Dance*. New York: Oxford University Press, pp. 41–53.

Rodosthenous, George (2016). 'Mamma Mia! and the Aesthetics of the 21st Century Jukebox Musical Genre.' In Robert Gordon and Olaf Jubin (eds), *The Oxford Handbook of the British Musical*. Oxford, New York: Oxford University Press.

Rodosthenous, George (2017). *The Disney Musical on Stage and Screen: Critical Approaches from Snow White to Frozen*. London and New York: Bloomsbury Methuen Drama.

Roesner, David (2016). 'Genre Counterpoints: Challenges to the Mainstream Musical.' In Robert Gordon and Olaf Jubin (eds), *The Oxford Handbook of the British Musical*. Oxford, New York: Oxford University Press.

Sanders, Julie (2006). *Adaptation and Appropriation*. London: Routledge.

Savran, David (2004). 'Towards a Historiography of the Popular.' *Theatre Survey* 45(2), pp. 211–217. doi:10.1017/S004055740400016X.

Schatz, Thomas (1981). *Hollywood Genres*. New York: McGraw Hill.

Siropoulos, Vagelis (2011). 'Megamusicals, spectacle and the postdramatic aesthetics of late capitalism.' *Studies in Musical Theatre* 5(1), pp. 13–34, doi: 10.1386/smt.5.1.13_1.

Smith, Susan (2005). *The Musical: Race, Gender and Performance.* London: Wallflower.

Symonds, Dominic and Taylor, Millie (eds) (2014) *Gestures of Music Theater: The Performativity of Song and Dance.* New York: Oxford University Press.

Taylor, Millie (2010). 'Experiencing Live Musical Theatre Performance: *La Cage Aux Folles* and *Priscilla, Queen of the Desert.*' *Popular Entertainment Studies* 1(1), pp. 44–58.

Taylor, Millie (2012). *Musical Theatre, Realism and Entertainment.* Basingstoke: Ashgate.

Wolf, Stacy (2002). *A Problem Like Maria: Gender and Sexuality in the American Musical.* Triangulations: Lesbian/Gay/Queer Theater/Drama/Performance. Ann Arbor: University of Michigan Press.

Wolf, Stacy (2011). *Changed for Good: A Feminist History of the Broadway Musical.* New York: Oxford University Press.

1

DRAG, ROCK, AUTHENTICITY AND IN-BETWEENNESS

Hedwig and the Angry Inch

Dominic Symonds

It is appropriate that a book about twenty-first century musical film should begin with a discussion of *Hedwig and the Angry Inch* (2001). Prior to the new millennium, the last few decades had seen a steady decline in the volume of film musicals being produced, so *Hedwig* – along with a handful of other movies such as *The Adventures of Priscilla, Queen of the Desert* (1994), *Dancer in the Dark* (2000), and *Moulin Rouge* (2001) – symbolically marked a comeback. While its independent origins, modest budget and limited release meant that the film's status was marginal, it made up for this with the stomping beat of its glam-punk score, the provocative identity politics of its storyline, and the forceful charisma of its platinum-drag title character. This is a story in which the characters are misfits and outsiders; not just marginalized, but 'at the margins of a margin', as Rosa Salazar has observed; yet 'in this story', she writes, 'the margin bangs at the center through an appropriation of the center's methods' (Salazar 2004: 70). Like many queer texts, *Hedwig and the Angry Inch* reoriented the page; and in doing so it thrust the film musical boldly onto twenty-first century cinema screens.

In this chapter I am going to explore how *Hedwig and the Angry Inch*, both as a text and a phenomenon, invigorates a thematic motif of 'in-betweenness'. Not only does Hedwig herself occupy an in-between position in terms of her gender identity, but she exists, as many scholars have noted, as a geographically in-between character in terms of her national identity. More than this, *Hedwig* as a musical occupies a curious position 'between' a number of different performance tropes and forms – notably those of the drag act and the rock concert on stage, and the rockumentary and reality TV on film. Still more, as a phenomenon *Hedwig* appeared at a poignant transitional moment in the turn from one millennium to the next, which also marked a shift between structural and post-structural preferences in culture. From the moment Hedwig is introduced to us in her band-member Yitschak's opening announcement, that theme of in-betweenness is confirmed:

'Ladies and gentlemen, Hedwig is like that wall, standing before you in the divide between east and west, slavery and freedom, man and woman, top and bottom.'

First, I will use a Deleuzean framework to introduce the notion of in-betweenness in *Hedwig*; then I will consider a number of in-between spaces that are magnified by the film's implied identity as a rockumentary. I will suggest that *Hedwig* blurs boundaries of drag/rock, authenticity/artifice, sincerity/pastiche, celebrity/ordinariness, fantasy/autobiography and gender/transition. In doing so, it articulates and embodies an ambivalence that characterizes post-millennial identity.

Hedwig and the Angry Inch on stage

Hedwig developed first as a stage musical conceived by John Cameron Mitchell and Stephen Trask. It had its beginnings in the early 1990s on the LGBT drag scene, but quickly gained cult status when it moved off-Broadway in 1998. By the early 2000s it was enjoying success internationally with productions in London's West End (2000), at the Edinburgh Festival (2001), in Toronto (2001), Berlin (2002) and at the Signature Theatre just outside Washington DC (2001–2002). But it wasn't until 2014 that *Hedwig* triumphantly returned to New York for its much-vaunted Broadway premiere, marking the acceptance of a show that had taken almost two decades to transition to the mainstream.

John Cameron Mitchell first met composer and rock musician Stephen Trask on a flight from LA to New York. Mitchell was already developing ideas, and Trask encouraged him to test material at New York drag club, Squeezebox!, where his band Cheater was the resident entertainment. Thus Hedwig was born as a drag act, at first performing cover versions of songs by David Bowie, Velvet Underground and others in the glam-punk scene. Gradually, lyrics changed to tell the story of an East-German émigré's migration to the US. As the show developed, Trask began to write an original score, and by 1998 a full-scale musical had been put together. The show, a pseudo-autobiography told through the schtick and songs of Hedwig and her band, was staged off-off-Broadway in the jaded ex-ballroom of the Riverview Hotel in Manhattan's West Village.

In her narrative, Hedwig recounts her story of growing up as Hansel, a young boy in East Berlin in the sixties who longs for the freedoms of Western life. Aged eighteen, he falls in love with an American GI posted in Berlin and is promised a new life in America. The sacrifice Hansel must make is to undergo a sex-change operation to become Ludwig's legitimate wife, Hedwig. When the operation is botched, Hedwig is left without genitalia and with the scarred 'angry inch' of the title. Soon afterwards, Ludwig ditches Hedwig and leaves her stranded in a Kansas trailer park, left to survive on babysitting and occasional prostitution. But in the meantime, Hedwig begins to perform, fronting the glam-punk band Hedwig and the Angry Inch. Through music, she falls in love with the teenage Tommy Speck and the two begin a troubled affair, played out through the songs Hedwig writes for him. Eventually, Tommy discovers the intimate secrets of Hedwig's gender identity and panics in horror. He goes on to become the international rock star

Tommy Gnosis, stealing Hedwig's songs and filling stadia while Hedwig and her mediocre band follow him around the country. Desperate to connect with Tommy, whom she poetically sees as her Platonic other half, Hedwig's narrative is a bitter account of her experience in becoming who she is.[1]

The notion of 'becoming' is a mainstay in the writings of Gilles Deleuze and Félix Guattari, whose work in general encourages us to reconceptualise the way we think about the world. For them – like most post-structuralists – conventional thought is problematic, leading to hierarchies and hegemony through its commitment to an ideology of progress. It is through such thinking that distinctions emerge between, for example, the mainstream and the marginal or, more simply, male and female; and anything falling in-between is simply not represented. 'How can one still identify and name things if they have lost the strata that qualified them …?', they ask.[2] Unconstituted, in a state Deleuze and Guattari call 'deterritorialized', anyone in-between is vulnerable to redefining by others and as Others. 'Outside the strata or in the absence of strata', they write, 'we no longer have forms or substances, organization or development, content or expression. We are disarticulated; we no longer seem to be sustained by rhythms.'[3]

The language Deleuze and Guattari use borrows significantly from ideas of place, employing terms like 'territorialization' and 'strata'. In theorizing ideas of in-betweenness, then, the most apparent points of reference relate to concepts of migration and belonging in a globalized world of nation states. These are certainly concepts germane to the narrative of *Hedwig and the Angry Inch* and the identity of

FIGURE 1.1 John Cameron Mitchell as Hedwig/Hansel Schmidt in *Hedwig*.

Credit: Collection Christophel/ArenaPAL.

Hedwig in transitioning from East to West. However, one of the virtues of Deleuze and Guattari's work is that it is easily transferable to other domains, and thus the identity of Hedwig in transitioning – and getting stranded – 'in-between' genders can also be viewed through their lens. Indeed, as Mat Fournier has argued, 'In the same way that spatiality for Deleuze and Guattari escapes the historical narratives produced by the state apparatus, the queer body disrupts the normative temporality controlling individual lives' (Fournier 2014: 45). Thus, 'Deleuze and Guattari's concern for biopolitics puts them in an interesting relationship with queer theory' (ibid.: 48).

The process towards reterritorialization is something they classify as a 'becoming'. Thus rather than being *in* a static existence, Hedwig's positioning 'in-between' various states of identity becomes transitive, always transitioning towards something. Yet importantly, Deleuze and Guattari also conceptualise this deterritorialization process as one that is 'disarticulated', suggesting that it is through articulating themselves that these 'Others' might be re-identified, reterritorialized. For becoming-Hedwig, whose transition from one State (and one state) to another is just such a deterritorialization, the re-articulation comes in the form of music, and the drag persona she adopts in both her onstage and offstage life.

Autobiographical glimpses: a performative journey towards identity

Drag evolved in part as a form of gay expression, standing as a metaphor for the masquerade historically enforced on homosexual behaviour through prohibition, social taboo or personal discretion. Principally performed by men dressed as women, drag is a popular performance form in gay urban communities.[4] Performances usually take the format of stand-up routines interspersed with songs, and adhere closely to the traditional performances of cross-dressing variety acts. Comic material often involves sexual innuendo, sometimes quite lewd in nature, and often draws attention to the gender charade at play; song material often draws similar attention to the charade by lip-synching to the recorded voices of torch singers such as Judy Garland or Bette Midler. As such, identities of gender and sexuality are writ large in the performance of drag, and the exploration of both in *Hedwig*'s own dramaturgy enables a focussed if rather self-conscious discussion to emerge.

In terms of musical theatre – which has traditionally favoured mainstream and conventional identity tropes – drag has remained a rather marginalised idiom, though there have been some important examples of drag identity in recent high profile shows. Most notably, drag hit Broadway with the romantic comedy *La Cage aux Folles* in 1983. Here, although the authenticity of drag identity was pronounced in the torch song 'I Am What I Am', in the end *La Cage* presents a muted challenge to gender identities, relationships and performance, with its central characters maintaining a rather clandestine alternative lifestyle. Thirteen years later, Jonathan Larson's *Rent* (1996) provided a smorgasbord of rather more open gender and identity types, including the ambiguous character Ariel who issues his own 'I am what I am' provocation in 'Take Me or Leave Me' ('Take me for what I am'). Ariel's slippage between genders and identities is further explored as he flits between life, death and rebirth in the musical's second act. This creates an interesting and highly stylised encounter with drag, calling on many intertextual layers that reference in-betweenness in everything from the music to the ethereality of the character's name.

Since *Rent*'s self-consciously postmodern take on drag in the run up to the Millennium, musical theatre has seen two other significant drag outings, now played with the irony of camp excess: *Priscilla, Queen of the Desert*, an adaptation of the 1994 film, originated in Sydney (2006) and then London (2009) before being mounted on Broadway by none other than Bette Midler in 2011; this was an unapologetic romp through the back catalogue of diva torchsongs and disco hits, with a Tony-award-winning costume design by Tim Chappel and Lizzy Gardiner. Meanwhile, Cyndi Lauper's *Kinky Boots* (2012) established its entire storyline around a boot factory owner who designs a special line of kinky boots for use by men in drag. Creating ample opportunity for the plot to be punctuated by kitsch and exuberant drag routines, this show was undoubtedly a camp success, though in terms of identity it was ironically built on the framework of an utterly conventional (straight) romance.

Drag is nothing if not a deliberately self-conscious performance of gender; and, like the platinum blonde persona of Hedwig, the drag characters performed are typically provocative and excessive in that conscious display. On the one hand, this defines drag as always an overt display of artifice; on the other hand, the forceful encounter of its queer performances also highlights the personal quest for an authentic self. In dressing up as women, drag queens are not (usually) trying to 'keep the illusion of being women', as Verta Taylor and Leila J. Rupp write, but instead to 'break it in order to accentuate the inherently performative nature of gender and sexual meanings' (Taylor and Rupp 2009: 115). And a sense of in-betweenness is key: 'Dragging up tends to involve a playful combination of traditional masculine and feminine signifiers, or the artful transcendence of established gender categories towards the performance of some kind of trans-human entity', suggests Gavin Brown (2009: 201). 'One of the main functions of drag performance', writes Rusty Barrett, 'is to expose the disunity between perceived or performed identity and underlying "authentic" biographical identity' (Barrett 1999: 316). Put in other terms, this exposure might be of the Otherness between the strata from which one is deterritorializing and towards which one is becoming.

Thus the performativity of drag foregrounds a dialogue of in-betweenness in its very act of performance, and in doing so it differs intrinsically from the conventions of dramatic performance. Although the performer is playing a character, and therefore acting in one sense of the word, drag performance does not establish the same relationship between performer and character. Where dramatic performance typically involves a suspension of our disbelief and a willingness to see actor and character as essentially different, drag requires us to see both as an amalgam of the performance identity. In contrast to dramatic performance, the artifice and the authentic cannot be so easily distinguished in terms of a binary, causing a particular awareness of the 'disunity' to which Barrett refers existing within the performative self of the individual.

This in-betweenness is not just a dynamic related to identity, but is woven into the practices and expectations of the performance act of drag itself. As in comedy, there is slippage between organised structure and improvised play; as in musical theatre, there is usually slippage between dialogue and song; as in cabaret, the mode of delivery slips between direct audience address and the bubble of performance; as in contemporary performance practice, there is an ambivalent relationship with notions of character, drama or script; and above all, the identity of the performer slips continuously within the blurred space of self-and-character.

Indeed, if there is one thing that stands out in *Hedwig and the Angry Inch* – especially now that the show has evolved over twenty years to become a cult show winning John Cameron Mitchell a coveted Tony award – it is that the subject of *Hedwig* and the identity of Hedwig is as much an embodiment of its creator as it is the projection of a character. *Hedwig* was originally rooted in an autobiographical account of Mitchell's own life,[5] and although we might simplistically follow the exploits of Hedwig and her band, the crossover between different identities, modes of engagement and styles of performance is so multi-layered that the person who is revealed in the end is a hybrid of all these personalities, including that of Mitchell himself.[6]

Given this complexity and the different nuances of these performative dynamics, it is hard to extract the performer's identity from the iconicity of the character, as if the entire performance is a demonstration of the becoming-Hedwig that the deterritorialized Mitchell seeks to find. Since Hedwig the iconic blonde of the film is also a complex amalgam of Hedwig the singer, Hansel the boy, and Helga the muse,[7] and since Mitchell's own identity has over time become a complex amalgam of unknown actor, cult writer/director/performer, recognisable celebrity, and (most recently) Special Tony Award winner (2015), the blurred identity he adopts in his performance as Hedwig is in almost every sense multiply defined and in-between. For the audience it is difficult – however rewarding – to follow the complex quest of Hedwig/Helga/Hansel/Mitchell in finding his/her/their true identity and authentic story. If this enigmatic identity seems to challenge conventions of character and performer, it also seems appropriate for a show emerging against a backdrop of post-identity politics, an aesthetic of post-dramatic performance, and a cultural landscape of celebrity and reality TV.

Owner of Squeezebox! Michael Schmidt comments on the tricky handling of this performative state for anyone unfamiliar with drag:

> At first, I was skeptical. John [Cameron Mitchell] was not an experienced drag performer and I wasn't keen on the idea of my stage being used to workshop an untested act. I was concerned the other drag and transgender entertainers wouldn't tolerate an actor who wasn't really interested in being

one of them. I explained that these other performers' drag personae were an extension of their lives, that they make their livelihoods from entertaining in drag, and that they take their craft extremely seriously. I told him essentially that this couldn't be a lark for him. He couldn't play Hedwig; he had to be Hedwig.

(Michael Schmidt in Wood 2014)

Stylistically, the real truth of drag identity is often explicitly exposed as the drag queen unmasks, at times by removing elements of costume such as the wig or false breasts; at other times by showing the application of make-up to effect a transformational act (consider 'A Little More Mascara' from *La Cage aux Folles*);[8] at still other times by refusing to adopt a female-gendered name (cf. Danny La Rue, Dave Lynn, Kevin Aviance), or even by confusing gender in the sporting of a beard (Conchita Wurst, Danny Beard). In these very acts, the idea of simplistic binaries of sexuality and gender are called into question, and the drag queen therefore inhabits a position that is consciously neither male nor female, straight or gay.[9] Hedwig sees herself as 'being in the middle of set categories'; 'a bridge, a connecting and necessary element', notes Rosa Salazar (2004: 77). Citing queer theory heavyweight Judith Butler, she sees this connecting middle-ground as integral to the 'vacillation between the categories' that is fundamentally implied by drag (ibid.: 75), and also fundamentally implied by the deterritorialized concept of becoming.

As it happens, Squeezebox! offered in itself a departure from conventional drag. Schmidt's whole premise in establishing the club had been 'a novel idea'. As the club's own account reports, performances were compèred by Mistress Formika, and involved 'drag queens dumping the lipsynching routine to sing rock and roll live onstage'; 'What began as a place for queer misfits who'd rather hear a guitar riff than a disco beat turned into a pansexual free-for-all. Straight or gay. Preppy or punk. Man or woman (or somewhere in-between). All were welcome at Squeezebox!' (Squeezebox! online)

Meanwhile, as a crossover between the aesthetics of musical theatre, punk and drag performance, *Hedwig and the Angry Inch* inhabits a similar in-betweenness, an ambiguous position that is reflected in its main themes. As we have seen, within its first few moments Hedwig is associated with this sort of ambiguity, 'standing before you in the divide between east and west, slavery and freedom, man and woman, top and bottom'. For some, this was an ambiguous status that was too challenging:

It was too rock and roll for the gay people and too gay for the rock and roll people … too music-y for the theater people and too theater-y for the music people. It was just in-between everything, in the same way that Hedwig is in-between genders.

(Michael Mayer in Wood 2014)

Between rockumentary and authenticity: Hedwig on film

Following cult success as a stage show, the writers signed with New Line Cinema and were given creative control over the development of the film. Mitchell adapted the screenplay, as well as directing and performing in the title role; Trask and the members of his band Cheater performed the supporting characters of Hedwig's punk band, the Angry Inch. Meanwhile, the actress Miriam Shor was cast as Hedwig's transgender lover Yitschak, another example of queering the production, offering a balancing character to Hedwig. The film was released in 2001, and despite modest takings at the box office, it went on to win a slew of awards, including Best Film at the Berlin International Film Festival and Best Director for John Cameron Mitchell at Robert Redford's Sundance Festival.

If the stage musical is presented as a cross between a drag act and a rock gig, with extended commentaries to the audience that narrate the story of Hedwig's life between songs, the film draws on other stylistic and narrative tropes from the rock world, particularly the rock documentary. *Hedwig* is set up as if a camera crew is following the small-scale tour of Hedwig and her band. We encounter them playing in a number of locations, most of them regional franchises of the Bilgewater restaurant chain. The band is not entirely unsuccessful – they have a press officer and a coterie of 'Hed-head' fans who follow the band around; but the captive audiences at the restaurants are uninterested and confused by Hedwig's drag-punk performances. In contrast to the rock star Tommy Gnosis, whose stadium tour Hedwig shadows, life on the road for the Angry Inch is unglamorous and often tense. Off-stage we see them in cramped motel rooms and caravan parks, replicating the sort of 'real-world' settings familiar from other rockumentaries. By way of illustrating the ongoing story Hedwig narrates about her life, the film flashes back periodically to her life as Hansel in East Berlin, her arrival as Hedwig in the US, and her early relationship with Tommy when he was still undiscovered and naive.

Establishing *Hedwig and the Angry Inch* as a rockumentary develops the rock concert premise of the stage show but taps into further aesthetics of the genre. Rock, on the face of it, could not be more dissimilar to drag. This is not so much in its performance of gender (which has been interestingly ambiguous throughout its development), but in its claim to be enabling the genuine voice of the rock star's authentic self. Rock status has traded on the degree of authenticity in the musician's performance, and this has become mythologized, as David Pattie remarks: 'the rock musician, as commonly implied, must be "real"; he or she must perform in such a way as to convey and confirm a sense of authentic investment in the music played' (Pattie 2007: vii). In the rockumentary form, magnified by the verité of a documentary style, access to privileged moments offstage and in private settings gives audiences the impression that they are encountering the real. Very often, grainy footage, black-and-white photography or hand-held camera shots add to the impression of exclusivity, intimacy and unmediated access. Such access to the reality of the rock lifestyle plays to the idea of the documentary being a 'truthful' genre, and it is implicitly in the moments away from the stage, away from the core reason for the rock star's status, that the greatest claim to finding the authenticity behind the star persona is often seen. According to Thomas F. Cohen, films like *What's Happening!: The Beatles in the USA* (1964),[10] capturing The Beatles' tour of America, and *Dont* [sic] *Look Back* (1965), following Bob Dylan's corresponding tour of Britain, 'established the rock documentary's form' (Cohen 2012: 55) as a blend of performance and intimate behind-the-scenes footage, and this is exactly what *Hedwig* offers, albeit in a fictionalized way. 'Paradoxically', writes Cohen of this type of film, 'truth is to be found off-stage rather than on' (ibid: 54), though he qualifies this assertion by acknowledging that both onstage and offstage portrayals of rock musicians are 'self-conscious presentations of their "true" selves' (ibid: 55). By the end of his discussion we deduce that any notion of stability is therefore called into question; any claim to authenticity is revealed as simply another performed trope.

Indeed, for all the impression of authenticity in rock music, the form is characterised by acts of very obvious performance, not to mention gendered play. Even if one aspect of rock is the overt masculinity of figures like Bruce Springsteen or Bryan Adams, rock's sexuality is itself blurred by a number of performative tropes: the sexualised use of guitars and microphones (Prince, Freddie Mercury); the ambiguous modalities of the body (Mick Jagger); the flamboyant and gender-bending costumes of certain performers (Elton John); the excessive manipulation of vocal registers (the Darkness); and in certain instances the actual use of cross-dressing personae (Alice Cooper, David Bowie, Marilyn Manson). Such complexities inevitably destabilize the identity of rock as a monovalent medium, and leave it very open to other manifestations of artifice and performative play. Moreover, the very fact that particular tropes have developed within the rockumentary genre as symbols of authenticity suggests a degree of coded artifice. The grainy footage, the mundane hotel rooms and the run-down streets indicative of the star's upbringing (consider U2) are all deliberately staged (however biographically accurate they might be). And – aside from the black-and-white aesthetic – *Hedwig* borrows all of these tropes in presenting an offstage world that is unglamorous, seedy and challenging.

The notion of truth – authenticity – is therefore positioned at the core of Hedwig's quest to understand herself, and the modes in which the film is delivered – the form of a rockumentary and the guise of a drag act – play against and with each other to address wider dynamics relating to authenticity. Drag implicitly questions the notion of an authentic (or at least monovalent) social self, yet the confessional delivery of the film's dialogue reveals candid (authentic) details about Hedwig's life, even while dismissing these through camp humour and carefree delivery. Meanwhile, the songs in their content explore ideas of emotional authenticity through music that trades on authentic expression. The soundtrack of *Hedwig and the Angry Inch* is eclectic, but within its diversity there is a notable lack of pop – a form often seen as inauthentic and the antithesis of rock. Instead, The Angry Inch's music stems from folk ('The Origin of Love') and punk ('Angry Inch'),[11] with the instrumentation of guitars rather than electronic or synthetic sounds. These styles, broadly categorised as derivatives of rock, have long claimed a sense of authenticity in comparison to pop. Some of the values on which that authenticity is based – notions of creativity, community, virtuosity, sincerity, politics, and anti-commercialism – can be seen very clearly in Hedwig's character, especially when she is compared to the dilettante Tommy. It is Hedwig, for example, who has written the songs that have made Tommy famous; she also creates her own musical sound by singing live rather than lip-synching, which in rock terms gives her authenticity as a musician. As Feffer reports, this authenticity is assisted in the way the film resists some of the conventions of pure drag: using punk as the signifier par excellence of truth, for example (Taylor 2009); filming the performance sequences live rather than over-dubbing them in the studio (Travers 2001: 70); using the implied veracity of site-specific performance rather than the implied artifice of a theatre (Feffer 2007: 241). Indeed, as Feffer argues, 'though Hedwig has had the sex change operation, and wears the wig and make-up', it is actually the character of Tommy (the straight white male) who 'appears as the inauthentic' (ibid.: 251).

Thus *Hedwig* combines a form that masquerades as artificial yet reveals an inner truth (drag), with another that claims authenticity yet constructs that authenticity through performance (rock); together, the aesthetics of drag and rock serve as performative idioms that magnify the tension of identity in this film. In the end, the lines between authenticity and artifice are more blurred than they may appear.

Between gender and transition: Hedwig's queer resolution

If this meeting of drag and rock creates a sort of yin and yang in the various ways in which we conceptualise their relationship, it is appropriate, and thematically modelled, in the central song 'The Origin of Love', which reflects the philosophy of *Hedwig*. Based on a story told by Aristophanes in Plato's *Symposium*, *Hedwig*'s most romantic song tells the story of how the Greek gods, in anger, split early mortals in half and cast their separated human bodies apart to be forever seeking their other half. In one sense, Hedwig's quest throughout the film is to find her other half – and she believes him to be Tommy Gnosis, which is why she trails him around the country. In Tommy, Hedwig finds her Platonic match, something for which the many motifs of in-betweenness have been preparing us throughout the film. More than this, though, the song is an allegory for the sort of identity Hedwig has in being neither man nor woman yet existing in-between. Thematically and symbolically, the song speaks for itself as voicing the emotional core of the musical and the transitional state of a becoming-identity. However, the brilliant conceit of the film in presenting this song is to move away from the aesthetic of the rockumentary to occupy a sort of dream-space indicated by the artifice of animation. As an illustrative accompaniment to the song, animator Emily Hubley created a primitive-style sequence of line animations that seem both childlike and profound. The beings from Plato's *Symposium* are clearly represented as jolly, rotund balls that morph as the independent identities of the separate half-beings are delineated as the traditional yin and yang symbols. Symbolically, this is a motif that represents both Hedwig's quest for completion and her identity of being already complete.

As John Cameron Mitchell has suggested, '[Hedwig is] more than a woman or a man. She's a gender of one and that is accidentally so beautiful' (Ouzounian 2014). In this sense, because of the three sexes of the early mortals (Children of the Sun, Earth and Moon), it's a story that lends itself to a queer philosophy: to Sharon Dean, the film positively 'emphasize[s] the playfulness of gender flux' rather than 'the angst of bi and trans gender confusion' (Dean 2006: 113); while to Salazar, 'the possible ways of desiring are slightly more open than those posited by the heterosexual matrix' (Salazar 2004: 72). If this reading of trans identity seems to open up the indeterminacy of identity even more ambiguously, without creating the chaos of confusion, it speaks to contemporary understandings of trans, which seek 'not to identify, consolidate, or stabilize a category'. Instead, write Susan Stryker, Paisley Currah and Lisa Jean Moore, '"Transing", in short, is a practice that takes place within, as well as across or between, gendered spaces' (Stryker, Currah and Moore 2008: 11, 13).

Between sincerity and pastiche: Hedwig and integration

With song serving as such a core thematic commentary on the emotional and narrative trajectories of this movie, it's clear that *Hedwig* is more aligned to the dramaturgy of the musical than that of the rockumentary. Unlike the songs of rockumentaries, or indeed, of other fictional rockumentary-style dramas such as *The Blues Brothers* (1980), *This is Spinal Tap* (1984) or *The Commitments* (1991), those of *Hedwig and the Angry Inch* are not just the playlist of the band. Instead they are fundamental to the drama in terms of their lyrics, their music, their performance and their purpose. This marks the film out as a musical rather than just a music film, and as Trask points out, is largely due to the dramaturgical background of Mitchell in conceiving the piece. 'To me, I write a neat song', Trask says, referring to his own work with Cheater and describing the typical approach to songs by (most) bands. 'I get up onstage, sing it and hope other people think it's a good song' (Fricke 1998: 56), he reports. A song in itself may have a narrative or trajectory, but the drama begins and ends within the unit of the song. By contrast, Mitchell's training as an actor meant that he 'needed a motivation' (ibid.) for each expression of the character, an instinct that informed both the placement and the performance of the songs within the narrative. This motivational impulse turns the songs into dynamic drivers whose lyrics, performance and musical style all contribute to the integration of the film.

Take 'Wig in a Box', which Peter Travers calls 'arguably the film's musical pinnacle' (Travers 2001: 70); the way the song is introduced into the drama is a clear example of integration. Left alone in a Kansas trailer park, Hedwig slumps onto her sofa-bed and reflects on whether any of her ordeal has been worthwhile: 'On nights like this', she sings plaintively, 'I get down, I feel had, I feel on the verge of going mad'. The music is sparse and introductory, a few piano chords idiomatically contributing an appropriate mood. After this preliminary verse, the tempo rises and Hedwig's resolution – to paper over her disappointment by dragging up – leads to a more up-beat refrain. A number of the other songs work in similar ways, introducing an appropriate mood-music from the drama of the scene before launching into the body of the song; the whole trajectory of the musical is also given an arc of resolution. In short, the structure of the piece in terms of its handling of the songs is dramaturgically that of an integrated musical, and therefore intrinsically different from the usual structuring of a rockumentary.

But it is also significant that there is anticipation in these opening bars, and no surprise when the song transitions into an upbeat refrain. We expect this because we have heard the device used many times before, and in trading on this sort of generic transition, *Hedwig* taps into the expectations of an audience immersed in the idioms of popular culture. (Just as rockumentaries tap into tropes of authenticity from popular culture.) Since we are familiar with the sort of material introduced at the beginning of the song, we recognise that its trajectory will lift into something stirring, reconciling, or emboldening.

The breathy vocals and plaintive piano accompaniment of 'Wig in a Box' shift as Hedwig makes her emotional and transformative transition into a far more defiant, glam-rock sound.[12] Yet here in the film the song also mischievously transforms, playing into the idiomatic camp of drag and deliberately juxtaposing the authenticity/integration of its opening with an overt display of artifice and pretence. By the time it gets going, the song has become a bouncy anthem, metatheatrically filmed to engage the audience in a singalong of its refrain: the band members' heads appear, framed in a window of their Kansas trailer, and they invite us to join in with the aid of on-screen lyrics and an animated bouncy wig telling us when to sing; then the whole side of the trailer hinges down to become a stage for their impromptu performance to a single fan in a field. The scene – like the film – oozes camp and self-deprecatory humour, fundamental characteristics of Hedwig and the ambivalent relationship she has with her band and her success, and characteristic too of the ambivalence of contemporary culture in slipping between sincerity and pastiche, and between the aesthetics of popular music and the musical. The song works on a number of levels and undoubtedly wears the trappings of pop videos, glam rock, drag and musical theatre on its flamboyant sleeves; yet by this stage it can hardly be considered an 'integrated' song. The same sort of analysis could be done for any number of songs throughout *Hedwig*, whose score is surprisingly strong in terms of integration yet consistently undermined by cinematic meta-devices that draw attention to the artifice.

Transformation: ambiguity, quest and becoming

It is in the final moments of the film that the real transformation, and at the same time the real blur between identities, takes place for Hedwig. In front of her audience, she rips off her wig and pulls away her clothes, daubs her forehead with a silver cross, and stands almost naked as what we take to be a man. 'Hedwig is thus transformed', writes Elizabeth Wollman, 'from a campy, second-rate glam act to an "authentic" rock artist who has shared herself so completely that (s)he becomes one with the audience' (Wollman 2006: 185). More than that, she becomes one with Tommy, the other half of her Platonic being whom she has been seeking throughout the narrative.

> He's the one. The one who was taken. The one who left. The twin born by fission. He'll die in fusion. Our fusion, cold fusion, unlimited power, unlimited knowledge… . The words to begin the sentence that began 'I am − '.
>
> (Mitchell and Trask 2014: 70)

I am what? Hedwig? Tommy? Or even John Cameron Mitchell? The question hangs in the air, as if articulating the many ambiguities that this film refuses to address. If Hedwig's realisation in this statement marks the fulfilment of her quest and a resolution to 'the angst of bi and trans gender confusion' (Dean 2006: 113), it is certainly not by selecting any of the binary positions of man, woman, straight or gay. Instead it is by situating Hedwig's identity fluidly in the middle ground, the terrain that has been established in querying the domains of authenticity/artifice, sincerity/pastiche, celebrity/ordinariness, fantasy/autobiography, and gender/transition.

Conclusions

It's perhaps not surprising that *Hedwig* has proven to be a popular movie at singalong events, often presented with a shadow cast performing live as the film is screened. In this intermedial guise, the sense of in-betweenness becomes even more magnified, with multiple identities performing the roles in ambiguous positions as spectators, shadows and performers. The format has been used before − notably with other queer texts such as *The Rocky Horror Picture Show*, which regularly screens singalong performances around the world. One cinema in Toronto even claims that this is 'the way [*Hedwig*] should be seen: big, loud and with hundreds of Hedheads singing along to every song' (Hedwig and the Angry Inch Singalong). At another event (see Ouzounian 2014), John Cameron Mitchell himself presided over affairs, creating yet another wheel within a wheel. Perhaps it's not surprising either that the popular 'Search for a star' TV format has been used in Korea to find a headline performer for the live theatre tour (2008), or indeed that online blogging platforms have spawned countless spinoffs of the character's exploits.[13]

For the musical of the twenty-first century, the shift between and across platforms and media is as much a part of its identity as its interdisciplinary fusion of music, drama and dance. And in responding so resolutely and positively to the possibility of such transitioning, *Hedwig and the Angry Inch* embraces the potential of what might be seen as the new millennium's emerging paradigm: a sort of universal queerness that is ambivalent to the stable and singular sense of self. We might not always phrase the contemporary mood in such terms, but how better could we articulate post-millennial identity than by acknowledging the plurality, diversity, multivalency and non-duality of a global world with porous borders, worldwide web networks and fluid understandings of self?

Notes

1 This synopsis reveals one of the challenges of writing about betweenness and gender identity; although I have chosen to use conventionally gendered pronouns that imply Hansel to be male and Hedwig to be female, alternative pronouns including ze/hir, ey/em/eir, or singular versions of they/them/their, are beginning to gain currency in LGBT+ and LGBTQ communities.

2 Deleuze and Guattari 1987: 78.

3 Ibid.: 554.

4 A significant history of 'drag kings' also exists, also stemming from music hall roots. See for example Torr and Bottoms 2010.

5 In fact, Mitchell based the character of Tommy Gnosis on himself and then went on to adopt the role of Hedwig as an acting opportunity: 'The mask of Hedwig – it's fun to leap into something. The specifics of her life are quite different from mine', he reports. Yet in turning to the role in conventional acting terms, he acknowledges one of the abiding complexities of actors playing a part: 'the emotional imperatives are mine', he concedes (Fricke 1998: 55), reminding us that in the world of performance there is a great deal of slippage between actor and character.

6 In this, I'm reminded of David Roesner's theoretical consideration of music theatre and music(al) film as '"fusional" phenomena'; he discusses the relationship 'between' the music and the film as tilting or flipping between one thing and another. He uses as visual metaphors the *Suchbild*, the *Kippfigur* and the illusions of M. C. Escher to explain the idea, and he considers the film *Dancer in the Dark* (2000), which features the Icelandic pop star Björk. 'The processual nature of this emerging, tilting and hovering is captured clearly in the musical sequences: you can practically watch Selma *and* Björk, as they amalgamate reality and fiction, day-to-day movement and dance, sound and music, and different layers of character, without finalising the process' (Roesner 2013: 174-5). And he quotes Kathleen Murray: 'Nothing is completed. No one is ever finished. There is no done. Everything and everyone is in a state of becoming' (Murray 2003).

7 Mitchell has talked about being influenced by his boyhood babysitter Helga, a prostitute on the side (see Wood 2014).

8 In particular, drag queen Randy Roberts' performance of this song within his stage set is notable, and available on YouTube here: www.youtube.com/watch?v=sSisCkkPSI_4

9 Developing trends in gender terminology can be seen in the coverage of this show; David Fricke's 1998 *Rolling Stone* article calls Hedwig 'gender-bent' (Fricke 1998); Peter Travers' film review from 2001 warily avoids any terminology; by 2014 in the same magazine Jennifer Wood is using the term 'transgender' (Wood 2014); in scholarly discourse both Rosa Salazar and Jillian Sandell usefully problematize categories of gender and refuse to label Hedwig (Salazar 2004; Sandell 2010); Sharon Dean talks of a 'bisexual aesthetic' in the film, but a 'portrayal of trans experience' (Dean 2006: 110); three years later Karin Sellberg considers Hedwig 'both a homosexual man and a transsexual woman, and also neither' (Sellberg 2009: 78); meanwhile, Steve Feffer orbits his

discussion around the musical language of 'queercore' (Feffer 2007), while the term 'genderqueer' gains some sporadic traction (Riley 2008; Whitesell 2013: 276). In short, categorization is difficult: even John Cameron Mitchell himself is ambiguous about his use of terminology, saying, 'I think Hedwig is under the trans umbrella', before going on to qualify Hedwig's sexuality as gay (Sasson 2015).

10 As Hugh Barker and Yuval Taylor state, 'The Beatles had a foot in both camps [pop and rock] for most of their career' (2007: 188). Their book, *Faking It: The Quest for Authenticity in Popular Music*, explores the diverging paths taken by pop and rock music in terms of authenticity, noting in particular how the approaches of The Beatles later in their career developed some of the dynamics that would subsequently become characteristic of a rock aesthetic.

11 'While its visuals pay tribute to a subgenre that gleefully disregards rock's imagined authenticity', Wollman notes, 'then *Hedwig* borrows musically from subgenres that tend to embrace it' (2006: 185).

12 This is a device also used in 'A Little More Mascara' from *La Cage aux Folles* (1983), trading in the musical aesthetic of a Broadway sound rather than pop/rock, but implying the same transition through the transformation of a character into drag. In *Hedwig*, the transition is further signalled by the figure of Skszp (played by Trask) standing incongruously outside the window of the trailer with a mini-keyboard at the ready to accompany Hedwig's every emotional moment.

13 See, for example, www.fanfiction.net/movie/Hedwig-and-the-Angry-inch/; http://archiveofourown.org/tags/Hedwig%20and%20the%20Angry%20Inch%20(2001)/works.

Bibliography

Barker, Hugh, and Yuval Taylor (2007). *Faking It: The Quest for Authenticity in Popular Music*. New York: W.W. Norton & Co.

Barrett, Rusty (1999). 'Indexing Polyphonous Identity in the Speech of African American Drag Queens.' In Mary Bucholtz, A. C. Liang and Laurel A. Sutton (eds), *Reinventing Identities: The Gendered Self in Discourse*. New York and Oxford: Oxford University Press, pp. 313–332.

Brown, Gavin (2009). 'Autonomy, Affinity and Play in the Spaces of Radical Queer Activism.' In Kath Browne, Jason Lim and Gavin Brown (eds), *Geographies of Sexualities: Theory, Practices and Politics*. Farnham: Ashgate, pp. 195–206.

Cohen, Thomas F. (2012). *Playing to the Camera: Musicians and Musical Performance in Documentary Cinema*. New York: Columbia University Press.

Dean, Sharon G. (2006). 'There Ain't Much of a Difference/Between a Bridge and a Wall.' *Journal of Bisexuality* 5(4), pp. 107–116.

Deleuze, Gilles, and Félix Guattari (1987). *A Thousand Plateaus: Capitalism and Schizophrenia*, (trans. Brian Massumi), London and New York: Continuum.

Feffer, Steve (2007). '"Despite All the Amputations, You Could Dance to the Rock and Roll Station": Staging Authenticity in *Hedwig and the Angry Inch*.' *Journal of Popular Music Studies* 19(3), pp. 239–258.

Fournier, Mat (2014). 'Another Map on the Wall; Deleuze, Guattari and Freeman at the Iron Curtain.' *Journal of Postcolonial Writing* 50(1), pp. 45–55.

Fricke, David (1998). 'Sex and Drag and Rock 'n' Roll.' *Rolling Stone* 801, pp. 54–56.

Hedwig and the Angry Inch Singalong. *Time Out Toronto* [online]. Available at: www.timeout.com/toronto.things-to-do/hedwig-and-the-angry-inch-sing-along.com [Accessed 7 October 2016].

Mitchell, John Cameron, and Stephen Trask (2014). *Hedwig and the Angry Inch: Complete Text and Lyrics to the Smash Rock Musical – Broadway Edition*. New York and London: Overlook Duckworth.

Murray, Kathleen (2003). 'Beyond Genre. Towards a Playful Grammar of Musicals.' MA thesis. New York: New School University.

Ouzounian, Richard (2014). 'John Cameron Mitchell to host Hedwig and the Angry Inch sing-along in Toronto.' *The Star.com* [online] Available at: www.thestar.com/entertainment/stage/2014/06/18/singalong_hedwig_and_the_angry_inch_comes_to_lgbt_film_fest.html [Accessed 7 October 2016].

Pattie, David (2007). *Rock Music in Performance*. Houndmills: Palgrave Macmillan.

Riley, Samantha Michele (2008). 'Becoming the Wig: Mis/identifications and Citationality in Queer Rock Musicals.' MA thesis. Chapel Hill: University of North Carolina.

Roesner, David (2013). 'Dancing in the Twilight: On the Borders of Music and the Scenic.' In Dominic Symonds and Pamela Karantonis (eds), *The Legacy of Opera: Reading Music Theatre as Experience and Performance*. Amsterdam: Rodopi, pp. 165–183.

Salazar, Rosa (2004). *Hedwig and the Angry Inch*: A radical affront to conventional renditions of gender. *Culture, Society and Praxis* 3(1), pp. 69–78.

Sandell, Jillian (2010). 'Transnational Ways of Seeing: Sexual and National Belonging in *Hedwig and the Angry Inch*.' *Gender, Place and Culture* 17(2), pp. 231–247.

Sasson, Eric (2015). 'John Cameron Mitchell on "Hedwig": "I have more rage than I thought I did at this age".' In *The Wall Street Journal* [online]. Available at: http://blogs.wsj.com/speakeasy/2015/02/02/john-cameron-mitchell-on-hedwig-i-have-more-rage-than-i-thought-i-did-at-this-age/ [Accessed 7 October 2016].

Sedgwick, Eve Kosofsky (1993). *Tendencies*. Durham: Duke University Press.

Sellberg, Karin (2009). 'Transitions and Transformations: From Gender Performance to Becoming Gendered.' *Australian Feminist Studies* 24(59), pp. 71–84, DOI: 10.1080/08164640802645158

Squeezebox! [online]. Available at: www.Squeezebox!themovie.com/ [Accessed 7 October 2016].

Stryker, Susan, Paisley Currah and Lisa Jean Moore (2008). 'Introduction: Trans-, Trans, or Transgender?' *Women's Studies Quarterly* 36(3 and 4), pp. 11–22.

Taylor, Jodie (2009). 'Spewing out of the Closet: Musicology on Queer Punk.' In Elizabeth Mackinlay, Brydie Bartleet and Katelyn Barney (eds), *Musical Islands*. Cambridge: Cambridge Scholars Publishing, pp. 221–241.

Taylor, Verta, and Leila J. Rupp (2009). 'Chicks with Dicks, Men in Dresses: What it Means to be a Drag Queen.' In Steven P. Schacht and Lisa Underwood (eds), *The Drag Queen Anthology: The Absolutely Fabulous but Flawlessly Customary World of Female Impersonators*. New York and Abingdon: Routledge, pp. 113–134.

Torr, Diane, and Stephen Bottoms (2010). *Sex, Drag, and Male Roles: Investigating Gender as Performance*. Ann Arbor: University of Michigan Press.

Travers, Peter (2001). 'Hedwig and the Angry Inch. *Rolling Stone*, 2 August.

Whitesell, Lloyd (2013). 'Trans Glam: Gender Magic in the Film Musical.' In Sheila Whitely and Jennifer Rycenga (eds), *Queering the Popular Pitch*. New York and London: Routledge, pp. 263–278.

Wollman, Elizabeth L. (2006). *The Theater Will Rock: A History of the Rock Musical, from Hair to Hedwig*. Ann Arbor: University of Michigan Press.

Wood, Jennifer (2014). 'Gender Bender: An Oral History of "Hedwig and the Angry Inch".' *Rolling Stone* [online]. Available at: www.rollingstone.com/movies/news/gender-bender-an-oral-history-of-hedwig-and-the-angry-inch-20140507 [Accessed 7 October 2016].

2

ALL THAT JAZZ

The difficult journey of *Chicago* from stage to screen

Robert Gordon

The huge critical and commercial successes of both *Moulin Rouge* (2001) ($179,213,414 gross against a budget of $50,000,000)[1] and *Chicago* (2002) ($306,776,732, with a budget of $45,000,000)[2] are widely regarded as responsible for the resurgence of the Hollywood screen musical in the twenty-first century. Ironically, it had taken twenty-seven years, a hugely successful Broadway revival (1996) and a number of failed attempts by Bob Fosse, Nicholas Hytner (with Wendy Wasserstein as screenplay writer) and others to finally transfer Kander, Ebb and Fosse's 1975 stage show to the screen. By examining both of the stage productions in their sociocultural contexts, this chapter will not only explain the appeal of *Chicago* as a film property but also identify the many difficulties posed for director/choreographer Rob Marshall and screenplay writer Bill Condon by its transfer from stage to screen.

On the face of it, the quintessentially theatrical conception of Fosse, Kander and Ebb's Brechtian meta-musical appears wholly resistant to film adaptation because the stage musical frames the entire narrative as a vaudeville performance, the audience itself being cast as the 'suckers' in a vaudeville theatre. In the theatre, the show begins thus:[3]

> *A* MASTER OF CEREMONIES *enters and addresses the audience from in front of the scrim.*
>   MASTER OF CEREMONIES. Welcome. Ladies and Gentleman, you are about to see a story of murder, greed, corruption, violence, exploitation, adultery, and treachery – all those things we all hold near and dear to our hearts. Thank you. (*He walks off. A solo trumpet plays, the* BANDLEADER *counts off the overture. The Scrim rises. We see an on stage* ORCHESTRA *on a platform suspended from a second level. They are seated above a Center Drum. The*

> *LIGHTS come up and* VELMA KELLY *enters. She walks forward to the audience.*
> *The Drum Doors close.*)

(9)

Bill Condon succinctly identified the challenge of transposing the 'musical vaudeville' to the screen:

> How is it possible to retain the vaudeville metaphor that informed every single moment of the play, when these characters had no reason to be on a stage? … On stage, all of *Chicago* is a vaudeville. Not only the numbers, but also the book scenes, which are highly stylized.
>
> (Marshall, Condon and Richards 2005: 16)

Unusually, the original idea for the musical *Chicago* originated with its star Gwen Verdon. Ever since seeing the film of *Roxie Hart* (1942), starring Ginger Rogers, on television in the 1950s, Verdon had considered Roxie a role that could be tailored to suit her own unique talents as a superb dancer who could act well and sing charmingly. After more than a decade, in 1969 she finally managed to purchase the rights from the estate of journalist Maurine Dallas Watkins, to the film's source play of 1926, *Chicago,* a fictionalization of the trial of infamous jazz singer Beulah May Annan, acquitted of murder with the aid of a clever lawyer (W.W. O'Brien) who exploited her feminine charms to manipulate the jury's sympathies.[4]

Vaudeville as Brechtian strategy

In fact it was Fred Ebb's idea to reconstitute the narrative of Watkins' play as a vaudeville show – at one and the same time to evoke the milieu of the Prohibition era and to create the metaphor of show business as life, a concept Fosse had become obsessed with since filming *Cabaret*. During the first week of rehearsals for the show in 1975, Fosse was rushed to hospital suffering from severe chest pains: it was discovered that he had almost had a heart attack and required open-heart surgery. This episode is represented in Fosse's autobiographical film masterpiece *All That Jazz* (1979); in any event his near-death experience is said to have transformed Fosse's cynical attitude into a view of life that was unrelentingly harsh, affecting his whole approach to *Chicago*.

In ironic counterpoint to its vaudeville format Fosse darkened every element of the show and his co-collaborators had a difficult time restraining him from over-emphasising the didactic point of the narrative: ultimately the entertainingly tongue-in-cheek quality of its satire of the judicial system would become a brutal exposé of the American dream as a sleazy capitalist nightmare, but the witty pastiche songs and the comic sensuality of the dances permitted an appropriate expression of social critique through the nostalgic prism of popular entertainment. Some reviewers and critics noted the parallels with Brecht/Weill's *Dreigroschenoper* (1928) in which Brecht and Weill's notion of gestic music determined the mocking counterpoint of music by lyrics and vice versa. A particularly good example of this strategy can be observed in the contrast between the mournful lamentation evoked by the music of 'Class' with its scatological lyrics:

> Everybody you watch
> 'S got his brains
> In his crotch;
> Holy crap,
> Holy crap;
> What a shame,
> What a shame
> What became
> Of class.
>
> (85–86)

While having no conventional academic or artistic education, Fosse had, somewhat unexpectedly perhaps, admired a production of *The Resistible Rise of Arturo Ui* in New York in 1963; with its fable-like device of enacting the rise of Hitler as if he were a Chicago gangster called Arturo Ui, this must have offered him a model for the doubleness that layers *Chicago* with irony and self-referentiality. In a direct parallel to the technique of Brecht in *Arturo Ui*, the vaudeville conceit reduces the portentous subjects of human cupidity and social corruption to a mock vaudeville show as savagely satirical as *The Threepenny Opera* and *Arturo Ui*. By appearing to reduce content to form, the musical implies what Billy Flynn the lawyer says in the lead-in to his appearance as ringmaster in a court represented as a circus ('Razzle Dazzle'): 'These trials ... the whole world ... show business'. The vaudeville show that constitutes a frame for the narrative is a metaphor for the fact that in a systematically mediatized society, everything is a performance. The forms of justice and government – in fact the whole social and political order – are a pretence. The only reality beneath the lies being spoken and enacted is what we literally see onstage: the power and gratification of bodies writhing in the orgiastic pleasure of illicit sex and ill-gotten gains.

   Chicago's meta-theatricality characterises most Kander and Ebb musicals from *Cabaret* (1966) to *The Scottsboro Boys* (2011). Even those shows that do not literally require the audience to view their narratives through the prism of a popular entertainment form – such as *The Happy Time* (1968), *Zorba* (1969), *Steel Pier* (1998) – do incorporate some type of epistemological distancing device that obliges a spectator to conceive the action as self-conscious artifice.[5] Fred Ebb explains *Chicago*'s vaudeville conceit:

> I made it a vaudeville based on the idea that the characters are performers. Every musical moment in the show was loosely modeled on someone else. Roxie was Helen Morgan, Velma was Texas Guinan, Billy Flynn was Ted Lewis, Mama Morton was Sophie Tucker.
>
> (Kander, Ebb and Lawrence 2003: 127)

What Fosse introduced to the partnership's idiosyncratic aesthetic in *Chicago* was the sleaziness of his own adolescent experience as a dancer in risqué nightclub entertainments and burlesque shows and his post-*Cabaret* view of show business as an inferno created by damaged souls and ruthless egoists. Kander and Ebb always explore serious and potentially disturbing subject matter but many of their musicals embrace such dark material without insisting that the characters can have no possible redemption.

Although *Chicago* lost every one of the eleven Tony's for which it was nominated to *A Chorus Line*, it later turned out to be the more successful show. The transfer of Walter Bobbie's semi-staged *City Center Encores!* production in 1996 finally ensured the show would become not only the longest-running American musical on Broadway but also the longest-running Broadway musical in the West End (1997–2012). According to Bill Condon,

> Like so much popular art of the time, it (the 1975 production) was informed by the twin traumas of Vietnam and Watergate. Then *Chicago* was revived in 1996, on the heels of the O. J. Simpson case, and the show business metaphor really came into focus. After all we'd just seen how the legal system could be manipulated by an expert showman.
>
> (Marshall, Condon and Richards 2005: 17)

While the show ran for a respectable 936 performances on Broadway and a different production ran in London for 600 performances (1979) it did not come close to matching *A Chorus Line*'s achievement as the longest-running show on Broadway (6,137 performances) before *Cats*. Why then was the more sentimental and far less hard-hitting *A Chorus Line* so much more successful at the time?

Fosse's stage production in its sociocultural moment

Perhaps Fosse's production happened too early and cut too close to the bone. The protracted horrors of the Vietnam War had only recently been comprehended as a tragedy of epic proportions. Although the revelation in 1973 of President Nixon's serial lying about his administration's involvement in the Watergate scandal led to his resignation in 1974, it had undermined Americans' trust in the rule of law.[6] The tarnishing of American society's self-image as moral guardian of the western world had only recently begun to register in the national consciousness:

> By 1975 most Americans had concluded that even though American troops had won every battle, they had lost the war … Surely both the military and the government were at fault, and Americans no longer completely trusted either … The image that the United States like to project to the world was as the victor, the champion of the underdog, of the oppressed, of the less fortunate. The outcome of the war … destroyed the 'feel-good' image that most Americans had of their country.
>
> (Wiest, Barbier and Robbins 2014: 1–8)

Chicago was metaphorically rubbing their noses in the duplicitous and corrupt nature of American imperialism at the very moment that Americans were being forced to come to terms with it in actuality. Psychologically, perhaps this was not the moment for cynicism or satire; the general cultural response to these traumas was characterized in films and plays by the style of tough journalistic reportage (*All the President's Men*, 1976) or mythic tragedy (*The Deer Hunter*, 1976; *Apocalypse Now*, 1979). Writing in the *New York Times* shortly after the destruction of the World Trade Center on 9/11/2001, Anne Taylor Fleming described the difficulty Americans have in coming to terms with the destruction of their heroic self-image:

> Americans have been serial innocents. Not just with Pearl Harbor ... but also with Vietnam, Watergate [...] Each time Americans have said, like abashed children: we've lost our innocence. Then that innocence is somehow re-donned like an alias or costume ... [...] there is a sense of the magic gift that is America. It is encoded in the national DNA ... and there is a sense that Americans cannot bear, in a collective and personal way, any transgressions against that magic, cannot bear that they might have tarnished it [...] So there is retreat back into innocence [...] If the country is going to go back, then let it be done in an uplifting, myth-reinforcing way.
>
> (Fleming, 23 September 2001)

In this context, it is perfectly understandable that *A Chorus Line* assumed pride of place on Broadway in 1975 as an apparent ritual of self-critique and renewed affirmation of the capitalist entertainment industry. Its backstage exposé of the emotional traumas and physical suffering that typifies the struggle to become a dancer on Broadway ends by celebrating the dancers' overcoming of those hardships in 'One', the glittering, golden paean to the star system at the musical's conclusion. In *Chicago,* by contrast, there is no recuperative valorization of show business – only mockery. After its satirical revelation of endemic corruption in the justice system, the show ironically celebrates the only value system that appears functional in America – celebrity. The two singing-dancing murderesses effectively thank the actual audience in the theatre for applauding their crimes:

> VELMA. (*To the audience.*) Thank you. Roxie and I would like to take this opportunity to thank you. Not only for the way you treated us tonight, but ... for your faith and your belief in our innocence ... You know a lot of people have lost faith in America.
> ROXIE. And for what America stands for.
> VELMA. But we are a living example of what a wonderful country this is. (*They hug and pose.*) ...
> VELMA and ROXIE ... God be with you. God walk with you always. God bless you. God bless you.

(Music up. They stand, bowing, throwing roses to the audience, waving and smiling as...)
THE CURTAIN FALLS (91)

This ending is an indictment of a whole society and its narcissistic culture of permanent immaturity. Anne Taylor Fleming draws on historian Michael G. Kammen's *Mystic Chords of Memory: Transformation of Tradition in American Culture* to analyse American society's 'collective amnesia':

> As a nation and a society, we do have very, very short memories [...] Most societies repress bad memories [...] But I do think there are reasons why short memory and collective amnesia are more pronounced and more problematic in our society. Tragedy is not part of the national self-image. But without that sense of the tragic, America is indeed "innocent," facing each new test or crisis with a combination of abashed patriotism and that feisty spirit. Without a sense of the tragic, its citizens are naked, unprotected, eternally childlike.
>
> (Fleming, 23 September 2001)

O.J. Simpson and the triumph of the 1996 stage revival

Why has the 1996 revival of *Chicago* become the longest-running American musical on Broadway? Was it simply that after 21 years of continuing disillusionment with violent crime, sex scandals and corruption, New York audiences were cynical enough to laugh at the unsparing denigration of their collective self-image? Was the televised trial of O.J. Simpson in 1995 – as has often been claimed – a catalyst for such a cultural shift? Simpson's huge celebrity as a retired football legend who became a movie star and TV personality is widely regarded as precipitating the first international trial by media, a trial that reinforced the black community's rooted mistrust of the LAPD by its exposure of the racism of Mark Fuhrman, a police detective on the case,[7] while at the same time totally undermining the white population's faith in a justice system that appeared to place celebrity murderers above the law.[8]

An estimated 95 million television viewers were watching as the television broadcast of a national football match was interrupted to show O.J. Simpson, recently charged with the murders of his ex-wife Nicole Brown Simpson and Ronald Goldman, holding a gun to his own head in the back of a white Ford Bronco in an attempt to evade arrest by fleeing to Mexico:

> National Football League teammate Al Cowlings [was] behind the wheel, and police cars were trailing slowly behind [...] [R]eality [was] playing out on jostling helicopter cameras [...] Simpson, a famous actor, running back and Heisman Trophy winner ... was one of the most recognizable personalities in the country [...] "What I realized is, this is entertainment,"

said Gerald Uelman, one of Simpson's defense attorneys. "This is not news."
In the years since, the lineage of so many cultural phenomena – the 24-hour
news cycle, a never-ending stream of reality television shows and many
Americans' unquenchable thirst for celebrity gossip – can be traced to this
nearly 16-month span.

(Kent Babbit 1995)

It was therefore fortuitous that the *City Center Encores!* production opened in May
1996, only eight months after the trial verdict was announced. The show's popular
and critical success was undoubtedly a reflection of the new climate of scepticism
concerning the uneasy relationship between celebrity and the law that followed the
Simpson case.

The new production created by Bobbie and Ann Reinking (the revival's star
and its choreographer 'in the style of Bob Fosse') did not slavishly reproduce Fosse's
original production but made it more user-friendly. The adaptations they made
subtly changed Fosse's gleefully tawdry exposure of the shabbiness of a justice
system indistinguishable from showbiz to a more chic and sexy visual spectacle of
capitalism as cat-walk show. The voguish costuming of sleek flesh in tight and
skimpy black plastic/leather fetishized the constantly undulating bodies of its
dancers, creating a visual metaphor that covertly valorised the narcissism of post-
O.J. Simpson culture. When the show transferred to Broadway for an open-ended
run, the creative team retained the black set with its gilt proscenium-style picture
frame surrounding the raised onstage band, leaving only a narrow strip of front-
stage floor for the minimalist staging and the nightclub intimacy of the dance. Not
only did the band watch the performers and the audience throughout, but a few
characters who were not immediately involved in a scene sat at the sides on black
bentwood chairs, a Brechtian strategy that went beyond even what Fosse had done
to stress the role of the audience as expert witnesses of a series of vaudeville acts.
The production – especially in London – speeded up the musical tempi so that the
music sounded more cheerful and the lyrics less explicit in their deadpan parody of
twenties clichés.

Audiences were still able to laugh at the pungent satire on the perversion of
justice by a celebrity-obsessed culture, but whereas in 1975 Fosse had cruelly
exposed two semi-naked middle-aged women on stage in the garish costumes of
striptease artistes, the revival displayed long-legged and comparatively young
women in sheer black stockings bumping cheeks and grinding groins with
muscular, bare-chested male dancers.[9] The intertextual play of imagery drawn
from show business, fashion and soft-core pornography created the spectacle of an
omni-sexual orgy of gyrating bodies whose indiscriminate pleasuring of gay and
straight male and female spectators seduced them into a complicity with the greed
and lust of the characters. In 1975 the colourful vulgarity of Tony Walton's
twenties period costume designs was reminiscent of the visual grotesquerie of
Fosse's film *Cabaret,* illustrating Billy Flynn's insouciant confession in the wittily
rhymed lyric,

What if your hinges all are rusting?
What if in fact you're just disgusting?
Razzle dazzle 'em,
And they'll never catch wise.

(75–76)

Here Fred Ebb and Fosse exposed the cynicism of routine self-disgust: the distancing of the audience from every character's tawdry cupidity in Fosse's production produced an authentic Brechtian *Verfremdungseffekt*; by contrast, the 1996 revival used an array of Brechtian techniques as putative distancing devices but at the same time undermined the effect of these by turning the audience into sexual voyeurs in thrall to the spectacle of the performers' self-gratification. In Fosse's production the spectators were detached observers of the characters' glorification of crime:

Who says that murder's not an art?
And who in case she doesn't hang,
Could say she started with a bang?
Foxy, Roxie Hart.

(45)

In the 1996 revival the audience became hedonistic accessories, the sexualisation of their investment in the performance collapsing the satirical attack on the cult of celebrity and the endemic corruption of the justice system into a tongue-in-cheek acknowledgement of their own selfish natures.

Transforming *Chicago* from vaudeville to gangster film musical

While the original stage production was only moderately successful, Liza Minnelli had rescued the show midway through its run by replacing Gwen Verdon as Roxie for four weeks when she became ill. Then at the height of her Hollywood fame, it was inevitable that Minnelli would be associated with the first attempt to film the musical, alongside Goldie Hawn as Roxie and Frank Sinatra as Billy Flynn. After Fosse's death in 1987, Nick Hytner was slated to direct Charlize Theron in a screenplay by Wendy Wasserstein, while in the nineties Madonna was attached to the film as Roxie. Ultimately it was Rob Marshall who kick-started the project again. While meeting Miramax executives to discuss filming *Rent*, he asked them if he could describe his concept for a film of *Chicago* and they introduced him to Harvey Weinstein who held the film rights. Marshall believed 'that it needed to take place in two worlds: a real one and an imaginary one' (Marshall, Condon and Richards 2005: 11), and after two hours he managed to sell the idea to Weinstein.

When Marshall interviewed Bill Condon as the movie's potential screenplay writer, the two men discovered they had very similar ideas concerning the approach to translating the stage musical to the screen:

> Our answer was to make the musical world of the film live in Roxie's imagination. Roxie is someone who's obsessed with being on the stage – being noticed … and when things get too unpleasant, she projects herself out of reality and re-imagines the experience as a vaudeville number. But the central conceit of the movie – that the musical numbers represent Roxie's escape from reality – meant that there had to be a real world for her to escape from.
>
> (Marshall, Condon and Richards 2005: 16, 17)

The approach permitted them to combine the conventions of the gangster film (representing 'the real world') with those of the backstage film musical, resulting in a movie that functions on its own terms while at the same time exploiting much of the material in the stage show.

The basic story of *Chicago* is retained. In reconstituting its vaudeville conceit as Roxie's escapist fantasy, director and screenplay writer revealed that they had learned from Fosse's *Cabaret* to adhere closely to the conventions of classic film realism by avoiding the inclusion of any musical numbers that were not diegetically motivated by being performed on a stage-within-the-film, even though that stage was the vaudeville theatre of Roxie's imagination. According to Bill Condon, 'Roxie became more central than she was in the play. After all, we're seeing everything through her eyes. And movies demand that a central character be someone you engage with on some level' (Marshall, Condon and Richards 2005: 17). In fact, the film opens with a close-up of Renée Zellweger's eyes accompanied by the 'slow, sexy wail of a jazz trumpet' (ibid.: 53), followed by the camera zooming and panning until her right eye fills the frame and dissolves to become the flickering middle 'C' of the electric CHICAGO sign that functions as the film title. Having established Roxie as a viewer of the vaudeville show cued by the black bandleader's 'A five-six, seven-eight', the editing creates the impression of movement across a panorama of auditorium and backstage views, reflecting an anxious stage manager's search for the Kelly sisters.

The overture from the stage production provides a soundtrack to the opening 'reality' montage in and around the vaudeville house, the camera cutting to an image of a woman's long legs as she walks from a taxi towards the theatre before ripping the name 'Veronica' off a bill advertising Velma and Veronica. This sequence cannot actually be part of what Roxie sees or imagines but establishes an independent perspective on the environment of crime and its detection that grounds the vaudeville performances in a historical reality. Her cryptic reply to the stage manager's question about where Veronica is ('She's not herself tonight') provides a motivation for Velma's solo performance of the Kelly sisters' intended double act. With dancers in orgiastic heaps on the floor, flailing legs and arms in all directions, silhouetted in glowing blue and lilac back lighting, 'All That Jazz' resembles a homage both to Fosse's *Cabaret* – although it is more glamorous and less grotesque – and a direct echo of the sleek black-and-white aesthetic of the stage revival of *Chicago*.

Roxie is then shown standing in the auditorium, apparently transfixed by Velma's performance, and for a moment her image and voice replace Velma's as she imagines herself a vaudeville star, before reality intrudes in the person of Fred Casely, who summons her to leave. The environment outside the auditorium is filmed in the sepia tones of old-fashioned photographs, stressing the contrast between the 'documentary' recording of events in the material world and Roxie's theatricalised fantasy. From here, images of Roxie and Fred having sex in her apartment are continually intercut with the stage act, revealing Roxie's fierce ambition to get into vaudeville and her violent reaction when Fred shatters her illusions.[10] Just before the end of the number a detective and police officer enter the auditorium, presumably to arrest Velma. The situation is later fully clarified by Velma's admission in the 'Cell Block Tango' that she had murdered her sister Veronica after catching her in bed with her lover, so that the viewer fully comprehends the bandleader's mistake in announcing 'All That Jazz' as performed by 'two jazz babes moving as one … the Kelly sisters'(Marshall, Condon and Richards 2005: 58).

The parallel set-up of Velma's and Roxie's crimes exemplifies the way the film attempts to ground every event witnessed on screen in a 'backstory', in order to supplement the sketchy, revue-like plot of the stage show with the realistic detail expected of Hollywood film narrative. The aphrodisiac nature of stardom is neatly suggested by the intercutting of the last few moments of 'All That Jazz' with shots of Roxie and her lover Fred Casely having sex in her apartment – 'You're a star, kid - my little shootin star'. The next shot reveals the post-coital couple in bed a month later. Now Fred no longer bothers to bolster Roxie's fantasy of becoming a headliner. When she reminds him of his promise to introduce her to his friend at the Onyx vaudeville theatre, Fred, having got what he wanted from her, brutally shatters Roxie's showbiz illusions:

> **ROXIE**
> And once I get a name for myself, maybe we can open a club of our own. You can run it and I'll be the headliner.
> *She reaches down to kiss him. Casely pushes her this time, hard enough to send her stumbling into the wall.*
> **ROXIE**
> Hey. What's the idea?
> **CASELY**
> Wake up, kiddo. You ain't never gonna have an act.
> …
> **CASELY**
> Face it, Roxie. You're a two-bit talent with skinny legs. And I'm just a furniture salesman.
> …
> **ROXIE**
> So you never told anyone about me?

CASELY

Sugar, you were hot stuff – I would have said anything to get a piece of that.

ROXIE

You are a liar Fred. You lied to me.

CASELY

That's life, sweetheart

ROXIE

You son-of-a-bitch.

(Marshall, Condon and Richards 2005: 68–70)

When Roxie shoots Fred three times, the spectator has already had a chance to grasp the details of a relationship that is more realistically motivated and more melodramatically conceived than it is in the stage version. Referencing the key conventions of the gangster movie, the incident of Fred's murder and Amos's subsequent attempt to take the blame for killing him 'to protect his home and his loved ones' (ibid.: 73) is explained in narrative terms that serve to humanise Roxie by making her attitudes and behaviour understandable as a response to Casely's cool rejection of her romantic overtures. Roxie's first song is visually motivated by the shining of a torch into first Fred's, then her face. While Velma Kelly sings 'All That Jazz' as a vaudeville performer on the bill of the Onyx theatre, 'Funny Honey' is the first of a series of songs in which Roxie imagines the action as a vaudeville act. The spectator's identification with Roxie's point of view is enhanced by her projection of herself as the twenties torch singer Helen Morgan, who famously sat atop an upright piano to deliver her poignant songs of unrequited passion. Roxie's shabby pink nightgown is transformed into a revealing pink satin dress in which she lounges and lies back sensuously on the piano in the manner of a glamorous Hollywood star. Although the showbiz fantasy is undermined by the intercutting of Amos's police interrogation, during which he realizes that Roxie has lied to him about Fred Casely, the film's revelation of both Amos's and Roxie's reactions is less comically detached than in the stage original, the comparative density of the narrative offering a far more three-dimensional representation of action and motive.

Intertexuality and editing: the aesthetics of the postmodern film musical

Bill Condon recognised that such a translation from theatrical into cinematic terms might risk sentimentalizing the characters:

> The challenge in the script was to create a world that was more real, and to create in the character of Roxie somebody with some psychological complexity, somebody you might feel more for. Personally, I felt the tough part of that was not to betray who she is. It's very easy to soften characters in movies, where suddenly you're told ... they have a pet, they're nice to their mother ... you think they're nice people, and ... you like them.

And we didn't want to do that with Roxie, because she's not. She's incredibly ambitious … But at the same time you kind of have to fill her out.

(Marshall, Condon and Richards 2005: 44)

What Condon's sharp self-reflection masks is the way in which the reification of stage types as three-dimensional cinematic characters blunts the social satire. When he claims that 'what makes her so compelling is that she's a shrewd, ambitious animal' (ibid.: 17), he reduces a critique of the society that romanticises Roxie to a comment on her own individual behaviour, betraying a modern tendency to comprehend fictional characters as virtual human beings by explaining their behaviour in the pseudo-psychoanalytic jargon of tabloid 'life-coaching'.

Casting younger actors than even the revival had done,[11] the film makes such characters plausible in the way classic Hollywood realism always does: viewers are induced to understand the circumstances of Roxie's crime because the killing is visually presented. Character and circumstance are concretely imbricated in the flow of narrative fiction, as opposed to the stage version's Brechtian enactment of the shooting with the gunshots being comically mimicked by a snare drum, a *Verfremdungseffekt* that enables spectators to judge the ethical standards of the society rather than to be engrossed in the violence.

The sepia-tinted visualisation of the Chicago crime narrative evokes the world of lawyers and police detectives, with the predominantly grey hues of the Cook County jail complementing the period newsreel style. Intercalated through the pseudo-documentary record of the sordid banality of historical reality is the highly theatricalized filming of the imagined vaudeville routines, in most cases directly figured as Roxie's escapist transformation of brute reality. These onstage sequences are lit by Broadway lighting designers Jules Fisher and Peggy Eisenhower, who contribute a vivid theatricality to the musical numbers, which are presented in starkly contrasting swathes of colour and darkness, sculpting the bodies of the performers in space and creating shadows through the use of lights from below and silhouettes by means of backlighting and sidelighting that heighten the subjectivity of Roxie's dream visions. The continuous contrast of cinematic realism with theatrical stylization, in conjunction with the hyperactive approach to editing, aestheticises the film, offering the pleasures of a dazzling variety of visual effects as an enhancement of the raucous jazz of the soundtrack.

The use of colour in both lighting and costumes is extremely artful, the key grey colour that signifies Roxie's first impression of the prison vividly contrasted with the golden amber glow of Matron 'Mama' Morton's 'When You're Good to Mama' number in which Roxie imagines her as a 'red-hot' mama à la Sophie Tucker. The comic shamelessness of the number as sung by Queen Latifah reinforces what Roxie has just been informed about the system of 'reciprocity' operating in the jail, by means of which Morton dispenses favours in a system of barter as immoral as it is transparent. Kander and Ebb's brilliant matching of vulgar lyrics with a burlesque-style bump-and-grind renders with cynical irony the crude philosophy that there is nothing that can't be bought:

> There's a lot of favors
> I'm prepared to do
> You do one for Mama
> She'll do one for you.

(Marshall, Condon and Richards 2005: 81)

As 'Mama' Morton flirts with a male customer, then with the woman beside him, the punning innuendo in the lyric hints at her lesbian feelings:

> They say that life is tit for tat
> And that's the way I live
> So I deserve a lot of tat
> For what I got to give.

(Marshall, Condon and Richards 2005: 81)

The warm light of the vaudeville stage gives way to the grey of the prison as the Matron welcomes Roxie and other new inmates, flirting with Roxie as she takes her to her dark cell.

Morton is transported to the stage of Roxie's imagination again, but now each chorus of the number is intercut with moments in the prison that is Roxie's actual environment. After she is escorted back to her cold cell, her request for a blanket ignored by Morton, Roxie lies awake, staring at a leaking faucet that is 'dripping relentlessly' (ibid.: 85). The regular drip of the water combines with other sounds (a guard's footsteps, a clock ticking and fingernails drumming on a metal bed frame) to produce a percussive rhythm that triggers Roxie's vision of the 'Cell Block Tango'. This song-and-dance sequence involves a virtuoso interplay of choreography, editing and lighting whose high stylisation emphasizes black bondage-style dance costumes, which are contrasted against red slashes made by the repeated appearance and vanishing of women's scarves; the ambient grey of the jail is replaced at intervals by a red screen signifying passion, blood and violence.

The complexity and speed of the cutting between images of historical reality and Roxie's fantasy throughout the film – and rather relentlessly during musical numbers – reveals the influence of the techniques used by Baz Luhrman in *Moulin Rouge* to emphasise the intertextuality of his film.[12] There is a visual reference to Elvis Presley's iconic 'Jailhouse Rock' number in the film of that name, although the extreme eroticism of the fetishised bodies and the garish red lighting against which dancers and prison bars are silhouetted in the 'Cell Block Tango' playfully conjure images of a brothel and an inferno.

This is the first musical number in *Chicago* that is not established as an interior scene performed before a lively audience in the Onyx vaudeville theatre. Marshall subtly alters the convention to permit the performers to refer to an imaginary audience or confidante when they dance with the 'dead' partners while confessing to justifiable homicide. The tango represents a stylized visual flashback to the past moment when each alleged crime was committed, while the lyrics and dialogue simultaneously suggest that these inmates are explaining the incidents to Roxie or others in the present. Although some interpolated shots of the 'real' prison portray actual conversations with the Matron and other inmates, the convention is not consistently maintained and most of the dancers speak directly to camera.

Critical reception

While a majority of reviews of the film were positive, cinema critics were divided in their response to Rob Marshall's filming of the musical sequences. According to *The Independent* film critic,

> The dancing is supple and athletic in the trademark style of Bob Fosse, though whereas one thrilled to the choreography on stage, director Rob Marshall relies here on trick editing and computerised imagery to lend an extra sheen of slickness. It belongs very much to the *Moulin Rouge* school of hoofing, where the smoke-and-mirrors of the cutting room effectively camouflage most of the dancers' efforts. Sometimes there is nothing more exciting, or more moving, than the sight of two people moving across a dance floor, but the magic evaporates once technology gets in on the act.
>
> (Quinn, *The Independent*, 27 December 2002)

After the 'Cell Block Tango', Roxie overhears a conversation in which Mama Morton offers to exploit Velma's notoriety in order to make her a headliner on the vaudeville circuit once her lawyer Billy Flynn has got her acquitted. Believing she has grasped the rules of the celebrity game, Roxie herself, with the aid of Morton, attempts to engage Billy Flynn to defend her in court. Before that, 'All I Care About is Love' envisions Roxie's fantasy of Billy as a caring and philanthropic charmer, but the number is staged as an elaborate burlesque striptease replete with white ostrich-feathered fans. Surrounded by scantily-clad female dancers in pink, Billy initially appears onstage as an Irish shoeshine boy in a tweed cap and open-neck shirt, an image that alternates with his impeccably groomed 'real world' manifestation in business suit and tie. Billy's mock striptease reveals his exterior appearance as man of the people to be fake: ironically he peels off layer after layer of clothing to expose the naked truth that his social performance is an act. In a reality sequence intercut during the number it becomes clear to Roxie that, contrary to the song lyric, 'all he cares about' is not love. Instead of the $5,000 he demands for his services, she offers him sexual favours only to learn that he is interested in nothing but money. When at the conclusion of the routine, surrounded by chorines whose fans mask Billy's supposed nudity as in a traditional burlesque number, he waves his underpants in the air, but there is no revelation.

The staging of 'All I Care About is Love' is taken directly from Fosse's original conception, as is the ingenious device of representing Billy Flynn, in 'We Both Reached for the Gun', as a puppeteer manipulating Chicago journalists like

FIGURE 2.1 Richard Gere as Billy Flynn in *Chicago*.

Credit: Collection Christophel/ArenaPAL.

marionettes and reducing Roxie to a ventriloquist's dummy who mouths his sentimental tale of her disadvantaged background as a convent girl in an attempt to minimize her criminal culpability. The only perceptible difference between stage and film versions of this number is that the film literally attaches bright red strings to the actors playing journalists, also adding garish make up to the puppet-journalists to create a grotesque circus-like impression. *Variety* reviewer David Rooney noted the film's indebtedness to the stage original:

> However the film version boasts few significant innovations. Much of the dialogue and jokes are word for word from the stage show, and conception of musical numbers strays very little … But too often the cross-cutting interrupts the rhythm of the songs to clutter the action, instilling a certain frustration at never seeing a song or dance number played out in full.
>
> (Rooney, *Variety*, 16 December 2002: 38)

Certainly the hyper-kinetic editing of the dance numbers, with their recurring colour motifs of blood red and cool blue and lilac, does tend to become repetitious, the kaleidoscope of images obviously designed to satiate the spectator with an embarrassment of riches. The continual effort to illustrate Mama Morton's observation that 'In this town, murder's a form of entertainment' (Marshall, Condon and Richards 2005: 106) betrays a fear of boring any spectator with a short attention span, imposing a frenetic pace to the whole film that threatens to submerge the ironic critique of the original production beneath a continuous stream of visual pleasure.

While a number of reviewers praised the relentless energy and flashy theatricality of the film as light-hearted comic entertainment, others observed that the obsessive naughtiness of the sexily costumed dancers becomes a cliché, its tongue-in-cheek jokiness undermining any potentially dangerous implications in the erotic spectacle and blunting the clear-eyed satire of Kander, Ebb and Fosse's original stage conception. Peter Bradshaw observed the problems created by Marshall's attempt to remain visually close to the musical staging of the revival:

> For great swathes of time, it looks like a very expensive record of the theatre production on a giant sound stage, rather than a living, breathing film on its own account ... what it does have are these showstopping numbers, properly embedded in the fabric of the show itself ... after seeing the principals ... striking choreographed poses with one knee bent and hat tipped with devilish sexiness over one eye, you begin to suspect a whiff of naff. Or ... sameness: familiar looking shots of supposedly louche nightclubs with a single spotlight in which the dust motes are circling, the camera doing an adoring and celebratory swirl around the leading lady as she belts out the final note – and it's all sugar-coated with ersatz glam-sleaze and unthreatening toughness.
>
> (Peter Bradshaw, *The Guardian*, 20 December 2002)

The super-abundance of stylish consumer images highlighted by Marshall's exploitation of the MTV pop video aesthetic of the 1980s and 1990s risks trivializing or even romanticising *Chicago*'s criminal milieu. This is particularly noticeable in 'Roxie', with its deliberate allusions to the mise-en-scène for Marilyn Monroe's 'Diamond's Are a Girl's Best Friend' from *Gentleman Prefer Blondes*. The sparkling projection of Renee Zellweger in a rhinestone-studded twenties dress, reflected by mirrors that multiply her image from a number of perspectives, creates the effect of a palimpsest, referencing both Madonna's exploitation of the Marilyn icon in the pop video 'Material Girl' and the manner in which Nicole Kidman is introduced in *Moulin Rouge*. The choreography surrounds Roxie – as it did Marilyn – with a phalanx of men, expensively attired in black tuxedos: by framing her as a desirable object, they celebrate her imagined triumph in a traditional showbiz trope whose 'Cinderella' conventions were established in 1920s musical comedies. The problem is that despite the intended irony, the *mise-en-scène* and filming of the number construct a glossy emblem of female stardom that is a deeply subliminal signifier of success. When Roxie climbs on the arms and hands of the male chorus as if supported by her worshipping fans, before standing on top of a glaring red neon sign spelling 'ROXIE', the theatrical apotheosis of the star is irresistible, representing an inevitable valorization of the over-determined notions of power associated with the image.

The only number in the later part of the film that might have a chance to compete with the emotional effect of 'Roxie' is Amos's desperate Bert Williams pastiche 'Mr Cellophane'.[13] The song's painfully comic demonstration that the honest and ethical behaviour of the ordinary citizen is a guarantee of social and material failure is brilliantly conveyed by John C. Reilly's delivery. While the unintended revelation of Amos's suppressed rage at being invisible in a world of fakes and con-artists is perhaps the only moment of genuine emotion in the film, the original song is shortened and what remains of it is regularly interrupted by the 'real life' scene in which Billy Flynn explains that Amos could not be the father of Roxie's 'baby'. The stage show's famous 'eleven o'clock' number, 'Razzle Dazzle', in which Billy Flynn defends Roxie while exposing the whole judicial system as a 'three-ring circus', appears in its cinematic context to be somewhat didactic. The constant alternation between the representation of Billy's 'real' performance in the courtroom and the comic illustration in song of his philosophy of life as show business flim-flam duplicates the expression of an idea that by this juncture seems superfluous.

Conclusion: a Hollywood compromise?

Chicago was filmed in the wake of the 9/11 terrorist attack (2001), the shock of which precipitated an escapist trend on Broadway in the first decade of the new millennium that was reflected in the enormous popularity of retro musical comedies such as *The Producers* (2001), *Thoroughly Modern Millie* (2002), *Hairspray* (2002), and *The Drowsy Chaperone* (2006). Although 9/11 did not have the same kind of effect on the film industry as it had on Broadway, the enormous commercial success of the *Chicago* movie less than two years after the attack suggests the cinema-going public's willingness to laugh cynically at adultery, corruption and even murder when represented in the escapist mode of musical comedy. The Bill Clinton–Monica Lewinsky scandal and the failed attempts between 1998 and 1999 to impeach the President reminded Americans once again of how the powerful are able to evade the law: by 2002 the whole episode had become a joke that might license knowing laughter at any satire on authority.

Although many aspects of the screen version of *Chicago* are brilliantly realized, Marshall's approach subtly reconceives the original in all sorts of significant ways. The viewer's connection with Roxie's point of view not only dissolves the distance established through the objective presentation of the stereotypical musical comedy character in the theatre, by generating excitement concerning the outcome of her role in the gangster narrative, but the fantasy vaudeville motif also promotes empathy for Roxie's aspirational desire to be a star. In the theatre, murder is presented as a vaudeville act, whereas on screen vaudeville becomes a necessary means of escape from the harshness of the criminal milieu. Most tellingly, the ironic reference to America that concludes the stage show, 'we are a living example of what a wonderful country this is' (91), is excised from the movie.

An additional new song for Roxie and Velma ('I Just Move On') written by Kander and Ebb at a late stage in the production process and played over the end credits, is a straightforward celebration of the art of survival that reinforces the film's shift in emphasis away from satire. Marshall's *Chicago,* while it preserves much (but by no means all) of the wonderful score, inevitably neutralizes the social critique of the original stage production in its – highly successful – drive to secure box office success. The homage to Fosse is visually exciting and comically entertaining, but Marshall replaces Fosse's dark world view with a more conventional cynicism. The surprising success of his Fellini-esque *All That Jazz* (1979) prompts the question of whether Fosse's intended film of *Chicago* might not have resulted in a screen masterpiece that somehow managed to retain both the abrasive vulgarity and the dazzling wit of his stage production.

Notes

1 Information provided by www.boxofficemojo.com/movies/?id=moulinrouge.htm. Accessed 30 April 2016.
2 Information provided by www.boxofficemojo.com/movies/?id=chicago.htm. Accessed 30 April 2016.
3 Page number refers to Fred Ebb, Bob Fosse, John Kander, *Chicago: A Musical Vaudeville* (1976). New York: Samuel French Inc.
4 The play had been adapted as a silent movie as early as 1927, produced by Cecil B. De Mille.
5 The photographs emblematising the photographer's fake memories in *The Happy Time,* the pseudo-Greek chorus that relates and comments on the narrative of *Zorba,* or the dance marathon that frames the action of *Steel Pier* are reminders that we are not watching unmediated reality on the stage (as in naturalism) but seeing action unfold through a representation of oneiric experience (dream or memory), the replay of a competitive ritual or the telling of a self-consciously fashioned tale.
6 'Senator John V. Tunney told the nation's top lawyers … that the Watergate scandal has caused Americans to lose faith in the rule of law … "Our tarnished self-image as a people governed by the rule of law derives from a profound loss of faith in the law as the protector of citizen against predatory government and citizen against predatory fellow citizen"' (*Bangor Daily News*, 14 August 1974).
7 In 1995 defence lawyers secured tape recordings that revealed Fuhrmann using racist language in reference to the case.
8 Simpson was acquitted on 3 October 1995.
9 At 50, Reinking was only four years younger than Gwen Verdon, but her height, her incredibly long legs and very slim figure made her appear much younger than Verdon onstage; Bebe Neuwirth was 38 as compared to Rivera (42) but in London, Ruthie Henshall as Roxie was 31, while Ute Lemper was 31.
10 This is another crib from Fosse's *Cabaret,* directly imitating the intercutting of stage performance with off-stage reality in 'Maybe This Time'.
11 Renée Zellweger and Catherine Zeta-Jones were both 33 when the film was released.
12 It is unlikely, however, that Rob Marshall had final cut on *Chicago* as a first time movie director working for the notoriously 'hands-on' producer Harvey 'Scissorhands' Weinstein.
13 Bert Williams was the first black vaudeville star to headline with white performers on Broadway in the *Ziegfeld Follies*. Himself a long-suffering victim of racist prejudice,

Williams' trademark 'Nobody' is a blues song, comically revealing his naïve 'Jim Crow' character's alienation from a society in which he seems invisible. Although written in the self-mocking manner of a minstrel-style representation of the nineteenth-century ex-slave, the song ironically exposes the injustice to African Americans that white people prefer to ignore.

Bibliography

Babbit, Kent (2014). *The Washington Post*, 9 June 2014, www.newsdiffs.org/article-history/www.washingtonpost.com/sports/redskins/how-the-ojsimpson-murder-trial-20-years-ago-changed-the-media-landscape/2014/06/09/a6e21df8-eccf-11e3-93d2-edd4be1f5d9e_story.html. Accessed 30 April 2016.

Bradshaw, Peter (2002). 'Review of *Chicago*' in *The Guardian*, 20 December 2002, www.theguardian.com/culture/2002/dec/20/artsfeatures2.

Ebb, Fred and Bob Fosse (Book), John Kander (Music) and Fred Ebb (Lyrics) (1976). *Chicago: A Musical Vaudeville*. New York: Samuel French Inc.

Fleming, Anne Taylor (2001). 'Aftermath: Innocence Lost; A Tragedy for an Optimistic Land.' *New York Times*, 23 September 2001, www.nytimes.com/2001/09/23/weekinreview/aftermath-innocence-lost-a-tragedy-for-an-optimistic-land.html. Accessed 30 April 2016.

Kammen, Michael G. (1993). *Mystic Chords of Memory: Transformation of Tradition in American Culture*. New York: Vintage.

Kander, John, Fred Ebb, Greg Lawrence (2003). *Colored Lights*. New York: Faber and Faber.

Marshall, Rob, Bill Condon, Martin Richards (2005). *Chicago: The Movie and Lyrics*. New York: Newmarket Press.

Quinn, Anthony (2002). 'Review of *Chicago*' in *The Independent*, 27 December 2002, www.independent.co.uk/arts-entertainment/films/reviews/chicago-15-137462.html. Accessed 11 July 2016.

Rooney, David (2002). 'Review of *Chicago*' in *Variety*, 16 December 2002, pp. 38–43.

Wiest, Andrew, Mary Kathryn Barbier, Glenn Robbins (eds) (2014). *America and the Vietnam War: Re-examining the Culture and History of a Generation*. Abingdon: Routledge.

3

READY FOR HIS CLOSE-UP

From horror to romance in
The Phantom of the Opera

Jessica Sternfeld

It took eighteen years for Andrew Lloyd Webber's *The Phantom of the Opera* to make the journey from stage to screen. Opening in London in 1986 and on Broadway in 1988, the show became one of the most successful musicals of all time, with dozens of foreign productions and tours, a chart-topping original cast recording, and a record-breaking Broadway run. In fact, *Phantom* is not only the longest-running Broadway musical, it can't be passed for many years to come, as its original 1988 production is still running. Lloyd Webber broke his own record (set by *Cats*), and the revival of *Chicago* and the original production of *The Lion King* are eight and nine years behind, respectively. The Broadway production shows no signs of closing; it has become a New York institution.

The film version was released in 2004, well into the show's run (indeed, runs, around the world), but seems not to have hindered sales of the live productions at all, despite the worry that film versions often cause. In fact it seems to have boosted sales for live show tickets around the world. Despite the trepidation of thousands of die-hard fans (or 'phans', as they are known) who feared a film version would destroy their beloved stage show, the reception of the film was strong among supporters, though tepid to poor among those who weren't already enamoured of the material. Director Joel Schumacher did indeed keep the loyal in mind, changing the score very little and retaining all of the central visual, aural, plot-based, and thematic elements of the stage version. While significantly opening up the look of the film, the fundamental ingredients – lushness, romanticism, dark shadows, lingering gazes, hushed whispers, lyrical singing – remain in place. And the plot is of course intact: young ballet dancer Christine Daaé, who dances at the Paris Opéra, has been taking mysterious voice lessons with a teacher – or ghost? or angel? – she has never seen. She tells her friend, fellow dancer Meg, that she thinks the voice is that of the Angel of Music, a figure her father had promised on his deathbed that he would send to watch over her. Meg's mother, the opera's ballet mistress Madame Giry, knows that the teacher is the Opera Ghost – a man, genius, monster, or creature (it remains largely unclear throughout) who resides in the opera house's dark underground lair, where he watches over his opera company. He demands a salary and artistic license from the opera's new managers, Messieurs André and Firmin, and he both scares and irritates the company, which includes Italian diva Carlotta, tenor Piangi, and stagehand Buquet.

When one of the Phantom's dangerous pranks – a crashing backdrop – annoys Carlotta, she quits, and in a star-is-born turn, Christine takes her place in that night's performance. Her childhood friend Raoul, Vicomte de Chagny, the opera's new patron, sees her perform and they fall in love. But Christine remains haunted by the Angel of Music. The Phantom lures her down into his lair, where he both woos and terrifies her. He demands Christine take the lead in the next opera, then kills Buquet and destroys the house's huge chandelier when he is not instantly satisfied. Next he composes the opera *Don Juan Triumphant* for the company, killing Piangi (who is meant to play Juan) and taking his place on stage. Christine finally stands up to him, unmasking him in front of everyone, and he, Christine, and Raoul have a final confrontation in his lair. He is completely undone when she kisses him, showing him pity and sympathy (though not the romantic love he desires). He frees the couple to go on with their lives, and disappears just as a vengeful crowd arrives.

Despite the loyalty of the film to the stage show, there is one element that is quite different, and that element has a cascading series of effects on what this story is actually about. In the stage version, the Phantom's face is deformed, in bold and very obvious ways. In the film, it is not; his disfigurement is mild to the point of being downright subtle. The ramifications of this change – the reasons behind it and the impact it has on the meaning and reception of the story – are far greater than a simple choice about makeup would suggest. The change affects the messages the show sends.

Thus this chapter will explore how the film reimagines the stage version in four significant ways. First, the Phantom's drastically different face renders him a potentially viable love interest for Christine, but eliminates the only justification for his evil deeds: that society would so obviously shun him. This change of the Phantom from horrifying creature to insecure loner led to three other changes: the complete erasure of all of the Phantom's magical unexplained powers and feats; the addition of a significant back story meant to create sympathy and justification for the Phantom's murders and isolation; and the steep lowering of the main characters' ages to render the story more of a youthful awakening than an adult love triangle. We will see that by making the Phantom more handsome, more human, and more sympathetic, the message that Christine could never choose him over Raoul is meant to be more romantic and heartbreaking, but becomes instead a harsh indictment of our own social expectations and stigmas about disability.

From novel to stage: parallels and opportunities

Gaston Leroux wrote the original novel (serialized from 1909 to 1910, published in novel form in 1910) as a gothic horror tale, and though there are plenty of romantic thrills included, the story is meant to be a scary one of a young girl, Christine, pursued by a terrifying ghost-monster-stalker-man. The many film versions played up the horror factor, most famously in the 1925 Lon Cheney version, featuring his terrifying sunken eyes, drawn face, and zombie-like persona. It is hard to say that the fundamental story is a love triangle when one of the three players – the Phantom – is more monster than man, but the story does indeed rest on the notion that Christine is being simultaneously pursued by the Phantom and wooed by the handsome, suitable Raoul. It is true that she eventually comes to pity the Phantom, briefly, but as he has become a murderer and kidnapper, she mostly simply wants to free herself, Raoul, and other victims from his clutches.

Composer Andrew Lloyd Webber happened across Leroux's novel in 1984, not long after the international success of *Cats* and the less well-received *Starlight Express*. He had in fact seen a stage version of the story earlier that year; his fiancée, Sarah Brightman, whom he had met when she was cast in *Cats* in London, had been asked to join Ken Hill's stage version of the tale that incorporated actual opera arias. She decided not to participate but Lloyd Webber and famed director Harold Prince had seen and liked the show. When Lloyd Webber read the novel, he saw it as an opportunity to create an original score, with plenty of opera influence, and with an eye toward what he repeatedly called the 'high romance' underneath the horror story. In other words, he saw something of a love triangle and immediately felt more sympathy for the Phantom than most other versions ever considered. The Phantom, a reclusive ugly genius hiding in the damp bowels of the opera house, is a composer, architect, magician, and social reject.

Not surprisingly, reporters and gossip columnists had a field day with the parallels: the geeky awkward composer writes a musical for his beautiful young wife, and that musical is about a reclusive composer who writes an opera for his beautiful young protégée. It is logical that Lloyd Webber related to the Phantom and felt comfortable telling the story with some of his perspective built in. Christine, in his telling (with lyricists Richard Stilgoe and Charles Hart), spends most of the show terrified of the Phantom yet continuously drawn to him, mesmerized by his voice, his seductive words about the magic of music, his clever and intentional confusion of himself with her father and with the amorphous Angel of Music. After spending nearly the entire show in a state of weepy, helpless fear and hypnosis, she stands up to him in the final scene, when his hideous face has been revealed and he has kidnapped her (and Raoul) yet again. She is no longer afraid, she pities him – and she kisses him. She knows he has never known love and she cleverly shocks him with her kiss; it undoes him.

There is never any question in the stage show that she will not end up with Raoul. Even as teenage girls may weep for the pitiable Phantom and his loneliness, no one could possibly expect her to give up Raoul, give up her life, and take up residence underground with the Phantom. Nor can he join society; having been rejected by everyone, starting with his own mother, who gave him his first mask, the story has made it clear that the world will not accept him. Along with Christine, we may pity him, we may even be drawn to his seductive ideas and his dark bad-boy persona, but he is nevertheless a murderer, a dysfunctional and unreformable reject of society. Christine has to go with Raoul.

Disability narrative and community

There are two underlying philosophical notions here that support the inevitability of Christine's decision. The first comes from the field of disability studies, and is known as the 'kill or cure' narrative. Presented by Rosemarie Garland-Thomson (2004) and taken up by many others, this rule states that, in nearly all stories (on stage, in novels, in films, and so on) with a disabled character, that character will end up either cured or killed/dead. The expectation is that such a character can be interesting, can propel the plot, can have an impact on both the other characters and on the audience – but that character cannot simply carry on being disabled. She or he must either be healed, and thus incorporated into society, or be eliminated, so that the society can carry on in a healthy and normative way. Tiny Tim gets healed, as does Colin in *The Secret Garden* (a common outcome for good-hearted children); Captain Hook gets eaten by a crocodile, Ahab killed by his whale. Richard III dies. Porgy leaves his community; so does Diana in *Next to Normal*. Nessarose, in *Wicked*, is both healed *and* killed, amazingly. The Phantom, with his incurable disfigurement, must be 'killed' – he chooses to disappear, in a seemingly noble act of self-sacrifice.

The second philosophical construct that makes Christine's choice inevitable is the notion that at all costs the community must be sustained. This idea contains the 'kill or cure' narrative under its umbrella. It states that every story begins with a community in which it is set, and that the community gets unsettled by the events of the story, but by the end will carry on – perhaps in a slightly new way – because we can't abide its total destruction. Thus whatever the force was that came to disrupt it – the disabled character, the new person in town, the oppressive political forces, the alien invasion – must be eliminated (killed) or assimilated (cured; that is, made normal in the society). Musicologist Raymond Knapp (2005) explains that many musicals rest on the 'marriage trope'; that is, they end with the reassuring merger of a boy and girl whose marriage, by extension, cements the community into a stronger, better whole. Many shows present

> a community threatened by something either within or outside the group, which grows wiser and more secure through pursuing an initially resisted approach to community-formation that is more inclusive than exclusive, with the marriage trope placed squarely at the center of the conflict and its resolution.
>
> (Knapp 2005: 122)

In *The Music Man*, the upsetting outsider Harold Hill earns the respect of Marian, his love interest, and – more importantly – brings the community together through music to form a band, a united town, a whole. In *Oklahoma!*, the sexually disturbing Jud must die in order to pave the way for Laurey and Curly to join together and – again, more importantly – for Oklahoma to move from rag-tag territory to united American state. In *RENT*, the incurably sick Angel dies, becomes an inspirational 'angel' to her friends, and by her absence creates a more bonded, close-knit community of friends.

For both of these reasons drawn from narrative expectations – that the disabled must be killed or cured, and that the community must carry on – Christine never really has a choice. She may be drawn to the Phantom, and fans may write hundreds of fan fiction tales in which she chooses him, but the rules of storytelling tell us she'll choose the socially acceptable option and the Phantom will martyr himself to give her the normalcy she needs to have a happy life. A frustrating rule, to be sure.

The Phantom's face: unmasking as anti-climax

So why does the Phantom's face matter so much, especially in the move from stage to screen? In the stage version, the Phantom's face is intensely deformed. This choice makes sense for a number of reasons, not the least of which is that the original novel tells us so. Buquet has seen the ghost:

> He is extraordinarily thin and his dress-coat hangs on a skeleton frame. His eyes are so deep that you can hardly see the fixed pupils. You just see two big black holes, as in a dead man's skull. His skin, which is stretched across his bones like a drumhead, is not white, but a nasty yellow. His nose is so little worth talking about that you can't see it side-face; and the absence of that nose is a horrible thing to look at. All the hair he has is three or four long dark locks on his forehead and behind his ears.
>
> (Leroux 1911: 11)

Certainly Lloyd Webber's Phantom does not look exactly like this, but the stage look is perhaps just as extreme, with licence granted to the poetic and exaggerated language of the novel. Also, for the reveal of his face to have any impact in a theatre, it must be changed and exaggerated enough to be visible from a distance. The stage Phantom wears a mask covering the entire right side of his face except for the jaw, and it crosses diagonally to the left side of his forehead. Even with the mask, some of his features and their unusual appearances are visible. His lips on the right are swollen and too large. His right eye is ice blue, glass-like. It is unclear if he can see out of it. Without the mask, we see that he has deep, large gashes on his cheek and forehead, dark and angry-looking. His nose is stretched, his eyebrow is gone, and dark vein-like scars emerge from under his hair onto his forehead.

The Phantom is actually unmasked twice in the course of the musical (and film). The first time, Christine is in his lair, having been swooped down there by the Phantom after he reveals himself in 'Angel of Music'. As they arrive in his home he incites her to sing ecstatically during 'The Phantom of the Opera'. He then sings her something of a lullaby or song of seduction, enticing her to enjoy the darkness and their collaboration, in 'The Music of the Night'. But just as she seems thoroughly hypnotized, he goes a step too far, revealing a mannequin in a wedding dress that looks exactly like her. She faints. The next morning, she awakens and cautiously approaches him, removing his mask out of curiosity. He immediately covers the right side of his face with his right hand, and turns his body away so that his right side remains mostly upstage – that is, Christine has briefly seen his face, but the audience has not. However, we know by her horrified reaction that we are meant to be scared and shocked. The second time she pulls off his mask is at the climactic moment of their performance of *Don Juan Triumphant*, the opera he has written for her and the company, in which he has taken (via sneaking and murder) the lead role, donning the costume and mask of an in-disguise Don Juan. She realizes it is him, and rips off not only his mask, but his wig as well. It turns out that his smoothed-back, debonair dark hair is fake, and underneath are dry, wild tufts of white hair sticking out in patches from his gray skull. The wig also reveals a huge crater on the side of his head. He looks deformed, old, pale, vulnerable, sickly. The gashes, craters, shadows, and bits of hair are visible from afar.

But even his impressive make-up job needed reinforcement to convey the horror; thus the second reveal, which shows everything, is done in public, on the opera stage, and can therefore be accompanied by screams of horror from the entire cast. Like audiences in any horror show or movie, we jump because the people in the story jump. An effective piece of theatrical business, undoubtedly. It is also a moment that arrives after two hours of expectation – after all, this is what we've come to see, is it not? Elsewhere (Sternfeld 2016) I have written about *The Phantom of the Opera* as a freak show, arguing that although it includes elements of romance, there is no question that the biggest thrill of the night is the revelation of his hideous face. Any pity or sympathy we may feel is easily justified by agreeing that his face is disgusting; that is, we need his face to be disgusting for us to be able to let him be a murderer with whom we sympathize, and we need his face to be disgusting for us to weep tenderly at his self-sacrifice. Of course he can't be with Christine, we reason. *Look* at him (see Figure 3.1).

It is quite shocking, then, that when the story got translated back onto film – after a long history of intense make-up jobs on film and in the stage version – Schumacher and company opted for such a mild look. The same two reveals occur in the film: first Christine sees him in his lair but we mostly don't. Near the end, she shows his face clearly to the camera and everyone on screen shrieks in horror. He seems to have a far more deformed appearance in this scene (and on through the rest of the film) than he did before; that is, things that should have been visible beneath his hand when she removes his mask the first time aren't there. Things that should be visible even with his mask on aren't there. It's as if his face gets worse when his mask is removed, and they didn't bother to make him up

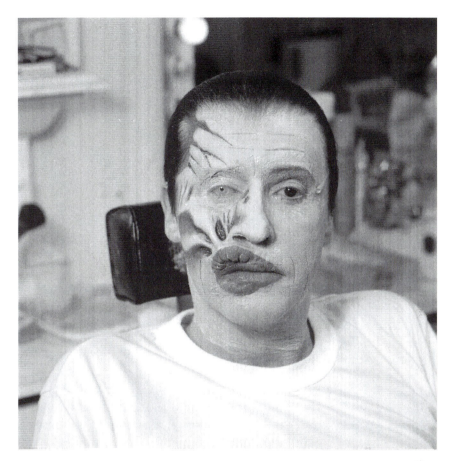

FIGURE 3.1 Michael Crawford in *The Phantom of the Opera* make up session.

Credit: Clive Barda/ArenaPAL.

fully when he had the mask and wig on. (This theory is confirmed by the 'fully authorized companion' book to accompany the film, which notes that indeed there was little or no make-up under the mask and it was only worn it when it would be fully visible: 'On the days when the Phantom was to be shot without the mask, Butler would spend many difficult hours in make-up, often starting work around 4am to be ready to go on set six hours later' (*Companion* 2007, 59).)

When he loses both the mask and wig in the second reveal, we see similar outlines to the stage design, especially the shadow of a sunken crater on his skull. But the whole effect is mild; the crater appears barely three-dimensional at all, more like a bruise than a hole. His eye droops slightly but is otherwise normal. His nose is symmetrical, his lips are fine. His skin on the affected side, on the cheek and forehead but not on his lower face, is somewhat textured – perhaps like a burn. There are no deep gashes, no nearly-black veins or scars or gullies. (To see the film's take on the Phantom's face, a sight almost entirely suppressed in promotional materials and published sources, the reader can do an internet search for Gerard Butler as the Phantom: https://musicalreviewer92.wordpress.com/phantom-of-the-opera-2004-movie-review-unmasked-gerard-butler-monkey-music-box-review-andrew-lloyd-webber-musical/ or www.pinterest.com/pin/396809417147027789/)

Critics took note. 'The Phantom's deformity', one film reviewer pointed out, 'looks like it could be solved with a little Clearasil' (Nestruck 2004). Another noted, 'when the mask comes off, he's simply not ugly enough' (Soergel 2004). This make-up choice renders the Phantom a viable choice for Christine, at least in theory. He is not terrifying to look at. One might think more of a heroic war veteran than a monster. He is young, tall, healthy in body, with a somewhat odd-looking skin condition and a few rather rakish scars, plus some unfortunate hair. Why wouldn't a teenage girl find him the rebellious bad boy she wants to tame? The film, then, seems to walk close to the line set by the two philosophical rules – the 'kill or cure' rule and the 'community above all' rule – and nearly tips over into allowing Christine to choose the Phantom. We know she never will, of course. Even if viability is presented by his appearance, it's not in the lyrics or the score. She pities him, she detests him, she manipulates him with her kiss into letting her be with the man she truly wants. But audience members can come much, much closer to disagreeing with her or even being surprised by her choice (should they happen not to know the story).

There are three other crucial factors in the film that make him a more viable choice than he is on stage, these three factors working together to make the whole film more romantic, realistic, and palatable to a broader audience than a musical or a horror movie might be. The film, in other words, changes three things from the stage show, in addition to the make-up, that result in this sweeping shift in tone: the role of magic, the addition of a back story, and the significant lowering of the leading players' ages. Let us see how these factors work to change the tone of the film.

A Phantom with no magic

In the stage show, the Phantom performs unexplained feats of magic. He's not simply called a magician by the opera's players, he does actual tricks that the audience can't explain, or doesn't see. A backdrop falls onto the stage near Carlotta. The Phantom's voice is heard, disembodied, without source, in Christine's dressing room and all around the theatre, moving from position to position in mid-sentence. The Phantom's mannequin figure of Christine bends forward and reaches out to her, seemingly on its own, causing her to faint. The Phantom's music box begins to play by itself, without winding or someone turning it on. When Carlotta takes Christine's role in the opera and calls Christine a 'little toad', the Phantom somehow makes Carlotta croak like a toad when she resumes singing. The chandelier falls when the Phantom cries out maniacally from above it. He simply appears and disappears at the masquerade ball.

In a rehearsal for *Don Juan Triumphant*, when the cast struggles to sing the challenging music, the piano plays the accompaniment on its own; the cast joins in, singing accurately but robotically, as if hypnotized. When Christine goes to her father's grave, the Phantom has somehow already arrived there, ready to woo her. Confronting Raoul in the graveyard, the Phantom shoots fiery electric bursts from a long staff with a skull on its top. We do not see how Piangi dies or how the Phantom takes his place, nor do we know how this could be accomplished backstage with dozens of people about. When Christine unmasks the Phantom on stage, he covers them both in his cloak and they disappear. When Raoul comes to confront the Phantom in his lair, the Phantom raises the gridiron gate with a gesture of his hand. He then tosses his magic lasso around Raoul's neck; the top end of it hangs tautly in space, attached to nothing. To make his final escape, he sits in his throne-like chair, wraps his cloak around himself, and disappears.

In the film, every single one of these feats of magic is given a mundane, logical visual explanation. Indeed, the Phantom does no magic at all in the film. The characters may not always see what he's up to, but the camera always does. To the audience watching the film, this Phantom is, at most, clever. He is a smart man – but not a monster and not an angel or magical creature. The backdrop falls because he cuts the rope from up in the catwalk. The Phantom's voice is heard around the theatre because he stands on a high walkway inside the roof's dome, or he hides down the hall from the echoing chapel. His voice does not move around the theatre in mid-sentence and does not take over the narration of his frequent letters. His Christine mannequin never moves. Carlotta croaks like a toad because he surreptitiously replaces her throat spray – which everyone knows (and the camera has established) she uses often – with something that damages her voice. The chandelier falls because he cuts its rope. The rehearsal scene is cut from the film entirely, so the opera cast never experiences the player piano or the musical hypnosis. The Phantom is at the graveyard because he has seen Christine leave the opera house and hail a carriage; he knocks out the driver and takes over, driving her there himself. Instead of shooting fireballs around the graveyard, he has a sword fight with Raoul. He kills Piangi by leaping on top of him in the wings and strangling him – as we saw him do with Buquet as well. When Christine unmasks him onstage, he leaps with her through a trap door in the stage to the space below; Raoul follows. The Phantom raises his gridiron gate with a lever. He ties Raoul to that gate with ropes and knots. When he leaves his lair, he simply walks out; he breaks a mirror and goes through a previously-hidden tunnel.

This complete erasure of the magical qualities of the stage Phantom render the film Phantom nothing more than a man; he has no inexplicable actions, he is simply clever. There is no 'gothic creepiness' remaining in the film, lamented *New York Times* critic A.O. Scott (2004); no 'mystery or strangeness' remains. While perhaps more realistic and easier for a film audience to swallow, the fantastic, other-worldly nature of the stage show (and novel) is completely lost.

A sympathetic back story

Thus the mild make-up and the explanation for all the magic tricks both help to render the Phantom entirely human. He is not angel, ghost, monster, or even magician; he is a (slightly) disfigured man with a sad past. Aiding this reading of his character is the most bold change made to the film version from the musical: the addition of a fully-realized back story for the Phantom. In the stage version, Raoul, in the midst of a frantic pursuit of the Phantom, corners Madame Giry who, as the opera's long-time ballet mistress, has always known more about the Phantom than anyone else. She tells Raoul, hurriedly, that she saw him when he was a child, locked in a cage as part of a travelling freak show. She maintains, though, that he is a genius, and clearly sympathizes with his plight despite his crimes. But the whole scene is brief, frantic, and – most significantly – unsung. In a show with barely any spoken dialogue at all, this scene feels like a throwaway, unimportant because unsung, its impact minimal. Raoul seems appropriately horrified that a person was in a cage, but then rushes off to attack or kill him nonetheless.

In the film, Schumacher and the screenwriting team have added an extended flashback scene, showing us the encounter between Madame Giry and the Phantom when both were children. Though still unsung, it plays over prominent underscoring and is visually arresting in the extreme – and thus given significance. In fact the brief dialogue is mostly cut, replaced by a complicated story told only through visuals and orchestral music. 'There was a traveling fair in the city,' Madame Giry tells Raoul. 'Gypsies. I was very young…' The camera zooms in on a photo of a pre-teen Madame Giry, and then morphs into a shadowy scene of a freak show. Young Giry and her fellow ballet-dancing friends skitter past leering gypsies and see a bearded lady, a contortionist, a fortune teller, fire-eaters, and other freak show staples, all shot with a sense of whirling chaos and fear. A tiny monkey, dressed in a circus outfit as one would see with a barrel-organ player, skitters about, in and out of the tents. The girls push into the 'Devil's Child' tent. In a cage, a bare-chested boy, his head covered in a sack, plays with a cymbal-playing monkey figure, similar to the real one running about and to the one that the grown Phantom (in both stage and film versions) has in his lair. A cruel and hairy guard whips and kicks the boy, who is tied to the cage with ropes. The man rips off the boy's hood; we do not see his face but the girls do. Some laugh nervously and cruelly, but young Giry looks horrified and sad. The crowd exits but Giry lingers, just in time to see the boy, his hood back on, use his own binding ropes to strangle his cruel master to death. He is free, and the two become a team, fleeing outside to a hidden side door of the opera house, where Giry lives (as Christine will later) as a resident ballet student. She guides him into the opera house's chapel (frequently visited by Christine; there she prays for her father and there she hears the Phantom's voice most often) and then shoves him deeper into the house's caverns, where we understand he will remain for ever. Back in the present, Madame Giry concludes: 'He has known nothing else of life since then, except this opera house.' She adds, 'He is a genius!' Raoul points out, 'But clearly, Madame Giry, genius has turned to madness.'

Thus the flashback scene, ostensibly, justifies his killings. The world could not have been more cruel to him. A child, a genius no less, treated like a monster, a prisoner, a beaten animal. It is quite a feat that we are meant to cheer when a boy of maybe ten years old commits his first murder. The guy deserved it, surely, and those early experiences scarred the boy's personality and his socialization for life. He is not, thanks to this information, ever expected to be normal. There is no way we can expect him to heal, or to integrate into society. Surely there is no therapy, no woman's love, that could fix what he went through and what it turned him into. Thus we are safe to pity him, to admire him even, but never to take responsibility for him or help him adapt to a realistic life. The flashback makes us more sympathetic to him than we are in the stage version, where we have so much less detail to feel sad about. But the flashback also exonerates the other characters, Christine included, and the audience as well, from any responsibility for what society turned him into, much less any responsibility for helping him. Thus, like Christine, we will weep prettily at his sad fate and his seemingly inevitable martyrdom.

Young and sexy

The final factor in the film version as compared to the stage version that renders the Phantom a more human, more viable candidate for Christine's love is a feature that both Lloyd Webber and Schumacher repeatedly played up in interviews and discussions of the film: the youth of the cast. Gerard Butler, cast as the Phantom when he was a mostly unknown actor then in his mid-thirties, came across as handsome, tall, and healthy-looking other than his mild skin issues. Broadway veteran Patrick Wilson was similarly young and dashing, sporting a Prince Valiant hair style and gaining, in the film, a sword fighting scene and even a bareback horse-riding moment. Thus, he becomes (or at least was intended to become) more of an action hero than a bland rich boy, as he often feels in the stage version. Emmy Rossum, cast at the age of only sixteen, brought huge round eyes, pale skin, and delicate features to Christine, making her – as she is in the novel – a teenage girl experiencing her first feelings of love and desire. Sarah Brightman was certainly young when she played the role, but it was understood that she was a grown woman, not a teenager, and that the Phantom was probably significantly older than her (as indeed Michael Crawford was).

Having the cast not just young but attractive and sexy was a requirement presented by director Joel Schumacher. He thought the story only worked if it was understood as Christine's sexual awakening, because her reaction to the Phantom – being drawn to this dangerous figure, naively not knowing how to deal with his attentions – marked her as a young girl. Raoul, then, is her first real love, and the Phantom her first sexual attraction. Lloyd Webber agreed readily to the notion of going younger, insisting in turn only that the cast do their own singing. They do; Emmy Rossum trained classically and had sung at the Met since the age of seven, Patrick Wilson had starred in several Broadway shows, and Gerard Butler – by far the least trained and skilled of the leads – sang in a rock band and underwent extensive vocal coaching for the film (Schaefer 2003). Lloyd Webber, a long-time fan of rock, especially heavy metal and other intense genres, seemed especially happy to cast a somewhat rough-sounding Gerard Butler; he 'fits my idea of the Phantom as somebody with an edge, the sort of dangerous man that has a rough, rock 'n' roll sensibility' (as quoted in Whipp 2004). Supporting the idea that this choice would only really be a dilemma for an inexperienced girl who hadn't yet outgrown her 'bad boy' phase, Schumacher described the two suitors as a 'stud muffin' and 'this insane, charismatic madman who has this incredible sexual pull on her', adding that the situation is 'every dad's nightmare come true' (as quoted in Whipp 2004; see also Stewart 2004).

Critics generally admired the cast even if they intensely disliked the material (the music, the story) and admitted that none of the three leads was given the opportunity for much depth or development but did their best. The youth factor surely helped: Rossum's near-perpetual damp-eyed stare of wonder would surely have played even more absurdly if she weren't a teen playing a teen.

Conclusions

The radically toned-down make-up, the absence of any magical powers, the sympathetic flashback story, and the emphasis on youth all combine to create a much more mainstream love-triangle story in the film than on stage. While a logical and probably smart series of choices, these factors also make a bleak statement about the reception of disabled people in our culture. We can excuse the idea that the Phantom could never be integrated into society by blaming it on the setting – he would never be integrated into 1870s society. But does the film make any case for the notion that things would be any different now? He may be younger, more handsome, and entirely without powers compared to his terrifying, hideous stage counterpart – but this leaves him simply a maladjusted murderer whom society can never accept, much less aid. We weep for him with Christine, and then abandon him as she does.

The stage version, therefore, makes something of a stronger case for his perpetual isolation, since he retains magical powers to the last and is understood to be too old and too strange – perhaps even too inhuman – to be socialized. The film instead unapologetically, romantically, abandons a disabled and abused orphan. While he may seem like a more viable choice in his film incarnation, we know – but should we know this, so readily expect and accept this? – that Christine and the audience can never end up with him.

Bibliography

Andrew Lloyd Webber's The Phantom of the Opera *Companion* (2007). London: Pavilion.
Barnes, M. (2004). '"Phantom" face-lift: No need to hide from screen version of much-improved musical.' *Austin (Texas) American-Statesman*, 22 December.

Garland-Thomson, R. (2004). 'The Cultural Logic of Euthanasia: "Sad Fancyings" in Herman Melville's "Bartleby".' *American Literature* 76(4), pp. 777–806.

Knapp, R. (2005). *The American Musical and the Formation of National Identity*. Princeton, NJ: Princeton University Press.

Leroux, G. (1911). *The Phantom of the Opera*. New York: Grosset & Dunlap.

Nestruck, J.K. (2004). 'Those who have seen it draw back in fear.' *National Post* (Canada), 22 December.

The Phantom of the Opera (2005) [DVD] Directed by Joel Schumacher. Warner Brothers.

Scott, A.O. (2004). 'Back With a Vengeance: The Music of the Night.' *The New York Times*, 22 December.

Schaefer, S. (2003). '"Phantom" to hit movie theaters with "young, sexy" look.' *USA Today*, 15 December.

Soergel, M. (2004). '"Phantom" ready for its close-up: Film version of Webber's [sic] beloved stage musical is purposely over-the-top.' *Florida Times-Union*, 22 December.

Sternfeld, J. (2016). '"Pitiful Creature of Darkness": The Subhuman and the Superhuman in The Phantom of the Opera.' In B. Howe, S. Jensen-Moulton, N. Lerner and J. Straus (eds), *The Oxford Handbook of Music and Disability Studies*. Oxford and New York: Oxford University Press. pp. 795–813.

Stewart, S. (2004). 'Theater Buff: How the Director Defied "Phans," Made a Movie.' *The New York Post*, 19 December.

Whipp, G. (2004). 'The Phantom Cometh: Music of the Night Finally Has Its Day On Film.' *Daily News of Los Angeles*, 19 December.

4

'BOHEMIA IS DEAD'

Rent celebrating life in the face of death

Mark Shields

Rent (1996), written by Jonathan Larson, focuses on a community living in New York City during the AIDS pandemic towards the end of the twentieth century. Based upon Giacomo Puccini's *La Bohème* (1896), *Rent* (1996) won four Tony Awards: Best Musical, Best Book, Best Score, and Best Performance by a Featured Actor in a Musical; and the Pulitzer Prize for Drama. Adapted for film in 2005 and directed by Chris Columbus for Sony Pictures, *Rent* (2005) featured the majority of the original Broadway cast returning to their roles.

In a loft apartment between 11th Street and Avenue B, roommates Mark Cohen and Roger Davis burn mementoes from their creative careers for heat while they despair at their impending eviction due to their unpaid rent. The homeless, artistic, multi-ethnic and queer communities occupying the surrounding area are also threatened with eviction to accommodate a 'state of the art, digital, virtual, interactive studio' (Larson 2008: 30). The plot unfolds between Christmases, told from the perspective of Mark, a heterosexual Jewish-American filmmaker, who documents the interwoven relationships of his ethnically and sexually diverse friends, many of whom are living with AIDS. This chapter will consider New York City as the cultural, political and ideological epoch for *Rent* (1996, 2005), its importance within the history of AIDS, and the audience's reception of *Rent* (2005) in a post-9/11 context.

Personal becomes political: experience, representation and authority

On 3 July 1981, *The New York Times* published the headline 'Rare Cancer Seen in 41 Homosexuals' (Altman 1981), a flashpoint in AIDS history that signified its official arrival in New York City, twelve years after the Stonewall Riots. By 1982 the Gay Related Immune Disease (GRID), renamed the Acquired Immune

Deficiency Syndrome (AIDS), was responsible for 752 diagnoses and 272 deaths in the city alone. Jonathan Larson graduated as an actor from Adelphi University in the class of '82, earning his Equity membership before moving to Manhattan. Larson grew up in suburban White Plains, Westchester County, to Jewish parents who took him and his sister to Broadway to see productions of *West Side Story* (1957), *Gypsy* (1959) and *Jesus Christ Superstar* (1971). Although he wanted to be an actor, Larson excelled in music during high school. At Adelphi, he performed in musical theatre, playing the lead in *Godspell* (1976), and had written political cabaret. During this time, Larson wrote to Stephen Sondheim, who advised him: 'I know a lot fewer starving composers than I do actors' (Leacock-Hoffman 2008: viii), believing that he was talented enough to succeed as a composer.

An early project of Larson's was *Superbia* (1989), a futuristic adaptation of George Orwell's *1984*. During this time, he worked at the Moondance Diner in SoHo, receiving tips and commissions and playing at open mic nights to pay his bills, while living in a fifth-floor walk-up in the Hudson Square district with a bathtub in the living room. *Superbia* (1989) received a concert staging in 1989, produced by friend Victoria Leacock-Hoffman, and won several awards and grants but did not see a full production due its ambitious set designs. In her introduction to Larson's book of *Rent* (2008), entitled '*Rent* Is Real', Leacock-Hoffman observes that 'AIDS seemed to be everywhere' (Leacock-Hoffman: vii) but it was yet to be 'better defined', and confessing that 'we were absorbed in trying to pay our rent and forge our careers' (ibid.: viii). Unfortunately, AIDS did become 'better defined' for Larson personally in 1986, when his childhood friend Matt O'Grady was diagnosed with HIV.

By 1989 AIDS was fully realised in the public consciousness, particularly in New York City as 19,482 of the city's population had died of the disease. The AIDS Coalition to Unleash Power (ACT UP) had already successfully performed several high-profile protests and in 1985 Hollywood actor Rock Hudson died of AIDS-related complications. Another of Larson's friends, Alison Gertz, was diagnosed with AIDS. Gertz's AIDS diagnosis drew international attention as an infection attributed to a white heterosexual female. Gertz's public image and media engagement brought AIDS into wider awareness, and she was hailed as a 'pioneer' of AIDS education (Lambert 1992). For almost a decade AIDS had existed at society's margins, devastating subcultures, with a hierarchy of stigmatising risk factors that mediated the public's understanding of the disease and their sympathy.

Larson included his experiences in an autobiographical rock monologue that addressed these new threats and his anxieties about his intermittent success. The result was *tick, tick…BOOM!* (1990), told from the perspective of Jon, a composer turning thirty in 1990, who wrestles with selling out to corporate America but is brought to his senses when his childhood friend is diagnosed with HIV. The plot concludes with a performance of 'Superbia' and an answerphone message from Stephen Sondheim, who remarks, 'You're going to have a great future' (Auburn and Larson 2009: 71) An off-Broadway production of *tick tick…BOOM!* was produced by Leacock-Hoffman and similarities between the rock score and

Larson's angst-filled lyrics now draw comparisons to *Rent* (1996). AIDS featured again in Larson's life when Pamela Shaw, who died in 1995 and had been dating Larson, was diagnosed with the disease, requiring Larson to have a HIV test. Leacock-Hoffman remarks that 'The grim reality that four of our best friends were infected with HIV, and three of them had developed AIDS, changed everything in our lives' (Leacock-Hoffman 2008: xiii), commenting that 'it would accelerate everything … it started an invisible stopwatch. Time could run out' (ibid.: x).

The real threat that HIV/AIDS now posed to Larson and the lives of his friends meant that the possibility of him bringing 'musical theater to the MTV generation' (Tommasini 1996) was in question. Fuelled by the death of his friends and his distaste for musical theatre at the time, he started work on *Rent* (1996). Larson had experienced moderate success with both *Superbia* (1989) and *tick tick…BOOM!* (1990), but was yet to write the 'transcendent' piece of musical theatre 'with the power to change your life' (Leacock-Hoffman 2008: viii). Larson had been recommended by Ira Weitzman to playwright Billy Aronson, who in 1989 wanted to adapt Puccini's *La Bohème* (1896) into a modern musical. Aronson worked with Larson and together they wrote the first draft of 'Rent', 'Sante Fe' and 'I Should Tell You', before Larson got Aronson's permission to continue with *Rent* (1996) as a solo work. In his review of *Rent* (1996), Dudley Saunders acknowledges (Saunders in Schulman 1998: i) 'some remarkable similarities' to writer and ACT UP member Sarah Schulman's fourth novel, *People in Trouble* (1990).[1] In her book *Stagestruck: Theater, AIDS, and the Marketing of Gay America* (1998), Schulman later recounts in remarkable detail her experience of challenging Larson's estate.

In a review of *Rent* (1996) that Schulman co-wrote with Don Shewey for the New York Press (reproduced in the book), she admits that she felt 'joyful recognition' of moments that she 'immediately recognised' (Schulman 1998: 10-11), acknowledging a sense of nostalgia in *Rent* (1996) and its effect on audiences that had experienced AIDS first hand in New York City. For Schulman, however, this sentimentality quickly dissipates as she notes that 'when *Rent* loses its specificities, it loses its meaning' (ibid.: 12). The representation of communities in *Rent* (1996) that are affected by AIDS, appear to be harmonious because they share the same geographical space and are affected by the same disease. Such communities' different and sometimes opposing experiences of AIDS are overridden by Larson for the sake of narrative so that they can be united in 'La Vie Bohème'. Schulman's personal experiences, evident in her work, offer an informed critique of these oversimplified representations which, she states, result in 'mediocrity … since any bit of complexity … would reveal immediately, the injustice of their dominant position' (Schulman 1998: 96). By Schulman's account, '[Larson] needed to steal from a lesbian and homogenize it … to falsely equate and banalize people of color, gay people, people with AIDS, and homeless people, everyone that he was not' (ibid.), going on to describe the different artistic responses and accounts of AIDS by queer, ethnic, and female artists who have been ignored in the history of AIDS that popular theatre provides. Schulman is clear that the oversimplification and fetishizing of people affected by AIDS in *Rent* (1996) not only contributes to the cultural erasure of these communities but is also complicit in its success.

New York City as a context for *Rent* (2005)

The representation of New York City on film in *Rent* (2005) is complicated by the social and political developments since its official theatrical preview at the New York Theatre Workshop in 1995. The medical advancements of highly active anti-retroviral therapy (HAART) for people living with HIV have significantly changed how audiences understand and relate to *Rent* and its discourses on screen in 2005.

The first drug made available to people with HIV/AIDS in New York City, Azidothymidine (AZT), was approved by the Food and Drug Administration (FDA) on 19 March 1987. Produced by pharmaceutical company Burroughs Wellcome,[2] AZT cost patients $10,000 a year and was the only drug licensed at that time to treat patients with AIDS. AZT is mentioned three times in *Rent* (1996); during 'Tune Up #3', on the black market in 'Christmas Bells' and between Mimi and Roger in 'I Should Tell You'. Both 'Tune Up #3' and 'Christmas Bells' are absent on screen, though some of the lyrics are used as dialogue. The exclusion of 'Christmas Bells' fails to represent the desperation of accessing the only expensive drug available to treat people living with AIDS at that time. The communities living with AIDS depicted in *Rent* (1996, 2005) are affected by poverty, unemployment, homelessness, and drug use, and on stage are unable to acquire AZT through legitimate means. Without 'Christmas Bells' on screen, it is unclear how the characters acquire treatment. Angel and Collins are not shown to have access to AZT, an omission which seems to favour the preservation of Mimi and Roger's climactic relationship for dramatic purpose.

On 7 December 1995, eight years after AZT was approved and 49 days before the official preview of *Rent* (1996) at the New York Theatre Workshop, the FDA approved Saquinavir, the first protease inhibitor to treat HIV infection, followed by Ritonavir four months later. These drugs became a new class of antiretroviral therapy, a precursor to the combined highly active antiretroviral therapy (HAART) for people living with HIV which halved death rates from AIDS in the United States within two years. After HAART was made available in the US, annual deaths from AIDS fell from 50,000 to approximately 18,000 (CDC 2011) with only 3,426 annual deaths in New York City in 1997, compared to the 6,004 recorded in 1996. The development of HAART to prevent and treat HIV crucially shifted its definition from a fatal acute infection to a long-term chronic condition which could be managed with access to medication that is now a matter of course for treating HIV infection. This immediately positions *Rent* (2005) as a historical representation of AIDS, which is somewhat vague, omitting the 'political and personal emergency' (Romàn 1998: 275) of the time before effective treatment was available.

The gentrification of the 11th Street lot is the opening plot point of *Rent* (1996, 2005). Sarah Schulman emphasises the significance of this in relation to AIDS in her book, *The Gentrification of the Mind: Witness to a Lost Imagination* (2012). Schulman recalls how the physical gentrification of New York City created a 'gentrification of the mind', providing two important perspectives for viewing *Rent* (2005). Firstly, Schulman points out that in practical terms the areas that experienced significant physical gentrification in the city had the highest rates of infection during the early stages of the pandemic and were left vacant because of high mortality rates. Secondly, Schulman recounts (Schulman 2012: 24-25) how the 'white flight' from post-war cities to the suburbs reinforced an ideological fear of the racial, sexual, religious and politically diverse communities that remained in inner city New York, and that city policy was subsequently developed 'with the stated goal of attracting wealthier people back to the city' (ibid.), which also marginalised the 'remaining poor, working-class, and middle-class residents [who] simply did not provide a wide enough tax base to support the city's infrastructure' (ibid.). Schulman describes how this process appealed directly to 'the children of white flight … with a nostalgic or sentimental familial attachment to the city: the place where they had gone to visit their grandmother or to go to the theater' (ibid.), mirroring Larson's path to Manhattan. The emergence of AIDS and the physical and ideological gentrification of New York City, however, is not purely a 'tragic example of historic coincidence' as suggested by Schulman (ibid.). The mayoralties of Ed Koch, David Dinkins, and Rudolph Giuliani and the global effects of 9/11 transformed New York City and changed how audiences would relate to it as a context for *Rent* (1996) on screen in 2005.

The mayoralties of Ed Koch and David Dinkins attracted wide criticism of their handling of the AIDS pandemic. As *The New York Times* observes;

> AIDS offers a rare insight into how well – or poorly – Mr Koch rose to a challenge that, unlike most city problems, unfolded entirely on his watch. The epidemic's severity is undeniable. New York has become the acknowledged world capital of AIDS, which is the city's third-leading cause of death, behind cardiac disease and cancer.
>
> (Lambert 1989)

Under Koch, AIDS emerged from obscurity to be the cause of death for 19,498 people in the city by 1990, when Dinkins assumed office. Both Koch and Dinkins took regressive action on preventative measures against infection when an estimated one in five in the city had AIDS and one-fifth of people living with AIDS in the USA lived in New York City, penalising both gay men and intravenous drug users through the closure of bathhouses and needle exchange programmes amid a crack epidemic. Both communities, which are disproportionately affected by HIV/AIDS, are significantly represented in the main cast of *Rent* (1996, 2005), though Larson's commentary on the politics that exacerbated the AIDS crisis in New York City is notable in its absence, and is only tangible in the capitalist vision of Benny, who later concedes to the romanticism of his bohemian friends. As the first African American Mayor of New York City, David Dinkins promised a 'gorgeous mosaic' of communities, a utopian vision similar to Larson's oversimplified representation of communities. Dinkins also signed a deal with the Walt Disney Corporation to gentrify Times Square and 42nd Street, transforming the Theatre District, once populated by pornographic theatres and sex work, into the family entertainment powerhouse it has now become. The gentrification of Broadway specifically had a direct impact on the marketing of *Rent* (1996) as it moved from its downtown beginnings to the Nederlander, now having to compete with conglomerates of the global entertainment market.

Rent on Broadway

The promotional campaigns for the Broadway opening of *Rent* (1996) solidified its status as a social phenomenon. The Broadway Ticket Lottery Model (now a fixture for theatre audiences globally) was developed by the producers of *Rent* (1996) to directly appeal to younger audiences who could not otherwise afford a ticket to see the show but identified with its characters. The near derelict Nederlander Theatre was redesigned to resemble a night club and the show benefitted from generous media coverage, celebrity audiences and a city-wide campaign of plain white billboards of the 'RENT' logo, which also doubled as an ironic comment on the gentrification and price of Manhattan real estate. The luxury department store Bloomingdales also created a fashion line inspired by *Rent* (1996), dressing the mannequins in the windows of their Lexington Avenue store in the 90s grunge clothing inspired by the characters of the show. The immediacy of the social issues represented in *Rent* (1996) spoke directly to the multiple communities in its audiences, particularly the Broadway community which had been devastated by AIDS. John M. Clum, author of *Something for the Boys: Musical Theatre and Gay Culture* (2001), importantly notes that 'Musicals were always gay. They always attracted a gay audience, and, at their best, even in times of a policed closet, they were created by gay men' (Clum in Shewey 1999: 54). With its multi-ethnic cast of 'Faggots, Lezzies, Dykes, Cross Dressers too' (Larson 2008: 84), *Rent* (1996) spoke to a generation still confronting AIDS, the biggest killer at the time of New Yorkers aged between 25 and 40. Although Larson was heterosexual, *Rent*'s (1996) offering of a less esoteric narrative of AIDS appealed to both the theatre community and the wider public, specifically a younger generation of audiences, through its marketing, rock score, subject matter, diversity and casting.

Theatre, *The New York Times* posits, was at the forefront in addressing the subject of AIDS, providing a purpose akin to 'Theater's ancient function as a public forum in which a community gathers to talk about itself' (Shewey 1987), though this is not without its contentions. David Romàn, in *Acts of Intervention: Performance, Gay Culture, and AIDS* (1998), examines the effects of AIDS on performance. AIDS, Romàn acknowledges, is still ongoing, and its beginning alludes a defining moment in which it arrived and was contained. Romàn attests AIDS as 'a crisis of such magnitude and boundless effect,' that needs 'little if any introduction' (Romàn, 1998: xiii), though he recognises that there are flashpoints of cultural significance when

AIDS exudes its clinical definition. The impact of AIDS on performance is unmeasurable, and 'its limits are not knowable' (ibid) partly due to the devastation of marginalised populations whose history remains uncharted and as a result, unofficial. Romàn writes, 'Narratives of AIDS are always representations of AIDS', quoting Cindy Patton (Patton in Romàn 1998: xix) that these representations are manifested in 'the effects of institutional process' and are 'multiple and discontinuous' (ibid.), of which *Rent* (1996, 2005) is one example. In theatre, several plays emerged out of New York City at the beginning of the pandemic, including amongst others *Torch Song Trilogy* (1982), *As Is* (1985), *The Normal Heart* (1985), *Love! Valour! Compassion!* (1994), *Elegies for Angels, Punks and Raging Queens* (1989), *Angels in America* (1993), and *Rent* (1996). These representations of AIDS that have survived are frequently revived to commemorate, fundraise and educate about AIDS globally. Their critical acclaim and popularity reinforce their dominance as authentic cultural representations of AIDS, almost becoming artefacts of this particular epoch, with some reaching wider audiences when adapted for film and television.

The representation of AIDS in *Angels in America* (2003),[3] broadcast for television by HBO, is multifaceted, seen through the internalised homophobia of right-wing capitalist Roy Cohn and closeted Mormon Joe Pitt, and in its visceral brutality as Prior Walter crawls across the floor of his apartment alone in the darkness, ravaged by disease. Although *Angels in America* takes place in New York City, the opening credits reaffirm that Kushner is addressing 'national themes', widening its appeal. Kushner's complex storytelling, still present, speaks beyond the immediate circumstances of the plot. Nancy Franklin, writing for *The New Yorker* (2003), discusses the navigation of multiple contexts in *Angels in America* through the process of adaptation. Franklin contends that 'America of 2003 isn't Clinton's America of 1993 when the play premiered' (Franklin 2003) and nor is it 1991 or 1992 when the play was in development. It is also not the 1985 of Ronald Reagan's second presidential term when the play is set. Franklin writes that watching the play on television 'reduces the work to the sum of its parts' (ibid.) emphasising the fragmentation of such representations of recent history for newer contexts.

The theatrical portrayals that represent the specificity of AIDS in New York City are dominated by narratives of gay men, the largest, but not the sole, demographic affected by AIDS during this time. Kushner constructs a narrative that expands this perspective somewhat through Roy Cohn as an antagonist, but he also delivers a much deeper and dexterous subtext. *Rent* (1996) is often credited with having the highest and most diverse concentration of main characters living with HIV/AIDS, though, as Schulman suggests, these are oversimplified and homogenise the reality of AIDS in New York City in favour of gaining a wider identification with its audiences.

Rent on film: casting, certification and nostalgia

Five months after *Rent* opened on Broadway on 29 April 1996 at the Nederlander Theatre, it was rumoured that Robert De Niro (credited as a producer for *Rent*

(2005)) and Miramax had secured the rights for its film adaptation, with Martin Scorsese as the director. When creating his musical film *New York, New York* (1977) Scorsese commented:

> In the city streets I'd seen in MGM and Warner Bros. musicals, New York curbs were always shown as very high and clean. When I was a child, I realized that wasn't right but was a part of a whole mythical city that they had created.
>
> (Scorsese in Grierson 2015: 70)

Scorsese's observation of how New York City is portrayed on film within the musical genre might support the realistic art direction of *Rent* (2005) by Keith P. Cunningham and Nanci Noblett. In the film, which was eventually directed by Chris Columbus, New York City is mythologised with nostalgia through its heightened realism of the past and homage to the original production.

On film, New York City is first seen through the lens of Mark, who narrates the footage with dialogue formed from the lyrics of 'Tune Up #1'. Mark's grainy footage depicts a New York City that is both past and familiar, including landmarks such as Radio City Music Hall, interspersed with scenes of the homeless and the East Village. The camera focuses on Giuliani's loathed squeegee man before panning out into colour and spinning back to Mark, who is seen capturing the moment on his 16mm Bolex, the Dziga Vertov of his day. The emergence of colour is recognisable in musical film, reminiscent of Dorothy's landing in The *Wizard of Oz* (1939). Avenue B, however, is not realised in Technicolour, but with neon lights, grime and inner city poverty. *Rent* (2005) was shot in New York City while San Francisco, Sante Fe and Los Angeles also provided locations for filming. The Avenue B first seen during the second production number 'Rent' was built on a soundstage in Los Angeles with the famous New York City skyline created using CGI in post-production. Columbus's use of establishing shots before a majority of scenes reasserts the city as the film's context. Wide shots of the graffiti-covered village emerge from the New York City steam system with walk signs and yellow New York taxis supporting the hyper-real garbage-strewn art direction. The use of CGI to insert breath, realistic light sources and diegetic sound during songs, and flashbacks to build characters' backstories, adds detail on film that theatre audiences are left to imagine.

The instances of direct address to the audience by Mark and in 'Voicemail #1-5', as they appear on stage, are omitted on film, adapted or cut, losing the immediacy of the theatricality of the stage production. The breaking of the fourth wall in *Rent* (1996) demonstrated Larson's pastiche of New York theatre community, specifically in 'Over the Moon' when Maureen urges the audience to participate. Although director Columbus uses television sets to reference 'the performance artists of the 80s' (Columbus 2005, 01:02:15), the action does not permeate the screen. 'La Vie Bohème', a riot of droll postmodern intertextuality, is supported on film by an anonymous ensemble that the audience have not connected with during an anguished 'Life Support' or 'Will I'. The result is a muted impression of the stage production, which is given a cinematic veneer. Columbus evokes nostalgia for *Rent* (1996) that, although recreated on film with much of the original cast, does not recapture the same fervent message of the 'La Vie Bohème' in 1996. Instead, it is stultified when retold with a rich mix of choreography, familiar tableaux and complex camera angles. On film, bohemia is dead. *Rent* (2005) fulfils, but does not transcend, the audience's expectations in the way that it redefined the musical genre on Broadway, relying heavily on the audience's nostalgia for the original production.

Columbus chose 'Seasons of Love' to open the film for the audience to 're-enter' the world of the musical, a function which served the same purpose at the beginning of Act Two on stage (Columbus 2005, 00:01:53). On film, 'Seasons of Love' acts as a prologue outside of the plot; it takes place on a bare stage, in an empty auditorium with a visible backstage area, before the house and spotlights fade to black. Aside from 'Seasons of Love', the plot throughout the film takes place outside of the theatre and inside the world of the characters. The only exception, apart from flashbacks and Mark's footage, is 'Tango Maureen', realised with full-scale ensemble choreography in Mark's imagination. This inclusion of stage life within the reality of the plot is inconsistent with Columbus's storytelling and is utilised more successfully in *Rent's* musical film predecessor, *Chicago* (2002).[4]

Reviewing *Chicago* (2002), Roger Ebert stated, 'The decision to use non-singers and non-dancers is always controversial in musicals, especially in these days when big stars are needed to headline expensive productions' (Ebert 2002). With *Rent* (2005) there was considerable speculation about possible casting choices.[5] Idina Menzel had won Best Actress in a Musical at the Tony Awards for *Wicked* in 2003, but was relatively unknown outside of the theatre community at the time of *Rent's* (2005) release. It would be her roles on Emmy and Golden Globe award-winning television series *Glee* (2009–2015) and Disney's *Frozen* (2013), which earned two Academy Awards, two Golden Globes, a BAFTA and a Grammy, that would bring her global acclaim beyond the stage. Rosario Dawson's portrayal of Mimi Marquez would also support *Rent's* (2005) claim to authenticity. Dawson, who had grown up in the East Village, also appeared in Larry Clark's *Kids* (1995), a gritty portrayal of teenage hedonism that results in an HIV infection. Clark made his film debut with *Kids*, 'shooting on location in the streets, placing his characters in their world' (Ebert 1995). With Clark's New York City, 'you can hardly even see Manhattan … the camera, like the characters, sees only this sad youth culture' (ibid.). *Kids* represents 'this culture in such a flat, unblinking detail that it feels like a documentary; it knows what it's talking about' (ibid.). Ebert wrote that the 'shadow' of AIDS gives *Kids* 'it's reason for being … intended as a wakeup call and for some kids it may be a lifesaver' (ibid.).

In *Rent* (2005), the only suggestion the audience has of how HIV is transmitted is through intravenous drug use seen during Mimi and Roger's flashbacks, leaving Collins and Angel's transmission ambiguous and inferred by their sexuality. Columbus felt it was important that *Rent* (2005) maintained its PG 13 certificate so that younger audiences could engage with its social message. Sony Pictures did not employ the same marketing tactics as *Rent* (1996) and had to compete with the franchise successes of musicals marketed towards significantly younger audiences, such as *High School Musical* (2006). Unlike *Rent* (2005), the message of *Kids* (1995) is clear, it is rated NC -17 and offers a stark observation of the tough realities of New York City during the 1990s.

Conclusions

Giuliani's election ended 16 years of Democratic mayoralty when he assumed office in 1994, continuing the rapid transformation of Times Square started by Dinkins, accommodating large media multi industries ESPN and MTV, further commercialising the area as a competitive entertainment destination. Aside from his role in the progressing of the gentrification of the city through his infamous zero tolerance policing strategy, Giuliani's mayoralty would come to be defined by a single global event, the Al Qaeda terror attacks on the World Trade Centre on 11 September 2001.

Like AIDS, the effects of 9/11, not only for New York but globally, are hard to define. '9/11', much like 'AIDS' has become an epitaph that signifies a multitude of meanings and experiences that extend beyond the initial events of that day. Giuliani played a visible role during the aftermath of 9/11 as 'America's Mayor'. He stated that New York was the 'most diverse city in the world' and that the events of 9/11 had affected 'every race, religion, and ethnicity', that 'it was an attack on the very idea of a free, inclusive and civil society' (Giuliani 2001). Though there were fatal terror attacks outside of New York on 9/11, ninety-two per cent of the victim deaths are attributed to the attacks in Lower Manhattan that day. The memory and discourse of 9/11 generally presides over the first bombing of the North Tower in 1993 during Dinkins's mayoralty. New York City was a more dangerous place in 1993, with 430,460 recorded crimes committed that year, including 1,946 murders. In 1993 such an attack was possibly more conceivable for global audiences compared to 2001, which had only 162,064 recorded crimes and only 649 murders (not including lives lost on 9/11). The two events are incomparable regarding scale, lives lost, and global ramifications; however, the significant difference in crime rate not only charts the success of Giuliani's policies but also changes the audience's perception of New York City when viewing *Rent* in 2005. Columbus chose to include an establishing shot of the World Trade Centre after 'I'll Cover You', which he justifies as a 'subtle' choice not included as 'any sort of a comment' (Columbus 2005, 00:59:00). However, New York City's transformation through the mayoralties of Koch, Dinkins, and Giuliani, from a city affected by AIDS, poverty, drugs, and crime to the epicentre of the neoliberal American dream, radically alters how the audience perceives and relates to New York City as the film's context.

Larson's tragically premature death from an aortic aneurysm on 25 January 1995, before *Rent's* (1996) official preview, means that he was unable to defend his work or contribute to its adaptation for film. It is evident from the autobiographical *tick, tick…BOOM!* (1990) and his friends' testimonies, that Larson was personally affected by the AIDS pandemic in New York City and that it did influence his work. However, the representations of the communities affected by AIDS in *Rent* (1996, 2005) are oversimplified, perhaps to support genre conventions and narrative structure, and the legitimacy of Larson's authorial voice and experience of AIDS is challenged by Sarah Schulman. The less intersectional and more romanticised representation of those affected by AIDS contributes to *Rent's* (1996, 2005) wider appeal. Unlike *Angels in America* (2003), *Rent* (2005) does not retain its theatricality or benefit from successful marketing to entice younger audiences as it did in 1996. The reunion of the original Broadway cast immediately renders the audience's relationship to *Rent* (2005) as nostalgic, through its homage to the original production, excluding newer audiences. The hyper-real art direction does not provide the same opportunities for the translation of stage life to screen as with Rob Marshall's *Chicago* (2002), and does not capture the harsh realities of AIDS for young New Yorkers in the same way as Larry Clark's *Kids* (1995).

The development of HAART to successfully treat HIV since *Rent* (1996) opened on Broadway historicizes the representation of AIDS, losing its urgency. The celebration of life in the face of death seems trite when AIDS and its affects are 'stripped' of their 'political and personal emergency' (Romàn 1998: 275) and the educational possibilities around depicting HIV is censored in favour of a PG 13 certificate. The exclusion of the politics that worsened the AIDS crisis in New York City is regrettably absent from *Rent's* (1996, 2005) narrative, paralleling how the physical gentrification of New York City created an ideological 'gentrification of the mind' as suggested by Schulman. The significance of New York City as the cultural, political and ideological context for *Rent* (1996, 2005) shifted dramatically in the aftermath of the terror attacks on 9/11. The threat of AIDS is surpassed by the threat of global terror in the audience's collective memory, and New York City now signifies prosperity, inclusivity and freedom, a place where *Rent* (2005) is harder to imagine.

Notes

1   Considered as one of the first fictional accounts of AIDS, *People in Trouble* (1990) includes characters such as 'a greedy landlord' and an 'interracial gay couple … both of whom are HIV positive', a drag queen who uses 'stolen credit card numbers to charge groceries for the poor', and a 'performance art piece' that 'leads to a riot' (Saunders in Schulman 1998: i).

2   The Gay Men's Health Crisis (GMHC) was established in January 1982 as one of the earliest proponents of health and social care for people affected by AIDS in New York City. Larry Kramer, a founding member of GMHC, felt it was politically ineffectual, condemning the lack of government action on AIDS. He wrote '1,112 and Counting' in 1983 calling for volunteers for civil disobedience. Kramer would later found ACT UP in March 1987, which was instrumental in lowering the price of AZT by 20 per cent to $6,400 by targeting both the FDA and the New York Stock Exchange with a

banner reading 'SELL WELLCOME' in September 1989. Dr Jean Scandlyn, in her article 'When AIDS became a chronic illness' (2000), recognises that 'Political activity by gay men … was effective in securing government support for research and treatment', though this is scarcely mentioned in *Rent* (1996, 2005).

3   *Angels in America: A Gay Fantasia on National Themes* (1993) had been revised several times before its opening on Broadway in 1993. Written by Tony Kushner, *Angels in America* was adapted by television network HBO in 2003 as a miniseries starring Meryl Streep, Al Pacino and Emma Thompson and directed by Mike Nichols. The television adaptation, retaining Kushner as its writer, manages to maintain the theatricality of the stage production in which some scenes happen simultaneously with characters moving between both scenarios.

4   The second longest running musical in Broadway history (as of 2016), *Chicago* (1975) was revived on Broadway six months after *Rent* (1996) opened. Tony-nominated director Rob Marshall created the film of *Chicago* (2002) 'more or less within Roxie's imagination, where everything is a little more supercharged than life' (Ebert 2002). Roger Ebert claims that *Chicago* (2002) 'continues the reinvention of the musical started with *Moulin Rouge!*' (ibid.), praising the art direction as 'high electric streamlined gloss'. *Chicago* (2002) balances songs and dialogue, delivered by an award-winning Hollywood cast, keeping a familiarity with the stage production but also managing to create 'its own spirit' (ibid.). The nightclub where Roxie Hart first encounters Velma Kelly and imagines herself as a jazz starlet makes for an easier translation of stage life to the screen. The physical context of the nightclub and stage on film supports the conventions of the musical genre and is also used in Baz Luhrmann's Oscar-winning dreamlike bohemian pastiche *Moulin Rouge!* (2001), and *Dreamgirls* (2006) directed by Bill Condon, who wrote the screenplay for *Chicago* (2002).

5   *The Washington Post* (2005) reported Justin Timberlake, Christina Aguilera and Usher as possible casting choices for *Rent (2005)*. The only absences from the original cast on film were Daphne Rubin-Vega as Mimi and Fredi Walker as Joanne, replaced by Rosario Dawson and Tracie Thom respectively. Thom continued the role of Joanne onstage in the final Broadway cast, which was filmed live and distributed by Sony Pictures in 2008.

Bibliography

ACT UP (2016). *AIDS Coalition to Unleash Power NYC.* www.actupny.org/. Accessed June 2016.

Altman, L.K (1981). 'Rare Cancer Seen in 41 Homosexuals'. *The New York Times.* www.nytimes.com/1981/07/03/us/rare-cancer-seen-in-41-homosexuals.html. Accessed June 2016.

Angels In America (2003). [Film] Directed Mike Nichols. United States. HBO.

Auburn, D. and J. Larson (2009). *tick, tick…BOOM!* New York: Applause Theatre and Cinema Books; Hal Leonard Corporation.

Bernstein, L., A. Laurents and S. Sondheim (1957). *West Side Story.* Directed Jerome Robbins. Winter Garden Theatre, New York, 27 June 1959.

CDC (2011). *HIV Surveillance – United States, 1981–2008.* www.cdc.gov/mmwr/preview/mmwrhtml/mm6021a2.htm. Accessed June 2016.

Chicago (2002). [Film] Directed Rob Marshall. United States: Miramax.

Clum, J.M. in Shewey, D. (1999). 'Kissed by Cole'. *The Advocate,* 21 December 1999. p. 54.

Dreamgirls (2006). [Film] Directed Bill Condon. United States: Paramount Pictures.

Columbus, C. (2005). 'Director's commentary: *Rent* (DVD),' directed by Chris Columbus. United States: Sony Pictures.

Ebb, F., B. Fosse, J. Kander, and D. Thompson (1996). *Chicago*. Directed Walter Bobbie. Ambassador Theatre, New York, 14 November 1996.

Ebert, R. (1995). '*Kids* movie review & film summary (1995).' www.rogerebert.com/reviews/kids-1995. Accessed June 2016.

Ebert, R. (2002). '*Chicago* movie review & film summary (2002).' Available from: www.rogerebert.com/reviews/chicago-2002. Accessed June 2016.

Ebert, R. (2005). '*Rent* movie review & film summary (2005).' www.rogerebert.com/reviews/rent-2005. Accessed June 2016.

Fierstein, H. (1982). *Torch Song Trilogy*. Director Peter Pope. Little Theatre, New York, 10 June 1982.

Franklin, N. (2003). 'America, Lost And Found'. *The New Yorker*. www.newyorker.com/magazine/2003/12/08/america-lost-and-found. Accessed June 2016.

Frozen (2013). [Film] Directors Chris Buck and Jennifer Lee. United States: Walt Disney Studios Motion Pictures.

Giuliani, R. (2001). *Giuliani addresses the United Nations*. 1 October 2001. New York City: United Nations.

Glee (2009–2015). Fox. 19 May 2009–20 March 2015.

Grierson, T. (2015). *Martin Scorsese in 10 Scenes*. Massachusetts: Focal Press.

Hoffman, W.M. (1985). *As Is*. Director Marshall W. Mason. Lyceum Theatre, New York, 1 May 1st 1985.

Kids (1995). [Film] Director Larry Clark. United States: Miramax.

Kramer, L. (1983). '1, 112 and Counting', *The New York Native*, 14 March, Issue 59.

Kramer, L. in Hevesi, D. (2014). 'Rodger McFarlane, a leader in the fight against AIDS, dies at 54.' *The New York Times*. www.nytimes.com/2009/05/19/nyregion/19mcfarlane.html?_r=0. Accessed June 2016.

Kushner, T. (1993). *Angels in America: A Gay Fantasia on National Themes*. London: Nick Hern Books.

Kushner, T. (1993). *Angels in America: Millennium Approaches*. Director George C Wolfe. Walter Kerr Theatre, New York, 4 May 1993.

Kushner, T. (1993). *Angels in America: Perestroika*. Director George C Wolfe. Walter Kerr Theatre, New York, 23 November 1993.

Lambert, B. (1989). 'Koch's Record on AIDS: Fighting a Battle Without a Precedent.' *The New York Times*. www.nytimes.com/1989/08/27/nyregion/koch-s-record-on-aids-fighting-a-battle-without-a-precedent.html?pagewanted=all. Accessed June 2016.

Lambert, B. (1992). 'Alison L. Gertz, Whose Infection Alerted Many to AIDS, Dies at 26'. *The New York Times*. www.nytimes.com/1992/08/09/nyregion/alison-l-gertz-whose-infection-alerted-many-to-aids-dies-at-26.html. Accessed June 2016.

Larry, K. (1985). *The Normal Heart*. Director Michael Lindsay-Hogg. The Public Theatre, New York, 21 April 1985.

Larson, J. (1989). *Superbia*. Producer Victoria Leacock-Hoffman. Village Gate, New York, September 1989.

Larson, J. (1996). *Rent*. Director Michael Greif. The Nederlander Theatre, New York, 29 April 1996.

Larson, J. (2008). *Rent: The Complete Book and Lyrics of the Broadway Musical*. New York: Applause Theatre and Cinema Books, Hal Leonard Corporation.

Laurents, A., S. Sondheim And J. Styne (1959). *Gypsy*. Director Jerome Robbins. Imperial Theatre, New York, 21 May 1959.

Leacock-Hoffman, V. (2008). '*Rent* Is Real'. In Larson, J. (2008) *Rent: The Complete Book and Lyrics of the Broadway Musical*. New York: Applause Theatre and Cinema Books, Hal Leonard Corporation.

Leoncavallo, R. (1897). *La Bohème*. La Fenice, Venice, 6 May 1897.

Lloyd Webber, A. and T. Rice (1971). *Jesus Christ Superstar*. Director Tom O'Horgan. Mark Hellinger Theatre, New York, 29 September 1971.

Marks, P. (2005). 'Hollywood's Rent Check'. *The Washington Post*. www.washingtonpost. com/wpdyn/content/article/2005/11/18/AR2005111800217.html. Accessed June 2016.

McNally, T. (1995). *Love! Valour! Compassion!* Director Joe Mantello. Walter Kerr Theatre, New York, 14 February 1995.

Moulin Rouge! (2001). [Film] Director Baz Luhrmann. Australia, United States: 20th Century Fox.

Murger, H. (2007) *The Bohemians of the Latin Quarter: Scenes De La Vie Bohème*. FQ Classics.

New York, New York (1977) [Film] Dir. Martin Scorsese. United States: United Artists.

NYC Department for Health and Mental Hygiene (2015). *New York City HIV/AIDS Annual Surveillance Statistics 2014*. www1.nyc.gov/assets/doh/downloads/pdf/ah/ surveillance2014-trend-tables.pdf .Accessed June 2016.

NYPD Crime Data Warehouse (2016). *Crime*. www.nyc.gov/html/nypd/html/home/ poa_crime.shtml. Accessed June 2016.

Original Motion Picture Soundtrack (2005). *Rent*. [Mp3] United States: Warner Bros.

Puccini, G. (1986). *La Bohème*. The Teatro Regio, Turin, 1 February 1896.

Rent: Filmed Live on Broadway (2008). [Film] Director Michael John Warren. United States: Sony Pictures.

Romàn, D. (1998). *Acts of Intervention: Performance, Gay Culture, and AIDS*. Indianapolis: Indiana University Press.

Russell, B. (1989). *Elegies for Angels, Punks and Raging Queens*. Ohio Theatre, New York, 1989.

Scandlyn, J. (2000). 'When AIDS became a chronic disease'. *Western Journal of Medicine* 172(2), pp. 130–133. www.ncbi.nlm.nih.gov/pmc/articles/PMC1070775/. Accessed June 2016.

Schulman , S. (1998). *Stagestruck: Theater, AIDS, and the Marketing of Gay America*. Durham, NC: Duke University Press.

Schulman, S. (1990). *People in Trouble*. London: Sheba Feminist Publishers.

Schulman, S. (2012). *The Gentrification of the Mind: Witness to a Lost Imagination*. California: University of California Press.

Schwartz, S. (1976). *Godspell*. Director John-Michael Tebelak. Ambassador Theatre, New York, 22 June 1976.

Shewey, D. (1987). 'Theater; Aids On Stage: Comfort, Sorrow, Anger.' *The New York Times*. www.nytimes.com/1987/06/21/theater/theater-aids-on-stage-comfort-sorrow-anger.html?pagewanted=all. Accessed June 2016.

The Normal Heart (2014). [Film] Director Ryan Murphy. United States: HBO.

Tommasini, A. (1996). 'Theater; The Seven-Year Odyssey that Led to "Rent".' *The New York Times*. www.nytimes.com/1996/03/17/theater/theather-the-seven-year-odyssey-that-led-to-rent.html?pagewanted=all. Accessed June 2016.

Wizard of Oz (1939). [Film] Directed Victor Fleming. United States: Metro-Goldwyn-Mayer Studios Inc.

5

WHERE DID WE GO RIGHT (AND WRONG)?

Success and failure in the adaptations of *The Producers* from and to the screen

Julian Woolford

Mel Brooks' popular movie *The Producers* (1967) underwent two major adaptations at the beginning of the twenty-first century: the first was to become the most successful Tony-winning Broadway musical; and then to become a screen version of the Broadway musical that was a box office and critical failure. Beginning with an understanding that the narrative is driven by notions of commercial and critical success and failure in the adaptation of *Springtime for Hitler*, this chapter considers the adaptations of *The Producers* from film to stage musical and then to movie musical.

This chapter will analyse adaptors' decisions, with reference to Linda Hutcheon's *Theory of Adaptation* and other discourse in the field, and critically evaluate and examine from a theoretical viewpoint certain decisions made in the translation from film to stage musical. It will consider whether an act of slavish copying across media, from stage to movie musical, can be considered a genuine adaptation or a lavish recording of the stage production. There then follows a further examination from a contextual viewpoint, including the musical's comic treatment of palimpsests of other stage musicals, and the appropriateness of these in the movie musical. Finally, there will be consideration of the cultural impact and symbolism of the stage musical in the geopolitical environment of the post-9/11 period, and the movie musical post-Iraq War. For the purposes of this chapter, the three remediations of the work are referred to as 'the film' (the original 1967 movie), 'the musical' (the Broadway 2001 production) and 'the movie musical' (as the 2005 movie was subtitled by its own producers).

Adaptations on the continuum of success and failure

The triumph of successful operas and musicals is how they reinvent the familiar and make it fresh.

(McNally 2002)

The Producers appeared first as a movie in 1967, written and directed by Mel Brooks and starring Zero Mostel and Gene Hackman. The narrative is overwhelmingly concerned with commercial success and failure: following a series of Broadway failures, producer Max Bialystock teams up with timid accountant Leopold Bloom to set out to create the most likely commercial failure in order to embezzle his investors. When the musical, *Springtime for Hitler*, becomes an unexpected success their plan unravels and they are jailed.

In 2001 *The Producers* was adapted as Broadway musical and opened starring Nathan Lane and Matthew Broderick; it received the most Tony awards in the history of Broadway and ran for 2,502 performances. In 2005 the Broadway musical was adapted into a movie musical, which retained Lane, Broderick, many of the Broadway cast, and the Broadway director, Susan Stroman, with her first, and to date only, movie credit. The film grossed $38 million worldwide (Hoad 2013), against an estimated budget of $45 million and is widely considered to be unsuccessful.

Central to the plot of *The Producers* is the commercial success or failure of the fictional adaptation of the events of the Second World War into *Springtime for Hitler, a Gay Romp with Adolf and Eva at Berchtesgaden*, a musical considered by Max Bialystock to be the 'worst play ever written', but which is hailed as 'satiric masterpiece' and 'The best new musical of the decade' by the fictional critics (Brooks and Meehan 2001). Notions of success and failure permeate the work, but it is obviously too simplistic to use Max Bialystock's own criteria to judge the success of the stage and later movie musical adaptations. As far back as 1957, Bluestone pointed out that commercial or critical success was too narrow a definition for judging adaptations (Bluestone 1957) and it is particularly ironic that in the case of *The Producers* the very benchmarks that the characters use within the plot become the obvious starting point for an analysis of the two adaptations.

Max and Leo produce for commercial reasons and therefore one must question Mel Brooks' motivation for adapting his own work not once, but twice. The remediation of the film to a stage musical was an obvious decision, coming as it did in a period when movie studios were actively exploiting their back catalogues for appropriate musical theatre adaptation source material: *The Producers* opened the same year (2001) as the screen to musical adaptation of *The Full Monty* and the year before *Thoroughly Modern Millie* and *The Sweet Smell of Success* (2002). *The Producers* also had the advantage of being a movie set on Broadway, It was a film about a musical, and a natural choice for a backstage musical. If content determines form, *The Producers* is more suited to a stage musical than the film medium. Co-bookwriter Thomas Meehan comments

> The movie itself was already partly a musical, featuring one of the funniest musical numbers ever put on film, "Springtime for Hitler", which I sensed could be at least as funny onstage.

> (Brooks and Meehan 2001: 22)

Although Brooks claims that he originally resisted turning the film into a stage musical, he was adamant in 2001 that there would not be a movie musical (Pogrebin 2001). Less than five years later he had changed his mind and the movie musical was released. Hutcheon reminds us that

> From another economic angle, expensive collaborative artforms like opera, musicals, and films are going to look for safe bets with a ready audience – and that usually means adaptations. They are also going to seek ways to expand the audience for their 'franchise', of course, though they have not been in the habit of thinking about it in quite those terms.
>
> (Hutcheon 2013: 87)

The profit motivation for the movie musical is obvious: According to Robin Pogrebin in *The New York Times,* the Broadway musical that 'cost $10.5 million to mount and runs at a cost of about $500,000 a week, would recoup its investment in a rapid 35 weeks' (2001: 34), and the show ran for six years (2,502 performances). The musical film grossed less than $20 million by the end of its initial US release. In the UK, on its opening weekend it grossed £1,311,179 across 347 screens, giving it an average of just £3,779 per screen.

Although the movie musical appears to be a commercial failure, there is a further consideration, which is the effect of a movie musical on the future worldwide licensing of the stage musical. Overwhelmingly, titles that are licensed in emerging stage musical markets are those that have movie versions, as it is through the screen version that the potential audience becomes aware of the stage version. *The Sound of Music, Grease* and, latterly, *Chicago* and *Mamma Mia!* have proven popular onstage in the emerging markets of Asia and the Middle East, driven largely by audiences familiar with the films. In some instances, this develops into the inclusion of material written specifically for the screen version (and after the original stage version) such as 'You're The One That I Want' and 'Hopelessly Devoted to You' being included in the majority of stage versions of *Grease* since the 1978 release of the movie version. The economic argument for a movie musical must therefore be considered as both a franchise building strategy, aligned with a simple profit motive from the movie, and in this context any financial losses of the movie musical might be offset against future stage musical income.

The sense of extending a franchise is particularly pertinent to *The Producers* because, unlike other screen to stage to screen adaptations, there is a uniformity of authorship for *The Producers* in the person of Mel Brooks. As writer of the film, for which he won the 1969 Academy Award for Best Screenplay Written Directly for the Screen, he was joined by Thomas Meehan as co-bookwriter for the musical and the screenplay of the movie musical. And although the producers of *The Producers* exploited the 'Mel Brooks brand' for both the musical and the movie musical – the advertising for the musical subtitled it 'the new Mel Brooks musical' – this underestimates the intensely collaborative nature of musical theatre creation. Brooks credits major collaborators in the musical as Meehan, musical supervisor and dance arranger Glen Kelly, director and choreographer Susan Stroman and also Stroman's late husband Mike Ockrent, who was to direct the musical before his sudden and untimely death in 1999.

Judged purely on profitability, both the film and, to a greater extent, the musical are undoubted successes, while the movie musical is clearly a failure. Whilst judging the critical reception is a more nuanced task, the website Rotten Tomatoes, which aggregates critical responses, scores the film with a 91 per cent approval rating and the movie musical with a 51 per cent approval rating.

Musical theatre as adaptation: extended intertextual engagements with the original

Although superficially, the movie musical is obviously a film version of the stage musical, one must question whether it should be considered a true adaptation. Hutcheon defines adaptation as

1. An acknowledged transposition of a recognizable work or works.
2. A Creative and an interpretive act of appropriation/salvaging.
3. An extended intertextual engagement with the adapted work.

(Hutcheon 2013: 8)

The stage musical is undeniably an acknowledged transposition of a recognizable work (the original movie) and the movie musical is undeniably an acknowledged transposition of the stage musical. But it is in examining the remaining of Hutcheon's criteria that we discover a divergence in the adaptation approaches firstly from the film to the stage musical, and then from the stage musical to the movie musical.

The creative and interpretive decisions undertaken in the adaptation to the stage musical are extensive. Co-bookwriter Thomas Meehan comments:

> We've taken *The Producers* … and changed it from start to finish. We've put in a new beginning and a new ending; we've cut entire scenes and lines that devoted fans have been laughing at for over thirty years; and we've even had the nerve to write brand-new scenes that hadn't been in the movie, along with scores of brand-new lines. Moreover, as the lyricist and composer of the show's score, Mel has stuck no fewer than sixteen brand-new songs into *The Producers*, to go with the two he'd already written for the movie, 'Springtime for Hitler' and 'Prisoners of Love'. What a monumental display of unabashed chutzpah!
>
> (Brooks and Meehan 2001: 14)

Notable among the many changes are not only the insertion of the songs, but the development of the role of Ulla, Bialystock's Swedish secretary, whose role is enhanced to that of the archetypical 'leading lady', and which serves as a useful example of the adaptors' decisions. In the original movie, she has barely ten lines and no character development. For the musical, she has a romantic relationship with Leo, a solo, 'If You Got It, Flaunt It', a love duet 'That Face' and a featured role in 'Springtime For Hitler'.

By contrast, it becomes apparent that the original film is remarkably 'male': all the major characters are men, women are underwritten sex-objects (Ulla and showgirls) or dirty-minded little old ladies with large cheque books. Enhancing the role of Ulla allows the development of romance that the Broadway musical's original dramaturg, Lehman Engel, deems one of the 'needs' of the musical. Kissel, in his notes to Engel's work, points out that the real romance of *The Producers* is not between Leo and Ulla:

> There's a Gershwin-esque charm to 'That Face', the one ostensible love song between the shy accountant, Leopold Bloom, and Ulla, the bombshell secretary. But the real romantic ballad comes at the end of the show, when Bloom expresses his affection for his unscrupulous business partner, Max Bialystock, in 'Til Him.'
>
> (Engel and Kissel 2006: 118)

Rocco Landesman, lead producer of the stage musical, comments in the Preface to Brooks and Meehan's libretto that he believes the adaptation into the musical

> had been greatly improved by developing what had been just a seedling in the movie, the relationship between Max and Leo, into a real love story. Mel and Tom had not only made the story funnier but had added the decisive element of human drama with an emotional payoff.
>
> (Brooks and Meehan 2001: 7)

The addition of the romantic aspect to *The Producers* musical is an excellent example of an 'extended intertextual engagement with the adapted work'. As Woolford points out 'Each artform has its own strengths and weaknesses and you need to understand how you are going to transform the source material by turning it into a musical' (Woolford 2012: 35). It is clear that this was precisely the strength of the adaptors in the case of the musical, where screenwriter and movie director Brooks enlisted the help of experienced Broadway professionals Stroman and Meehan. This facilitated both the intertextual engagement and a 'creative and an interpretive act of appropriation'.

Commercial success affecting remediation

Having scored such a success onstage, it is easy to assume that the creators wished to recreate the stage success with a movie musical but failed to undertake a requisite adaptation. Whilst successful movie musical adaptations of the early twenty-first century such as *Chicago*, which took $306 million worldwide (nearly eight times

The Producers gross), and *Sweeney Todd* (which took $152 million) successfully remediated the libretti of the stage musical sources into movies, Stroman's approach to the movie musical appears to be precisely that of the movie musicals of the 1940s and 1950s:

> In the wake of [stage successes] *Oklahoma!, Carousel, Annie Get Your Gun, My Fair Lady*, and other long-running Broadway successes, Hollywood returned to the late-twenties practice of bringing book musicals to the screen relatively untouched ... the adaptations of the fifties and sixties stick painfully close to the Broadway version. The freedom from scenic construction achieved by Lubitsch and Mamoulian a quarter-century earlier is here abandoned in favour of a staginess that testifies more to a poverty of taste than to a limitation of means.
>
> (Altman 1987: 196)

This is exactly the issue with Stroman's movie musical; there is a failure of remediation. In his commentary on the creating of the musical Meehan emphasises the importance of establishing that 'The Producers [onstage] was going to be its own thing and not simply a slavish copy of the movie' (Brooks and Meehan 2001: 30), but the movie musical is precisely a 'slavish copy' of the stage musical, from its casting right through to its staging.

If we consider the screenplay first, we see that it is an edited version of the stage libretto, with some scenes being relocated to take advantage of the flexibility of the medium of film. Four numbers are removed – 'King of Broadway', 'In Old Bavaria', the reprise of 'Opening Night' and 'Where Did We Go Right?'– presumably for reasons of running time, as the movie musical is also experienced in single sitting, rather than in the two sittings with an intermission common in stage performance. The reference to 'Where Did We Go Right?' in the number 'Betrayed' is retained, but meaningless. With the exception of the interpolation of the song 'You'll Find Your Happiness in Rio', which was written for and cut from the musical (but here provided an eligible song for the Academy Awards, though it was not nominated) and is here sung by an off-stage chorus over images of Leo and Ulla in Brazil, there are only fifteen lines in the film musical that do not appear in the stage libretto. Some of these appear to be adlibs improvised between the publication of the musical libretto and the release of the movie musical. The work is edited, but not remediated.

Secondly, there is the casting, which retains all of the major (and some of the minor) original Broadway cast except Brad Oscar as Liebkind and Cady Huffman as Ulla, replacing them with 'bankable' movie stars Will Ferrell and Uma Thurman respectively. A total of twenty alumni of the Broadway production appear in the movie musical, invariably recreating their stage performances. It must be recognised that the two Broadway stars, Nathan Lane and Matthew Broderick, both have substantial movie credits, so the retention of them for the movie musical is unsurprising.

If 'the most widespread misconception about the process of adaptation of a work from one medium to another is the myth that the adaptation should be faithful to its source' (Gordon and Jubin 2015: 5), then Brooks, Stroman and Meehan, having fully understood this in the creation of the stage musical, consciously or unconsciously ignored it with the movie musical, creating a work that was criticized for its overwhelming fidelity.

Critical responses and the embodiments of excess

Where other examples in collection cite successful stage to screen adaptations, *The Producers* is viewed as a failure on nearly all criteria. Whilst overall critical opinion of the movie musical included some positive reviews, the negative reviews were strident. As Stephanie Zacharek wrote in *Salon*:

> *The Producers* is essentially a filmed version of a stage play, in which none of the characters' expressions or line readings have been scaled down to make sense on-screen. Every gesture is played out as if the actors were 20 feet (or more) away in real life, which means that, by the time the performers are magnified on the big screen, they're practically sitting in your lap.
>
> (Zacharek 2005)

and *The New York Times*, which had heaped praise on the musical, wondered 'how come the movie feels, in every sense, like a rip-off?'(Scott 2005).

Comparing the critical reception of the musical and the movie musical, it becomes apparent that Feuer's 'contradiction between live performance in the theatre and the frozen form of cinema'(Feuer 1977: 320) is illustrated in the two versions. The stage performances, which were hilarious when viewed from the auditorium of the 1,710-seater St. James Theater in New York or the 2,196-seater Theatre Royal Drury Lane in London, are monstrous when filmed in close-up and projected onto large cinema screens.

In 1987, Tambling commented that 'In stage musicals, the music has often been called "The embodiment of excess"' (Tambling 1987: 101), but this might also be considered relevant to the entire performance of a musical. Much has been written about how 'life cannot be contained by its ordinariness but must spill over into rhythm, singing and movement' (ibid.), but this is the theatrical language of the genre, and in the retention of both the stage cast and performances for the movie musical this theatrical excess is overwhelmingly apparent.

For an audience, viewing a stage musical and a film musical is experientially different. The suspension of disbelief required for a stage musical's theatrical language becomes more challenging in the circumstances of the more naturalistic film medium and in not inhabiting the same physical space as the live performers. Feuer's 'frozen form', in which audiences are aware that editing has taken place, generates a different excitement to the sense of risk in live performance, which is necessarily absent. This excitement is most notably absent in the major performance in which the performer embodies the emotional excess, so that a song such as 'And I'm Telling You I'm Not Going' from *Dreamgirls* (2006), which is thrilling in the theatre for its test of the singer's emotional and technical ability, becomes static when robbed of the element of live performance. The test for performers in *The Producers* is whether the comic performance can be consistently maintained, and the excitement of this is lost in a cinematic version. Similarly, in the remediation Lane and Broderick are robbed of their ability to judge and 'play' an audience in a comic sense, that was so apparent in their stage performances. For this reason, musical comedy has proven a difficult sub-genre to adapt to the screen, and the stage to screen adaptations on the list of the American Film Institute's *25 Greatest Movie Musicals of All Time* (AFI 2016) reveal that only *Guys and Dolls* can be classed as a musical comedy movie, whilst *West Side Story*, *Cabaret*, *The Sound of Music* and *The King and I* are musical dramas or romances, and even those stage musical comedies such as *Grease* are remediated to emphasise the romantic aspects.

Although Hutcheon reminds us that 'multiple versions exist laterally, not vertically' (Hutcheon 2013: xv), she is also clear that

> Like classical imitation, adaptation is not a slavish copying; it is a process of making the adapted material one's own. In both, the novelty is in what one *does* with the other text.
>
> (Hutcheon 2013: 20)

At the stage musical, audiences relished the intertextual pleasure of recognising the palimpsests of the original movie alongside the creative decisions and new experiences of text, song, staging and performance that the remediated musical afforded. At the 'slavishly' copied movie musical those decisions lacked the appropriateness to the medium and originality that a truly remediated movie musical could have afforded.

Gordon and Jubin caution that neither critical nor commercial success is a satisfactory benchmark of an adaptation, and that

> Far more illuminating is the exploration of the shifts in emphasis that come about as the result of sociocultural factors that affect the process of adapting any material in different countries, for any theatre system, and in any era – or simply as an expression of different artistic temperaments, attitudes and ideologies.
>
> (Gordon and Jubin 2015: 6)

Using this as a series of benchmarks for consideration of the adaptations of *The Producers* reveals a more complex understanding of the work, but their interpretation is focussed on a sociological interpretation of the adaptations in context, dismissing personal artistic choices as being of secondary importance.

Key to the artistic decisions made in the adapting of the film to the musical is the alteration of the historical setting. Whereas the film was set in its present (1967), the musical and movie musical are set in 1959. This sets them firmly in the 'Golden Age' of Broadway and the musical shares similarities with musical comedies of this age, particularly those set in workplace environments such as *The Pajama Game* (1953), *Promises, Promises* (1960) and *How To Succeed in Business* (1961). Brooks has created a score that reminds Thomas Meehan 'of songs from some of the great Broadway musical comedies of the 1940s and 1950s, like *Where's Charley?, High Button Shoes*, and *Guys and Dolls*' (Brooks and Meehan 2001: 21).

Altering the historical setting avoids the influence of rock music of 1967's revolutionary Broadway musical *Hair* and also the flower-power inspired interpretation of Hitler of the original film, in which the actor chosen to play the role was named Lorenzo St Dubois, shortened to L.S.D. in a clear reference to the popular recreational drug of the 1960s. The musical, and subsequent movie musical, are depoliticised and the context of a hippy version of *Springtime for Hitler*, with its inherent anti-Vietnam war messages, is sacrificed on the altar of high camp as the Broadway audience is invited to interpret references to Judy Garland in director/performer Roger de Bris' impersonation of Hitler/Garland.

The moment of de Bris' appearance as Hitler, then as Hitler/Garland, is so loaded with references that it can be considered as the ultimate indicator of all that Brooks and his collaborators set out to achieve in the stage adaptation. Whilst the film's Max Bialystock is a down-at-heel producer scrabbling to make a living, there is little reference to the real Broadway in which he is presumed to operate. The real-life producer of *The Producers*, Rocco Landesman, described the musical as 'a valentine to Broadway, its ridicule cocooned in a deep and sustaining affection'(Brooks and Meehan 2001: 7). The musical becomes a series of routines in which the palimpsests of other musicals are parodied. Thus there are references to 'Rose's Turn' from *Gypsy* in Bialystock's 'Betrayed'; to *Follies'* 'Loveland' sequence in the 'Little Old Lady Land' references in 'Along Came Bialy'; to *42nd Street* in the Finale; and, as the *New York Times* review pointed out,

> There's even a dancer-reflecting mirror à la "Chorus Line," for the big Nazi numbers, which then turns into a crucial visual aid in Ms. Stroman's answer to Busby Berkeley-style formation dancing. And you can find gleefully over-the-top reworkings of the classic Ziegfeld beauty parades and the office as prison routines of "How to Succeed in Business Without Really Trying."
>
> (Brantley 2001)

These palimpsests are combined with those from the original movie, most notably 'Springtime for Hitler': the first half of this number is staged by Stroman in a close copy of the film choreography by Alan Johnson, and for the movie musical Stroman closely recreates her adaptation of the stage choreography. Other palimpsests from the movie include the development of the throwaway number 'Haben Sie Gehört das Deutsche Band' into a more substantial song for Franz Liebkind, and the appearance of Leo Bloom's blanket.

In making the movie musical Stroman does not alter any of the creative decisions made in the remediation of movie to stage musical, but attempts to recreate some visual quotes from the original movie. In some cases, she is hampered in this by the very decisions already made. One famous moment from the movie is Max and Leo deciding to embark on their fraudulent scheme by jumping in the Lincoln Centre fountain. This moment is referenced in the stage musical with a brief water 'display' at the climax of the 'We Can Do It' reprise. Following the alteration of the historical setting from late 1967 to the 1950s, the movie musical sets this moment at the less impressive Bethesda Fountain in Central Park because the Lincoln Centre was not built until 1964.

The Broadway audience was sophisticated in its reading of these palimpsests. Data from the Broadway League illustrates the importance of regular theatregoers, who account for nearly a third of tickets sold:

> The average Broadway theatregoer reported attending 4 shows in the previous 12 months. The group of devoted fans who attended 15 or more performances comprised less that 5.65 of the audience, but accounted for 32% of all tickets (4.2 million admissions).
>
> (Broadway League 2016)

This group, who can be expected to account for a higher percentage of the audience during the early years of a run, can also be expected to understand references to other Broadway musicals. Data does not exist for the cross over between the audience for Broadway musicals on tour across America, but it can assumed that those living outside New York who are regular theatregoers in their home cities also attend Broadway musicals whilst visiting New York and view these musicals with a sophisticated understanding of references. The sophistication of the audiences, and the possible lack of sophistication of other audiences, geographically and culturally further from Broadway, may account for the commercial failure of *The Producers* in some territories; a British regional tour in 2007-8 was curtailed and a Toronto production ended early (Jones 2004) and, despite its record-breaking Tony awards and successful Broadway run, *The Producers* has not replicated the worldwide success of franchising experienced by *Mamma Mia!* and *The Lion King* of the same period, being produced in twenty territories but often not in a replica production of the original.

One must also consider the stage musical in both its context within Broadway history and in a global context. Brooks has commented that the intention of the adaptation was to create a new musical comedy, a form that had been in decline:

> For that's what we wanted *The Producers* to be … for some reason, along about 1960, the musical comedy went out of vogue, became passé, and for the last forty years only a handful, mainly revivals, have made it to town. Unhappily, as far as I'm concerned, the musical comedy was replaced by

what might be called the musical tragedy, the kind of show, often from
London, in which you sit in the dark all evening without laughing once.

(Brooks and Meehan 2001: 23)

Meta-musical comedy: the impact of 9/11

The critical and commercial success of the musical led not only to a further
musical by Brooks, *Young Frankenstein* (which was not a success), but also to a
revival of musical comedy on Broadway. A survey of Tony Award winners in the
period reveals that the Tony Award for Best Musical had not been won by a
musical comedy since *Crazy For You* in 1992, and that from 1993–2000 the
winners had been tragedies (*Kiss of the Spiderwoman*, *Passion*, *Sunset Boulevard*,
Rent, *Titanic*) or dance shows (*Fosse*, *Contact*). Only *The Lion King*, one of the most
serious of Disney's adaptations, cannot be classed in either category. As a broader
indicator of musicals produced on Broadway during this period, a survey of
nominees rather than winners reveals that only *The Goodbye Girl* and *Beauty and
the Beast* can be considered musical comedy, whilst other productions of the
period include *Blood Brothers*, *Tommy*, *Chronicle of a Death Foretold*, *The Life*,
Ragtime, *The Civil War*, *Parade* and *James Joyce's The Dead*. A similar survey
conducted for the period after *The Producers'* win reveals that the musical can be
credited with beginning a revival of musical comedy, the next four Best Musical
winners being *Thoroughly Modern Millie*, *Hairspray*, *Avenue Q* and *Spamalot*; and
within the nominees over the next nine years there is a strong evidence of musical
comedy on Broadway, including *Mamma Mia!*, *Urinetown*, *Dirty Rotten Scoundrels*,
the 25th Annual Putnam County Spelling Bee, *The Drowsy Chaperone*, *Curtains*,
Xanadu and *Rock Of Ages* (Tony Award Productions 2016). In contrast, the movie
musical does not have such a context; its 2005 release was the same year as the
movie version of *Rent* and in a season of comedies including *Wedding Crashers*,
The 40 Year Old Virgin and *Mr and Mrs Smith* – evidence that the movie musical
lacked an equivalent cultural impact.

With regard to the referencing of other musicals, it is also possible to consider
The Producers as the beginning of the period of meta-musical comedy, the self-
referencing of musicals for comic effect evident in *Spamalot*, *Avenue Q* and
Urinetown, which reached its apotheosis in *Title of Show*. Throughout the movie
musical, however, the references continue to be to stage musicals, rather than
utilising the opportunities to reference and parody film musicals, which might have
created a satisfying adaptation.

This revitalisation of stage musical comedy cannot be considered in isolation, as
if Broadway exists in a vacuum. The stage musical opened on 19 April 2001, less
than six months before the terrorist attacks on New York of 11 September, and
played to capacity business prior to 9/11. A survey of Broadway grosses reveals
that it was playing at 105.4 per cent of financial capacity for the week ending
9 September 2001; in the first full week of performances after the attack, ending
23 September 2001, it played to 94.3 per cent financial capacity, the highest

capacity of any production, closely followed by *The Lion King* at 92.8 per cent, but a week where long-running musicals played to very small houses, such as *Phantom of the Opera* (37.1 per cent), *Chicago* (35.9 per cent), *Beauty and the Beast* (32.6 per cent) and *Les Miserables* (27.7 per cent)(BroadwayWorld 2016). In the aftermath of the attacks Mayor Giuliani made a speech in which he emphasised the importance of Broadway to the economy of New York:

> People call us from everywhere asking us how they can help, I tell them it's simple: come to New York. Come here and spend money. Go to a restaurant, a play – you might actually have a better chance of getting tickets to *The Producers* now … The life of the city goes on.
>
> (Giuliani 2001, quoted in *Daily Telegraph*)

Giuliani's imploring worked: Broadway, the epicentre of global commercial theatre, reopened for business before Wall Street. The revitalisation of American musical comedy after 2001 must be considered in the historical context of the changed geopolitical landscape following 9/11.

Rugg comments that

> For a city devastated by loss and fear, it made sense to put forth a symbol of resilience. Broadway now seems an obvious choice, but there were others: Korean delis that never closed could, for instance, have been heralded as a symbol of New York's staying power. But the everyday patriotic associations of Broadway positioned it perfectly to take up the mantle of symbolic victory.
>
> (Rugg 2009: 93)

And what could be a more patriotic experience than the musical that had already been heralded as an homage to classic American musical comedy. Where popular musicals prior to 2001 had often been thought-provoking and challenging, popular musicals produced in the next ten years emphasised escapism and Americana. More importantly, as Rugg continues,

> When death is already on the minds of audience members because of events outside the theatre, I would argue, the experience of live connection among people with the theatre is further heightened.
>
> (Rugg 2009: 94)

The importance of this live connection, of people performing, experiencing and, importantly, laughing together gave *The Producers* on Broadway a patriotic context for America recovering from the shock of 9/11. By contrast, the movie musical, released four years later (by which time America had become less secure and embroiled in the protracted aftermath of the Iraq War), also lacked the vital sense of live performance that a stage musical can embody.

A conclusion of intertextual ironies

Devoid of the sociological context of live performance during a period of national tragedy, the slavish copying of the movie musical, with its unimaginative translation from stage to screen, is most appropriately considered an extremely lavish and costly exercise in recording the stage musical. This exercise might have more in common with video recordings of existing musicals, such as the commercially available *Cats* or *Jesus Christ Superstar*, rather than with other remediated film versions of stage musicals of the same period such as *Chicago* or *Dreamgirls*. Whilst it is 'an acknowledged transposition of a recognizable work', it is neither 'a Creative and an interpretive act of appropriation/salvaging' nor 'An extended intertextual engagement with the adapted work'.

Of the film musicals of the early twenty-first century, *The Producers* and *Rent* were the two commercial and critical failures. Whilst these two stage musicals were the most commercially and critically successful of the period and were considerable interpretive acts and extended intertextual engagements, the movie musical versions were not. In both cases the creative teams largely failed in the adaptation as either a creative and interpretive act or as an intertextual engagement. It must therefore be considered that imaginative acts of adaptation can be the governing factor in the commercial and critical success of stage and movie musicals. And in the highly commercialised business ecologies of Broadway producing and Hollywood film-making, this can be an important lesson. The irony, of course, is that just as Max Bialystock had underestimated the effect of a*dapting* the events of World War Two in *Springtime for Hitler*, so Brooks and Stroman underestimated the effect that truly adapting *The Producers* a second time could have had.

Bibliography

AFI (2016). *AFI's 25 Greatest Movie Musicals Of All Time*. Available: login.microsoftonline.com/login.srf . Accessed 19 August 2016.

Altman, R. (1987). *The American Film Musical*. First edn. Bloomington, IN: Indiana University Press.

Bluestone, G. 1957, *Novels into Film,* First edn. Berkeley: University of California Press.

Brantley, B. (2001). 'Theater Review: *A Scam That'll Knock 'Em Dead*.' New York: *New York Times*.

Broadway League (2016). *The Demographics of the Broadway Audience*. Available: www.broadwayleague.com/research/research-reports/. Accessed 16 July 2016.

BroadwayWorld (2016). 11 July 2016–last update. *Broadway Grosses*. Available: www.broadwayworld.com/grosses.cfm. Accessed 14 July 2016.

Brooks, M. and T. Meehan (2001). *The Producers: The Book, Lyrics and Story Behind the Biggest Hit in Broadway History!* First edn. New York: Roundtable Press.

Engel, L. and H. Kissel (2006). *Words With Music: Creating the Broadway Musical Libretto*. First edn. New York: Applause Theatre and Cinema Books.

Feuer, J. (1977). 'The Self-reflective Musical and the Myth of Entertainment.' *Quarterly Review of Film Studies* 2(3), pp. 313–326.

Giuliani, R. (2001). 'Mayor urges: "Come to New York".' London: *Daily Telegraph*.

Gordon, R. and O. Jubin (2015). 'Telling the tale: Adaptation as interpretation.' *Studies in Musical Theatre* 9(1), pp. 3-11.

Hoad, P. (2013). 'How film and musical theatre formed a lucrative bond.' London: *The Guardian*.

Hutcheon, L. (2013). *A Theory of Adaptation*. 2nd edn. London: Routledge.

Jones, K. (2004). *Playbill* 4 July 2004–last update. 'Lack of Summer Tourists Helps Sink *The Producers* in Toronto; 33-Week Run Ends July 4.' Accessed 13 October 2015.

McNally, T. (2002). 'An Operatic Mission: Freshen the Familiar.' *New York Times*, 1 September 2002.

Pogrebin, R. (2001). 'Ticket Sales For "Producers" Set A Broadway Record.' *New York Times*, 21 April.

Rugg, R.A. (2009). 'Mission Accomplished: Broadway, 9/11, and the Republican National Convention.' In K. Solga, S. Orr and D.J. Hopkins (eds), *Performance and the City*. First edn. London: Palgrave Macmillan, pp. 92–109.

Scott, A.O. (2005), *New York Times* 16 December 2005–last update. '*The Producers* Again (This Time With Uma).' Available: www.nytimes.com/2005/12/16/movies/the-producers-again-this-time-with-uma.html?_r=0. Accessed 11 July 2016.

Tambling, J. (1987). *Opera, Ideology and Film*. First edn. Manchester: Manchester University Press.

Tony Award Productions (2016). *Tony Awards*. Available: www.tonyawards.com. Accessed 14 July 2016.

Woolford, J. (2012). *How Musicals Work*. First edn. London: Nick Hern Books.

Zacharek, S. (2005). *Salon* 16 December 2005–last update. '*The Producers*'. Available: www.salon.com/2005/12/16/producers/. Accessed 11 July 2016.

6

'BIG, AS IN LARGE, AS IN HUGE'

Dreamgirls and difference in the performance of gender, blackness, and popular music history

Todd Decker

In September 1982, with *Dreamgirls* approaching the start of its second year on Broadway, director and choreographer Michael Bennett issued a casting call for 'Equity and non-Equity black performers' that included specific instructions as to skills and style.

> We are looking for attractive musical performers who are between the ages of 18 and 32 who sing, dance and act well. Women must be 5´4″ to 5´8″ and must move well. Men must be 5´8″ to 6´1″ and must dance well. Be prepared with *two* pieces of contemporary music (rhythm and blues, rock or pop). One should be a driving up-tempo number. The second should be an emotional ballad or love song showing your style and range. Do **NOT** sing jazz or theatre songs. … Come looking your best.[1]

Bennett's call precisely parses both the difference between the men and the women in *Dreamgirls*' cast and the distance between *Dreamgirls'* score and standard Broadway music of the time. *Dreamgirls'* music, by white composer Henry Krieger, is fuelled by a range of black popular music styles from the 1960s and 1970s as recreated by a Broadway pit orchestra. The show's larger tale of black music's success on the pop charts – or, in racial terms, with the mass white audience – requires almost every character to perform several popular music styles (ranging from rhythm and blues to pop to soul to disco) in a variety of settings (from recording studios to concert, nightclub, and television venues). Bennett's warning *not* to prepare theatre or jazz songs for the audition makes it plain that he was after musical theatre actors who had convincing popular music skills. The possibility that actual popular music performers might fill the cast of *Dreamgirls* – as happened in the 2006 film version starring pop superstar Beyoncé Knowles and *American Idol* finalist Jennifer Hudson – is implicit in this early casting announcement.

The difference between the men and the women in *Dreamgirls*, as articulated in the casting call, comes down to movement: while the women must merely 'move well', the men are called upon to 'dance well'. The different verbs point towards Bennett's dramaturgical approach to the show and reveal that the original Broadway *Dreamgirls* was a dance show as well as a platform for powerful singing. When viewed as a dance musical, the gender distinction in *Dreamgirls* proves crucial. While the women moved in ways that tapped into popular dance styles matched to the popular music styles that drive the plot, the men in *Dreamgirls* danced in more individually eloquent fashion, their strong movements not linked to popular culture but instead expressing masculine power and agency in Bennett's choreographic Broadway vernacular. Given the show's story of African American success in the business of popular culture, Bennett's choreography for the men in *Dreamgirls* put a danced embodiment of heterosexual black male power on the Broadway stage – in retrospect, one of the standout achievements of this underappreciated show.

Bennett's gender-differentiated approach to movement in *Dreamgirls* relies on a body-centred dramaturgy. For while the original production – with automated, moving light towers and stage-spanning bridges descending from and rising into the flies – was received as a triumph of computerized lighting and technologically-complex continuous staging, in essence *Dreamgirls* was, like Bennett's 1975 success *A Chorus Line*, made of strongly contrasting characters who sing and dance in distinctive ways on a nearly empty stage. Indeed, for the national tour and a return Broadway engagement in 1987, Bennett simplified the technological apparatus of the original production, opting for a simpler (and less expensive) staging – minus the bridges and automated towers – that set the cast's performances into even greater relief. *Dreamgirls* was fundamentally built on the expressive bodies and voices of the performers. This approach sprang directly from Krieger's score, which – with book and lyrics by Tom Eyen – includes lengthy, dramatically effective sung dialogue, usually to a driving beat, as well as a narratively integrated matching of vocal style and character trajectory. In schematic fashion, the characters in *Dreamgirls* sing contrasting kinds of blackness and dance or move along gender-defined lines of power. Differences in the performance of blackness and gender define the expressive strategies and aesthetic nature of the show. These differences also express the show's larger mythic tale of American popular music history across the 1960s and 1970s, a story centred on African American protagonists. The tension between different types of performed blackness proves crucial to the show's tale, which is more symbolic than historically accurate.

This chapter begins with a consideration of Krieger and Eyen's text and Bennett's choreography and direction as captured in three sources: the 1981 original cast recording, which preserves only pieces of the score; a live recording of the complete score from a 2001 concert performance featuring major Broadway stars; and, most importantly, a 1985 video of the original stage production (featuring only one original cast member in the leading roles) in the collection of the Theatre on Film and Tape Archive (TOFT) at the New York Public Library for the

Performing Arts.² A close reading of the vocal and gender dynamics of the show as performed on Broadway is followed by an analysis of the 2006 film *Dreamgirls*, written for the screen and directed by Bill Condon with choreography by Fatima Robinson. Condon's film fundamentally altered the stage original, miniaturizing and muddling Krieger and Eyen's boldly sung story of contrasting black singing styles and shrinking to nearly nothing Bennett's presentation of a dynamic black masculinity. Furthermore, Condon's effort to nail down the specifics of *Dreamgirls'* story and characters relative to actual events and people – including social and political as well as popular music history – put undue pressure on Krieger and Eyen's symbolic narrative of black music history. In sum, the big screen *Dreamgirls* – in retrospect ironically dedicated to the memory of Michael Bennett – fails to re-create in a new medium the defining differences between vocal styles and gendered movement that lent the original stage production great power and size. Condon's attempt to link the *Dreamgirls* narrative to historical specifics (and his addition of more detailed individual plotlines for several characters) lessens the resonance of the story. The resulting contrast with Bennett's more evocative, chronologically vague staging of a similar, differently nuanced tale reveals how the musical stage, in this instance, offers a more welcome context for the performance of mythic stories of national and racial identity than does the musical screen.

Singing black femininity: a dramaturgy of contrast

Bennett's 1982 casting call hardly needed to note that everyone in *Dreamgirls* had to sing well, some extraordinarily well, and many in specific ways. The three central women – Effie, Deena, and Lorrell, the original members of the girl group the Dreamettes, later the Dreams – had to offer contrasting vocal styles situated within the plot along a tonal spectrum of blackness. The Broadway audience for *Dreamgirls* was assumed to bring with them into the theatre a comparative knowledge of post-1950s popular music, specifically an ear for the differences between rhythm and blues, pop, gospel-inspired soul, and disco. This was a reasonable expectation on Krieger and Eyen's part. *Dreamgirls* is a period show set in the recent past, ending just shy of the present for the show's original audiences. The suggested historical span of the story – early 1960s to late 1970s – remains legible for a broad spectrum of the theatre and film audience, thanks to the continued presence of 1960s and 1970s popular music in American media more broadly, be it on radio, film, or television.

The defining differences in performance style and function between Effie, Deena, and Lorrell are juxtaposed early on in the song 'Fake Your Way to the Top', when each woman sings the fill 'running around' in a markedly different manner. Effie White, originated by Jennifer Holliday, attacks the moment with power, planting her musical flag solidly in the realm of gospel exhortation. Holliday, who received the Tony Award for Best Leading Role in a Musical for Effie, had only one previous Broadway credit, the 1980 revival of the 1976 black gospel musical *Your Arm's Too Short to Box With God*, and has appeared in only three other Broadway shows (as a brief replacement for featured roles in revivals of *Grease*, *Chicago* and *The Color Purple*). Her gospel voice and style are not standard for American musical theatre. That *Dreamgirls* fits a voice like Holliday's into a musical narrative marks the show as both unusual for Broadway and especially embedded in post-rock and roll popular music history. Effie's voice, alongside that of *Dreamgirls*' unreconstructed James Brown, soul-singing, stand-in James 'Thunder' Early, offers the 'blackest' sound in the show, a sound the plot argues could not 'crossover' to the white pop charts. (Early is referred to below as Jimmy, following the script.) In fact, this voice did crossover in the later 1960s careers of singers such as Aretha Franklin. But *Dreamgirls* onstage is not interested in accurate history. Instead, the plot runs on defined racial types played off each other in a tale of contrasting styles. Effie and Jimmy (in his soulful numbers) represent a black vocal power that will not be contained nor, the story goes, be embraced by white audiences. Jimmy is called upon to modulate his blackness, adopting a 'mellow sound' to attain crossover success. His ultimate refusal to be contained by the requirements of crossing over – Jimmy sheds his 'sad songs', along with his pants, in his soul number 'The Rap' late in Act Two – proves an important indicator of how stage and film versions deal with black music history.

Deena Jones exemplifies the lighter pop sounds that propel the Dreams to superstardom in both 1960s girl group and 1970s disco styles. Deena sings 'running around' on a light and smooth mechanism, rhythmically correct and lyrical, earning the comment from Jimmy, 'You fit right in there.' Indeed, Deena's role will be to fit right in to white audience tastes. But it is crucial to the dignity granted every character and musical style in *Dreamgirls* that Deena's light approach should not be framed as a rejection of blackness. Deena is never condemned for being a pop star or disco diva, nor is her performance as either framed as anything less than thrillingly professional. *Dreamgirls* has no time for a black politics of musical authenticity: the only concern is commercial success and every character in the show, whatever style they perform, is rewarded with applause, wealth, and fame. As a trio of male characters sing at one point, 'There are so many sounds we love to hear'. *Dreamgirls* refuses to moralize about African American musical history, opening the way for audiences to enjoy each style offered in turn, all of which are presented in polished performances. Still, there are moments in the dramatic score, especially during intense stretches of sung dialogue, when the actress playing Deena needs to show some vocal power. For example, late in Act One, just before Effie's solo 'And I Am Telling You I'm Not Going', Deena must match Effie's forceful delivery in a moment when diva confronts diva. But this exchange proves the most intense moment in the show for Deena. Her declaration of independence from husband and manager Curtis Taylor Jr near the end of Act Two is a simple spoken 'goodbye'. Deena never sings a so-called 'I Am' or 'I Feel' song. As written for the stage, Deena's role includes singing almost entirely as part of her professional embodiment of a malleable black pop diva. When singing as a pop star Deena maintains a light sound and style, lacking the growling chest voice and improvisation techniques that define Effie's musical persona virtually every time she raises her voice in song.

Lorrell Robinson, the only Dream to remain a backup singer throughout the story, sings 'running around' without calling attention to herself musically, showing she's paying attention and doing her job. Lorrell's consistently supportive contribution to the Dreams breaks explosively open during her dramatic Act Two solo, 'Ain't No Party', when the character erupts in frustration after years of being the married Jimmy's lover. Lorrell's part is deceptively difficult, requiring a vocal and dramatic flexibility that surprises the audience. Loretta DeVine, who originated the role, can be seen on the TOFT video. DeVine played Lorrell with a comically high, slightly daffy, almost over-the-top speaking voice that charmed the audience and concealed a sharp-minded character. Heather Headley's approach in the 2001 concert version was less of a caricature but no less powerful in the dramatic scenes. Both women garnered wild applause during 'Ain't No Party' and on Lorrell's sung exit from the plot, when she leaves Jimmy with a gospel-style, unmetered arioso beginning 'Lorrell loves Jimmy' and ending 'Lorrell and Jimmy are through'. Such moments invest Lorrell's offstage self with a musical intensity similar to Effie's, even if her onstage persona as a Dream is always smiling and restrained. In contrast to both characters, Deena's offstage feelings are largely confined to dialogue.

Like the girl groups for whom they are fictional stand-ins – Lorrell names the Chiffons, the Marvelettes, and the Supremes in the show's first minutes – the Dreams combine singing with simple moves, many derived from familiar social dances. For example, in their first number, 'Move', the Dreamettes – still teenagers, after all – do the Mashed Potato and the Swim. As they edge into the white pop charts as Jimmy's backup singers, the trio moves less, avoiding calling attention to their bodies, sometimes just swaying. When they emerge as the Dreams, their gestures grow expansive and sweeping, often with arms extended full out to the sides, their simple sway to the music now an assertion of the entire body. And the Dreams' disco numbers in Act Two – with Michelle Morris in Effie's place – are largely about strutting in high heels and posing seductively.

Bennett's changing movement vocabulary for the Dreams was supported throughout by Theoni V. Aldridge's costumes, which situated the trio along three overlapping trajectories: (1) historical changes in fashion from the early 1960s to the late 1970s, (2) the characters' maturation from teenagers into women, and (3) a racial mapping of their journey from a desexualized black respectability (body-obscuring dresses for an all-white Miami Beach nightclub) to an elegant made-for-television persona for their national media breakthrough (two stunning full-length gowns for the song 'Heavy') to provocative, hypersexualized disco outfits (the Act Two opener and the up-tempo 'One Night Only'). Throughout the show, the Dreams 'move' within the changing contexts of their performing careers. They do not dance to express their own identities or emotions. In this, they are physically constrained even as their voices set them free. Late in Act Two, while ostensibly performing an elaborate dance number to their latest hit, 'One Night Only', each of the Dreams in turn sings lyrics about their personal state of mind. Deena articulates the dramaturgical strategy of the moment, singing 'All of us got other things than singing on our minds'. Crucially, while their voices might express their wandering thoughts, their bodies do not stray from the performance of a theatrical black pop femininity.

Dancing black masculinity: a dramaturgy of agency

The Dreams' career is shaped by the pop music marketplace and dictated, for the most part, by the men who manage their professional lives: their manager Curtis Taylor Jr and their songwriter C.C. White. As figures with creative power, Curtis, C.C., and (sometimes) Jimmy, do more than just move: all three also dance – Curtis by far the most. Dancing as well as singing proves central to this trio's embodiment of a striving and powerful black masculinity that seeks, as one lyric goes, to 'make this country change'.

The moment when black male dance as historical agency kicks in is built on a musically-supported change in dramaturgical mode: a smooth yet sudden and surprising shift from everyday walking and standing to dancing. Having convinced the Dreamettes to let him be their manager and secured their position as Jimmy's backup singers, Curtis begins trying to sell Jimmy and his agent Marty his own vision for the future of blackness in pop music. Curtis, a car salesman after all, initiates his pitch with the sung line 'Big, as in large, as in huge'. These words set the stage for Curtis's overarching goal: he wants to produce black artists who

FIGURE 6.1 Marty (Roy L. Jones) watches as C.C. (Kevyn Morrow), Jimmy Early (Herbert Rawlings Jr) and Curtis Taylor Jr (Weyman Thompson) sing and dance about creating a 'smoother sound' in the first section of 'Cadillac Car' (*Dreamgirls* international tour, NYPL).

crossover to the white charts, where big money and fame await. Any such move demands that black performers, in Curtis's words, 'got to get a smoother sound'. This phrase – sung three times, once each by Curtis, C.C., and Jimmy in overlapping vocal entrances, all arriving together at a shared cadence – initiates dance as central to Bennett's conception of black masculinity (see Figure 6.1). Curtis, C.C., and Jimmy dance to express the inner lives and drives of their characters, not, like the women, as the action of characters who are performers. Here, *Dreamgirls* becomes a danced as well as sung musical, a show where crucial information about character motivation is communicated in a jazz dance-derived theatrical choreographic vocabulary that draws on Bennett's *A Chorus Line*, like *Dreamgirls* a show that defines male dancing in a narrative context as a particular kind of male power.

Curtis, C.C., and Jimmy dancing their shared ambition in a sung dialogue scene during the first section of 'Cadillac Car' yields to an even more stunning moment of danced black masculinity in the next number, a dream ballet cum symbolic representation of Curtis using payola – paying DJs to play a record – to turn Jimmy's new recording 'Steppin' to the Bad Side' into a hit. 'Steppin'' begins with Curtis, C.C., Jimmy, and Curtis's assistant Wayne standing in a row in deep shadow. They move both individually and in unison during the slow, sung introduction, adopting dynamic, powerful poses incorporating deep lunges, strong and straight arms, and aggressive and proud, long-lined body postures. It's an arresting moment where black men perform their masculine power as dance without presenting their bodies as objects for the viewer's gaze so much as declaring in movement their intention to act in history, to literally change the world (see Figure 6.2). As the number develops, Curtis acts on his plan by handing four,

FIGURE 6.2 Curtis, C.C., Jimmy, and Wayne in the first section of 'Steppin' to the Bad Side' (*Dreamgirls* international tour, NYPL).

identically-dressed male chorus members physical totems of the payola scheme to make Jimmy's record a hit: each man holds aloft a single 45 disc in a tableau-like expression of black cultural power that kicks off an extended dance sequence (see Figure 6.3). Curtis initially dances with the four men, then steps out so that the quartet from the dance chorus can push the choreography to a further degree of difficulty. Throughout this initial section of 'Steppin'', Bennett draws on the isolations, sharp moves, and jazz extensions seen in *A Chorus Line*. This is Broadway jazz dance bearing no evident relationship to the popular social dance styles performed by the women in *Dreamgirls*. In short, the men in *Dreamgirls* are granted a non-historically contained sort of movement that expresses individual intention to change the world – which, indeed, Curtis manages to do with Jimmy's, the Dreams', and Deena's success.

'Cadillac Car' and 'Steppin' to the Bad Side' begin as what a film scholar might call non-diegetic song and dance, led by the non-performer character Curtis whose ambition fuels the plot for most of the show. Both numbers then transition into the diegetic performance of songs framed as pop recordings performed by the characters who play performers: Jimmy and his backup singers, the Dreamettes. In a further development of black masculinity as theatrical dance, Jimmy's all-male band is played in both numbers by a group of dancers holding trumpets, trombones, and saxes. Their exuberant jazz-informed musical theatre dancing offers a further contrast to the historically-defined social dance moves of the women.

FIGURE 6.3 Black power in a 45 single, as Curtis initiates his payola scheme in the second section of 'Steppin' to the Bad Side' (*Dreamgirls* international tour, NYPL).

Credit: Martha Swope. Billy Rose Theatre Division. The New York Public Library for the Performing Arts.

'Cadillac' and 'Steppin'' combine to offer a potted racial history of American popular music in the post-rock and roll era that does not quite align with any actual historical chronology. Between the two numbers, 'Cadillac Car' is treated to an all-white, slow dance version sung by a Pat Boone lookalike. This white record supposedly bests Jimmy's grooving R&B 'Cadillac Car' on the pop charts, leading to Curtis's decision to use payola to make their next single, 'Steppin' to the Bad Side', a national hit. Pat Boone did, indeed, cover two early black hits: Fats Domino's 'Ain't That A Shame' (1955) and Little Richard's 'Tutti Frutti' (1956). Marty mentions Boone's 'Ain't That a Shame' and Elvis Presley's 1956 cover of Big Mama Thornton's 'Hound Dog' in the short dialogue scene between 'Cadillac' and 'Steppin''. Another example would be 'Sh-Boom', initially released by the black doo-wop group The Chords, then covered within weeks, to greater chart success, by the white group The Crew-Cuts in 1954. But the historical window for whites to remake black hits and expect superior chart performance was very narrow – over by the late 1950s at least. And Boone's covers of Domino's and Little Richard's hits were nothing like the white 'Cadillac Car' in *Dreamgirls*. Boone knew these songs were not ballads and he tried, in his way, to rock. *Dreamgirls* Act One is purportedly set in 'the early Sixties', when the show's 'Cadillac Car' and the characters' reaction to it would be thoroughly out of date, even naive.

Still, precise chronology doesn't matter all that much on the musical stage, where Krieger, Eyen, and Bennett are sketching in mythical post-rock and roll figures who negotiate a symbolic cultural landscape: Curtis as the black record producer dealing with the white-run music industry; Effie as the large, dark-skinned, gospel-style singer; Deena as the thin, light-skinned, pop-style singer. On stage, where Bennett and his design team present a vague chronology defined mostly by costuming, this schematic narrative points indirectly towards an implied racism over which the characters in the story triumph without specific comment. On screen, with period detail in the production design and precise placement of story events in the flow of well-known social, political, and musical history, *Dreamgirls*' story of black popular music history fails to convince.

Vocal contrasts lost: Hudson's Effie, Beyoncé's Deena

The film version of *Dreamgirls* offers abundant evidence that writer/director Bill Condon and choreographer Fatima Robinson knew Bennett's original staging. Jimmy's dancing male band shows up in 'Fake Your Way to the Top', as do Bennett's flying bridges and silhouetted figures in the performance sequence of 'Steppin' to the Bad Side'. In another recycling of visual concepts from the stage, the Dreams perform 'One Night Only' in front of a massive, grid-like wall of headlamp-like lights. And while the film is committed to a detailed production design, microphones to amplify singers in the act of performance are only selectively present, often following practice within the stage show: for example, all the acts in the opening talent contest sing without mikes (even though these performers would clearly have required amplification at the time) while the onstage announcer uses a mike. Also following the stage, the Dreams are mostly held in place by three microphones on stands during the title number. The one-arm extended wave to the audience during the film's final number is also taken from Bennett.

However, the above choices drawing on Bennett prove little more than tips of the hat: the movie *Dreamgirls* departs significantly from the stage original. Entirely predictably, the balance of vocal power between the three leading women was upset by the casting of Beyoncé Knowles as Deena and Jennifer Hudson as Effie. With room for only two divas, the role of Lorrell (taken by Anika Noni Rose) was downgraded to a supporting figure in the story of Jimmy (played by above-the-title star Eddie Murphy). Additions and cuts to the score – new songs for Beyoncé and Hudson; the elimination of Lorrell's 'Ain't No Party' as well as almost all the sung dialogue – fundamentally recalibrated the show, resulting in a flattening of the musical and vocal style distinctions that fuelled the stage original and a lowering of the dramatic temperature of the whole. Lost entirely is the show's danced black masculinity as performed by leading male characters. Indeed, Jamie Foxx as Curtis hardly sings – and does so in a restrained, almost embarrassed fashion – and dances not at all. Finally, the film's obsession with period production design and precise dating of specific events contrasts strongly with the more generalized *mise en scène* of the stage.

The role of Effie as re-made for Hudson remains largely unchanged in terms of song content except for the addition of a new song in the film's first half. 'Love You I Do' is a bouncy AABA pop tune with a lyric expressing, by implication, Effie's love for Curtis, her lover until she is forced out of the Dreams. The song's arrangement has a strong backbeat but offers little in the way of 1960s pop sound. The tune provides Hudson with little room for gospel embellishment or powerhouse singing and ends with a jazzy deceptive cadence close. The addition of 'Love You I Do' adjusts the film Effie to a softer, more pop-oriented style and, in the process, casts doubt on Curtis's insistence that Effie as lead singer could not cross over to the pop charts, that her voice, as C.C. says later, 'is too special. We need a lighter [meaning less black] sound to cross over to the pop charts.' Curtis even comments of 'Love You I Do', 'It's too light. We want it light but not that light.'

In the stage version, Effie never has a moment like 'Love You I Do', where she sings lead in a performed black pop context – the Dreamettes' talent show number, 'Move', is hard-hitting R&B – much less in a number described by Curtis as 'too light'. Instead, Effie manages just barely to blend in when singing backup and is consistently aggressive and forceful during sung dialogue. When told Deena will sing lead, Effie says, 'she can't sing like I can'. This rings true onstage, where the vocal contrast between the roles has consistently defined casting choices. For example, the Julliard-trained Audra McDonald works as Deena in the 2001 concert version in part because explicitly 'black' singing styles have never been a hallmark of her career. It is as difficult to imagine McDonald singing Effie as to imagine Lillias White (the 2001 concert Effie) or Jennifer Holliday singing Deena. But the difference between Beyoncé's and Hudson's voices – mostly a matter of timbre rather than style – is simply not on this order of contrast. The pop quality of 'Love You I Do', put over nicely by Hudson, makes Curtis's decision a false choice – at least on musical grounds. The accusation, levelled by Effie, that Curtis is choosing Deena to sing lead because she's prettier and thinner becomes, practically speaking, the only reason for the decision – readable in star text terms as Foxx preferring Beyoncé to Hudson. (Indeed, Condon shows Foxx and Beyoncé in bed together but Foxx and Hudson's sex life is confined to a dialogue scene among the women taken directly from the stage script. A sexy kissing episode for Effie and Curtis, the latter on the phone, was cut in the film.) And given Beyoncé's casting, Effie's subsequent statement that 'Deena's beautiful and she's always been beautiful but I've got the voice, Curtis. I've got the voice', falls flat. Beyoncé's multi-talented career in popular music belies any notion she's nothing but a pretty face. 'Love You I Do', together with the film's star casting, upsets the delicately calibrated popular music style plot used throughout the stage version to differentiate Deena and Effie.

A second added song for the film – 'Listen' for Beyoncé as Deena – furthers the musical style confusion introduced by Hudson's 'Love You I Do'. 'Listen' comes near the end, inserting a big number for Deena where the stage version has the character exit with a curt 'goodbye'. 'Listen' is a declaration of female independence from a controlling man that maps onto Deena and Curtis's relationship, expressing the opposite sentiment of Effie's parallel number 'And I Am Telling You I'm Not Going'. 'Listen' welcomes, and Beyoncé indulges in melismatic, ecstatic gospel singing, a black vocal idiom appropriate to so momentous an occasion. Pop or disco stylings could not carry the serious weight of the sentiment: soulful melismatic singing gives Deena's character power and agency at exactly the moment she breaks free from Curtis. Except, of course, in *Dreamgirls'* schematics of singing style, this thoroughly black approach to singing belongs to Effie and lies outside of Deena's competency. Refashioning Deena's role to more directly feature Beyoncé's star persona likely made 'Listen' or something like it a required addition to the film. Revealingly, remaking Deena to fit Beyoncé's talents effectively reveals the compromise inherent in Beyoncé's own vocal style: she has a light voice but also regularly sings 'black'. She is – like Whitney Houston, the defining post-disco black pop star, a figure emerging in the decade after *Dreamgirls'* narrative closes – a cross between Deena and Effie, her voice more naturally the former but her expressive choices consistently touching on the latter. That 'Listen' welcomes a heavier voice – that it is, in essence, an Effie number – is abundantly clear on a fragment of the number sung by Hudson on a radio show.[3] While the reasons why 'Listen' was added for the film are obvious, the number – like 'Love You I Do', although with even greater impact – calls into question the very foundation of Krieger and Eyen's symbolic equation of Effie with blackness and Deena with lightness.

Eliminating sung dialogue and male dancing: smaller characters on the big screen

Condon largely rewrote *Dreamgirls* to contain passionate vocal utterance in set piece, diegetic solos for Beyoncé and Hudson, the film's female stars. Almost all the show's sung dialogue was cut. Characters burst into song outside of performed contexts on only six occasions, sometimes for just a line or two.[4] Minus these moments, *Dreamgirls* the film is hardly a musical at all, but instead a movie about musical performers. This decision had far-reaching consequences for the relative size of *Dreamgirls* on the big screen. The only extended stretch of sung dialogue precedes Effie's 'And I Am Telling You I'm Not Going'. This sung fight for all the characters comes as a jarring shift in the film's default narrative mode, instead of the escalation of a battle engaged already by characters who, in the stage version, sing as much or more than they talk. Coming a few scenes earlier, 'Heavy' in the contrasting stage and screen versions captures the loss of character size in the latter.

In the stage show, the Dreams perform 'Heavy' in two contexts: a rehearsal for a television show and at a San Francisco hotel, with heated stretches of sung dialogue between the two and after the hotel performance. The set for the television show featured a huge sign reading 'DREAMS'. Bennett flipped the sign around to economically take the story backstage, where diegetic singing of the song 'Heavy' yielded seamlessly to sung dialogue at the same tempo and to the same beat. A similar verbal fight after the hotel performance is brought to a fantastic momentary halt when Effie sings, 'I don't care. Let 'em all hear', to which Lorrell responds just as loudly and at an even higher pitch 'You're impossible'. It's a signature moment of diva confrontation, eliciting audience cheers on the TOFT video and 2001 concert recording. The pace of the 'Heavy' sequence onstage is breakneck. Indeed, between the television and hotel performances the women execute a lightning-quick full costume change in a moment of theatrical magic. The pressure on these women to perform their crossover pop music selves while also dealing with intrapersonal crises is presented economically and powerfully, especially in terms of how the three women relate to each other.

In the film, Condon shortens the 'Heavy' sequence. The women are first seen recording the song. Effie disrupts the session by singing too loudly (and heavy) and then walks out. Outside, she finds herself in the midst of violent rioting on the streets of Detroit. Condon's effort to locate the narrative in social history disrupts the unfolding personal tension among the characters. In the next scene, the Dreams are rehearsing for the television show – a big sign reading DREAMS behind them, as in Bennett – and Effie again walks out. Deena and Lorrell, followed by Curtis, exit the soundstage – effectively silencing the music, losing the beat – and the women speak lines that are sung on stage. Hudson's much smaller scale Effie tosses away a spoken 'Let 'em all hear' while Lorrell and Deena just look sad or frustrated. Condon rips out the dramatic guts of the 'Heavy' sequence, specifically the continuity that comes from the show's serial juxtaposition of orderly public performance of a pop song with meaning-laden lyrics that can be applied to the plot, and explosive private confrontations that threaten to rip the group apart. Hudson and Rose are robbed of yet another great moment from the original score. The radical difference in scale between show and film inheres in exactly these small moments.

The characters who are not performers are greatly diminished by the loss of Krieger and Eyen's abundant sung dialogue. Curtis, in particular, loses size. On the stage, Curtis makes his first entrance exultantly singing the character-defining line, 'Are you interested in the style of tomorrow?'. In the film, Foxx initially appears in the shadows, watching backstage events, hatching a plan but lacking the physical presence that makes the stage Curtis a tremendously vital presence. Key moments in Curtis's stage role are excised, including the sung first section of 'Cadillac Car', described earlier, when Curtis pulls C.C. and Jimmy into a shared dance and the danced display of black masculine agency in 'Steppin' to the Bad Side'. In the case of 'Steppin'', montage replaces movement, with Curtis liquidating the inventory of his car dealership and gambling on boxing matches and in behind-closed-doors poker games to finance a nationwide payola effort. Anxiety over black masculinity in 'Steppin'' is evident in the replacement of Bennett's danced black power with a musicalized boxing match observed by Curtis and C.C., where a sequence of two blows and a knockout are cut to the syncopated rhythm of the tune, creating a 'danced' sequence by way of sound effects and editing and removing Curtis and C.C.'s bodies from the dance. C.C. is briefly seen teaching a group of black male back-up dancers moves to the song but the dance, seen in fragments intercut with shots of Curtis at a desk, has none of the character assertion inherent in seeing Curtis himself dance the moment in the show. Condon's strategy of casting dramatic actors with little musical theatre experience in leading musical roles – evident in his trio of film musical adaptations: *Chicago* (Catherine Zeta-Jones and Renée Zellweger), *Nine* (Daniel Day-Lewis), and *Dreamgirls* – perhaps makes the above displacement of dance content necessary. Foxx, a television and movie star with a music career located within hip hop, likely would not – perhaps could not – have danced at the level expected of any Curtis cast in a stage production of *Dreamgirls*. It's hard to imagine Foxx making Bennett's 'dance well' cut. And the image of a man dancing onstage, where such expressive action is expected, would have been stunningly risky on screen.

Screen specifics versus stage mythologies: *Dreamgirls* and popular music history

A third added song for the film brings into relief Condon's strategy of tying down Krieger and Eyen's schematic tale of popular music history to the specifics of social and economic history. Part of this effort involves making direct links between the characters in *Dreamgirls* and the history of Motown Records, the phenomenally successful 1960s black-owned record label based in Detroit. The film is, from the start, firmly located in Detroit instead of New York City. Like Motown chief Barry Gordy Jr, Curtis releases an LP of Martin Luther King Jr's 'I Have a Dream' speech. From the formation of the Dreams forward, Beyoncé plays Deena as a knock-off Diana Ross, directly situating the Dreams as stand-ins for The Supremes, Motown's top girl group who, at their height, were as successful on the pop charts as their exact contemporaries The Beatles. Especially during the title number,

Beyoncé's slightly hunched posture and small, isolated head movements, combined with costuming and wig choices, create the suggestion of a straightforward imitation of Ross that is entirely lacking in Bennett's staging. The Motown label featured a rainbow and the slogan 'The Sound of Young America': Curtis's label in the film is called Rainbow Records and bears the slogan 'The Sound of Tomorrow'. And like Gordy and Motown, Curtis and Rainbow relocate to sunny California in the early 1970s.

Around that time, Gordy resisted releasing Motown artist Marvin Gaye's song 'What's Going On', a socially engaged, lyrical exploration of current events that as single, and later album, would become one of the biggest hits of the era. In similar fashion, Curtis rejects the third added new song in the *Dreamgirls'* film score: 'Patience', a song of hope and assurance addressed by a black voice to a black audience. C.C. introduces the song as a new number for Jimmy, who is then seen recording the number with Lorrell and a black gospel chorus. 'Patience' also accompanies a montage of Effie living with Magic, her and Curtis's daughter, in inner city Detroit: initially without a job and in despair, Effie goes to Marty for help restarting her singing career. Listening to the demo recording of 'Patience', Curtis rejects the record as a 'message song'. C.C. pleads, 'Isn't music supposed to express what people are feeling?' Curtis shuts the discussion down with a curt reply: 'Music's supposed to sell.' 'Patience' and the brief debate it sparks introduce a moralizing over popular music that is entirely absent in the show.

The conversation over 'Patience' makes Curtis look insensitive and greedy. Indeed, the film goes to some length to make Curtis a bad guy, detailing his crooked dealings beyond simply stopping Effie's recording of 'One Night Only' and, somewhat incredibly, enlisting Deena in the legal plot to bring Curtis down. Eliminating most of Curtis's sung dialogue and all his dancing opens the door to making the character an unsympathetic figure, in effect not only destroying a powerful black male figure from the stage original but inverting that figure into a stereotypical corrupt music industry executive. Indeed, Curtis's refusal to release 'Patience' is presented as the proximate cause for Jimmy's descent into drug abuse. After being fired by Curtis in a subsequent scene, Jimmy dies of a heroin overdose. On the stage, Jimmy makes a defiant final departure after being fired, proclaiming in his sung exit line, 'I don't beg. 'Cause I was here long before you. And I'll be here long after you all.' In its way, Jimmy's sung exit proclaims a soul-based black popular music authenticity narratively expressed in the character's rejection of Curtis's long effort to make him 'mellow'. But the stage Jimmy does this crucially – without denigrating the success of any of his performing peers, without rejecting his own success in earlier scenes singing, to his own amusement, like 'Tony Bennett', and without descending into drugs and death. Jimmy leaves the stage back in touch with the black sources of his style, his talent and self-worth intact. The audience is given the chance to applaud Jimmy's resilience as a performer even if they also cheer Lorrell leaving him. While the show declares in sung dialogue that soul – a close cousin to the blues – is a life-affirming force, the film subjects Jimmy to a personal demise more reminiscent of (white) rock and roll narratives.

Conclusions

The bows for Bennett's *Dreamgirls* concluded with the show's ten leading and supporting characters standing in a line. In turn, beginning with the less prominent roles, each individual stepped forward for a solo bow then exited the stage. By process of elimination, Effie alone remained as the curtain fell for the final time to the sound of the still roaring audience. The building of Bennett's show on individual voices and bodies could hardly be more explicitly acknowledged. Bennett's extremely flexible staging created a dynamic context for the sung and danced performance of Krieger and Eyen's schematic story of black popular music's rise to success with white audiences. Relying on the overwhelmingly white Broadway audience to understand the vocal style differences between the characters of Effie and Deena, Krieger, Eyen, and Bennett also trusted the audience to fill in the social and political context, to intuit what the ambitious characters in *Dreamgirls* mean when they declared in song 'We're gonna make this country change.' Along the way, the theatre audience was invited to play the audience for the many performances offered as part of the narrative, while also enjoying privileged access to the passionate (and passionately sung) backstage drama of Effie, Deena, Lorrell, Curtis, C.C., and Jimmy. The result is a mythic musical tale of major shifts in American popular music and culture: the mainstreaming of black music with the white mass audience; the move from 60s pop to 70s disco. On stage, the story of *Dreamgirls* is performed – sung and danced by male and female characters in meaningfully contrasting ways – in a manner that keeps the focus always on the work of the performers themselves, directing the audience towards popular music history as the creative physical labor of individuals striving to get audiences to respond, in turn, by clapping and cheering.

The end credits for Condon's *Dreamgirls* begin with the above-the-title stars Foxx, Beyoncé, and Murphy. With much fanfare in the music, Hudson's 'and introducing' credit rounds out the cast. Multiple images of each actor juxtapose, via rapid and always changing split screen montage, the dramatically different hair, clothing, and make-up styles of the film. The dizzyingly fast return of these images, viewed all out of chronological order, continues into the credits for the creative team, with, for example, costume sketches shown beside finished costumes as seen in the film. The credits celebrate by making visible the creative labor behind the film, the achievement of the cast and designers' recreation of various and specific popular culture pasts. Condon's film version is hobbled by the need to cater to Beyoncé, Foxx, Murphy, and Hudson – stars who hail from outside musical theatre and whose personas and talents do not, on the whole, match the characters as drawn in the show. Eliminating most all the sung dialogue shrinks all the characters and even evinces a modest embarrassment about the storytelling mode of the musical as a genre. Tying the stage version's mythic story to the specifics of popular music history (Motown) and literalizing the social and political historical context (the civil rights era) led to a reliance on production design and narrative detail that crowded out the vital, performance-centered energy of Bennett's original. As a result, the tremendous scale of *Dreamgirls* on stage – the show's fantastic size, founded throughout on the singing and dancing of a large and varied cast of characters – is greatly diminished on the big screen.

Dreamgirls on stage and *Dreamgirls* on screen alike tell a story of African American achievement across decisive decades in American political and cultural history. They do so, however, by very different means. Condon's film strives to pin down specific connections between the fictional characters in the story and the viewer's knowledge of real historical actors, while also emphasizing dramas of personal betrayal and loss. This effort, as suggested by the film's end titles, rests primarily on the surface elements of design, how the film looks rather than how it sounds. Bennett's stage version, built on Kreiger and Eyen's masterful text, worked along more evocative and more visceral lines, foregrounding by its very dramaturgy the explosive and enduring talent of black performers as the force that changed history, embodying thereby the essence of the show's story.

Notes

1 *Variety*, 22 September 1982.
2 *Dreamgirls* (original Broadway cast album), Los Angeles: Geffen Records, 1982; *Dreamgirls in Concert*, New York: Nonesuch, 2002; *Dreamgirls* (videorecording, 7 August 1985, Imperial Theatre, New York City), Theatre on Film and Tape Archive, New York Public Library for the Performing Arts.
3 www.justjared.com/2014/12/24/jennifer-hudson-covers-beyonces-dreamgirls-song-listen-kills-it-listen-now/. Accessed June 2017.
4 The first hint that *Dreamgirls* is more than a film about characters who happen to be performers – that it is, strictly speaking, a musical, where singing is an expected replacement for speaking – comes some thirty minutes into the film during 'Steppin' to the Bad Side'. Curtis, Wayne, and C.C., all dressed up sharp, walk in time to the music down a dramatically lit alleyway towards a poker game. Here – for the first time – a character sings instead of speaking and not as part of a performance within the film story. Given the framing, camera motion, and editing, it is easy to miss the fact that Curtis has just burst into song. But the moment passes quickly and Condon returns to a storytelling approach that almost entirely contains singing to diegetic contexts, effectively reducing the mythic proportions of *Dreamgirls* as a tale of black power.

Bibliography

Anonymous, www.justjared.com/2014/12/24/jennifer-hudson-covers-beyonces-dreamgirls-song-listen-kills-it-listen-now/. Accessed March 2017.
Dreamgirls (original Broadway cast album), Los Angeles: Geffen Records, 1982.
Dreamgirls in Concert, New York: Nonesuch, 2002.
Dreamgirls (videorecording, 7 August 1985, Imperial Theatre, New York City), Theatre on Film and Tape Archive, New York Public Library for the Performing Arts.
Variety, 22 September 1982.

7

AT THE INTERSECTION OF MUSIC, SEXUALITY AND RACE

Hairspray's generic and aesthetic variances

Linda Mokdad

Unlike many popular contemporary film musicals that draw upon Broadway stage plays, *Hairspray* (Adam Shankman 2007) in fact originated as a film (John Waters 1988). *Hairspray*'s transformation from film to stage play and film again constitutes a complex intertextual history and process of adaptation for a variety of reasons. While the 2007 film employs the medium-specific resources of cinema, its adoption of the score and slightly modified story line of the 2002 stage play (book by Mark O'Donnell and Thomas Meehan, lyrics and music by Marc Shaiman and Scott Wittman) distances it from the original film. Furthermore, even though all three versions of *Hairspray* more or less resemble one another narratively, their deviating generic and aesthetic strategies help to explain their divergent constructions of otherness.

All three versions of *Hairspray* center on the plump and perky Tracy Turnblad, a white working-class teenager who, growing up in 1960s Baltimore, dreams of dancing on 'The Corny Collins Show'. Despite not conforming to conventional standards of beauty, Tracy's dance moves and bubbly personality earn her a spot on the show. Soon after this initial success, she works to put an end to the show's policy of segregation, seeing no reason why whites and blacks should not dance together. Ultimately – with the help of Seaweed, a black fellow student she befriends in detention (who happens to be the son of Motormouth Maybelle, a radio personality and host of 'Negro Day' on 'The Corny Collins Show'), best friend Penny Pingleton, and the object of her affection, Link Larkin – Tracy succeeds in doing just that.

In acknowledging that all three iterations of *Hairspray* engage with the history of racial segregation in the United States, this chapter will consider how medium specificity converges with aesthetic and generic demands to produce profoundly dissimilar projects in regard to their handling of this history. How the various iterations of *Hairspray* mobilize genre to produce and articulate space is central to their focus on marginalization and, in turn, their configurations of gender, sexuality, and especially race. However, while the original *Hairspray* mobilizes genre and other aesthetic resources to trouble and destabilize normative categories of identity, the successive versions of *Hairspray* increasingly rely on conventional tactics to recuperate the disruptions and challenges posed by the 1988 film. This chapter will first address how the restaging of *Hairspray* and a repurposed nostalgia impact its subsequent constructions of gender and sexuality. It will then move into a discussion of how the various versions of *Hairspray* address and reframe their racial identity politics, before ending with an analysis of *Hairspray*'s transformation at the formal level (in particular emphasizing the handling of space).

Gender and sexuality: nostalgia, shock and camp

Broadway has long furnished Hollywood with source material and, although to a lesser extent the cinema has also provided material for a number of stage musicals, ranging from *42nd Street* (1933), *Seven Brides for Seven Brothers* (1954), *Thoroughly Modern Millie* (1967) to *Saturday Night Fever* (1977), *Footloose* (1984), *The Lion King* (1994) and *Billy Elliot* (2005). While musicologist Jessica Sternfeld has ascribed a 'literal-mindedness' to the failures of some film-to-stage adaptations such as *Footloose* and *Saturday Night Fever* (Sternfeld 2006: 352), critics such as Ethan Mordden have more categorically denounced the stage play's reworking of a movie musical as 'perhaps the worst aspect of Broadway's attempt to revive bygone art'.[1] Furthermore, Mordden refers to this form of adaptation as a 'franchise extension' because of the actual 'lack of adaptation' (Mordden 2013: 255). Unlike the historical (and now disparaged) legacy of fidelity criticism, which has privileged a faithfulness to the original (Stam 2005: 3), these comments point to anxieties about adaptations not reworking or departing far enough from the original work. The notion of these types of Broadway stage plays as 'franchise extensions' or 'tourist stops' (Mordden 2013: 256) also suggests that these revivals are less about revisioning previous works of art than capitalizing on a certain nostalgia for them. This revivalism, in fact, is exceptionally complicated in the case of *Hairspray*, where the original film itself participates in a nostalgia for the 1960s that also depends on a reworking of film genres.[2] However, while the subsequent versions of *Hairspray* engage nostalgia to present audiences with a now identifiable product, and one reassuringly tempered by more mainstream conventions and the passing of time, the original *Hairspray* uses nostalgia as an apparatus to poke fun at our often generic and comfortingly whitewashed constructions of the past.

An American auteur who specialized in cult and exploitation cinema, John Waters made a name for himself as the 'pope of trash' – one who 'effectively redefined what's "good" taste and what's "bad," what's beautiful and what's not, what's permissible and what's forbidden' (Levy 2015: 268). One of the key queer filmmakers of the 1970s, Waters worked to upset 'middle-class sensibilities' and 'expose and satirize the shallowness of the American Dream' (Benshoff and Griffin 2006: 161). With its PG rating, *Hairspray* marked a foray into more mainstream cinema and a departure from his earlier underground films such as *Pink Flamingos* (1972), *Female Trouble* (1974) or *Desperate Living* (1977), collectively known as the Trash Trilogy (Aufderheide 1990/2011: 118). However, rather than simply viewing this trajectory as a dilution of Waters' politics, the director's move into the mainstream opens up the possibility of another political space – where audiences not familiar with his previous work 'will not necessarily have shown up ready for a shock' (Tinkcom 2002: 159).

The 'shock' provided by Waters' *Hairspray* risks being neutralized or mitigated for a Broadway audience and, later, a more mainstream Hollywood audience due to a number of factors – be they aesthetic differences, a greater willingness in contemporary public discourse to engage with queer and/or transgender politics, and the familiarity or 'in-the-know' positionality that the process of adaptation may encourage. Regarding *Hairspray*'s aesthetic decisions, the diminishment of the original film's subversive potential occurs at the level of casting. Waters himself has acknowledged the power of his casting: 'The cast in itself is weird enough – if there's a gimmick, that's it' (Lally 1988/2011: 112). In addition to retaining the basic plot developments and primary characters of the 1988 film, the stage play and 2007 film continue the tradition of a man in drag performing the role of Edna Turnblad, Tracy's mother. While everything from conventional fare such as *Mrs. Doubtfire* (Chris Columbus 1993) to the far more challenging *The Adventures of Priscilla, Queen of the Desert* (Stephan Elliot 1994) features men in some form of drag, all of these examples provide a diegetic explanation or logic for such an appearance. For example, in the former a man disguises himself as a female housekeeper and in the latter actors are playing drag queens or transgender characters. However, Waters offers no such explanation for why an actual drag queen (Divine) is playing the role of a domesticated housewife, thus refusing to address or even acknowledge any incongruities. While the man-in-drag component is handled quite differently in each of the versions, its continuation in subsequent versions of *Hairspray* might suggest its humor is more about an intertextual play and recognition that points us back to the original text, and less about the destabilization of gender identity that Waters delivers.[3] Real-life drag queen and Waters regular, Divine, plays the role of Edna Turnblad 'straight', particularly troubling the boundary between male and female because no one in the diegesis acknowledges this incredibly conspicuous slippage. The 2002 stage play's casting of Harvey Fierstein as Edna also exploits Fierstein's star text by making use of a gay actor, one well known for writing and starring in *Torch Song Trilogy* (1982), a collection of plays that center on the life of a gay drag queen. But Fierstein's Edna is a kinder and gentler one; as one critic put it, 'She's every forgotten housewife, recreated in monumental proportions and waiting for something to tap her hidden magnificence' (Brantley 2002).[4]

While Waters mobilizes camp to critique and revise conventions and formulas related to Hollywood genres such as melodrama or the 'woman's picture' (Tinkcom 2002: 157), subsequent versions of *Hairspray* reproduce the generic structures that associate women with suffering with far more sincerity, sentimentalism, and conciliation. At the same time, Broadway's greater willingness to engage with topics that work against and outside of heterosexual norms might mean the role of Edna carries less weight in this regard. The 2007 film's casting of John Travolta for the role moves the characterization of Edna into an entirely different realm. And perhaps unsurprisingly for a $75 million project, Travolta's performance seems more focused on the feat and spectacle of a straight white male actor performing the role of a female (complete with prosthetics, fat jokes, and close-ups of Edna's behind) than illuminating femininity as performance. Travolta's own reflections on the films illustrate this shift in meaning well: 'Playing a woman attracted me. Playing a drag queen did not' (Green 2007).[5] Casting and characterization, and their impact on the film or stage play's encounter with genre, hint at how *Hairspray* moves incrementally from an emphasis on, and even a celebration of, the marginalized to the more comfortable and mainstream politics of assimilation.

History and race: historical fantasies and segregation

One of the most profound changes that *Hairspray* undergoes in its transformation from the 1988 film to the stage play is the removal of popular songs by black artists such as Dee Dee Sharp's 'Mashed Potato' and 'Gravy (On My Mashed Potatoes)' or The Five Du-Tones' 'Shake a Tail Feather'. The original film's soundtrack is replaced with a score by well-known composer Marc Shaiman and co-lyricist Scott Wittman. Subsequently, as an adaptation of the stage play, the new film adopted most of its songs and music. Whether or not the absence of black popular music undermines the idea that a black popular culture ever existed, as Matthew Tinkcom points out in his excellent essay, '"Dozing Off During History": *Hairspray*'s Iterations and the Gift of Black Music' (2010: 206), what is certain is that the Shaiman–Wittman score shifts its focus from a recognition of actual black popular music to an emphasis on narrative events, with most of the songs providing commentary on the characters and the unfolding plot.[6] This change undercuts the original attention to race – with the exception of Seaweed's 'Run and Tell That' and Motormouth Maybelle's 'I Know Where I've Been', the score comments on the relationship of mothers to their daughters ('Mama I'm a Big Girl Now'), the relationship between Edna and her husband Wilbur ('You're Timeless to Me'), introduces the teen dancers on 'The Corny Collins Show' ('The Nicest Kids in Town'), and so on and so forth. In other words, the songs express and elaborate on narrative developments that encourage us to focus our attention inward, rather than outward and beyond the text as the Waters film does.

Because the original *Hairspray* avoids any earnest attempt at being a social message film, its music participates in crucial cultural work that extends beyond narrative. In other words, the original *Hairspray* is able to mock the social message film while still acknowledging the powerful contributions of black music from that era. The stage play and 2007 film incorporate 'live' (or diegetic) black music, while the 1988 film mostly denies us the body from which the songs emanate. I would argue that it is Waters' way of pointing out how the black voice has been alienated from the black body – a point that is all the more emphasized considering the film's attention to white bodies dancing to black music, and the simultaneously imposed invisibility of black ones. Remarkably, then, the 1988 film version both 'showcases' and points out the absence of the black talent responsible for the music.

Taking into consideration that the stage play and 2007 film de-emphasize black popular music in general and recorded music in particular, the live (actual or diegetic) performances of Motormouth Maybelle and Seaweed do not function in the same manner. The 1988 film sets up a problem, a kind of disembodiment and repression of the black body, and it acknowledges and 'corrects' this problem in a crucial scene that finally unites the black body and voice. In what is perhaps one of the most moving and unexpectedly sincere moments in the 1988 film, Tracy, Link, and Penny accompany Seaweed to a black dance club where real-life R&B singer Toussaint McCall appears in a cameo, performing his hit song 'Nothing Takes the Place of You'. Unlike every other moment in the film that provides us with black music (accompanied by images of white bodies dancing to it) or marginalized black bodies, this moment presents us with a (diegetically) 'live' voice, thus bringing the body and voice together in the same space.

Considering the camp aesthetics that inform Waters' *Hairspray* and his canon at large, the scene stands out for its incredible sincerity. Eschewing the camp or irony that permeates the rest of the film, this tonal shift is meaningful for a number of reasons. First, although it functions pivotally in the diegesis, it also summons meaning at the extra-diegetic level. Like the actual popular black music that the 1988 film includes, this moment, too, acknowledges the real historical contributions of black artists. But perhaps more importantly, its odd and unexpected emotional tenor, which stands out dramatically from the tone of the rest of the film, also self-consciously suggests that this historical solution is the work of fantasy and cinema. Moreover, while a number of critics have pointed out the scene's anachronism (the film is set in 1962 but McCall's song was not actually released until 1967), the temporal disconnect seems to confirm the historical projection and fantasy of the scene.

Tinkcom examines how both the 1988 and 2007 versions of *Hairspray* function as historical 'fantasies' about 'black musical performance in the US post-World War II period' (2010: 206). He writes:

> [W]e might wonder how even seemingly progressive accounts of race in dominant depictions do not in fact seem to service the sense that non-white perspectives can move entirely into a Hollywood product; they appear too often to frame their depictions through the sense that changes – and especially positive changes – in race in US culture are consistently brought about by the motives and intentions of well-meaning white people.
>
> (2010: 200)

While Tinkcom's description applies to a large number of mainstream films, given Waters' attention to genre or the role of genre in Hollywood's production of history it seems unlikely that the director is seriously advancing the idea of Tracy as some kind of redeemer. In fact, rather than redeem the reality of segregation, the 1988 film acknowledges that the solutions it provides (such as McCall's cameo) are only made possible by contemporary (and adult rather than adolescent) as well as generic (the teen pic and melodrama) sensibilities about segregation and the history of racial politics in the United States. Waters' own ideas also suggest that the film attempts to offer this type of critique: 'How serious is it to come out for integration in 1962? Who would say, "I was really against it in '62?" It's a joke on message movies. That's what happened, I lived through it – Baltimore was the South, and there was a lot of segregation there' (Lally 1988/2011: 113).

The 1988 film pays tribute to popular black music while parodying the generic conventions that often redeem history. The stage play and the 2007 film, on the other hand, handle history quite differently. Near the end of the stage play's narrative, Motormouth Maybelle sings 'I Know Where I've Been', a song that, like the McCall cameo in the 1988 film, offers a rare moment of solemnity. At the most basic level, and as the lyrics, 'There's a light in the darkness … Showing me the way, but I know where I've been', aptly demonstrate, the song attests to Tinkcom's critique regarding 'well-meaning whites' functioning as the agents of progressive change. The permutations of stage performances leave more room for ambiguity in regard to this metaphor of Tracy as the 'light' (for instance, in one Broadway production, Motormouth Maybelle does not look at Tracy when singing these lyrics). In the 2007 film, however, soon after Tracy takes up a leadership position in the demonstrations against segregation, Mothermouth Maybelle does looks directly at Tracy while singing the song. While it might be tempting to compare the earnestness of this scene to McCall's cameo in the 1988 film, it is worth noting that although Tracy is otherwise a likeable character, the film never asks us to take her role as a civil rights activist seriously. Indeed, the stage play and 2007 film employ and carry out much of the camp aesthetics of the original, but they do not fully sustain its irony or distance to history, privileging a conclusion that (unintentionally or not) diminishes a political critique of form.

Space and the musical: marginalisation, boundaries and parody

While the various versions of *Hairspray* embrace parody or sincerity somewhat differently in their approach to history, they are profoundly different at the formal level of genre. The 1988 film includes a number of songs and features a lot of dancing, but ultimately it is a film about music rather than a musical – the latter being the generic form taken by both the stage play and the 2007 film. This transformation has several important implications. In becoming a quasi-sung-through musical, the act of singing in the stage play and 2007 film becomes distributed among a multitude of characters, both major and minor. Instead of being a specific tribute to black music, the stage play and 2007 film ask that we take the singing and dancing for granted as part of the logic of the musical, whether or not the story centers on the topic of music or not. Simply put, in its transformation into a musical, the diegetic (and historical) music are downplayed as *Hairspray* becomes less interested in showcasing that music and more invested in the generic use of song and dance as vehicles to express or enact the story's oscillation between narrative and spectacle.

This adoption of the musical form also has a huge impact on *Hairspray*'s configuration of space, both in the stage play and the 2007 film. All of the numbers in the 1988 film are diegetically motivated, unlike those in the most recent iterations of *Hairspray*, existing as they do in the musical's liminal space that blurs the boundaries between the diegetic and non-diegetic. In the tradition of the musical genre, this indeterminacy between diegetic/non-diegetic permits the stage play and 2007 film to have a far more expansive, spectacular, and affective relationship to space than the more diegetically anchored 1988 film. The medium-specific differences between theater and film further complicate this relationship to space, so that while the stage play and 2007 version are, unlike the 1988 film, both musicals, they rely on dramatically different techniques and resources to produce and arrange space (for example, film's recourse to editing). In addition, the configuration of space in the musical has always been deeply connected to its ideological inclinations. Richard Dyer's seminal work on the genre illuminates its impact of space on the construction and legitimization of white racial identity:

> Blackness is contained in the musical, ghettoized, stereotyped, trapped in the category of 'only entertainment'. Yet containment is the antithesis of the entertainment that the musical offers. Bursting from the confines of life by singing your heart out and dancing when you feel like it, this is the joy of the musical. It is in whites' privilege to be able to do this, and what it tells us about the white dream of being in the world, that the musical most disturbingly constructs a vision of race.
>
> (Dyer 2002: 39)

It might be said that in its focus on a white girl's intervention in the history of segregation all versions of *Hairspray* privilege a white perspective, but each mobilizes space differently to construct a 'vision of race', and each engages with or reproduces structures of containment to varying effects. This encounter with containment at the formal level is markedly important, given *Hairspray*'s investment in containment and marginalization at the level of content.

Like so much of Waters' output, *Hairspray* champions the people who live on the margins of society, and his protagonists are ones who challenge and sometimes choose to live outside the codes of white heteronormative culture. The film's rejection of standard notions of beauty, sexuality or gender might be viewed as an empowering alternative to assimilating or conforming to middle-class values; however, marginalization is a thornier issue in a film whose topic is about imposed racial segregation. *Hairspray* is certainly not asking that we view a painful history of institutionalized and legally enforced segregation as some kind of joke, but it does not hesitate to make fun of the generic conventions that make these types of history easier to digest. Despite Waters' insistence on parodying genres, he invests a lot of effort in demarcating and contrasting the spaces of black and white neighborhoods through editing.[7] Moreover, he sets up the conflict between these spaces in humorous but relentlessly uncomfortable terms. For instance, he does not hesitate to show the irrational fears that racist white characters such as Penny Pingleton's mom have of blacks – or to make fun of her hysterical and fearful flight during which she searches for her daughter in a black neighborhood – or even to point out some of the misinformed ideas about race held by Tracy, the film's benign if naive heroine. Simply put, Waters is not interested in producing an image of the past that comforts or eases the conscience of white audiences.

The 1988 film's willingness to use space to unsettle its audience becomes even more apparent if we consider how the stage play produces and registers space. Without recourse to editing, and in its more limited capacity to construct and parallel a variety of different settings, the stage play largely does away with the spatial contrasts the film provides. But even beyond the medium-specific conditions or restrictions of the theater, the stage play does not really mobilize the space of its mise-en-scène to suggest the impact of segregation. Again, given the musical's absence of a clear boundary between the diegetic and non-diegetic, the stage play does not confine itself to the logic of a diegetic world. While blacks and whites are segregated in terms of the story line, their performances as singers and dancers occur in the same space and with one another. In this way, the stage play does not exploit formal elements to express the segregation that informs its content.

The 2007 film exploits editing to produce space and the affect that accompanies it, while also setting up comparisons between the white and black characters. For instance, the 'New Girl in Town' number cuts from Amber (Tracy's rival) and two other white females performing on 'The Corny Collins Show' to a trio of black female singers called The Dynamites who perform the same song on the show during 'Negro Day'. Thus, in addition to maintaining the physical space of segregation, the editing allots screen time to, and develops contrasts between, the two groups without defying any diegetic logic. In other numbers that do blur the boundary between diegetic/non-diegetic, such as 'Welcome to the 60's', The Dynamites go from a diegetically anchored performance on television to magically entering the same physical space as Edna Turnblad as she undergoes her dramatic makeover by shopping for new clothes. This scene illuminates the ambivalence that frames much of the film's encounter with race. While first the voices and later the bodies of The Dynamites powerfully transcend their original physical space and help inspire Edna's metamorphosis, the trio also trade in their glamorous garb for employee uniforms belonging to the store where Tracy's mother is shopping. In other words, their move into Edna's physical space does not happen without them also being relegated to the background, there to motivate and support her transformation.

Other scenes in the film further confirm Richard Dyer's point about a musical legitimizing and making pleasurable the traversing and occupation of space by white characters. For instance, Tracy's opening number 'Good Morning Baltimore' functions as an unabashed love letter to the city ('I love you Baltimore/Every day's like an open door/Every night is a fantasy/Every sound is like a symphony'). Showing Tracy on her morning routine of heading out to school, the scene presents her moving in and out of several neighborhoods. Unlike the 'Welcome to the 60's' number, the fantasy space of the scene does not use its liminality or transcend the logic of the diegesis to feature black characters. Instead, the film is inconsistent regarding when or not it mobilizes the space of the diegesis to depict the reality of segregation. But perhaps more telling is Tracy's unrestricted movement through the various neighborhoods she traverses. While the number begins with tight close-ups and medium shots of Tracy in her bedroom getting ready for school, it increasingly opens up both in terms of shot scale (gradually with long shots and extreme longs shots that provide space for her movements) as well as a constantly moving camera (her departure from her home is met with a tracking movement) that expands and energizes the spaces Tracy encounters. In fact, she determines and motivates much of the camera movement that follows her as she produces and maps the space of the city with her singing and dancing. Mobility and freedom of movement are never an issue for Tracy; when she misses her school bus she hitches a ride on top of a random truck, and at that moment the number reaches a crescendo that is accompanied by a crane shot that further expands space and augments the affect and euphoria of the scene.

Tracy's privilege and ecstatic occupation of space becomes even more apparent if we examine Seaweed's 'Run and Tell That' musical number. After Tracy and Penny express their excitement about being invited to an event by 'colored people', Seaweed launches into a song that addresses his racial identity ('The blacker the berry/The sweeter the juice/I could say it ain't so/But darlin' what's the use'). The scene begins with Seaweed restricted with Tracy, Link, and Penny to the space of the detention room, where, shortly after he begins to sing, he is accompanied by a group of black students that are also in detention. The film then alternates shots of Seaweed and the group dancing with shots of Tracy and her friends watching them. In a move that seems to potentially match some of the dynamism of Tracy's opening number, Seaweed leads the group out into the hallway and, subsequently, outside of the school – with shots from a number of different angles adding to the scene's dynamism. However, this sense of movement and expansion is once again quickly restricted as Seaweed and his friends move their performance into the confined space of a school bus, all while Tracy, Link and Penny sit back and watch them admiringly. Even if we allow that the film is not asking audiences to take seriously the lyric's exoticism and essentialism, the scene's formal strategies reproduce many of the same structures that have marginalized or contained blacks in the musical genre. We should acknowledge the unintended irony of Seaweed's lyrics ('And there's those that try to help/God knows/But always have to put me in my place'), by recognizing that one of the few musical numbers to privilege the performances of the film's black actors also restricts their movement and confines the space they inhabit by reducing them to objects of a (reassured and entertained) white gaze.

Conclusions

Although the various iterations of *Hairspray* do not reflect any significant changes in the narrative, their divergence in terms of formal and generic strategies impact their meaning in substantive ways. The 1988 film can hardly be described as invested in realism and the historical accuracies of segregation; it does, after all, approach this history via a teenage dance show. However, in parodying the conventions of genres well known for their easy solutions or manipulation of sentiment (the teen pic, melodrama, and the musical), the film lays bare the inadequacy of these genres to engage with history. The more recent versions of *Hairspray* might appear to be more inclusive at the level of content (providing heartfelt moments and earnest reflections on racism), but they are often guilty of reproducing and perpetuating the generic structures that privilege white heteronormative ideologies (especially in terms of how they produce space and exploit affect vis-à-vis the musical).

In the case of *Hairspray*, the process of adaptation contributes to its depoliticization, both through repetition and increased familiarity with its narrative, and as a more commercial product that mobilizes the star system to encourage spectatorial identification and disavow the discomfort of the original. In addition, *Hairspray* returns to the workings of the musical, reproducing its spatial conventions and the racial divisions that the genre has helped to reinforce and perpetuate. Therefore, while the 1988 film consistently emphasizes how both society and genre work to produce and regulate sexuality, gender, or race, the other versions of *Hairspray* – particularly the 2007 film – pair the politics of assimilation with the exuberance of the musical form to absolve and redeem the troubling history of segregation.

Notes

1 It is worth noting that *Hairspray*'s run on Broadway was certainly no failure – it won eight of thirteen Tony Award nominations, including Best Musical, Best Original Score, Best Direction, Best Actor (Harvey Fierstein), and Best Actress (Marissa Jaret Winokur) – which may or may not be attributed to the stage play's creative reimagining of the 1988 film.

2 Waters has stated that *Hairspray* was inspired by the black popular music he listened to and loved as a teenager growing up in Baltimore, as well as his recollections of watching 'The Buddy Deane Show' – a show that ultimately failed in its efforts to integrate (Lally 1900/2011. 112, 113).

3 Unsurprisingly, the 2007 film mobilizes recognition and capitalizes on the nostalgia of the 1988 version by featuring cameos by Ricki Lake (the original Tracy), Pia Zadora, and John Waters himself (as a neighborhood flasher), as well as role by Jerry Stiller (who played Tracy's father in the original).

4 It is worth noting that the ephemerality and variability associated with the acting (every show will offer some form of permutation) and number of actors also form an important difference from recorded film acting. Perhaps in this medium-specific capacity, the theater offers an element of destabilization in regard to the character of Edna.

5   Leaving aside rumors calling into question Travolta's sexuality, his casting as Edna stirred up controversy given his associations with the Church of Scientology – and it prompted a boycott of the film by Kevin Naff, the editor of a gay newspaper, *The Washington Blade*, who described Scientology 'as a cult that "rejects gays and lesbians"' (Green 2007).

6   The stage play and 2007 film do, however quickly, reference 'the Detroit sound', and the latter includes a contemporary R&B song by Chester Gregory, which Seaweed uses to teach Tracy a dance called 'The Peyton Place'.

7   Tracy seems able to negotiate these various spaces the best, as we often see her moving in and out of them, unlike most of the white dancers such as Amber Von Tussle (Colleen Fitzpatrick), who is mostly confined to, and associated with, the artificiality of 'The Corny Collins Show' set.

Bibliography

Aufderheide, Paul (1990). 'The Domestication of John Waters.' *American Film 15*, no. 7 (April 1990), pp. 32–37.

Benshoff, Harry M. and Sean Griffin (2006). *A History of Gay and Lesbian Film in America.* Lanham, MD: Rowman & Littlefield.

Brantley, Ben (2002). 'Through Hot Pink Glasses, A World That's Nice'. *New York Times* (16 August 2002).

Dyer, Richard (1992/2002). *Only Entertainment.* London: Routledge.

James Egan, J. (ed.) (2011). *John Waters: Interviews.* Jackson: University Press of Mississippi.

Green, Jesse (2007). 'John Travolta In "Hairspray": Keeping His Rhythm, Even in Drag,' *New York Times* (18 July 2007).

Lally, Kevin (1988). 'Hairspray Gets a "Shocking" PG as Waters Looks Back to '62.' *Film Journal* (February/March 1988).

Levy, Emanuel (2015). *Gay Directors, Gay Films? Pedro Almodóvar, Terence Davies, Todd Haynes, Gus Van Sant, John Waters.* New York: Columbia University Press.

Mordden, Ethan (2013). *Anything Goes: A History of American Musical Theatre.* Oxford: Oxford University Press.

Smith, Susan (2005). *The Musical: Race, Gender and Performance.* London: Wallflower.

Stam, Robert (2005). *Literature through Film: Realism, Magic, and the Art of Adaptation.* Malden, MA: Blackwell.

Sternfeld, Jessica (2006). *The Megamusical.* Bloomington: Indiana University Press.

Tinkcom, Matthew (2002). *Working Like a Homosexual: Camp, Capital, Cinema.* Durham and London: Duke University Press.

Tinkcom, Matthew (2010). '"Dozing Off During History": Hairspray's Iterations and the Gift of Black Music.' In Steven Cohan (ed.), *The Sound of Musicals.* London: British Film Institute, pp. 200–211.

8

'WITH A BIT OF ROCK MUSIC, EVERYTHING IS FINE'

Mamma Mia! and the camp sensibility on screen

Helen Deborah Lewis

In 2008 Universal Pictures released the film version of the 1999 West End stage show *Mamma Mia!*, one of the most popular and lucrative 'jukebox musicals' of the last twenty years, featuring a whimsical plot woven between songs by Swedish pop band ABBA. Phyllida Lloyd directed both the film and the original Broadway production of the musical comedy, set on the Greek Island of Skopelos where the action takes place in a kind of fairytale, escapist atmosphere. Critics almost unanimously panned the film for its unapologetic garishness and superficiality, while some scholars and academics praised both the primarily female production team and the plot's feminist themes.[1]

Another movie that employs ABBA's music as the narrative soundtrack to parallel a female protagonist's journey to independence and self-fulfillment is the 1994 Australian comedy *Muriel's Wedding*. Both *Muriel* and *Mamma* are imbued with a camp sensibility, not in the queer sense but as aesthetic choice, with ABBA songs as the driving force behind both films. In this chapter, I posit that both films use ABBA music as the cornerstone of a distinct campy theatricalism. Unlike *Muriel's Wedding*, which applies the self-consciously brazen and exaggerated elements of camp, *Mamma Mia!* the film transforms theatrical camp gaudiness into a cinematic fairytale escapism that hampers the feminist elements of the plot. Both the film and the stage version of *Mamma Mia!* present flamboyant fantasy worlds without apology or irony, but the film especially does not recognize its own kitsch value and loses the sense of joyful, carefree camaraderie of the show.

Camp, kitsch, or fluff: terminology and context

Often, the term 'camp' gets equated with a number of other terms that may relate to camp or to a camp sensibility. It is almost impossible to give the word a singular, definitive meaning, given its multitudinous definitions and manifestations across cultures, genres, and media. The progenitor use of 'camp' was in Susan Sontag's landmark 1964 essay 'Notes on Camp', in which she fleshed out the term and its derivation, describing it as both a sensibility and an aesthetic choice. For Sontag, camp could not be defined as either genre or concept because it is something 'felt' rather than 'declared' or consciously prescribed. (Sontag 1966).

Since the publication of Sontag's essay, numerous scholars have challenged her interpretation of camp as denying its socio-political potential and valuing camp's form over its substance. Esther Newton's 1972 anthropological analysis of drag, *Mother Camp*, recognizes camp's manifestation in drag performances as a political act because drag highlights the performativity and artificiality of gender. Eve Sedgwick describes camp as an inherently queer directive with overtly subversive elements and notes camp's need for 'reader recognition' in order for it to have a significant effect (Sedgwick 1990: 156). David Bergman emphasizes camp's aesthetic value, defining camp as 'a style that favors "exaggeration," "artifice," and "extremity",' recognized and appreciated by a select population 'outside the cultural mainstream' and connected to gay culture (Bergman 1993: 4–5). For Bergman, camp's historical connection to queerness makes it both a stylistic and political choice. Moe Meyer's 1994 book *The Politics and Poetics of Camp* defines camp as 'the total body of performative practices and strategies used to enact a queer identity, with enactment defined as the production of social visibility' (Meyer 1994: 5). In *Feeling Backward*, Heather Love suggests that camp is a form of queer 'backwardness', or a reflection upon queer history's simultaneous negative, tragic elements related to social and cultural oppression as well as its affirmative response to such traumas. (Love 2007: 2–3) Love notes camp's 'tender concern for outmoded elements of popular culture and … refusal to get over childhood pleasures and traumas', or nostalgia as an act of reliving both joy and pain (ibid.: 7). These scholars reclaimed and asserted camp's role as both an aesthetic and political performance of queerness and identity, even as the definition began to shift after its appropriation into mainstream culture.[2]

Now, 'camp' is almost entirely part of postmodern vocabulary, separate from a queer connotation. In *Guilty Pleasures: Feminist Camp from Mae West to Madonna*, Pamela Robertson points to postmodernism's similar values to camp, notably the overvaluing of the flamboyant, the theatrical, and the 'lower' arts, and deconstruction of the hierarchy of art values systems, as one of the reasons for the change in the definition of camp and its movement into a non-queer paradigm. She writes, 'The various values attached to notions of postmodernity need to be acknowledged and accounted for as part of the cultural current that shapes the discourse around contemporary notions of camp, parody, kitsch' (Robertson 1996: 121). An audience's perception, valuation, and analysis of a performance or text seem to determine its camp categorization.[3]

Andrew Ross's article 'Uses of Camp' makes the distinction between terms and their valuation:

While schlock is truly unpretentious—nice, harmless things—and is designed primarily to fill a space in people's lives and environments, kitsch has serious pretensions to artistic taste, and, in fact, contains a range of references to high or legitimate culture which it apes in order to flatter its owner–consumer.

(Ross 1988: 145)

'Schlock' might be equated with 'fluff', in that both terms connote the 'harmlessness' of vacuous content, whereas 'kitsch' is in the eye of the beholder. A work or object's legibility as 'kitschy' to the consumer/spectator/audience is based on his/her knowledge of the hierarchy within popular culture that informs one's appreciation of kitsch value. Kitsch, a word derived from the German *kitsch* meaning tacky or tasteless, has become invisible in favor of the word 'camp' as a descriptor not only of self-conscious, flamboyant performativity with a queer sensibility but also of content or material objects that are 'kitschy.' A camp sensibility, comingled with a queer sensibility, in some definitions values and appreciates 'kitsch' for its aesthetic pseudo-value and its adherence to camp principles. Certainly, 'kitsch' embodies aspects of postmodern discourse that question how we evaluate and designate what is 'good' versus 'bad' art, and challenge essentialist arguments about art's worth and value.

Indeed, appreciation for 'kitsch' is often congruent if not equivalent to camp in the connection to a queer sensibility. David Halperin makes this distinction between what he describes as 'ascription' versus labeling:

Camp ascription … produces an effect precisely opposite to that of kitsch labeling. It marks the person making the judgment as an insider, as someone who is in the know, who is in on the secret of camp, already initiated into the circuits of shared perception and appreciation that set apart those who are able to discern camp and that create among such people a network of mutual recognition and complicity.

(Halperin 2012: 189)

Here, Halperin contends that one who appreciates something for its 'kitschiness' does not connect to a camp sensibility, because an appreciation for bad content is not enough; camp as a performed, theatrical entity makes the spectator part of the same crowd or coterie, connected by the ability to detect and identify campiness. Kitsch is for the uninitiated while camp is for those 'in-the-know'.

One word that might best describe the dramaturgy of the musical *Mamma Mia!* is fluff. 'Fluff', in the colloquial sense of the word, connotes media and entertainment that is vacuous and devoid of depth. In the hierarchy of popular entertainment, *Mamma Mia!* would be considered neither high nor low art; rather, it is categorized as pedestrian popular entertainment.[4] It is a work meant for mass production and consumption, non-threatening to multiple types of audiences and overall benign. While 'fluff' does not pack as strong a political punch as other subcategories of camp, it is how the audience receives and interprets the 'fluff' that could imbue it with socio-political implications.

In a world of postmodernist perspective, is it fair to dismiss some work as simply 'meaningless fluff'? Or 'schlock'? Or what some critics of musical theatre describe as pure and simple 'stupidity'? Are not all works of art, devoid of an antiquated values system, worthwhile to some degree? It is the development of 'camp', connected to a gay theatrical context, that proscribed the notion of appreciation and valuation of the tacky, trite, and tasteless. Add to this the pop art sensibility recognizing and codifying mass-produced cheap content, and 'meaningless fluff' becomes an entity worthy of critical examination and ironic appreciation by an *au courant* audience. Using the more current, postmodern definition of 'camp' and its sub-genres, 'fluff' is a form of camp that lacks depth and kitsch is an object-driven kind of camp that, to an audience, is more substantive. Ultimately, camp appears to come down to the 'value' of the work and audience reception of its execution, or how the culture, both scholars and the general public, interprets and classifies the work.

Mamma Mia!: camp exemplified?

Most of *Mamma Mia!*'s central elements fall into a modern textbook definition of 'camp'. First: it is a jukebox musical featuring the music of ABBA, whose uncomplicatedly written songs are upbeat disco dance numbers produced with theatrical orchestral flourish and a focus solely on a few subjects: love gained, love lost (with hope of regaining it), the power of dance, and the power of song. Second: the narrative takes place on a Greek island, a location representative of escapism and an alternate universe from the normality of everyday life's responsibilities.[5] Third: the plot centers around a woman trying to figure out which of the three men from her past could possibly be the father of her adult daughter who is about to get married. The story's superficiality, fantastical setting, disco music, and musical theatre framework combined together might be the reason that the show's campiness goes without saying. However, what we in the twenty-first century take for granted about 'camp' is its roots in queer history, theatre, and the postmodern zeitgeist, relying on the definition based on audience reception/ valuation of the work.[6]

At first glance, the ABBA soundtrack reads as the most 'campy' element of *Mamma Mia!*, as it does for the film *Muriel's Wedding*. *Muriel's Wedding* features an all-ABBA score to which the main character Muriel listens religiously and uses as a proverbial security blanket against the mundanity and disappointment of her everyday life. For the most part, the original songs play behind the action, but in several instances characters actively listen to ABBA recordings or sing along to the tracks. *Muriel's Wedding* is not a movie musical; characters do not perform the songs but experience and engage with the music as a separate entity. The songs affect the characters emotionally while also driving the plot forward and letting us into Muriel's failures, successes, and self-discoveries.

In *Mamma Mia!* characters perform ABBA songs in the traditional movie musical form: the songs express and explain characters' feelings and experiences to other characters or to the audience and break the 'realism' of the rest of the film. The setting and plot do not serve the story; the story serves the ABBA songs and the audience's experience of them in a Broadway or West End setting. The songs do somehow fit the plot, which isn't difficult since the ABBA lyrics are open-ended enough for wide romantic comedy interpretation. Songs like 'S.O.S.' (performed by Pierce Brosnan as Sam responding to Donna's insistence that she is happy being romantically unattached) contain the lyrics, 'Where are those happy days/They seem so hard to find/I try to reach for you/But you have closed your mind/Whatever happened to our love/I wish I understood/It used to be so nice/It used to be so good' (Johnson 2008). The lyrics could be placed in any number of narrative contexts, making the songs similar to the 'trunk songs' of early Broadway: written without context by a composer then wedged into a show's score. In between musical numbers, ABBA instrumentals play over the action as if the music itself must umbrella all of the action in the film, rather than serving as a realistic extension of everyday life.

An example of this distinction is illustrated in the film's use of the crowd-pleasing song 'Dancing Queen'. In the stage version of *Mamma Mia!* Tanya and Rosie perform the song to remind Donna of her younger days as 'the life and soul of the party' and 'el rock chick supremo' after Donna laments the appearance of her three former lovers, all potential fathers of her adult daughter (Johnson 2008). Through their playful rendition of the song, using costume pieces and a hairdryer as a microphone, the women rediscover their bond and youthful vibrancy while bolstering Donna's confidence. In the film version, the number begins much the same way, with the women dressing up and romping about in Donna's bedroom, and then moves out into the town where local women throw away their chores and other business to join in the musical celebration. It culminates in a dance sequence on the dock that ends with all of the women leaping happily into the Aegean Sea. Regarding the 'Dancing Queen' number in the film, director Phyllida Lloyd remarked, 'Time works in such a different way on-screen and we wanted every song to really earn its place in the story … 'Dancing Queen' became an epic, Pied Piper journey that really filled the space that was allowed to it' (Phyllida Lloyd interview, IndieLondon). In both versions of the musical, 'Dancing Queen' is meant as an anthem of female empowerment and strength. However, by moving the number outside of the intimate bedroom scene into a public space, the film version of the number becomes a generic 'Go, Girl' celebration of womanhood taken away from the narrative context and losing its dramaturgical power.

In an interview about her first experience of seeing *Mamma Mia!* on Broadway in October 2001 (a month after the 11 September terrorist attacks on New York), as part of her daughter's birthday celebration, Meryl Streep commented on the show's positive energy-inducing power:

Everybody was really dimmed spiritually after 9/11. I thought, 'What am I going to do with the kids?' So I took all these 10-year-olds to see a matinee of *Mamma Mia!*. They walked in and they sat there with their heads in their hands. Dimmed is the word – they were sad all the time, you know? The first part was really wordy, and then 'Dancing Queen' started up. And for the rest of the show they were dancing on their chairs and they were so, so happy. We all went out of the theatre floating on the air. I thought, 'What a gift to New York right now.'

(Jeffries 2008)

Streep commended the show as a welcome burst of cheer during a time of tragedy and national mourning. *Mamma Mia!*, which opened on Broadway one month and one week after the 9/11 terrorist attacks, became for some audience members the best form of escapism: an optimistic, upbeat contrast to the sadness and fear pervading New York. Assessment of the show's schlockier elements may not have been as important as one's pure enjoyment of them, without irony.

More negative reviews gave the show even less benefit of the doubt. In his 2010 review of the Winter Garden production in New York, blogger Christopher Caggiano simply called the musical, 'Bad. Really, really bad,' and went on to unpack the definition of the show's badness, including some choreography that was 'laughably amateurish, featuring pointlessly intricate footwork with no sense of flow or stage perspective' and the book's humor limited to a few 'hoary jokes', none of which landed 'except the ones (and there are many) that involve[d] characters touching their own or someone else's boobs or buns' (Caggiano 2010). Of the film version, Anthony Lane of *The New Yorker* wrote, 'The legal definition of torture has been much aired in recent years, and I take 'Mamma Mia!' to be a useful contribution to that debate' (Lane 2008). Even so, the plethora of negative reviews for the stage and film versions of *Mamma Mia!* do not acknowledge that any of the unfavorable elements are campy, intentionally or otherwise. In only a few reviews did critics admit the kitschiness of the film but immediately apologized for the pleasure they took in it, as one reviewer wrote in *The Telegraph*: 'Only in the last third does Mamma Mia! degenerate into the best available version of itself – a so-bad-it's-good, never-mind-the-singing campathon' (Robey 2008). Rather than celebrating the film's unintended campiness, critics only portrayed the film as a guilty pleasure.

The aspects of *Mamma Mia!* with the most camp potential are in the eye of the beholder. For some audiences Meryl Streep bouncing around on a bed in overalls might be a lighthearted, uncharacteristic moment of comedy that fans of the Oscar-winning actress can appreciate; for others, Streep's bed romp is an exercise in grotesquery and an un-Streep-like lack of decorum. Spectators may see Streep's role in the film as separate from the medium of the story and a moment of levity or shame for the actress, depending on interpretation. Streep's participation in *Mamma Mia!* as a campy performance ties into a more queer perception of the term: if Streep is American cinema royalty, her performance in *Mamma Mia!* could be read as a carnivalesque reversal of social hierarchy in which one of the most respected actresses of a generation performs in a perfunctory movie musical. While audiences might interpret the film this way and identify Streep's work in *Mamma Mia!* as camp, Streep's explanation of the experience (at least in the press) does not acknowledge this 'reversal'. Streep stated that the film 'wasn't hard work' but 'a joy', and that she appreciated her foray into movie musicals (Meryl Streep interview, IndieLondon).[7]

ABBA and nostalgia as dramaturgy: wedding scenes compared

Musical theatre composer and critic Ethan Mordden, who unabashedly characterizes *Mamma Mia!* as a 'piece of stupid junk', admits the appeal of ABBA, who 'always had a lot of energy even when singing about nothing', whose songs have the 'balance and polish that careful studio work achieves' (Mordden 2004: 226). Even for writers like Mordden, who devotes an entire chapter of his book on late-twentieth-century musical theatre to shows like *Mamma Mia!*, titled 'Junk is a Genre', the international success and unyielding popularity of the show comes from the likability of the music. Ben Brantley of the *New York Times* wrote about the musical score that '[t]hey're the sort of songs that seem to belong to some hazy collective memory. And it's amazing how much cumulative emotional clout they acquire here' (Brantley 2001).

ABBA has multiple meanings in both *Muriel's Wedding* and *Mamma Mia!*. In *Muriel's Wedding*, songs like 'Dancing Queen' and 'Waterloo' represent all at once escapism, joy, personal fulfillment, and independence. *Mamma Mia!* enlists the songs for their generic messages and themes. Both movies use ABBA music to perform escapist fantasies in different contexts. They also employ ABBA music to add to the camp aesthetic of the film. In both cases, camp-like content enriches the films' comic and fantasy elements. However, *Mamma Mia!* lacks the self-conscious camp potential visible in *Muriel's Wedding*.

In *How to Be Gay*, Halperin writes about the Swedish pop quartet ABBA and its appeal to queer consumers: 'ABBA itself, of course, was not a gay band, being comprised of two married heterosexual couples, but some of its songs were popularized in gay clubs and became gay anthems – before being reappropriated by straight culture' (Halperin 2012: 135). Music by groups like ABBA, made popular in both gay and straight disco settings, has cultural cachet for its gay fandom as well as its 'campy' potential due to the over-the-top, theatrical quality of the music and the overproduced bubble gum pop aesthetic. Some of ABBA's songs declare self-affirmation in the spirit of the band's disco contemporaries like Gloria Gaynor's 'I Will Survive' or Chaka Khan's 'I'm Every Woman'. Celebratory songs of personal empowerment performed by female singers have historically fallen into the category of gay iconicity and ABBA music, performed by lead singers Agnetha Fältskog and Anni-Frid Lyngstad, fits well into that category.

Interestingly, both of these ABBA-scored films have weddings as a major theme. *Muriel's Wedding* upends the wedding fantasy fairy tale entirely. If the island in *The Tempest* might be Prospero's dreamscape, Skopelos might be that of Muriel. In her bedroom, Muriel murmurs along to 'Dancing Queen' as she holds a wedding bouquet. Using Heather Love's interpretation of camp as cultural nostalgia, Muriel experiences ABBA songs as nostalgia for the cultural past, allowing her to remain stuck in a childhood fantasy of fairy tale weddings. In contrast, *Mamma Mia!* is a nostalgic experience not for the characters but for the audience, whose job is to escape into the comfortable familiarity of the music. The audience must otherwise do the 'work' of interpreting the film as kitsch or camp.

Mamma Mia! could be read as the performance of Muriel's marriage fantasy. After moving to Sydney, Muriel reinvents herself as 'Mariel', a more sophisticated version of her old self that has a job, goes dancing, and goes to bridal boutiques pretending to shop for a gown for her upcoming wedding. After she is confronted by her friend Rhonda about this charade, Muriel cries:

> I want to get married! I've always wanted to get married. If I can get married, it means I've changed, I'm a new person ... And if someone wants to marry me, I'm not [Muriel] anymore, I'm me ... Muriel! Muriel Heslop! Stupid, fat, and useless − I hate her! I'm not going back to being her again. Why can't it be me? Why can't I be the one?
>
> (*Muriel's Wedding* 1994)

Muriel spends her life in Sydney pretending she is a bride-to-be, having her picture taken in various dresses at multiple shops around town, continuing to live in a fantasy world that does not exist. Arguably, *Mamma Mia!* could be that fantasy world, one in which men clamor to claim women as their own while ABBA music plays constantly.

The wedding scenes in both films exemplify this interpretation. During the wedding scene in *Mamma Mia!*, after Sophie has called off her marriage to her fiancé Sky, Sam sings 'I Do I Do I Do' as a surprise marriage proposal to Donna in the chapel. While Sophie and Sky's idyllic island wedding has been canceled, another wedding takes place and provides the audience with a lighthearted, domestic-comedy happy ending. Conversely, 'I Do I Do I Do' plays during Muriel's sham marriage to a South African swimmer who is getting married for Australian citizenship and cares nothing for his bride-to-be. The upbeat tune does not fit or belong as Muriel joyfully walks down the aisle toward a groom who neither knows nor loves her, and vice versa. The marriage is an ill-fitting fantasy being played out against a stark, unfeeling reality and 'I Do I Do I Do' plays awkwardly in the background as the groom grimaces at his pending fate and Muriel plays a dress-up game. The scene has an uncomfortably comical and grotesque atmosphere bolstered by the irony of the song's simple naiveté.

In *Mamma Mia!* there are only two overt demonstrations of nostalgia; otherwise, the characters appropriate the songs in the moment and the songs function as an extension of character dialogue. The first moment takes place during the reunion performance of Donna and the Dynamos, 'the world's first girl power band' made up of Donna (Streep) and her two best friends (Christine Baranski and Julie Walters) at Sophie's bachelorette party. The women perform 'Super Trouper' and nostalgically experience their feminist pop group heyday. In this instance, the song is diegetic: the characters are aware it is a performance, rather than an extension of their everyday dialogue. The other moment of self-conscious, performed nostalgia comes at the end during the 'encore/current calls', when the six principal actors sing 'Waterloo' while dressed in spandex, spangled ABBA-style costumes (complete with bell-bottoms). Famously, the original stage show contains multiple encores that would allow audience sing-along participation (clapping along is strongly encouraged) and certainly 'Waterloo' could be considered the logical song choice, as it likely could not find a home within the show's plot. In the film, the actors perform 'Waterloo' on what appears to be an empty sound stage. Toward the end of the song, the camera cuts to a brief cameo for original members of ABBA dressed as Greek gods and goddesses, giving due diligence to the show's composers and providing spectators a moment of conscious nostalgia outside the film's primary narrative. In the stage version of *Mamma Mia!* the encore gave performers a chance to 'karaoke' ABBA songs in concert-style, encouraging audience members to sing along and engage directly in the performative nostalgia, much in the way Muriel does in *Muriel's Wedding*. These moments are potentially the only 'campy' parts of the show, consciously flamboyant self-parody that does not necessarily give the film full camp 'street cred'. After all, not all camp must be diegetic in order for it to be successful, but what makes entertainment more plausibly campy is its self-awareness.

On this repurposing of ABBA music, Malcolm Womack writes,

> The music of ABBA is no longer the sole property of the terminally square or the knowingly camp, but rather, and once again, that of a popular audience. Nowhere is this clearer than in the massive success of *Mamma Mia!*.
>
> (Womack 2009: 201–2)

ABBA reached its popularity peak in the 1970s, as Womack notes, and then went through a number of shifts in audience reception before it gained a new acceptance as nostalgia. George Rodosthenous (2016) contends that ABBA music has never lost its appeal: 'It is the music of ABBA, with its diachronic, refreshing and celebratory qualities, that is mainly responsible for *Mamma Mia!*'s success; people have been listening and dancing to it for the past forty years.' Music from the 1970s as an impetus for cultural nostalgia can be found in other musicals and music theatre plays from the last twenty years, including *Saturday Night Fever* (1998), *Disco Inferno* (1999), *Xanadu* (2007), *Disaster!* (2012), and Diane Paulus's production *The Donkey Show*, a reimagining of *A Midsummer Night's Dream* in a 1970s disco in the spirit of New York's Studio 54. As a jukebox musical repurposing popular 1970s music, *Mamma Mia!* is in good company.

In her article 'Memories That Remain: *Mamma Mia!* and the Disruptive Potential of Nostalgia', Naomi Graber suggests that nostalgia was repurposed in the film *Mamma Mia!* specifically to accentuate the film's feminist themes. She references the use of ABBA music as a form of 'feminist nostalgia' harking back to the liberal feminist movement of the 1970s (Graber 2015: 188). For Graber, the show 'rewrites the past it remembers' by 'changing ABBA's music from bubblegum pop to feminist anthems' (ibid.: 191). Relating to the show's themes around age, love, sex, marriage, and family, she describes the musical overall as a 'cheeky response to the postfeminist voices that proclaim the feminist project completed' through its celebration of sisterhood, singledom, and the possibility of sexual reawakening in middle age. Graber also notes how nostalgia allows consumers and spectators to re-assess original content and put new meaning and value onto it, allowing non-political material like ABBA music to be reframed for its socio-cultural value. Certainly, such an analysis of *Mamma Mia!*, placed within the context of a larger socio-political moment to understand its feminist potential, adds a layer to audience understanding and experience of the film. The question is whether or not audiences received the film as such, and there is little evidence to suggest that fans of the film specifically appreciated it as an exercise in feminist nostalgia. What is more, the film describes itself as a fairy tale in the opening number. One might argue that Donna's independence and female-centered world on Skopelos reads as whimsical fantasy on the outskirts of mainstream society. It is only when three men from the 'mainland' infiltrate the idyllic space that Donna moves to rescind her single life and get married, returning to a more traditional reality.

Queer readings and camp potential

Perhaps it is the powerful female figures in *Mamma Mia!* that make it not only legible as a feminist film but also as a queer-friendly one as well. On *Mamma Mia!*'s camp potential, Georges-Claude Guilbert writes:

> Camp is the key word to describe *Mamma Mia!*, but not in the debased sense it has unfortunately acquired in the US in recent decades – not in the reductive sense of so-bad-it's-good, strictly associated to kitsch. It is camp rather in the sense that queens and drag queens are camp, incorporating associations to kitsch and queer.
>
> (Guilbert 2013: 181–2)

Guilbert then argues that *Mamma Mia!*, separate from the gay content that appears in the film, is gay as both a movie musical and a work of gay iconography, given the all-star female cast including Meryl Streep and Christine Baranski, both of whom could be read as female drag queens (Guilbert 2013: 184–8). This queer reading of the film evokes Esther Newton's notion of drag as an exemplary form of camp, therefore making three principal female roles in the show campy because they read as surrogate drag queens. As the brassy, outspoken 'cougar' of the film, Baranski's character Tanya has all the right parts to be mistaken for a drag persona, especially in her song 'Does Your Mother Know', during which she seductively teases Pepper (a young bartender and the groom-to-be's best man):

> You're so hot teasing me/So you're blue/But I can't take a chance on a kid like you/It's something I couldn't do/There's that look in your eyes/I can

read in your face/That your feelings are driving you wild/Ah but boy you're only a child.

(Johnson 2008)

As an older woman seducing a much younger man, Baranski's character invokes the 'comic dame' drag persona (also known as 'dame comedian'), historically performed by a male comedian as a caricature of a grotesque, tawdry, and vulgar older woman.[8] However, 'Does Your Mother Know' suggests nothing of the dame character's absurd, boorish sexuality. In a red bathing suit and a floral sarong, Baranski winks and flirts her way across the beach with a chorus of young, muscular men in swim trunks. She teasingly pushes Pepper away from her and lifts her arms in dominating, confident poses, calling to mind a female iconic performer or 'diva' far more than a comic dame. The 'tongue-in-cheek distance' of drag performance that Guilbert suggests Streep and Baranski are reflecting in their characters seems entirely absent. Both women are sexually confident but neither actress plays the role as tongue-in-cheek or wildly exaggerated; they are sincere in their romantic comedy performances.

Conclusions: critical response and interpretation

For fans of *Mamma Mia!* the delightfulness of the show and the film is a result of the joy the musical espouses and the pleasure in experiencing a musical with familiar, lovable music, and does not derive from an ironic pleasure in the cheapness of the product. Even critics of the stage show and the film failed to demonstrate an appreciation for the presumed 'camp' or 'kitsch' qualities of either. Of the West End original production, Katy Thompson wrote, 'This wedding celebration with a twist is worth attending. Just make sure your tongue is wedged firmly in your cheek' (Thompson 1999). Charles Isherwood of *Variety* proclaimed the Broadway premiere of *Mamma Mia!* 'a thoroughly preposterous show, but ... also a giddy guilty pleasure' (Isherwood 2001).

The extreme financial success of the film version of *Mamma Mia!* and the popularity of the stage version of the show on Broadway, in the West End, and on multiple national tours (both Equity and non-Equity) ultimately helps us understand how popular culture receives 'camp'. In a postmodern world, now perhaps a 'post-postmodern' world, all media content is subject to parody, pastiche, and irony, seemingly within milliseconds after its dissemination. For some spectators, *Mamma Mia!* is ripe material for mockery and derision, particularly because of its earnestness and unironic glow. For other audience members, however, that glow is a refreshing respite from a callous, cynical worldview to which most creative content is subject. No doubt, the 2018 release of the film's sequel, entitled *Mamma Mia!: Here We Go Again!*, shows Universal Pictures' belief that their audience's craving for more unabashed positivity will result in yet another box office triumph.

Romantic musical comedies are, perhaps, one of the last bastions of sincerity. *Mamma Mia!* takes its pure sentimentality very seriously and for this reason it is not inherently campy until we prescribe cultural meaning to it. Even so, most people fall into the same category as Tim Robey of *The Telegraph* (2008), who noted, 'Finding the film a total shambles was sort of a shame, but I have a sneaking suspicion I'll go to see it again anyway.'

Notes

1   For recent scholarship on the film adaptation of *Mamma Mia!*, see E. Aston (2013). 'Work, Family, Romance and the Utopian Sensibilities of the Chick Megamusical *Mamma Mia!*', in Elaine Aston and Geraldine Harris (eds), *A Good Night Out for the Girls*, 114–33, Basingstoke: Palgrave Macmillan; G. Rodosthenous (2016), 'Mamma Mia! and the Aesthetics of the 21st Century Jukebox Musical Genre', in Robert Gordon and Olaf Jubin (eds), *The Oxford Handbook of the British Musical*, Oxford: Oxford University Press; L. Fitzgerald and M. Williams (eds) (2013), *Mamma Mia! The Movie: Exploring a Cultural Phenomenon*, London: I.B. Tauris.
2   Writing about the birth of Off-Off-Broadway and the development of underground queer theatre in the 1960s, Don Shewey described camp's use in live theatre as a political act in disguise: 'a subversive strategy, cultural critique, and identity formation described as child's play'. He notes that the politically subversive nature of camp faded as mainstream culture embraced both it and postmodern principles in which 'all pop culture quotes other pop culture' (Shewey 2002: 129). Yet the connection between camp and theatricality remains intact, as Jack Babuscio describes it: 'To appreciate camp in things or persons is to perceive the notion of life-as-theater, being versus role-playing, reality and appearance.' (Babuscio in Bergman 1993: 24).
3   Various disciplines including popular culture studies, queer and gender studies, and theatre and performance studies have unpacked the definition of 'camp' to understand its relationship to popular entertainment and creative content, and in the last few decades some musical theatre scholars have employed 'camp' as a subgenre of the musical theatre form. Even within queer studies or theatre studies, the definition of 'camp' is the work of scholars, whereas camp in the popular imagination encompasses mostly low or 'bad' popular entertainment, as well as ostentatious or flamboyant content. Usually, a work will be called 'camp' whether or not the writers, composers, artists, directors, actors, performers, etc. intended it to be camp in the first place.
4   Oxford Dictionaries define the term as 'entertainment or writing perceived as trivial or superficial' (Oxford Dictionaries 2016), while Merriam Webster's definition is 'something inconsequential' (Merriam-Webster Collegiate Dictionary 2016). The Cambridge Dictionary simply describes fluff as 'useless or unimportant information' (Cambridge Dictionary 2016).
5   If we think of the island of Lesvos today, with the refugee crisis, this is becoming a different kind of association – an ironic one. Paradise becomes an in-between place for forced displacement.
6   The musical and its subsequent film seem to fall into the 'unintentionally campy musical' category that includes glitzy, flamboyant, guilty-pleasure shows like *Starlight Express* (1984) and *Joseph and the Amazing Technicolor Dreamcoat* (1972). However, these shows are only one version of camp. There are shows that are purposefully campy, musicals that deconstruct and parody original musical theatre forms, including *The Rocky Horror Show* (1973), *Little Shop of Horrors* (1982), *Batboy: The Musical* (1997), *Reefer Madness* (1998), and *The Toxic Avenger: The Musical* (2009). Then there are the shows whose

notoriety for both failed ticket revenue and universal panning by critics have given them cult status and are considered 'camp' because of the joy spectators might get from experiencing them: *Carrie: The Musical* (1988), *Jekyll and Hyde* (1995), or *Spiderman: Turn off the Dark* (2001) are the most memorable examples. By definition, *Mamma Mia!* doesn't fall into the latter category because of its overwhelming commercial success on such a global scale. Still, the very aesthetic of *Mamma Mia!* – with its ABBA music, Greek Isle fantasy environment, and general silliness – could give it a 'camp' identification. One could argue that all musical theatre, an already flamboyant and heightened medium by definition, is a safe venue for camp or camp-like entertainment.

7   Conversely, the campiness of *Muriel's Wedding* was not lost on reviewers, who noted the film's camp as one of its strongest selling points. Roger Ebert recognized the film's use of ABBA music as a representation of Muriel's need to escape from her mundane, lifeless existence and the overall aesthetic of the film as one 'that walk[s] a careful line between satire and misery' (Ebert 1995). A *New York Times* critic wrote:

> Some may wonder why ABBA also turns up in *The Adventures of Priscilla, Queen of the Desert*, and how triumphant-misfit stories like these (another is *Strictly Ballroom*) manage to be so intensely campy whether their characters are straight or gay. When Muriel and a girlfriend don white satin jumpsuits and blond wigs to lip-sync 'Dancing Queen' (the song Muriel equates with life's highest pinnacles), it takes work to remember that neither of them is actually in drag.
>
> (Maslin 1995)

For this reviewer, the film's camp, combined with its story celebrating the coming-of-age of social pariahs, keeps the narrative open for queer interpretation, which is perhaps what makes the overall movie more palatable. The overly theatrical aesthetic of the film, through the ABBA music, flamboyant costumes, and amplified gaudiness of the characters, makes *Muriel's Wedding* a queerer film if not in terms of the sexuality of the characters but in the composition as a whole.

8   A comprehensive documentation and analysis of the comic dame drag archetype can be found in L. Senelick (2000), *The Changing Room: Sex, Drag, and Theatre*, London: Routledge, 228–52.

Bibliography

Barlow, H. (2014). 'Toni Colette looks back at 20 years since Muriel's Wedding.' SBS Movies, 12 November. www.sbs.com.au/movies/article/2014/11/11/toni-collette-looks-back-20-years-muriels-wedding. Viewed 18 April 2016.

Bergman, D. (ed.) (1993). *Camp Grounds: Style and Homosexuality*. Amherst: University of Massachusetts Press.

Brantley, B. (2001). 'Theater Review; Mom Had a Trio (And a Band, Too).' *New York Times*, 19 October.

Caggiano, C. (2010). 'A Broadway Milestone … For Me.' *Everything I Know I Learned From Musicals* blog, 9 February 2010. www.everythingmusicals.com/ everything_i_ know_i_ learn/2010/02/a-broadway-milestone-for-me.html. Viewed 1 May 2016.

Cambridge Dictionary [online] (2016). Cambridge: Cambridge University Press. Available from http://dictionary.cambridge.org/. Viewed 10 June 2016.

Carnevale, R. (2008). 'Mamma Mia: The Movie – Phyllida Lloyd interview' and 'Meryl Streep interview.' IndieLondon. www.indielondon.co.uk/Film-Review/mamma-mia-the-movie-phyllida-lloyd-interview; www.indielondon.co.uk/Film-Review/mamma-mia-the-movie-meryl-streep-interview. Viewed 10 May 2016.

Ebert, R. (1995). 'Review: "Muriel's Wedding".' *Chicago Sun Times*, 17 March.

Graber, N. (2015). 'Memories That Remain: *Mamma Mia!* and the Disruptive Potential of Nostalgia.' *Studies in Musical Theatre* 9(2), pp. 187–198.

Guilbert, G-C. (2013). 'Dancing Queens Indeed: When Gay Subtext is Gayer Than Gay Text.' In L. Fitzgerald and M. Williams (eds), *Mamma Mia! The Movie: Exploring a Cultural Phenomenon*. New York: I.B. Tauris.

Halperin, D. (2012). *How to Be Gay*. Cambridge: Belknap Press.

Isherwood, C. (2001). 'Review: Mamma Mia!' *Variety*, 18 October. http://variety.com/2001/legit/reviews/mamma-mia-7-1200553290/. Viewed 5 September 2016.

Jeffries, S. (2008). 'A Legend Lights Up.' *The Guardian*, 2 July. www.theguardian.com/film/2008/jul/02/features.culture2. Viewed 14 May 2016.

Johnson, C. (2008). *Mamma Mia!: Cast Script & Vocal Book*. New York: Music Theatre International.

Lane, Anthony (2008). 'Euro Visions.' *The New Yorker*, 28 July. www.newyorker.com/magazine/2008/07/28/euro-visions. Viewed 25 April 2016.

Love, H (2007). *Feeling Backward*. Cambridge: Harvard University Press.

Mamma Mia! (2008). Motion picture. Universal City: Universal Pictures.

Maslin, J. (1995). 'Film Review: Cinderella Makes Over Her Life.' *New York Times*, 10 March.

Matthews, N. (2000). 'Kitsch on the Fringe: Suburbia in Recent Australian Comedy Films.' In R. Webster (ed.), *Expanding Suburbia: Reviewing Suburban Narratives*. New York: Berghahn.

Merriam-Webster Collegiate Dictionary [online] (2016). Springfield: Merriam-Webster, Inc. Available from www.merriam-webster.com/. Viewed 10 June 2016.

Meyer, M. (ed.) (1994). *The Politics and Poetics of Camp*. London: Routledge.

Mordden, E. (2004). *The Happiest Corpse I've Ever Seen: The Last 25 Years of the Broadway Musical*. New York: Palgrave Macmillan.

Muriel's Wedding (1994). Motion picture. Melbourne: Film Victoria.

Oxford Dictionaries [online] (2016). Oxford: Oxford University Press. Available from https://en.oxforddictionaries.com/. Viewed 10 June 2016.

Robertson, P. (1996). *Guilty Pleasures: Feminist Camp from Mae West to Madonna*. Durham, NC: Duke University Press.

Robey, T. (2008). 'Film reviews: Mamma Mia! and more.' *Telegraph*, 11 July. www.telegraph.co.uk/culture/film/filmreviews/3556138/Film-reviews-Mamma-Mia-and-more.html. Viewed 12 May 2016.

Rodosthenous, G. (2016). 'Mamma Mia! and the Aesthetics of the 21st Century Jukebox Musical Genre.' In Robert Gordon and Olaf Jubin (eds), *The Oxford Handbook of the British Musical*. Oxford: Oxford University Press.

Ross, A. (1988). *No Respect: Intellectuals and Popular Culture*. London: Routledge.

Sedgwick, E.K. (1990). *Epistemology of the Closet*. Berkeley: University of California Press.

Shewey, D. (2002). '"Be True to Yearning": Notes on the Pioneers of Queer Theater.' In Alisa Solomon and Framji Minwalla (eds), *The Queerest Art: Essays on Lesbian and Gay Theater,* pp. 124–134. New York: New York University Press.

Snetiker, M. (2015). 'How ABBA (and that "Waterloo" scene) made it into *Muriel's Wedding*.' *Entertainment Weekly*'s EW.com, 13 October. www.ew.com/article/2015/10/13/how-abba-waterloo-scene-made-muriels-wedding. Viewed 2 May 2016.

Sontag, S. (1966). *Against Interpretation*. New York: Farrar, Straus & Giroux.

Thompson, K. (1999). 'Review: *Mamma Mia!*.' *Billboard*, 10 April, p. 22.

Womack, M. (2009). '"Thank You for the Music": Catherine Johnson's Feminist Revoicings in *Mamma Mia!*.' *Studies in Musical Theatre* 3(2), pp. 201–211.

9

8½ TO *NINE* TO *NINE*

Evolutions of a cinema classic

Arthur Pritchard

As a film musical Rob Marshall's 2009 movie *Nine* can boast not only a remarkably complex process of development, but also a profoundly polarised reception. Marshall's grandiose project, a virtual remake with songs of Federico Fellini's widely acclaimed (and sometimes deeply deplored) 1963 cinematic extravaganza *8½,* probably draws more on the stage musical of the same title than on Fellini's film. Fellini's choice of title was based on his calculation that he had by then directed six feature films and three shorts, not quite nine. By the time he began work on *8½,* Fellini was well known as the director of *La Strada* (1954) and the neo-realistic *La Dolce Vita* (1960), 'that elaborate fresco of modern Rome, with its brilliance and its vulgarity … and its facile symbolism (a helicopter-borne statue of Christ to begin with; a dead fish on a dawn beach to end)' (Houston 1963: 32-33). It is a reflection on the maestro's status and kudos that the 1950s Italian aristocracy were prepared to queue for bit parts in movies that would satirise and eventually destroy their pretentious way of life. The introspective, personal material explored in *8½* would not make it an obvious choice for musical adaptation, but Fellini's cinema had been adapted previously. Bob Fosse's 1966 Broadway show *Sweet Charity*, about the near-prostitute who hopes to reform herself through a good marriage, originated in Fellini's 1957 film *Le Notti di Cabiria*, with the action relocated to New York City, and was itself filmed in 1969 with Shirley MacLaine in the title role.

8½, much loved by cinephiles as 'the best film ever made about filmmaking' (Ebert 2000), was adapted for Broadway under the title *Nine* by Maury Yeston in 1982. With a book by Arthur Kopit, 'innovative staging' (Laird 2002: 211) by Tommy Tune (his real name), for which he won a Tony award, and with Thommie Walsh as choreographer, the original Broadway production played 729 performances from May 1983 to February 1984. This was followed by a moderately successful national tour of the US. At the time of its first airing on

Broadway, *Nine* was competing with *Dreamgirls*, the show that celebrated Motown and female Rhythm and Blues groups such as The Supremes and The Shirelles. *Dreamgirls* appealed to mainstream pop audiences, had the better songs and ran for twice as long, winning the award for the most popular musical of its season, and indeed retains its popularity today, with a new West End production opening in the autumn of 2016.

This chapter[1] will explore some of the issues of adaptation and dramaturgy that underlie the progress of Fellini's original film from screen to the musical stage and back to the screen again. Through examination of two stages of adaptation, and comparing the visual and narrative elements of *8½* and the stage version of *Nine,* it will ask why Rob Marshall did not manage to re-generate the powerful impact and subsequent commercial success achieved by his previous musical film, *Chicago.*

8½ as source for adaptation: *Nine* on stage

Fellini's cinema has deservedly generated a significant body of critical literature for its diversity of content, its depth of engagement with wide-ranging subjects and the perspectives it generates on Italian cultural history. Howard Hughes (2011) describes the film as 'Fellini's most autobiographical film' in which

> Director Guido Anselmi is planning a post-nuclear sci-fi film at a health spa. Survivors are leaving earth to escape an atomic plague. Pressured by financiers and cast, he escapes into flights of fantasy and reveries. As there is no film, is what we see all Anselmi's fantasies as he waits trapped in a traffic jam?
>
> (Hughes 2011: 131)

Roger Ebert summarises this opening scene:

> It is told from the director's point of view, and its hero, Guido is clearly intended to represent Fellini. It begins with a nightmare of asphyxiation, and a memorable image in which Guido floats off into the sky, only to be yanked back to earth by a rope pulled by his associates, who are hectoring him to organize his plans … Much of the film takes place at a spa near Rome, and at the enormous set Guido has constructed nearby for … the science fiction epic he has lost all interest in.
>
> (Ebert 2000)

It's slow, rambling and unpredictable, but we gradually gain understanding of how Guido the director has been driven deeply into his inner world and his own past. Through a surreal, other-worldly visioning of the effects of stress and his attempts to escape from them, the sequence graphically projects the terrors of depressive anxiety in a distinctive cinematic form. Once back on the ground, Guido is obliged to face his personal demons, the film's producers, the press and his women.

Landy sees *8½* as an 'instance of Fellini's metacinema' in which Marcello Mastroianni is provided with 'an exemplary text to explore the protean dimensions of his star persona'. He continues:

> Marcello as Guido is the consummate figure of power and desire – a film director who seeks actors for a film and situations in which to film them. He is a decadent, bored and restless but an attractive image of vulnerable masculinity who is a wielder of power and object of desire because he can create stars. He … confronts women whose images blur one into the other. However his inaccessibility is an invitation to women and a goad to make him experience love for them. At the same time, he is a childlike man who lives in his fantasies – fantasies of childhood and youth, surrounded and tended by women, and of adulthood, surrounded by bevies of women who seek to rebel against, but ultimately succumb to his whip.
>
> (Landy 2000: 37)

There is a radical contrast in the treatment of the material in Yeston's stage adaptation. The show exploits a theatre of limited means, where simple non-specific settings of steps, rostra, and moveable chairs enable spectators to imagine the presence or absence of locations for the liminal experiences between the director's actual world and the dream world into which he escapes. The director Tommy Tune identified the problem of the storyline: 'I went about trying to figure out how to do it, because nothing happened' (Bryer and Davidson 2005: 250).

Ebert, whose film criticism has legendary status in the US, repudiates a frequent criticism of *8½*:

> The film weaves in and out of reality and fantasy. Some critics complained that it was impossible to tell what was real and what was taking place only in Guido's head, but I have never had the slightest difficulty, and there is usually a clear turning point as Guido escapes from the uncomfortable present into the accommodating world of his dreams.
>
> (Ebert 2000)

The absence of location in the stage show comfortably facilitates these transitions. Yeston, who originally conceived the stage musical *Nine* as a class-project in Lehman Engel's BMI Music Theatre, notes that the title not only represents a small step on from *8½*, but also that this was the first song he composed for the show. In an interview with Michael Riedel of the *New York Post* for *Theater Talk* in 2011 Yeston describes the vivid sequence in *8½* when the nine-year-old Guido, the subject of traditional Italian adulation by his mother and a bevy of adoring females, is taken from his bath and wrapped in a womblike shelter of towels and sheets. Yeston's song encapsulates a possible cause of the adult Guido's psychological state, suggesting that his relationships with women are a continuing symptom of his need for female attention. It is this that will return him to this comfortable childhood existence. In the song, the women celebrate little Guido's birthday, expressing the wish that he will always be nine years old.

The stage show of *Nine,* with no really memorable songs (excepting perhaps 'Be Italian') appears to have had no recent revivals. For his film Marshall cut all but eight of the show's musical numbers but added three new Yeston songs including 'Cinema Italiano' and 'Guarda la Luna'. Marshall seems to have struggled to find an appropriate cinematic language with which to reformulate a fusion of the show and Fellini's visual imagery, but elected to rework the extensive film studio as a much more literal scene location than in *8½*. Hence the lyrics and music of the stage version manage to suggest, rather than illustrate, the evocative, surreal visual world of Fellini's original, while in Marshall's version these evolve into extravagant show numbers that seem at times arbitrary and disconnected and lack the disorientating power of Fellini's extraordinary imagery.

Maury Yeston's stage version of *Nine* did enjoy some success on the London stage. It was first given a concert performance in 1992 in the Royal Festival Hall in London, with a cast of 165 including Jonathan Pryce and Anita Dobson, and in 1996 a successful small-scale performance ran for three months at the Donmar Warehouse. It may have deserved a more fully resourced production, but depending as it did on simple staging and low-tech production values, it was unlikely to compete for audiences with the burgeoning mega-musicals that had then begun to dominate the West End repertory. However, the original Broadway show had won five Tony awards including Best Musical, and was revived a few years later. Although now rarely performed, *Nine* has travelled widely, with international productions in Australia, Argentina, The Netherlands, Japan, The Philippines, Greece, and Brazil, as well as its limited success on both sides of the Atlantic.

But the two separate stages of development of *Nine,* where a 60s film classic by a director of outstanding imaginative vision is first adapted for the musical stage, and then re-imagined as a highly colourful cinematic spectacle, vividly demonstrate how interpretation of a dramatic text can evolve to suit current performance styles and audience tastes. In considering the ways in which dramatic texts are reinterpreted in new productions (even without the radical genre change from cinema to musical theatre), Jonathan Miller 'sponsor(s) the idea that the afterlife of a play is a process of emergent evolution, during which meanings and emphases develop' (Miller 1986: 35). While it is self-evident that an important work for the cinema will not necessarily convert convincingly to a live performance, the musical stage may offer a more conducive environment for reworking the highly subjective material that constitutes the content of Fellini's film. It may be that the problems of treating Fellini's complex mix of childhood memory, fantasy and personal struggles with his own creativity and his complex relationships with the opposite sex, adapt more convincingly to the live stage.

Marshall's *Nine* enjoys what David Calhoun describes as 'fetishising the look and feel of '60s Italy so that the mood of artistic melancholia … comes dangerously close to the look and feel of an Italian coffee ad' (Calhoun 2010: 763). The glossy artificiality of these 'authentic' Italian locations contrasts strikingly with the precisely constructed reality/fantasy sequences that reflect the dark psychological condition of the central character in *8½*. It is through the strange black and white imagery and grotesque characterisations that Fellini creates a nightmarish utopian other-worldliness to convey the inner struggles of a director in personal and professional crisis. Such suggestive, conceptual imagery might adapt more effectively to the theatre's 'empty space' than to the contemporary screen, where it is hard to escape the camera's tendency towards literal representation (unless by recourse to editing techniques and colour-tinting, as with the pervasive orange and blue cast favoured by some recent cinema on mythological themes). Fellini's idiosyncratic visual language enables access to the director Guido's chaotic inner experiences through 'an intricate structure of highly original, highly imaginative scenes whose conjunction creates an unprecedented interweaving of memories, fantasies, and dreams' (Sesonske 2010: 1). Perhaps acknowledging contemporary obsession with celebrity and associated glamorous lifestyles, Marshall chooses to fashion glitzy period locations for the external, visible world of the protagonist, and to explore his personal challenges in more mundane terms through on and off-set encounters that are then extended and amplified through musical numbers and other scenes from the film in production.

In developing the stage musical Yeston took the decision to realise a character totally dependent on the women in his life, by removing all the male roles in Fellini's film except Guido as adult and child, and the boys (who express their adulation for the *femme fatale* in the beach scene by following her around the stage on all fours). In 'Guido's song', Yeston contrives a musical distillation of the dramatic situation at the opening of the film, where the director, harassed by his cast, his backers, numerous journalists and all the various operatives involved in the project, wants to take a break at a spa with his wife but receives an unexpected visit from his mistress. The opening number, 'Overture delle Donne' is a languorously choreographed, sexually-charged episode in which the women characters in chorus variously tease, challenge, torment or attempt to seduce Guido. His reaction is ambivalent: he is at once master and victim, challenged by possibility and at once irresistibly enticed and disgusted by the overwhelming power of female sexuality.

In her memoir, Deena Boyer describes how she became press officer, or in her phrase 'script girl', during the development and production of the Fellini movie (her story bears close parallels with Eddie Redmayne's role in the 2012 film *My Week with Marilyn*). In her account of finding actors and screen testing, the planning of costumes and settings and other practical production issues, it is evident that the extravagances of Fellini's working day, with the lunches, speeches and celebrations that are carried into the film itself, are in effect an extension of Fellini/Contini's indulgent childhood experiences, a little boy in middle age who has yet to grow up. As his song will tell us, part of him wants to remain forever nine; another part of him effectively does so.

Nine on film: celebrity casting, numbers and a troubled narrative trajectory

The film script of *Nine*, though largely rewritten from the stage book by Anthony Minghella, is substantially derived from Fellini. The artist in crisis, now dubbed Contini rather than Anselmi, hides from his producer as a splendid but pointless multi-level constructivist set grows around him. While a sequin-clad chorus and a score of stars stand by ready for action, we learn, if we can believe it, that there is no script. Eleven days are allocated for filming and expectations are running high. Deeply conscious that his last films have flopped, the maestro teases the assembled press that he will not tell them a thing about the new movie. Cast and chorus are rehearsed and ready, but such story as there is remains securely locked inside the director's head.

Clearly Marshall recognised possibilities in fusing the content of both sources, reworking Yeston's songs and music and Walsh's choreography to reimagine Guido's inner world and facilitate reflection on some of theatre's oldest preoccupations: the clash between seeming and being, illusion and reality, between what is thought and what is said. Thus Fellini's distinctive vision could be made accessible to audiences who four decades later might well reject the self-indulgent propensities of *8½*, finding it slow paced, over-stated and confusing.

Nine treats the character's emotional journey in a standard expressionist scenario. Using flashback and fantasy, real and imagined worlds are contrasted. Contini's unwillingness and/or helplessness to resolve his personal crisis throws him back into himself, to seek support from the intimacy of his most cherished and significant memories. Through the film he comes to recognise the shallowness of his lust for each starlet that makes it as far a screen test. Contini's aspirations and fears are mediated through his relationships with his many past lovers. The ever-present chorus of showgirls serves to project his fantasies. He can only react to the songs as they are experienced inside his head. He is a victim of his own loss of inspiration, and the audience soon gathers he is unlikely to escape from it. The *Italia* project is doomed from the start. When the crisis comes and the movie has to be abandoned, Day-Lewis's big number is delivered in *Sprechstimme*. His illusions shattered, he has a near-tragic outburst of burning insights: in his rage of self-discovery he recognises that it is through his film making, and its search for illusion, that he has destroyed his marriage and deeply damaged himself.

The central premise creates a structural problem. In the standard backstage musical, stage or screen, there is a golden rule: the show must go on. There are few exceptions. Personality clashes, Bronx accents or broken ankles may delay the performance, may cause major recasting or even a complete rewrite of the show but the outcome is certain: a show will go on, maybe a different one from what we started with, but ultimately the film will be finished, the star will be born. With *Nine* Marshall's problem is that the narrative trajectory is counter-intuitive: with everything set and film ready to roll, the opening sets up all the expectation of a grand finale, the triumphant screening of the new film, the awards ceremonies, the happy union of lovers, and, in the experience of blogosphere would-be critics who are used to predictable scenarios, it lets us down. The climax finds a character in near-tragic mode shouting at the sky as he calls the company together to announce the abandonment of the film. Does Marshall intend to make us think more deeply about the causes of Contini's failure? Can an art form built on the energy of creating a new work of cinematic art and used to celebrating success carry comfortably the story of a failed project and a dysfunctional character?

In spite of its lukewarm critical reception and poor box-office returns, Marshall's film had its admirers, winning Oscar and BAFTA nominations as well as some lesser awards. At the planning stage the project generated considerable interest and the stellar female cast assembled for the film certainly bears witness to this, not least Nicole Kidman's willingness to begin filming only four weeks after giving birth. With an $80 million budget and his reputation on Broadway as a choreographer for *Zorba* and *Kiss of the Spiderwoman*, as director of *Cabaret* on stage and *Annie* (1999) and *Chicago (2002)* for the screen, Marshall needed no introduction to artists' agents. In an interview with The Hollywood Times Marshall declared:

> To work with the best actors in the world on difficult, challenging, complicated material, an adult musical, is like, unheard of and the process of it, for me, was thrilling. It's important for me to give actors a place to be able to really do their best work – that's one of the things I really try and do, to create a safe environment for them to really be great – because many times I'm working with actors who are new, for instance, to singing, which is very exposing.
>
> (Feinberg 2015)

When challenged that audiences seem to have preferred *Chicago* to *Nine,* Marshall remarked, 'What I try and do is follow my heart and follow my gut, that's all. All you can really do is tell a story you want to tell that's personal, that you're connected to in some way, that means something to you' (Feinberg 2015). There is simple candour here, and certainly his female leads enjoy plenty of opportunity to express themselves, but Marshall's response here does not comment on the narrative and dramaturgical problems of *Nine,* and it may be that directorial decisions are at the heart of the disappointing reactions of audiences to the film. With his *Chicago* adaptation, the clearly established vaudeville frame against which the narrative is played out enables the film to succeed through the ingenious, ironic interplay of these two aesthetic components.

Disruptions of the dramatic narrative: dreams, backstage and nostalgia

At the time he came to plan *8½* Fellini had moved on from the neo-realism of his early work and become strongly influenced by the ideas of Karl Jung, particularly the nature and interpretation of dreams. The 'oneiric' imagery of the movie owed much to Jung's thinking on the role of archetypes and the collective unconscious and his writing enabled Fellini to identify what he described as 'extrasensory perceptions', as 'psychic manifestations of the unconscious'. In film musicals song enables characters to articulate deeply felt emotions. As Jane Feuer wrote, 'In becoming song language is in a sense transfigured, lifted up into a higher, more expressive realm' (Feuer 1993: 52). By analogy, therefore, song can function as an effective vehicle for non-literal subject matter, and Yeston clearly recognises and exploits the possibility, economically crafting episodes into lyrics and music that shift between the dramatic present and the dreamlike sequences of Fellini's movie. Yeston goes on to argue that Guido is a character who is 'deeply in love with three women, his wife, his mistress and Claudia, the actress who appears to audition for the film' (Theater Talk interview: 12). In the song 'Only with you' Guido declares his belief that he could be happy if he were to live his live 'only with you…and you…and you'.

The number 'Guido's Song' opens with the female cast, all individually costumed, singing as they move elegantly, casually, provocatively on a simple set consisting of a white circular table and a number of transparent plastic chairs. All appear to be attracting the attention of Guido in a brief prelude that finally reveals him rising from the back to commence his solo:

> I would like to be here
> I would like to be there
> I would like to be everywhere at once

The number fuses the 'I am' and 'I want' tropes of traditional musicals, offering character information out of narrative time and space. Here, the chorus watches silently for most of the song, remaining still until the closing section when they reprise their opening refrain and then extend it in a musical counterpoint to Guido's melody. Behind the set in the 2003 Broadway revival (accessible on YouTube) is a vast backdrop in triptych, the centre panel being a projection of the left side of Botticelli's allegorical painting *Primavera,* depicting the three Graces in diaphanous silken drapes, placed centre stage. The painting's interpretative ambiguities provide an apt extension of the *tableaux vivants* of the chorus, incorporating Guido's fantasies, his conflicting needs and the dramatic situation in a single set of images. To the sides are two further panels in abstract geometric designs reminiscent of those stylised cityscapes that feature in 1930s Hollywood musicals. As Guido's song continues (performed here by Antonio Banderas), Yeston's lyrics develop the director's persona by articulating his sense of personal dissatisfaction:

> I would like to have another me
> To drum it along with myself
> I would like to be able to sing a duet with myself

and, by extension, how desirable it would be if he could also conduct a relationship with more than one woman at once (which of course he is already doing). The song closes with Guido trying to resist the now very physical attentions of the girls, who have closed in and are kissed, dismissed, delayed or rejected in turn. As a synopsis of Guido's personal relationships in Fellini's film the song is simplistic, but its comedic slant effectively debunks the character's tendency for indulgent self-absorption. It is in such episodes as these that the stage musical shows its potential: the dispensing with extravagant staging and special effects, the focus on a limited number of central characters, and the distilling of narrative into the songs liberates the imagination and generates exciting possibilities for each audience member to create a personal reading of the content.

In spite of the film's visual appeal, audiences found it hard to empathise with the central character or sustain interest in his decline. In reworking the Fellini in the language of a 'backstager', Marshall may have failed to recognise that a character on the way down lacks the attraction of one on the way up. *Nine's* opening montage, like a musical dumb-show, is a condensed flash-forward of the film's main fantasy sequences. Marshall confidently manipulates the interplay between the inner world of the central character and the frenzied, media-powered cinema production machine he is supposed to control. The new film project is *Italia,* the latest aspiration of legendary film director Guido (Daniel Day-Lewis), whose legacy was to have shaped the experience and understanding of Italy for the world of his contemporaries (as, arguably, did Fellini himself). The affinity of the title to *Fellini's Roma,* the director's rambling, at times just silly, 1972 fantasy on Italian life is surely no accident.

Nine is rich in its creation of a period, as was well demonstrated in Marshall's earlier output. There are nostalgic, almost reverential, overtones in the treatment of 1960s Rome, and the black and white scenes depicting Contini's childhood reinforce the Fellini connection in a virtual carbon-copy of the original. We see this in the over-reaction of family and church to the 'sinful perversion' of young Contini and a group of his pals who head to the beach to draw out the reclusive prostitute who for a bundle of coins will offer a glimpse of the forbidden mysteries of adulthood, an experience no more corrupting than watching her mildly provocative dance on the shore and joining in a few steps.

Marshall varies the sequence slightly by intercutting between the studio set and the beach. But he extends the sexual associations of Fellini's original scene through the song 'Viva Italia', a relatively innocent childhood memory slowly transforms into an aggressively sexual showpiece. With sultry provocative attitudes, the chorus magnifies and multiplies the images, as each girl trickles handfuls of sand through her fingers. In a display of female sexual power, the falling veil of sand teases and tantalises, carrying with it associations of mortality as in an hour glass, and perhaps offering hints of the excitement and danger of the bullring. As in the original, the sequence concludes with the seminary brothers hauling the nine-year-old Contini back to school for a confrontation with his mother and a good muscular Christian beating.

This and other black and white sequences in *Nine* allow the viewer to access Guido's formative past, and some of the repressive circumstances of his/Fellini's childhood. The experience is replayed when, in continued frustration with the project and to escape from producers, crew and press, Guido flings himself on his hugely understanding costume-maker (Judi Dench) for ideas and help. She tells him he must create a show with spectacle and music (could this be Marshall's film?), and again Marshall intercuts past and present through Dench's 'Folies Bergères' number. She trails an endless red feather boa across the set, and in a remarkable image, Guido, a little boy again, gazes with wonder at the extraordinary spectacle of tights, basques and sequins as he runs entranced among the dancer's legs.

In turn each of the female stars sings her song. Each is a female archetype, wife, mother, mistress, whore, idol. Each has helped form the person the director has become. Their interventions may spur him forward or threaten to distract him. His muse (represented by Nicole Kidman), his principal star, who could once be depended on to stimulate the flow of his creative juices, deserts him in disgust. Frustrated by a dearth of ideas, and in a peaceable (or desperate?) gesture, he invites his wife (Marion Cotillard, 'My husband makes movies') to join him at the studio location and help reinvigorate his creativity. But his mistress (Penélope Cruz, whose phone-call morphs into a provocative corset and tights number and is described to the medics examining Contini as 'A call from the Vatican'), desperate to spend more time with her lover, and perhaps help him through the crisis, inconveniently turns up. Contini installs her in a run-down, back-street *pensione*.

FIGURE 9.1 Nicole Kidman in *Nine*.

She is thrilled at the prospect of playing his sex games in her new love-nest but her attentions, rather than driving him to new creative heights, induce panic attacks. In her desperation to be near her genius lover, Cruz gate-crashes the lavish production team dinner. Cotillard dubs him a habitual liar and walks out, leaving the new marital harmony foundering irretrievably.

Contini seeks an interview (or perhaps a confessional?) with a cardinal who is known to be a fan of his early films. As they converse in a shared (public) bath the cardinal chastises him for the prevalence of sex in his films and the poor example this sets to the wives and mothers of the Italian nation. But the church, in the person of the cardinal, also fails to find a direction for the film project, and the moral and artistic void opens wider as Contini's crisis deepens. At each stage a new facet is added to the director's decline towards inadequacy and despair. Perhaps his most moral act comes later when he walks out of the bedroom just as the voluptuous journalist (Kate Hudson, 'Cinema Italiano') is removing her underwear in preparation for an in-depth interview with the maestro. Paradoxically, as audience, we experience delight at his failure to consummate this particular encounter.

The dramatic action of *Nine* faces constant disruption by the sequence of solo songs Contini's women sing. Vagelis Siropoulos points out (2009: 90) that the song's 'autotelic nature always disrupts and retards the flow of events', even in the most successful integrated musicals, 'creating an antagonistic relation between the narrative and musical sequences that results in a stop-and-go discontinuous structure.' Although all are showy and voluptuous, and many teasing, the richly orchestrated and powerfully presented numbers are not especially memorable. While they do have links with the dramatic action, they tend to underline ideas that the dramatic narrative has already provided: chiefly that Guido's sexual obsessions are purely escapist fantasy, behaviour to be indulged in when thinking and work becomes too painful. For the film audience, though, the repeated presentation of glamorous women on a catwalk becomes tiresome. The comic irony that enhances *Chicago* is missing. Contini's obsessions and fantasies are quickly understood, and we don't need the repetitions the film gives us to grasp them. Unless, of course, this is the reception the director intends: that Contini's sexual preoccupations can only be understood through overdosing on a surfeit of glamour to the point of stultification.

However, Marshall can make his moments work wonderfully, as when Marion Cotillard, as Contini's wife Luisa, decides to leave him. Through her song 'My husband makes me riot' we hear the voice of a woman struggling with her husband's incessant lying; in her second song, prompted by the showing screen tests, we realise that Guido's chat-up line as he unpins the debutante's hair is trotted out to every aspiring actress who comes for audition. Importantly, this is another moment, like many in the film, where our empathy with Guido diminishes. Day-Lewis invests his character with a degree of charm, but his incessant womanizing, his chain-smoking, and his cool demeanour make it hard for us to believe he could have any real power to attract women. Day-Lewis manages to find touches of a fading charisma but his compulsive, loveless philandering eventually palls: he must stink of tobacco, there is no hope for his project, and he seems devoid of decent human qualities. Should we still find his failure interesting? 'There is no movie,' he tells the crew near the end of the film. We knew this from the start.

Conclusions: inversions, critical reception and the vulnerability of moments of failure

By contrast to the critical reception afforded to *8½*, responses to Marshall's film version towards the end of 2009 were lukewarm. Erik Childress (2009) complained: '*Nine* is a film about a director who has no clue what film he wants to make – made by a guy who also has no understanding of the film he's making.' Chris Barsanti (2009) described *Nine* as a 'wandering, sporadically entertaining adaptation' with 'a script that could charitably be described as drifting'. In *Chicago* Marshall had exploited the self-reflexivity of the backstage musical for satirical effect. Through rapid-shot cinematic montage in 'a theatrically stylised world where breaking into song seems natural' (Blumenthal, Taymor and Monda 2007: 265). Marshall glamorised Roxie Hart's showbiz ambitions in ironic contrast to the 'reality' of her actual predicament. The opening sections of *Nine* appeared to promise another essay in postmodern cinema on the lines of *Chicago*. In *Nine*, as in *8½*, the project is in crisis. The director's memory, fantasies and personal introspections collide as he engages in a hopeless search for an elusive muse that will fuel and reignite his creativity. The glamorous imagery of the showgirl chorus contrasts with the darkness of his mental state, and through the interaction of these elements we watch him driven into decline, breakdown and failure.

Nine's closing scene moves on from *8½*. It reads as an epilogue, reflective and downbeat. Two years after the *Italia* project has been abandoned and, we may assume, long enough for a near-full recovery from a nervous breakdown, Day-Lewis and Dench converse about Contini's future. The sequence is moody and slow-paced, filmed in grey, cold weather. There is no red-carpet event, or the opening night triumph that would signal the ending of a conventional musical. Contini tells his costume designer that his next film must be about a man who wants to win back his wife. There's a germ of hope. Then in the imagination of one or both characters, the music begins to play again as gradually the cast and chorus reassemble to revive the lavish spectacle of the abandoned film and reprise one of the show numbers.

Feuer noted that in backstage musicals 'the synthesis between the two levels (the stage and the world) depends on the marriage of the couple in the realm of the narrative occurring simultaneously with the success of the show in which they star'. She goes on to say that there is a marriage of the world of reality with the world of the imagination, where often the latter 'is obliterated by the force of the film itself' (1993: 71). In *Nine* Marshall attempts to invert the predictable fusion of the heterogeneous worlds of film and 'life' and leaves us in a less comfortable place. When failure is heroic in scale, and because we are repelled by the details, we can be touched personally; then we can come to realise that without due care we too can be drawn into those dark places. There is grandeur of a kind in Day-Lewis's big number, a celebration of his failure on a grand quasi-tragic scale. It's a powerful sequence which seems to embrace what O'Gorman and Werry (2012) call 'the vulnerability of moments of failure'. They contend that failure 'stands against the imperialism of hope, generates a reflexive understanding of the inherently agonistic space of learning and change.' As in great tragedy, when there is no hope we can learn, 'there is no temptation to try to escape: argument is gratuitous: it's kingly' (Anouilh 1966: 35).

Note

1   Part of this research was presented in A. Pritchard (2012), 'Rob Marshall's Nine: A film musical disaster or a celebration of failure?' *Studies in Musical Theatre* 6(2), 247–253; doi: 10.1386/ smt.6.2.247_1.

Bibliography

Anouilh, J. (1960). *Antigone*. Trans. Lewis Galantière. London: Methuen.

Barsanti, C. (2009). 'Review of *Nine*' in Filmcritic.com, 18 December.

Blumenthal, E, J. Taymor and A. Monda (2007). *Julie Taymor: Playing with Fire*. New York: Abrams.

Boyer, D. (1964). *The Two Hundred Days of 8½*. New York: Macmillan.

Bryer, J. and R. Davison (2005). *The Art of the American Musical: Conversations with the Creators*. New Brunswick, NJ: Rutgers University Press.

Calhoun, D. (2010). 'Nine.' In *Time Out Film Guide 2011*, p. 757.

Childress, E. (2009). 'Review: "Life's a Stage...Again...and Again".' efilmcritic.com, 24 December.

Ebert, R. (2000). 'Review: "8½" Great Movies,' RogerEbert.com. Accessed 10 September 2016.

Feinberg, S. (2015). 'Rob Marshall on Movie Musicals and His Journey "Into the Woods" (Q&A).' *The Hollywood Times*. Accessed 10 September 2016.

Feuer, J. (1993). *The Hollywood Musical*. 2nd edn. Bloomington: Indiana University Press.

Houston, P. (1963). *The Contemporary Cinema*. Harmondsworth: Penguin Books.

Hughes, H. (2011). *Cinema Italiano*. London and New York: IB Tauris and Co Ltd.

Knapp, R. (2006). *The American Musical and the Performance of Personal Identity*. Princeton, NJ: Princeton University Press.

Laird, P. (2002). 'Choreographers, directors and the fully integrated musical.' In W. Everett and P. Laird, *The Cambridge Companion to the Musical*. Cambridge: Cambridge University Press.

Landy, M. (2000). *Italian Film*. Cambridge: Cambridge University Press.

Miller, J. (1986). *Subsequent Performances*. London: Faber and Faber.

O'Gorman, R. and M. Werry (2012). 'On Failure (On Pedagogy).' Editorial introduction, *Performance Research: A Journal of the Performing Arts* 17(1).

Pritchard, A. (2012). 'Rob Marshall's Nine: A film musical disaster or a celebration of failure?' *Studies in Musical Theatre* 6(2), 247–53. doi: 10.1386/ smt.6.2.247_1.

Sesonske, A. (2010). '*8½*: A Film with Itself as Its Subject.' *Criterion Collection* website www. criterion.com/current/posts/173-8-1-2-a-film-with-itself-as-its-subject. Accessed 13 October 2016.

Siropoulos, V. (2009).'Historicizing *Chicago*'s Resurrection of the Film Musical, or, Thinking in Fragments, from Vaudeville to MTV.' *Image & Narrative* 10(3), pp. 83–96.

Theater Talk: Maury Yeston, composer/lyricist. 'Nine.' Pt. 1. YouTube interview uploaded 13 May 2011. Accessed 14 September 2016.

Yeston, M. and A. Kopit (1982). *Nine* Broadway revival 2003. YouTube. Accessed 14 September 2016.

10

'YOU WANNA HEAR THE REAL STORY?'

(Mis)remembering masculinity in Clint Eastwood's adaptation of *Jersey Boys*

Sarah Whitfield

'Walk like a man my son' – a musical about men?

At the risk of stating the obvious, *Jersey Boys* is about men. It is the story of the eponymous 'boys', Frankie Valli and the Four Seasons (Bob Gaudio, Nick Massi and Tommy De Vito), who tell us their versions of how it was, or perhaps more accurately, how 'it never ever was' (Sondheim 1986). Their story is well-worn, a rags-to-riches tale of four blue-collar guys singing on street corners and ending up in the Rock and Roll Hall of Fame, 100 million record sales later (Rolling Stone 2016). Given their fame, the relative anonymity of the band members is somewhat surprising, though Gaudio, Massi and De Vito eventually left the band and were replaced by a rolling line-up of musicians. While Gaudio continued writing for them, only Valli remains in the line-up as front man and in 2016 is still performing, so the band is now in its sixth decade. Their individual obscurity has been blamed on their working-class status; the show's US education-pack quotes Valli's explanation for why their stories were unknown: 'We were just a bunch of working stiffs, not fashion magazine pretty boys' (Harper 2006: 8). Even so, their songs remain an undeniable part of the soundtrack of Western cultural memory. I am sure I am by no means alone when watching the musical in thinking 'Oh I didn't know I knew *that*… I didn't know *that* was by the Four Seasons … I didn't know I knew this many of their songs.' The publicity for the stage musical specifically focuses on the audience's memories, real or otherwise: one of several talking-heads on a promotional clip from an official YouTube channel says 'I find I'm nostalgic about it even though I wasn't born when some of it was released' (Jersey Boys UK 2016).

In the beginning the Four Seasons were a doo-wop band, although their sound shifted towards the generic commercial pop of the early 1970s (listen to the difference between 'Sherry Baby' released in 1962 and 'Will You Still Love Me

Tomorrow' in 1968). Their stylistic features are that of doo-wop: 'simple lyrics, usually about the trials and ecstasies of young love, sung by a lead vocal against a background of repeated nonsense syllables' (Goldblatt 2013: 105). Doo-wop music is an African-American form that originated from young men singing on street corners. Goldblatt explains that this 'implies that those who occupy [the corner] have no private place to go' (2013: 103). The image of the group singing under a street lamp appears on the film's marketing, and a street lamp prop is flown into the stage show several times. Many of the Four Seasons' songs are about growing up and being a 'real' man: 'Walk Like a Man' (1963) or 'Big Man in Town' (1964), whether it's being a young man in love or dealing with no-good girlfriends, 'Big Girls Don't Cry' (1962), or having a girlfriend from the right side of the tracks, 'Dawn (Go Away)' (1964). The male harmonies in the band contrast the almost implausibly vast difference between Nick Massi's bass voice and Frankie Valli's soaring falsetto. Doo-wop emphasizes this disparity with call-and-response lines and Massi's accompanying nonsense syllables to Valli's lyrics. For example, 'Walk Like a Man' uses the lowest part of Massi's tessitura, almost a growl, to repeat 'he said', indicating the voice of the father who is telling the son: 'No woman's worth/ Crawling on the earth/So walk like a man my son' (Original Broadway Cast 2005).

In this chapter, I want to consider the particular version of masculinity that the film presents, and argue that the choices made in moving from stage to screen have exacerbated the work's underlying problems in its presentation of gender, sexuality and race. I quote David Savran here, since he offers such a compelling description of the anxiety the musical historically provoked in academic scholarship because it is 'a little too gay, too popular, too Jewish, and too much damned fun' (Savran 2004: 216). A musical that Clint Eastwood makes about four men from New Jersey apparently cannot run the risk of being too gay or too fun.

Broadway success and Hollywood disappointment

Whatever the connection to the band or their songs, the show worked: it opened on Broadway in 2005 and by March 2014 had taken a reported $1.7 billion in worldwide grosses (Michael David, a co-producer of the show, quoted in Ng 2014). When it closed on Broadway in January 2017 it had played 4,642 performances (Paulson 2016), and during this decade has had long-running parallel productions around the world, including in Las Vegas, London, Chicago, Melbourne and multiple national tours in the US and the UK. Its success was not just financial: it was nominated for eight Tony Awards, winning four including Best New Musical and another '57 major awards worldwide' (PremierComms 2016). The show incites a level of joy in its audience that critics and academics alike have struggled to convey to their readers, let alone explain. Ben Brantley's original review of the Broadway production concentrates on the perfect reconstruction of the Four Seasons' sound, and in particular John Lloyd Young's performance as Valli, which 'crossed the line from exact impersonation into something more compelling' (Brantley 2005). Lloyd Young won the Tony that season for his performance. Brantley notes that the audience get what they demand, 'a mimetically precise rendering of [the Four Seasons'] songs' (ibid.). In her work on how the musical creates pleasure in its audience, Millie Taylor explores *Jersey Boys* at some length. She considers the broader role of the performance of music and the construction of identity, and argues that the very form of the jukebox musical makes it a particular vehicle of nostalgic pleasure: 'it is the voluptuousness and excess of these texts that flow into contemporary life and allow audiences the transcendental pleasure of attachment, intelligent interpretation and nostalgic recreation' (Taylor 2012: 165).

Given its phenomenal stage success, and the precedent that *Mamma Mia!* (2008) set for box office takings for stage-to-film jukebox musicals, a film adaptation of *Jersey Boys* must have looked like easy money for potential producers. Yet if the adaptation was inevitable, the choice of Clint Eastwood to direct the film seemed to surprise many: even pre-release press coverage tried to reassure the potential opening weekend ticket buyer that it did make sense because, if you think about it, *Jersey Boys* is not really a musical. *Rolling Stone* explained that the best way to think of the show was 'not so much a musical as a drama' (Ebiri 2014). John Lloyd Young (who also plays Valli in the movie) explained the choice of Eastwood as director by agreeing that it 'felt odd', but this was because of an underlying 'strange communication problem' that the show has:

> It won best musical at the Tony Awards and people call it a jukebox musical. But it's unlike any other jukebox musical. When you look what Jersey Boys is – a drama about a band – you see the connection of Clint Eastwood to a Broadway musical in this instance makes complete sense. There is a compelling biographical story.
>
> (Teodorczuk 2014)

It is worth noting that there was similar coverage querying why musical theatre actors were cast in a Clint Eastwood film (see Lee 2014). The question remains, is it bad or confusing if *Jersey Boys* the musical was 'a musical'? And what does Eastwood have to do with that? Apparently, even serious film critics felt they should explain: Richard Brody writes with some relief in *The New Yorker* that *Jersey Boys* is 'gendered', noting that '[Eastwood's] film is a masculine tearjerker, a melodrama from a male perspective that's set in a milieu of unchallenged gender roles, and he makes those roles the source of the drama' (Brody 2011).[1]

Clint Eastwood as an 'icon of masculinity'

Eastwood is usually described along the lines of 'the icon of macho movie stars' (IMDb 2016). His prodigious list of film credits as actor and director has solidified the connection between Eastwood and American masculinity for over half a century. As an academic discipline, film studies largely confirms these ideas: 'the Eastwood persona represents probably the single strongest icon of heroic masculinity in popular cinema over the past quarter-century' (Beard 2000: ix). Though some have focused on Clint Eastwood as a 'cultural production' through his acting career (see Smith 1993), more recent approaches have considered Eastwood's directing output. His work on the other side of the camera is supposed to challenge the earlier *Dirty Harry* period, in what Baker calls the 'post-macho Eastwood' (Baker 2001: 159). Baker's argument that 'the traditional Hollywood myth of masculinity is thus challenged and undone by the icon of the screen patriarchy himself' (ibid.: 158) is echoed elsewhere. Berkowitz and Cornell's 2005 paper considers similar themes in response to *Mystic River* (2003), ideas which are later developed by Cornell into her book *Clint Eastwood and Issues of American Masculinity*:

> Eastwood's interests and choices have stamped his work with a distinctive trajectory that builds upon, disrupts, and re-envisions the very masculine stereotype for which he is known so well. Indeed, what makes Eastwood's work so interesting is how he engages with accepted genres and pushes them to their limits.
>
> (Cornell 2009: ix)

Others doubt that Eastwood successfully destabilizes concepts of masculinity. Indeed, Modleski notes the frequency with which Eastwood returns to what she calls a particular kind of 'white male melancholia' (Modleski 2010: 152). This responds to what we have already seen, noting the positioning of his films as 'masculine tearjerker[s]' (Brody 2014). Modleski focuses on *Gran Torino* (2008) and the way in which it is 'unambivalently devoted to the perpetuation of the [white] patriarchal order' (Modleski 2010: 154). It is worth noting that *Jersey Boys* was released only two years after Eastwood's infamous 'Empty Chair Speech' at the Republican Convention in 2012, during which he encouraged Obama to step aside for Mitt Romney, whom he described as 'a stellar business man' (Foxnews. com 2012). Continuing to perpetuate the white patriarchal order seems a fairly safe bet for this period in Eastwood's career.

So we find ourselves with a phenomenally successful musical (musical-ish) about men, and Clint Eastwood as icon of masculinity at the helm of a film adaptation – a sure-fire hit? Something somewhere went wrong, since the film did not continue the trend of financial success – one report cited a 'middling $67.6m on a production budget of $40m' (Child 2015). And while critics found that the film had many problems, no one would point the finger at the film being 'too much damned fun' (Savran 2004: 216). Its dour tone received attention in several reviews: one explains that 'rather than embracing the jangling song-and-dance numbers that made the live version box-office catnip, Eastwood sheepishly tidies them into the background' (Collin 2014). Others note how unlike *other* musicals the film is; 'Not an umbrella is twirled, not a lamppost swung around' (Davies 2014), or comment that 'Eastwood makes no concessions to glitzy, show-biz razzle-dazzle' (Eagan 2014). Mark Kermode notes the overall gloom, describing it as a 'somewhat plodding but still sporadically entertaining affair … underpinned by an indestructibly infectious songbook to which only the director himself appears able to turn a deaf ear' (Kermode 2014).

Removing the musical from the musical: anti-theatricality and masculinity

As a result, *Jersey Boys* as film explicitly excises the musical-theatre-ness of *Jersey Boys* to avoid any risk to its own masculinity. To be clear, the collaborative method of production for a Hollywood film (as indeed for all art) means that this is clearly not just Eastwood's doing. As a cultural materialist, I am nervous of reduction for easier prose, when such reductions might imply the movie is doing anything on its own terms – it is not a sentient being, it has come into existence through the work of hundreds of people who have made thousands of decisions and compromises at every stage of its production and reception.[2] Yet contemporary naming practices mean it is known as an 'Eastwood film', something which implies a particular presentation of hegemonic masculinity. The process of adaptation from stage to film allows us to examine a clear nervousness about what turns out to be quite a fragile masculinity – given the need to avoid a series of threats to its own dominance. These 'threats', such as they are, move by degrees from the misguided to the egregiously offensive. The threat of the musical's silliness and fun brings with it the perception (and clearly the risk) of campness. By camp I mean not the presence, as Sontag suggests, of a 'degree of artifice, of stylisation' (Sontag [1964] 2009: 277), which the musical assuredly does utilise, but the reductive, and offensively frequent, conflation of 'camp-as-survival-strategy' with camp-as-homosexual-expression that supposedly perniciously threatens masculinity. R.W. Connell's explanation, now over two decades old, is depressingly still relevant: 'to many people, homosexuality is a *negation* of masculinity, and homosexual men must be effeminate. Given that assumption, antagonism toward homosexual men may be used to define masculinity' (Connell 1992: 736).

In order to present its own hegemonic masculinity, the film adaptation of *Jersey Boys* actively seeks to limit the 'damage' to masculinity that the musical genre as cultural product threatens. The film takes a regressive position as a result of this nervousness, minimising 'otherness' and in particular the role and presence of women and gay men, and suppressing any African-American presence or musical practice. While the stage musical also does this to an extent, the film goes much further with its extreme suspicion of theatricality; what are cracks in the stage musical become fully-fledged fault lines in the film. Imagine a deeply troubling Venn diagram with two separate circles: 'Things that belong to the hegemonic masculinity of *Jersey Boys*' and 'Things that do not' – musicals are in the do not category. And, whether inadvertently or not (and as an excuse that is neither here nor there), it also specifically pushes gay men, women and African-American musical practice into this 'do not' category.

I want to pause to address what the hegemonic masculinity of *Jersey Boys* actually is, and to establish the key terms I am using. I use Connell's model of the understanding of masculinity as a dual approach that does not ignore either the 'radically cultural character of gender or the bodily presence' (Connell [1995] 2005: 52). Connell, perhaps above any other scholar, has established a careful understanding of how masculinit(ies) operate, and the ways in which they are understood. She has established a critical model that incorporates cultural constructs of masculinity alongside embodied presence, arguing that 'True masculinity is almost always thought to proceed from men's bodies – to be inherent in a male body or to express something about a male body' (ibid.: 45). She defines her concept of hegemonic masculinity as suggesting 'the configuration of gender practice which embodies the currently accepted answer to the problem of the legitimacy of patriarchy which guarantees (or is taken to guarantee) the dominant position of men and the subordination of women' (ibid.: 77). *Jersey Boys* is explicitly presenting its masculinity through the soft focus lens of nostalgia. It is somewhat of a relief that contemporary hegemonic masculinity permits a wider range of expression under its auspices, even within a patriarchal and repressive society. Yet the film version romanticises and looks back at a simpler time, when being a man, and being a man from New Jersey, meant... well what exactly? Try using the movie-trailer voice-over-man voice in your head to finish that sentence: meant being 'a man of your word', 'a tough guy' – the fact that we *know* what is being implied with this nostalgia indicates the ubiquity of this 'golden age' of masculinity. The film offers a safe retreat to contemplate a simpler time when 'men were men'. Yet all this begs the question, a safe retreat for *whom*? Certainly not anyone who has been pushed into the film's 'not masculine' category.

'Oh, What a Night!': what kind of masculinity is being modelled?

To establish what kind of masculinity is being presented, I want to consider one significant scene in both the film and stage show versions, and how they recount Bob Gaudio's first sexual encounter. The adaptation from stage to film vividly illustrates how theatricality has been minimised, since we can so easily compare what has been lost and what remains in the two different scenes.

The film uses 'Walk Like a Man' (Eastwood 2014, 1:01:45 onwards) as a backing track and accompaniment, and nothing about what follows is subtle. Firstly, we see Tommy (played as dumb here – which I will attend to later on since it clearly draws on racist anti-Italian-American stereotypes) fail to understand what the song is about. As Gaudio tries to explain to him, Bob Crewe interrupts: 'It's a metaphor, it's an anthem for every guy who's ever been twisted round a little girl's little finger. And if I'm explaining that to you, we're in trouble. Now knock off the bullshit and sing the song' (Eastwood 2014). Crewe actually co-wrote the song, but no mention is made of that in favour of the joke that even a gay man can understand what Tommy does not. As the boys start to record the track, we cut to the POV of the room-service trolley approaching the hotel room, as the camera lingers on the name plate – the 'Frank Sinatra suite' bedecked with a Christmas wreath. Gaudio talks to the camera, recalling that Frankie really knew how to throw a party, and we see an appropriately debauched scene play out (Eastwood 2014: 1:03:32). Gaudio is avoiding the party, shut in his room watching Clint Eastwood in *Rawhide* (1959) on TV.

As Eastwood as icon-of-masculinity is contrasted with the pitiful, virginal Gaudio, Tommy interrupts the viewing by 'giving' him a woman (listed in the film credits as 'Party Girl'). Tommy says as he gently pushes her into Gaudio's room: 'Bring the boy to the party, now I gotta bring the party to the boy' (Eastwood 2014). The contrast between Gaudio as *boy,* in comparison to Eastwood's rugged man (and presumably the man in the lyrics), clearly indicates what we are meant to know, that only when he has sex for the first time will Gaudio be a man. As she turns off the TV, she introduces herself as his 'Christmas present'; the camera remains fixed, the couple drop out of frame onto the bed. Still playing as the backing track, 'Walk Like a Man' abruptly stops, and we cut to the eager crowd of partygoers opening the door to Bob now in a dressing gown, transformed and having a post-coital cigarette. The crowd cheers (Eastwood 2014).

In the stage show, 'December '63 (Oh, What a Night)' is used to bookend the same scene. As in the film, the band has just recorded 'Walk' and Frankie and Bob Gaudio have set up their off-the-books partnership outside of the band. The song is a hit, and we transition into the Christmas party. Gaudio tells us that 'The label is raking it in, so they send over some girls when we hit Chicago at Christmas. And that night, I rack up a personal first' (Original Broadway Cast 2005). Rather than backing music, song is used as direct comment on the action – as Gaudio transitions into the memory that is being enacted on stage. Since he is on stage the whole time, narrating what is happening requires him to slip into the scene (and for us to see this transition). While both film and stage show use direct audience address to break the fourth wall *GoodFellas* style (1990), theatre has a sense of physical presence to contend with and cannot easily intercut with another scene. If someone talks to the audience about a memory that they then enact, they have to physically transition into the playing space. So here, the song allows for Gaudio to transition back into his memory. Dramaturgically the song functions simultaneously as diegetic backing track and as arising out of the events – which, since it is about remembering in the first place, creates a very slippery space between memory and events happening for the first time. This slipperiness is exacerbated by the band members (Valli is still absent from the party here), who when they sing 'What a Night' are clearly referring both to the party that is currently happening, and the innuendo of the song being about remembering a first sexual encounter. After Gaudio emerges from his bedroom, Tommy uses the lyrics of the song to taunt Gaudio's lack of sexual prowess: 'As I recall it ended much too soon' (Original Broadway Cast 2005).

Scott McMillin, in his unpicking of the way the musical functions dramaturgically, suggests that the book of a musical operates in one order of time – 'progressive time' (2006: 6) in contrast with what he calls 'lyric time' (ibid.: 9) which 'interrupts' the action. In the stage musical at least two orders of time are running simultaneously – the story is progressing through the song as we are aware that Gaudio is offstage having sex and 'becoming a man'. Additionally to these two orders of time, something else is happening, something which relates back to Taylor's ideas about the jukebox musical as inviting transcendental pleasure of recreation (Taylor 2012:165). As soon we hear the opening hook of 'What a Night', we know exactly what is going to happen because we already know the song – it is simply a question of the details. So the song interrupts, in that it is delaying us finding out how Gaudio's personal first played out, and it is also progressing the narrative since the scene is playing out in front of us. But we already know the music and words. Even if any member of the audience had managed to make it to the theatre without having heard the song, they would have heard it as the opener for the show, since it somewhat incongruously begins with a fully staged performance of French hip-hop performer Yannick M'Boloa's 2000 cover of 'Oh What a Night' ('Ces Soirees-La'). No one is left in any doubt that this is a song about remembering a *particular* night.

Jersey Boys on stage explicitly invites its audience to dispense with time altogether – less entering 'nostalgia time' than what I am going to call 'nostalgia-land'. We are explicitly invited to enjoy the fun of the youthful memory and to freeze time while we do so. Taylor, in her framing of the jukebox musical somewhat overlooks this pleasure of simply being in this nostalgia-land – without having to do anything very much at all. The stage musical indulges in theatricality, allows us to luxuriate in just having a good time. While Taylor is absolutely right, the jukebox musical does rely on the pleasure of watching virtuosic re-performances and reconstructions, it invites another kind of enjoyment, a safe place to daydream. We are meant to enjoy the fun of the memory (and in reference to this scene, certainly not be a spoilsport and think too hard about how creepy the whole situation actually is). The stage musical embraces theatricality and spectacle and deploys it to make the audience enjoy the musical *more*. The carefully controlled rapturous responses from the audience are no accident – the time taken before an actual Four Seasons song is sung in Act One in any recognisable form is surely about teasing the audience and delaying the gratification of seeing the band perform as 'the band'. When the audience finally do see the band play, the applause is heightened, and the audience slip easily between receiving two different kinds of performance; as Taylor notes, the audience 'engaged with experience both as concert and theatre piece' (Taylor 2012: 153).

The film version carefully controls its use of direct address – we do not see Gaudio slip back into the scene. Instead there is a long sequence of shots: Gaudio sticks his head out into the party, and tells us directly that Tommy could throw a party; we cut back into the studio, then cut back into Gaudio's lonely room where he is really is watching TV. He is certainly not addressing us (see Eastwood 2014: 1:03:29). The film version can dispense with the theatricality, it never needs to have Gaudio 'slip' back from one scene to another, instead he can cut between modes because of the cuts. The film has Gaudio in three concurrent times: the studio (the day of the recording), the lonely bedroom (the day of the recording), and the direct to camera address (where he is reliving some memory in talking to us both afterwards and during the day of the recording). The stage musical shows Gaudio slipping into the memory in the same physical stage space. Dyer has noted the use in film musicals of one song intercut with other scenes and locations to move the plot forward; he explains that these kinds of songs in film musicals can convey 'a sense of time expanding or contracting in the length of a song. In the course of a number a great deal of diegetic time may pass ... but it is musical time and length that determines screen time' (Dyer 2012: 24).

The stage version has the band members sing 'What a Night' to Gaudio, and to us the audience, without anyone asking too many questions about the switch between modes of storytelling. This shift into singing might be better described under the remit musical-theatricality, and it embodies the most egregious kind of theatricality that the film musical attempts to avoid. I am intending this term to mean the specific mechanics of theatricality in the form of the musical. The mechanics of theatricality are accentuated in the jukebox musical, since in negotiating the shift from speaking to singing, most of the audience know the whole song as soon as the actors start singing. It recalls Sontag's description of camp, of 'the degree of artifice, of stylisation' ([1964]2009: 277). While the jukebox film musical does utilise and invite its audience to enter nostalgia-land, *Jersey Boys* does so without the theatrical exuberance of its stage version. The film largely restricts song to diegetic concert performance, removing the very few songs in the musical that function as 'normal' musical songs. In the stage musical, after Frankie's daughter dies he sings 'Fallen Angel' – and summons her ghost or her memory onto the stage so he can sing to her; while she does not sing back there is a physical intimacy and connection in this poignant moment. This is not in the film version; instead a withdrawn Frankie is coaxed back to performance after his daughter's death by Gaudio.

'Not-masculinity': homosexuality as difference and women on the margins

Ultimately, both stage and film versions present men's sexuality as a defining feature of masculinity; specifically, men's sexual needs are insatiable and relentless. I want to consider now what is in the other side of the Venn diagram – since the hegemonic masculinity here largely defines itself against things it is not. Firstly, in terms of the presentation of homosexuality (to be clear, the invisibility of all other aspects of LGBTQ+ here is sadly typical). *Jersey Boys* is by no means alone in its problematic presentation of gay characters. In films or stage musicals such characters are played primarily for comedic effect: the roughly contemporaneous *The Producers* (2001) has 'flamboyant' director Roger de Bris singing 'Keep it Gay' in a camp spectacular. Yet what is perhaps striking in a musical which has a self-identified gay writer on its creative team (Rick Elice – who co-wrote the book with Marshall Brickman) is the way in which Bob Crewe's contribution is so egregiously minimised. While one could counter that he was not in the band, almost every opportunity to give Crewe credit for the band's success is missed in favour of using his sexuality as a joke.

Both stage and film versions feature a troubling scene where Frankie is chided by record producer Bob Crewe (then 29), who he obviously knows from school days. Crewe circles his index finger in the air and says 'Hey hey Toto, you're not in Newark anymore' – a reference to Dorothy not being in Kansas anymore. Frankie introduces Crewe to the band's keyboard player and songwriter, Bob Gaudio (then 17). Crewe rather lasciviously says: 'Hello young man ... you young, young, young, young man', guesses his star sign and calls him a 'silly goose'. Now alone to the camera/stage audience, Gaudio explains: 'I remember thinking at the time there was something a little off about this guy, I mean, this was like 1959, people thought Liberace was just, you know, theatrical.' (This whole sequence runs from Eastwood 2014: 0:44:30 onwards.) In both versions, Crewe's campness-as-gay is emphasised in order to jar with the straightforward hegemonic masculinity of the band. This is not to unsettle the masculinity, or present any kind of valid alternative, but to make his being gay a joke. Eastwood's film exacerbates the problems in the original text, and both stage and film version rely on the misrepresentation of homosexuality as inseparable from camp, and as camp as inseparable from theatrical flamboyance (misunderstanding gender and sexuality). In this faulty logic, to be theatrical and/or to be gay is to be not masculine. A review published in a reputable newspaper echoes these sentiments, in asking why the film was 'so reluctant to throw off caution and embrace fabulousness?' (Collin 2014). The 'fabulousness' referred to again conflates musical-theatricality as something different to the serious masculinity Eastwood represents.

Women are almost entirely absent from the film version, and when they are there, they generally play the tropes of haranguing mothers, nuns, sweet and largely silent daughters, and angry (ex-)wives. Again, this is largely the same situation in both versions. While Frankie's wife is played in both versions as telling him to style his name with an 'i' (Valli not Valley) and not hide away his Italian background, she ends up a stereotypical drunk wife having shouting matches with him for being away on tour. I have noted the 'Christmas gifts' in the Gaudio sex scene, and women appear as decorative sex objects throughout. In one unpleasant moment in the film, Tommy tells two identically dressed young women in a bar who are getting in the way of his conversation: 'I'm gonna shut my eyes and count to three and when I open them, you're gonna disappear' (Eastwood, 2014: 0:38:15 onwards). One reviewer noted that in film: 'female characters are either short-term playthings or long-term irritants, while queeny record-industry types are something to be endured with a raised eyebrow' (Collin 2014).

What masculinity is not: masking African-American musical cultures

The most egregious removal in the film is of African-American musical identity – or even actual existence. In the stage version, the hip-hop 'What a Night' performed as Yannick M'Boloa ensures the presence of one black actor in the cast (and given the nature of doubling, this means he will appear throughout the play, albeit in minor roles). Eastwood's movie does not have a single line spoken by an African-American actor, though 'jazz musicians' appear throughout playing trumpets or vocalising in the background (sometimes as literal set dressing – see Eastwood 2014: 0:43:42). There are other non-speaking roles played by ethnically diverse performers: at the Four Seasons' induction in the Hall of Fame there are two black women journalists, yet they remain uncredited, unlike the white male journalist who asks the questions. Quite apart from the minimisation of actual people, the suppression of music is staggering. The Four Seasons were a doo-wop band, and black music is extensively referenced in both stage and film versions. The stage musical shows the proto-Four Seasons performing a number of songs either written by or known as standards for African-American groups, including 'Earth Angel', a song by doo-wop group The Penguins, and 'I'm in the Mood for Love'. When Gaudio hears Frankie sing, he tells the audience he had been on the road with Chuck Berry, Sam Cooke, The Everly Brothers and Jackie Wilson and never heard a voice like Frankie's. In the film version, when Frankie and Bob Gaudio visit the Brill Building to follow up on their demos, a producer at 'Tropical Rhythms Music' expresses his surprise that, given their sound, they are not 'a coloured group' (Eastwood 2014: 0:44:19). The stage version has a similar list of references to 'coloured groups'.

Dyer has addressed the ways in which the film musical *Singin' in the Rain* (1952) seems obsessed with the idea of authenticity in crediting performers for their work, while at the same time dubbing its actual performer's voices. He notes 'so many slippages to affirm the truth of what we are seeing suggest just how important it is and perhaps how anxiety-inducing is any sense of it not being so' (Dyer 2012: 18). He draws heavily from Clover's earlier study of the movie, she argues that the frequency of the slips act 'as a sign of repressed anxieties that underwrite the text but are denied' (Clover 1995: 737). Elsewhere, Dyer has explicitly considered the 'absence of reference to whiteness in the habitual speech and writing of white people in the West' (Dyer [1997] 2013: 2). The absence of African-American voices in a story about a musical form dominated by black groups is constantly referenced by 'slips' in *Jersey Boys*, slips which serve to highlight a racism so well established and accepted in the musical that is has largely drawn little comment. In actively excluding (and forgetting is the same thing as excluding), the film further serves to demarcate what counts within its extremely limited portrayal.

There is of course a question as to whether the Four Seasons were seen as 'white' in the extremely racially coded 1950s America, perhaps unlikely, given the racism faced by Italian-Americans in the period. Goldblatt explains that there were many other ethnic doo-wop groups including 'working-class Italians and Hispanics' (Goldblatt 2013: 101). Whether a contemporary audience are now aware of this rigidly enforced racist society, the film reinforces racist Italian-American stereotypes (such as a lack of education – Tommy at one point threatens Vivaldi for stealing the Four Seasons' name). While the band has acknowledged their real connection to organised crime, many casual short-hands are used throughout both stage and film versions: Frankie goes shopping 'Jersey style' to get some jewellery for his wife (i.e. to acquire stolen goods). La Gumina notes that linking Italian-Americans with criminality 'remains the predominant feature of stereotyping' (2010: 111). In addition, Frankie's honour and heroism is played as a result of his origin, his unbreakable 'Jersey contract' is idealised within both versions. I am unconvinced that any kind of accuracy has been attended to in favour of an overall nostalgia for this particular performance of masculinity.

What a very special night for me: anti-theatrical to a point?

Eastwood's film almost entirely succeeds in pulling *Jersey Boys* away from the risky business of theatricality, until all of a sudden it can bear it no longer. The carefully controlled world we have seen throughout collapses, and tries to briefly return us to the theatricality of the stage musical – but it is too little too late. Both film and stage version end with the band's reunion some twenty years after their split – in the film version, the passing of time is illustrated with somewhat unconvincing wigs. Together (and without rehearsal) we see them perform 'Rag Doll': during this number, as has been the case throughout the film, each member of the band directly addresses the camera to tell us how it *really* was, before turning away from the audience, spinning back to the microphones and singing 'Who Loves You Baby?' They are once again young, rejuvenated by performance. The film cuts to black, and there is a second transformation. We hear the familiar opening notes of 'Sherry', and see a bird's eye view of the street lamp. Underneath, wearing their distinctive red jackets, we hear them singing 'Sherry' a-capella, which quickly shifts into 'What a Night'.

As would be expected in any traditional jukebox musical 'megamix', characters reprise numbers largely as an ensemble. Taylor notes the function of this section in a bio-musical, 'during which audiences are encouraged to sing, dance and join in' (Taylor 2012: 153). In the film, it functions in lieu of bows; through choreographic addition to the ensemble line we re-meet the full company as the strictly controlled internal world of the musical collapses as theatricality and fun takes over. The film world fully collapses when Christopher Walken's character, mob boss Gyp De Carlo, joins in the dancing (and Walken really can dance). We are meant to enjoy this – as an apparent burst of musical-theatricality. When the song has finished, there is silence where in the theatre there might have been applause. The camera, in ground angle shot, replicates the view of looking up the stage from the orchestra seats. We see sweat on bodies and performers trying to catch their breath, entirely frozen but still breathing, maintaining poses with effort and cigarettes still burning – the film is not frozen but the performers are. Cut to credits. In his *Telegraph* review of the film, Collin says that this 'may be the most miserably heterosexual musical routine in the history of cinema' (Collin 2014).

In attempting to minimise theatricality from a film adaptation of a musical, Eastwood reveals the fundamental workings of a jukebox musical. The process of adaptation exposes the form of the musical as a vehicle for pleasure, albeit with some underlying problems. It invites us to pay attention to these uncomfortable shortcuts, the unlovely features of the musical's presentation of diversity, gender and sexuality. Even if, especially if, we are busy enjoying ourselves and singing along with the words we did not know we knew.

Notes

1 Note the idea that the audience need not worry, some musicals might not be for men but *this one* is acceptable.
2 It is worth noting that the film has entirely male producers (and executive producers), writers, director and choreographer (though there are women in the design team and as assistant directors) (IMDb, 2016a).

Bibliography

Baker, R. (2011). 'Deconstructing Dirty Harry: Clint Eastwood's undoing of the Hollywood myth of screen masculinity in Play "Misty" for Me'. In G.O. Glabbard (ed.), *Psychoanalysis and Film*. International Journal of Psychoanalysis Key Papers Series, London and New York: Karnac Books, pp. 153–160.

Beard, W. (2000). 'Introduction'. In W. Beard (ed.), *Persistence of Multiple Vision: Essays on Clint Eastwood*. Alberta: University of Alberta, pp. ix–xv.

Berkowitz, R. and D. Cornell (2005). 'Parables of Revenge and Masculinity in Clint Eastwood's Mystic River'. *Law, Culture & The Humanities* 1(3), pp. 316–332. Humanities International Complete, EBSCOhost, viewed 31 August 2016.

Brantley, B. (2005). 'Theater review: *Jersey Boys*'. *New York Times*. www.nytimes.com/2005/11/07/theater/reviews/from-bluecollar-boys-to-doowop-sensation-a-bands-rise-and-fall.html?_r=0. Accessed 8 June 2016.

Brody, R. (2014). '"*Jersey Boys*" and the Lost Mainstream of America'. www.newyorker.com/culture/richard-brody/jersey-boys-and-the-lost-mainstream-of-america. Accessed 2 September 2016.

Child, B. (2015). 'Frankie Valli faces trial over rights to own life story for Four Seasons musical *Jersey Boys*.' www.theguardian.com/film/2015/oct/02/frankie-valli-faces-trial-for-stealing-life-story-on-four-seasons-film-jersey-boys. Accessed 2 September 2016.

Clover, C. J. (1995). 'Dancin' in the Rain.' *Critical Inquiry* 21(4) (Summer, 1995), pp. 722–747.

Collin, R. (2014). 'Review: "Miserably heterosexual".' www.telegraph.co.uk/culture/film/filmreviews/10911447/Jersey-Boys-review-miserably-heterosexual.html. Accessed 15 August 2016.

Connell, R. W. (1992). 'A Very Straight Gay: Masculinity, Homosexual Experience, and the Dynamics of Gender.' *American Sociological Review* 57(6) (December), pp. 737–751.

Connell, R. W. ([1995] 2005). *Masculinities*. 2nd Edition. Cambridge: Polity Press.

Cornell, D. (2009). *Clint Eastwood and Issues of American Masculinity*. New York: Fordham University Press.

Davies, S. (2014). 'Jersey Boys.' *Sight & Sound* 24(8), p. 76. International Bibliography of Theatre & Dance with Full Text, EBSCOhost. Accessed 15 August 2016.

Dyer, R. (2012). *In The Space Of A Song: The Uses of Song in Film*. New York: Routledge.

Dyer, R. ([1997] 2013). *White*. London: Routledge.

Eagan, D. (2014). 'JERSEY BOYS.' *Film Journal International* 117(8), pp. 89–90. International Bibliography of Theatre & Dance with Full Text, EBSCOhost. Accessed 15 August 2016.

Eastwood, Clint (2014). *Jersey Boys* (2014) [Film]. Directed by Clint Eastwood. California: Warner Bros. Pictures.

Ebiri, B. (2014). *Dirty Harry vs. Clint Eastwood*. www.rollingstone.com/movies/news/dirty-harry-vs-clint-eastwood-20140620. Accessed 2 September 2016.

Foxnews.com. (2012). 'Transcript Of Clint Eastwood Speech At Rnc.' Text Article, *FoxNews.com,* 30 August. www.foxnews.com/politics/2012/08/30/transcript-clint-eastwood-speech-at-rnc.html. Accessed 2 September 2016.

Goldblatt, D. (2013). 'Nonsense in Public Places: Songs of Black Vocal Rhythm and Blues or Doo-Wop.' *The Journal of Aesthetics and Art Criticism* 71, pp. 101–110. doi: 10.1111/j.1540-6245.2012.01546.x

Harper, S. (2006). 'Jersey Boys The Story of Frankie Valli: The Four Seasons Discovery Guide.' Los Angeles: Center Theatre Group, LA's Theatre Company.

IMDb. (2016) 'Clint Eastwood – IMDb'. *Internet Movie Database*. http://gb.imdb.com/name/nm0000142/. Accessed 2 September 2016.

IMDb. (2016a) 'Jersey Boys – full credits – IMDb'. *Internet Movie Database*. www.imdb.com/title/tt1742044/fullcredits?ref_=tt_ov_st_sm. Accessed 26 November 2016.

Jersey Boys UK (2016). *Jersey Boys/Gala Night – 12 April*. www.youtube.com/watch?v=lyt65T6qqk0. Accessed 1 September 2016.

Kermode, M. (2014). 'The New Review: Critics: Film: FILM OF THE WEEK: "Angelic voices, unpleasant vices: Clint Eastwood's take on the Four Seasons story isn't quite the joyous celebration it could have been: *Jersey Boys* (134mins, 15)".' *The Observer*, 22 June. Retrieved from Proquest. Accessed 15 August 2016.

La Gumina, S. J. (2010). 'Prejudice and Discrimination: The Italian American Experience Yesterday and Today.' In W.J. Connell and F. Gardaphé (eds), *Anti-Italianism: Essays on a Prejudice*. London: Palgrave Macmillan, pp. 107–116.

Lee, A. (2014). LAFF: 'Clint Eastwood defends casting musical's actors in "Jersey Boys" film at premiere.' www.hollywoodreporter.com/news/jersey-boys-premiere-clint-eastwood-713739. Accessed 2 September 2016.

McMillin, S. (2006). *The Musical as Drama : A Study of the Principles and Conventions behind Musical Shows from Kern to Sondheim*. Princeton, NJ: Princeton University Press.

Modleski, T. (2010). 'Clint Eastwood and Male Weepies.' *American Literary History* 22(1), pp. 136–158.

Ng, D. (2014). '"Jersey Boys" has been a windfall for all involved.' *LA Times*. www.latimes.com/entertainment/arts/la-et-cm-ca-jersey-boys-musical-20140622-story.html. Accessed 19 July 2016.

Original Broadway Cast (2005). *The Jersey Boys Original Broadway Cast Recording*. Audio CD. Burbank, CA: Rhino.

Paulson, M. (2016). '*Jersey Boys* Announces Its Closing Date.' *The New York Times*, 6 September. www.nytimes.com/2016/09/07/theater/jersey-boys-will-close-in-january.html?_r=0. Accessed 7 September 2016.

PremierComms (2016). 'Jersey Boys, London – the story of Frankie Valli and the Four Seasons.' www.jerseyboyslondon.com/about-the-show.asp. Accessed 31 August 2016.

Rolling Stone (2016). *The Four Seasons Biography*. www.rollingstone.com/music/artists/the-four-seasons/biography. Accessed 1 September 2016.

Savran, D. (2004). 'Towards a Historiography of the Popular.' *Theatre Survey* 45(2), pp. 211–217. doi:10.1017/S0040557400016X.

Smith, P. (1993). *Clint Eastwood: A Cultural Production*. Minnesota, University of Minnesota Press.

Sondheim, S. (1986). *Merrily We Roll Along*. Sound recording original cast CD, RCA.

Sontag, S. ([1964] 2009). 'Notes on Camp.' In S. Sontag, *Against Interpretation and Other Essays*. London: Penguin, pp. 275–292.

Taylor, M. (2012). *Musical Theatre, Realism and Entertainment*. Basingstoke: Ashgate Interdisciplinary Studies in Opera Series.

Teodorczuk, T. (2014). 'Jersey Boys cast admit Clint Eastwood was a "strange choice" to direct movie.' www.independent.co.uk/arts-entertainment/films/features/clint-eastwoods-jersey-boys-9544382.html. Accessed 17 August 2016.

11

THE ETHICAL EXCULPATION OF MORAL TURPITUDE

Representations of violence and death in *Sweeney Todd* and *Into the Woods*

Tim Stephenson

Sondheim's auteuristic domination of musical theatre wrestled the genre away from staid family entertainment formulas, establishing him as *the* 'avant-gardist artist working in *the* populist form' (Gordon 2014: 1). He writes musicals considered 'way ahead of the commercial audience for which they are designed' (Sutcliffe 1987), recognised for their 'dark, astringent sensibility, their focus on various kinds of ambiguity, alienation, and misanthropy' (Kirsch 2011). He explores themes of loss, morality and fate, providing 'ephiphanic justification' (Banfield 2014: 9) for the violence and death within his narratives. Yet within the perfect crafting of each song he also imbibes dark humour and acerbic wit, where 'the psychological gestalt of audience expectation is placed in ironic relief' (Gordon 1992: 9). But Sondheim's work continues to polarize opinion, ranging from the uncritical hyperbole adopted by aficionados who proclaim 'he's the greatest musical theater composer of all time' (Peitzman 2015), through to those who condemn his work as, 'sterile, cynical, over-intellectualized, and arid' (Gordon 1992: 3) For some, the intellectualism of Sondheim's work defines it as 'the antibody of the blockbuster, the antithesis of mass taste' (Lebrecht 2015) but how can this be, as for Sondheim consideration of audience was always key and his lifelong engagement with Broadway has always been commercially predicated?

Sondheim's friendship with Hal Prince began when they were both in their teens. It was Sondheim who persuaded Prince to produce *West Side Story* when the show looked destined for oblivion. They collaborated throughout the 1970s, with Prince directing the works that are now recognised as the staple components of his musical language; *Company* (1970), *Follies* (1971), *A Little Night Music* (1973), *Pacific Overtures* (1976), *Sweeney Todd* (1979) and *Merrily We Roll Along* (1981). The partnership worked because they shared a common philosophy on the direction music theatre should take:

> He's the best around by far. He has a sense of the function of music in a show. He takes it seriously and is more daring, imaginative and endlessly creative.
>
> (Sondheim in Ilson 1992: 23)

This 'middle period' in Sondheim's career established him as 'an accomplished composer and lyricist … receiving mostly favorable critical notices and multiple Tony Awards' all of which emanated from their 'extraordinarily fruitful working relationship' (Knapp 2016: 352)

Perhaps the most influential artistic collaboration was with James Lapine. Lapine was entrusted with both writing the book and directing *Sunday in the Park with George* (1984), *Into the Woods* (1987) and *Passion* (1994). Sondheim now assumed the role of elder statesman and Lapine the up-and-coming intellectual, having taught at Yale School of Drama and with a broad range of professional interests including photography, design, film-making as well as writing and directing.

> Rarely have two people of such vastly different backgrounds, temperaments, and levels of experience joined forces so successfully, nor left such an indelible impression.
>
> (Leavitt 2015)

Thus Sondheim, the 'over-reaching auteur genius' (Banfield 2014: 19) with a purported obsession over controlling all aspects of production, would seem to have spent his entire life creating work through engaging with traditional musical theatre collaborative practices. So even though his work may appear auteuristic, isn't this just a convenient shorthand applied by critics because the description of Sondheim as obsessive or controlling doesn't bear scrutiny?

> The stories come from the librettists; the themes and the atmospheres are theirs; the sentiments (or lack thereof) expressed in the songs belong not to Sondheim but to the characters the book writers have created.
>
> (Schiff 1993)

Given his manner of working it is not surprising that Sondheim would agree to relinquish control of his work and facilitate film adaptations by Hollywood of *Sweeney Todd* (2007) and *Into the Woods* (2014). Although some staunch Sondheimites might consider he sold his soul to the devil by taking the Californian dollar, it was the logical next step for a collaborative auteur. Yes, the studios were keen to capitalise on the resurgence of interest in musical theatre,[1] but Sondheim also wanted to connect his work with new, younger and non-theatre-going audiences.

This chapter will therefore discuss the myth of Sondheim's purported isolationist and auteristic approach to his art by considering the creative genesis and subsequent cinematic transformation of two of his most established theatrical triumphs, *Sweeney*

Todd and *Into the Woods,* through a focus on the disambiguation of the moral rectitude inherent in both narratives.

Moralistic fallacies: from concept musicals to *Sweeney Todd* on stage

Retrospective analysis has labelled many of Sondheim's works from the 1970s and 1980s as 'concept musicals', where the show's underlying metaphor or political message is considered more important than the narrative. It could be argued that both *Sweeney Todd* and *Into the Woods* fall into this category given *Sweeney Todd's* central tenet of moral ambiguity and *Into the Woods* being an extended metaphor for 'the dark, hidden, near-impenetrable world of our unconscious, ... that leads us from the safety of our parents' homes into the world at large' (Kakutani 1987) If this is the case, then any musical that demands more of its audience than a simple retelling of a narrative tale is capable of falling into the 'concept' category, making any such distinctions spurious. What is evident is that both *Sweeney Todd* and *Into the Woods* force the audience to consider both the moral and ethical repercussions of the drama unfolding before them; yet, given their absolute reliance on narrative exposition, they surely fit more comfortably with the traditional book form of an integrated musical – a structure that is equally sympatico with film.

> Musicals that are regarded as integrated present a coherent narrative, but that the narrative might be signified through individually disjunctive or alienating elements that audiences read as 'integrated'. The interpretation of a text relies on genre understanding that sets up expectations of readership as much as on the material itself.
>
> (Taylor 2012: 56)

However, both are moralistic fallacies where the justification for action overwrites usual ethical norms to satisfy unrealistic perceptions of justice or need. Yet as the body count rises we slowly realise that Sondheim has cleverly reversed the flow, and is now challenging the rectitude of ethical exculpation whilst demonstrating its causal symbiosis with moral turpitude. In Sondheim, one cannot exist without the other.

Although Sondheim's works are uniquely conceived and conceptually different, this belies the plethora of thematic and structural similarities evident between *Sweeney Todd* and *Into the Woods*: both revel in twisted narratives, both address adult themes of death and the deviant manipulation of others, and both unfold narratives steeped in 'misery' (Kirsch 2011), anger and violence. Yet they remain lyrical, engaging, gripping and laced with wit, irony and humour.

To unfold his challenge to the audience, Sondheim deliberately selected genres steeped in contemporary culture (horror and fairy tales/fantasy), modifying them to become the perfect vehicles for his particular brand of musical and narrative subversion. This cultural familiarity is also the reason why both works transfer so readily onto film. But what separates *Sweeney Todd* and *Into the Woods* from the formulaic horror stories and fantasy-adventures that have littered the cinema in recent years, is Sondheim's focus on the moral dilemmas and ethical dichotomies, deliberately challenging our voyeuristic enjoyment of the violence and death even if the transference of medium from stage to screen means that the fourth wall has been partially rebuilt.

Sondheim's work has always abandoned the rigid adherence to heteronormative dualities and the affirmation of patriarchal hegemonic moral rectitude, leaving his audiences unable to fulfil the traditional fictive certitude of the genre. So whatever the story, we don't expect a happy couple to wander off into the sunset, or for everything to be neatly and happily resolved by the end of the second act. As Gordon points out, Sondheim's musicals tend to, 'begin after the traditional happily ever after has run into trouble' (Gordon 1992: 5), lacking the verisimilitude of traditional Broadway fare. In *Sweeney Todd* and *Into the Woods* he teases us throughout with allusions to formulaic romantic and happy-ever-after endings, before destroying them through the slash of a razor or the rampaging clumsiness of a vengeful giantess. Thus, the inherent omphalic forms of both narratives work in perfect accord with the ebb and flow of Sondheim's macro-compositional structure and his love of musicological symmetry.

Arguably *Sweeney Todd* owes more to Brecht and Weill's *Threepenny Opera* and prewar horror movies than anything from the Broadway canon. The sensationalism of Victorian melodrama combines with allusions to Jacobean-style revenge tragedies in an operatically conceived, sensationalised penny-dreadful narrative that demands that the audience directly addresses the central dilemma of whether ethically exculpated vengeance can ever justify Sweeney's appalling anti-social activities.

> As the corpses pile up we develop an empathy with the moral turpitude of the cannibalistic antihero, whilst delighting in the illicit depravity of our 'immoral collusion'.
>
> (Banfield 1993: 7)

Can there ever be justification for unconscionable, indiscriminate mass murder, even for a man so wronged by Judge Turpin? We loathe the judge for raping Todd's wife (and apparently causing her to commit suicide) and for incestuously lusting after his ward who also happens to be Todd's daughter, but does this justify mass-murder? We know the answer, of course, as we watch Sweeney become increasingly consumed with revenge before reaching the point where his own destruction is assured in the aptly named 'Epiphany'.

> We all deserve to die,
> Even you, Mrs Lovett, even I …
> And I'll never see Johanna,
> No, I'll never hug my girl to me – finished!

The unrequited affection of the disturbing sociopath Mrs Lovett accompanies Todd's attempt to fight off the madness of vengeance. At the start he is portrayed as 'as moral a hero as one could ask for in a dystopian world' (Libresco), yet as the X-rated narrative slashes its way to its inevitable conclusion, we are enthralled to witness the destruction of the 'happy family' trope (so aptly parodied in 'By the Sea') as Todd abandons his only hope of reconciliation with, or redemption from, his daughter Johanna, and then sets about murdering the judge and seriously reducing the viability of the rest of the cast. The finale sees him 'accidentally' murder his wife (the judge exacting revenge on Todd even after death?) as the narrative descends into a 'morality fable for a world that doubts the very existence of good and evil' (Libresco). We are swept along by the orgy of violence despite understanding that Todd's moral turpitude can never be justified. We search for crumbs of comfort in the exculpation that at least his daughter has been 'rescued' from the judge, and remains oblivious to the fact that Todd is her father. Then, as if to thumb his nose at tradition once more, Sondheim constructs a deliberate parody of the usual happy ending by allowing Johanna and Anthony to squelch off into the sunset over the bloodied corpses of Todd and his numerous victims. Todd's sanguinary carnage is therefore moderated through Anthony and Johanna's salvation, providing an ironic blood-splattered nod to the usual 'terminal' romanticism of the Golden Age.

> From its first ominous notes to its blood-soaked finale, *Sweeney Todd* creates a complete, almost suffocating atmosphere of dread and terror. *Into the Woods*, on the other hand, is all about uncertainty.
>
> (Watts 2008)

Into the Woods: narrated fairy tales and uncomfortable symmetries on stage

Outwardly, *Into the Woods* and *Sweeney Todd* appear to come from parallel universes. From X-rated slasher horror we are transported into an illusory utopian village where everyone is destined to live happily ever after; or are they? Of course Lapine and Sondheim's inspired interweaving of familiar childhood fairy tales creates the perfect frame to explore the inherent moral justification for the actions of the various characters. The underlying meta-narrative is that wishes do come true, but only if you are prepared to face the consequences: should Jack really slay the giant, will Cinderella really find true love with Prince Charming, and does Little Red Riding Hood deserve to be rescued from the Big Bad Wolf? Add to the mix a baker and his wife desperate to end their curse-induced sterility, a witch in search of her youth and maternal absolution, and an imprisoned kidnapped child (Rapunzel), and it is no wonder that the moral dilemmas mount as the various protagonists become increasingly detached from the consequences of their actions, and more and more frantic in their selfish pursuit of guilt-free happiness.

Although the stories are familiar, these are not the sanitised fairytales of Disney cartoons but the darker Grimm by name and grim by nature originals, where Cinderella's maliciously tormenting stepsisters force on the golden slipper in a bloody maelstrom of dismembering podiatry, and her unrequested post-ball retribution is served cold via a blinding avian attack. Similarly, the pastry pilfering Red Riding Hood's perambulations into the woods are insinuated with paedophilic overtones throughout her salacious encounter with the duplicitous Wolf. Their meeting is 'a coded narration of sexual initiation' (Menton 2000: 66) reinforced by her complicity in her own demise as the lupine gormandizer metaphorically seduces her, making her feel simultaneously 'excited and scared'. Even Rapunzel, who escapes her prison, is seduced by the prince and then banished by her 'mother' the witch, to die alone in a swamp, whilst her heroic beau is blinded by thorns and left to wander aimlessly in the woods. Perhaps only the larcenic Jack, with his obsession with stealing from the bone-crunching behemoth in the sky, along with Lapine's wonderfully allegorical creation of the witch, emerge relatively unscathed from a first act which Sondheim described as being, 'about moral responsibility – the responsibility you have in getting your wish not to cheat and step on other people's toes, because it rebounds' (Lipton 1997).

In *Into the Woods* Sondheim's love of structural symmetry is made overt in the cyclical adaptations of the opening 'Into the Woods' and 'I wish' material. The cast gradually dismiss their moral qualms in 'First Midnight' and 'Second Midnight', driving the plot towards the Act One finale 'Ever After'. It may not be as 'epiphanic' a pivot point as that in *Sweeney Todd* but the coded warnings are clear,

> Narrator: And it came to pass, all that seemed wrong
> Was now right, and those who deserved to
> Were certain to live a long and happy life …
> And they reached the right conclusions
> And they got what they deserve!

leaving us wondering who the narrator thinks 'deserve' to live a 'long and happy life'? The sardonic irony of the last two lines is not lost as Sondheim careens over this pivot point, accompanied by a resurgence of the skipping 'Into the Woods' motifs. We now realise the equivocation of his 'happy ever after' construct: the falsehood of the apparent resolution where the baker and his wife have a child, Cinderella marries Prince Charming, Red Riding Hood is rescued from the Wolf, Rapunzel elopes with her Prince and even the witch regains her beauty. Yet we also know all this has been achieved without addressing the moral dilemmas inherent in their actions.

As a consequence, it is inevitable the narrative will descend into a catalogue of self-induced mayhem, mishap and death. Seeking retribution for the murder of her innocent husband, the giantess now presents a new and deadly moral dichotomy. She has been wronged and demands they hand over Jack to satisfy her need for revenge. Her grieving rampage destroys the village and kills Little Red

Riding Hood's mother. Apparently continuing health can only be assured by acceding to the Giantess's demands, or at least until the survivors collude to lure her to a tar-splattered demise. The rights and wrongs of their decision to murder the giantess dissipate in an accusatory downward spiral of blame, demonstrating how morally justified behaviour ebbs and flows. Each of the cast is made to address the effect of their moral collusion aided and abetted by the lethal clumsiness of the giantess. Soon the baker's wife is dead, killed by a falling tree in apparent retribution for the immoral act of allowing herself to be seduced by the Prince: a moralistic fallacy that completely ignores the needs of the newborn child and the unquestioning love of her husband. Jack's mother is also 'accidentally' killed by the steward whilst defending Jack from the giantess; can a son really do no wrong? Rapunzel is driven mad by her maternal banishment and her feckless Prince, who only five minutes ago was blindly searching for his hirsute true love, is now lusting after Sleeping Beauty. Rapunzel's rejection of the cloying safety of the witch's imprisonment, driven by her desire for true love and freedom, is dashed as Sondheim exposes the ravaging pain of parental love, explodes the falsehood of instantaneous heterosexual fairytale attraction and has her 'accidentally' crushed to death by the giantess. The steward and the royal family flee to take their own chances, and to add to the carnage even the narrator is dragged into the narrative, given to the giantess in the hope she'll think he's Jack, before falling to his death. Finally, the witch, disgusted with their refusal to accept responsibility for the situation, demands they give her the blame. Her desire to lift her mother's curse has cost her a 'daughter', her magic powers, her house and garden and has acted as a catalyst for all that has followed. She therefore chooses to sacrifice herself, and leaves the few remaining survivors alone in the woods whilst offering no remorse or resolution for her actions. Thus, from the apparent midway satisfying point of resolution, Sondheim has systematically unraveled each and every one of the mythologies of 'happy ever after', and we are again left challenging whether the purported ethical exculpation justifies such apparent indiscriminate violence and slaughter.

We already know that Sondheim 'is not interested in happy endings, rather in perfect outcomes' (Lebrecht 2015), and that happiness, for Sondheim, is symmetry. Through examining the consequences of each of the character's wishes the *Woods* evolve from the mystical, magical place of endless possibilities of the opening into a place where one is forced to develop moral discrimination in a desperate fight for survival and redemption. In the process the *Woods* becomes a metaphor for confusion, loss, separation, death and ethical confusion, which are only escapable once the survivors are prepared to address and accept the consequences of their actions. 'No-one will leave the woods feeling comfortable or reassured, which is just as the composer intended' (Lebrecht).

As in *Sweeney Todd*, the ending parodies the 'happy ever after trope' through Sondheim's enforced construction of a fairy-tale nuclear family comprising the baker, Cinderella and the baby, and with the orphaned Jack and Little Red Riding Hood thrown in for good measure. This further exaggerates the hidden layers of analogy as the cast concludes by outlining their understanding of the moral lesson they have learnt,

> Into the woods, each time you go,
> There's more to learn of what you know …
> To heed the witch, to honor the giant,
> To mind, to heed, to find, to think, to teach, to join …
> Then out of the woods, And happy ever after!

and Cinderella wistfully concludes with a final reprise of 'I wish', ending this 'darkly lighted parable for our times' (Kakutani 1987).

From stage to screen: *Sweeney Todd* with no chorus

The symbiotic relationship between stage musicals and the silver screen has a long and well established history. The conveyor belt of Tony Award winning musicals in the 1950s and 60s to Hollywood was a given. Yet for every triumphal cinematic success, like the ten times Oscar winning *West Side Story* (1961), there was a poorly conceived *Rent* (2003), where even the most supportive critic had to admit, 'I don't think the movie really works on its own, without reference to the theatrical version' (Ebert 2005). The process of adaptation can be fraught with difficulties; even on *West Side Story* the disagreements between Broadway maestro Jerome Robbins and cinematic debutant Robert Wise became legend.

Films are a director's medium, controlled by a single vision (which is seldom the author's), and movie musicals in particular 'require a director with an understanding of both forms and a respect for the material' (Flahaven 2008). With both *Sweeney Todd* and *Into the Woods* it is hard to conceive of directors better suited to the transformation and adaptation of Sondheim's material than Tim Burton and Rob Marshall. Although Burton had never worked on a musical before, he had developed a directorial genre recognised for dark macabre films, developed within gothic sensibilities and with a quirky sense of humour; the perfect animateur for *Sweeney Todd*.[2]

Some critics seemed taken aback that Sondheim finally agreed to give Hollywood access to arguably his two most famous musicals, but the reality was that throughout his career he repeatedly dabbled in both genres. He started, of course, as lyricist on the Broadway hits *West Side Story* and *Gypsy* at the end of the fifties, yet by 1961 and 1962 both of these had turned into cinematic triumphs, even if his artistic contribution to those films was negligible. The first Broadway hit where he was credited as both composer and lyricist was *A Funny Thing Happened on the Way to the Forum*, which similarly transferred to film within a few years of its premiere. Although the historical satire was a hit at the Broadway box office, Sondheim's role within the production was hardly a pronounced critical success; 'I don't think I'd give you much for the music, by Stephen Sondheim, but the lyrics, also by him, aren't bad' (Hewes in Gordon 1992: 28). Despite this, the show went on to win six Tony Awards in 1963 for Best Musical, Best Director, Best Producer, Best Author, along with two acting awards, yet the award for best original score that year went to Lionel Bart for *Oliver!* Sondheim wasn't even nominated. Therefore, it was hardly surprising that his engagement in the subsequent film version was equally marginalised. The irony is that music director Ken Thorne (engaged by the studio to adapt Sondheim's work for the big screen) won the film's only award, an Oscar for Best Music – Scoring and Adaptation, whilst Sondheim himself again failed to trouble the judging panel.

Given those early experiences it is hardly surprising that Sondheim developed a reputation for being fiercely critical of most film musicals, particularly because of the manner in which they destroyed the performer/audience dynamic that he had been so insistent on challenging.

> There's something inimical about the camera and song. Musicals are, by nature, as far as I am concerned, theatrical, meaning poetic, meaning having to move the audience's imagination and create a suspension of disbelief, by which I mean there's no fourth wall. Whereas the camera is different, you can put the camera at different angles and it's all realistic.
>
> (Sondheim in Edwardes 2006)

He did, however, have another brief dalliance with Hollywood in the 1970s, co-writing the thriller *The Last of Sheila* with Anthony Perkins for Warner Brothers. This film reflected his obsessive love of games and scavenger hunts, as the parlor games within the plot descend into murder. It was well received critically, and did well enough at the box office for further scripts to be prepared, although none came to fruition. So Sondheim was obviously conversant with the cinematic art, and even gave his agreement for some of his stage shows to be filmed,[3] yet the debacle of his exclusion from the film of *A Funny Thing Happened on the Way to the Forum* meant it would be almost forty years before he again acceded to Hollywood.

By this point his fame and status within the theatrical canon meant his inclusion in the transformation process was assured, and although directorial authority for *Sweeney Todd* lay with Burton, it is clear that Sondheim was fully engaged with the adaptation and actively aided the process. He was asked to approve the choice of screenwriter, John Logan,[4] and of course Tim Burton's reputation was well-established. Sondheim knew that Burton was a fan, having approached Sondheim some twenty years earlier about the possibility of making a film of *Sweeney Todd*. Burton had always been struck by how cinematic the musical was, and was committed to maintaining the prominence of Sondheim's score in order to confirm the suspense and horror he had musically infused into the unfolding narrative. Thus, both the stage show and the film are '*infused* with music to keep the audience in a state of tension ... and to prevent them from separating themselves from the action' (Lipton 1997), and to achieve this Burton kept dialogue to a minimum, allowing the pseudo-spoken yet operatic delivery of Sondheim's Bernard Herman-inspired score to dominate throughout his silent horror movie inspired vision.

Now adapting a two-and-a-half-hour stage show into the shorter medium of film meant differing emphases would automatically come to the fore, supplemented by the added realism of the cinematic art (especially close-up work). This meant that much of the chorus work was eliminated, with Sondheim expressing a temporary regret at the exclusion of the recurring chorus of 'The Ballad of Sweeney Todd', yet accepting that its role in the stage show of externally commenting on the action was superfluous and 'ineffective in films, where the focus lies more on dramatizing interior emotions than creating theatrical spectacle' (Burns 2009). Therefore, they cut songs 'that were overtly theatrical or cinematically superfluous' (McGill 2014: 55) and removed sections from other songs to help 'get from this point to that point more quickly (Sondheim in Hutson 2007). Sections were removed from numerous numbers, including the middle section of 'Green Finch and Linnet Bird' and large parts of 'A Little Priest', and although,

> only ten of the original score's twenty-seven songs remain substantially intact, Sondheim, as his contract stipulated, approved every change … altering certain lyrics and expanding instrumental sections so that they tallied with the structural and narrative alterations made by Logan.
>
> (Philpotts 2008)

The major dramatic change was the added emphasis on the potential relationship between Sweeney Todd and Mrs Lovett afforded by the casting of Johnny Depp and Helena Bonham Carter. The sexual potential of the film was largely absent from the stage show,[5] but the smouldering passion of Depp's Todd (even if misplaced) is constantly responded to by Bonham Carter's 'emotional neediness' and 'erotic longing' as 'she's barely able to rein in her heaving bosom' (Sandhu 2008). Whilst some have criticised the fact that 'the stars did not have the vocal training to adequately perform … Sondheim's music' (Nogee 2015), this adds to the intimacy of some of their exchanges. The use of close up shots and shooting Bonham Carter from above (to make her look needy) comes to a fantastical and satirical conclusion in 'By the Sea', which Burton transforms into a classic dream sequence. This provides a momentary hiatus in the descent to the inevitable murderous final rejection, as Bonham Carter's duplicity is revealed and she is thrown into the furnace by a remorseless and hideously blood spattered Depp.

> What Burton's adaptation does do, and rather convincingly, is draw us into the personal world of Todd and Mrs. Lovett in an unsettling way by inducing ambivalent responses to its principal characters.
>
> (Riley 2010)

The other primary change is that the socio-political edge of the original is diminished in favour of the elevation of the revenge narrative. The removal of much of the chorus is largely responsible for the resulting 'grotesque juxtaposition of horror with broad, music-hall-style comedy' (Riley 2010), and yet the satirical

FIGURE 11.1 Johnny Depp and Helena Bonham Carter in *Sweeney Todd*.

Credit: Collection Christophel/ArenaPAL.

element remains in Mrs Lovett's representation of corrupt capitalism, 'We've got a nice, respectable business now!', and exemplified by her justification for robbing one of the corpses with "Waste not. Want not.' So Burton's film is different to the stage show in numerous ways and yet Sondheim, the collaborative auteur, not only approved all of the changes, he actively assisted in the cinematic recreation of his anti-hero. 'Those of you who know the show– - forget it. Just go along with it, and I think you will have a spectacular time. It is its own animal' (Sondheim in Wloszczyna 2007).

Into the Woods: musical puzzles and complex narratives on film

Marshall started as dancer and choreographer on Broadway. He was nominated for five Tony Awards for his choreography and directing, working on numerous productions including revivals of *Damn Yankees* in 1994 and *Cabaret* in 1998. Sandwiched between these productions were new productions of Sondheim's *Company* (1995) and *A Funny Thing Happened on the Way to the Forum* (1998), so when Disney came looking for a film director for *Annie* (1999) he was the obvious choice. Marshall is now recognised as *the* contemporary master of the film musical, winning a plethora of awards for his star-studded adaptation of *Chicago*

(2002) and critical plaudits for the financially disappointing *Nine* (2005). He then more than regained his fiscal popularity with Disney by putting over \$1billion into their coffers by directing the fourth in the *Pirates of the Caribbean* series (*On Stranger Tides*) in 2011. Thus Marshall was Disney's obvious choice for *Into the Woods*, another appointment fully endorsed by Sondheim, as was James Lapine, the author of the original book for the Broadway show, who was asked to write the screenplay.

Once again, some critics were initially horrified: 'it's the antidote to Disney … how could Disney possibly adapt the show without betraying its dark spirit?' (Schulman 2014), but the tenebrosity of the moral retribution within *Into the Woods* concurred with Disney's increasingly adult approach to the reinterpretation of their stock-in-trade through films like *Alice in Wonderland* (2010)[6] and *Maleficent* (2014). Marshall and Lapine were committed to ensuring that the complex mixture of divergent narratives, arising from Sondheim's understanding of the symbiotic lyrical, harmonic and structural possibilities of fairytales, transferred more or less intact onto film.

The Sondheim voice may have been modified, yet the rhythms, rhymes and recurrent motifs are all maintained within another almost through-composed, re-orchestrated score that is 'a puzzle-master's trove of overlapping motifs, internal rhymes, and psychological nuance' (Schulman 2014). The complexity of the narrative is only marginally simplified, retaining its humour from the interplay of stereotypical characterisation (as in 'Agony'), acerbic wit (Prince Charming justifying his infidelity to Cinderella with 'I was raised to be charming, not sincere') and ingenious word play: 'We've no time to sit and dither, While her withers wither with her' (Jack's Mother, Prologue). Yes, there are some cuts and some obvious omissions (Rapunzel's demise and the diminution of the role of the baker's father) and even some new material written by Sondheim (Meryl Streep's Rainbows) yet the film 'honors both the slicing humor and underlying menace of the tale' (Dabkowski 2014).

> [Marshall] didn't want to change the story he wanted the story just the way it was … he didn't want to change the character, he didn't want to change the ending; he didn't want to change anything about the telling of the tale and that's enough.
>
> (Sondheim in Hutson 2007)

Nevertheless, there are obvious differences between stage and screen. Some aspects of the satirical and socio-political comment are lost, as is the intimacy of the audience dynamic, which revelled in cutting asides, direct address and the deliberate comedic interventions between the narrator, cast and audience. The purposeful irony of dual casting is also lost. On stage Prince Charming also plays the wolf, insinuating the underlying lascivious nature of his character. Similarly, on stage the recently demised narrator is resurrected as the revelatory baker's father. Yet such obvious deceits seldom work in film, although I rather doubt that dual casting was dropped simply 'to squeeze in a few more prospective Golden Globe nominees' (Collin 2015).

Marshall therefore maintains the central concerns of the morality tales whilst creating a commercial triumph in which the adult consequences of action are not Disneyfied. Even the notorious seduction and consequent death of the baker's wife, which led to so much press speculation prior to the film's release, are maintained. Lapine noted, 'it was a given that it would have to be edited down. We did a lot just to make it cinematic' (Burlingame 2014). For example, Rapunzel's tale is greatly simplified and her dalliance with the second prince and resultant almost spontaneous combustion of twins is omitted.

As with *Sweeney Todd,* it certainly helped that much of the original show was already cinematic in many aspects of its production. For example, the opening triptych of simultaneous 'wishes' from the stage show is strengthened by its transfer to an intercut, scenery changing, individualisation of the wants and desires of the characters. Other examples are the integration of the narrator's role into the thoughts and words of the baker, the wonderful scenic tableaus of tangled undergrowth, castle exteriors and the crashing realism of the giant (as opposed to the pantomime gestures of the cast responding to off-stage sound effects), all of which are more in keeping with contemporary expectations of fantasy storytelling. Thus *Into the Woods* abandons its vaudeville roots and is reinvented for the cinema with affection, but without sentiment, in a film which 'transforms classic fairy tales into reflections of modern fears and psychoses ... [and with] ... casting so perfect it had to have come from the musical theater gods' (Dabkowski 2014). With provenance like that, how could it fail to be another success?

Transformed narratives

The adaptations from stage to screen of both *Sweeney Todd* and *Into the Woods* were successful because of their homogeneity with horror and adult fantasy conventions, their familiar narrative structure and the cleverness of the musical adaptations. Obviously one expects films to create different meanings and provide differing audience experiences to the stage versions, with differing emphases, changing thematic interpretations, star casting, the emphasis on design, cinematic techniques, changing cultural references and a myriad of other variables all potentially altering the meaning within the process of adaptation. Yet, unusually for Sondheim, both works appear to have been conceived with cinematic overtones within their stage productions.

Both films connected Sondheim's work with new audiences, and both succeeded because Sondheim demonstrated a 'willingness to forego fidelity to its theatrical source in favor of doing what works cinematically'(Riley 2010). Yet both were far more than simple cinematic recreations, with Sondheim, the directors and Hollywood finding an appropriate balance between the commercial necessities of the genre, the artistic integrity of the source material and the necessity to reinvent Sondheim's work for a media-savvy twenty-first century audience. As a result,

> The intermedial aspects of both stage and screen … present an interesting case study of how adaptations can successfully transform … to reflect an intra-cultural web of contemporary interests, desires and fears.
>
> (McGill 2014: 60)

'It's strange to think that a man so honored could remain a minority taste' (Kirsch 2011); but is this true? Sondheim has certainly lived through a period of enormous upheaval in the genre, with the formulaic certitude of the golden age replaced by 'the deluge of "jukebox musicals", overblown crowd-pleasers and "theme-park" spectacles that now dominate the Broadway stage' (Brown 2010). But Sondheim *has* moved with the times and *has* challenged and developed the form, creating a canon of adult-oriented musicals that offer socio-political commentaries designed to inform and entertain. Whilst protective of his oeuvre, Sondheim has always created something new for every project with which he's been engaged; not for him the staid regurgitation of past triumphs or the prostitution of reality TV to keep the impresarios and box office satisfied. Sondheim remains eloquently aloof yet paradoxically accessible, always able to connect with his audience narratively, emotionally and sagaciously.

> Sondheim's lyrical work in this field is the best there is. It is intellectual, analytical, funny, cynical, moving, adult, and above all, deeply thoughtful.
>
> (Goodhart 2000: xv)

Sondheim's love of melodrama provided him with the means to 'dig beneath the mundane appearances of everyday life in order to reveal and dramatize the hidden moral core of experience' (Ito 2008: 5). *Into the Woods* 'is an adult morality tale for the modern era' (Frank 1990), whilst Libresco explains that in *Sweeney Todd* Sondheim 'succeeded in writing a morality fable for a world that doubts the very existence of good and evil'. Both narratives address protagonists torn apart by the moral choices that lie at the centre of melodrama's hyperbolic sentiments. They challenge the audience, as voyeur, to justify the qualities of baseness, vileness and depravity portrayed, whilst the addition 'of pathos … intensifies the binarity of its disposition and struggles' (Shevchenko 2008: 35). As such we are challenged to assess their moral legibility, to assign both guilt and innocence, and, arguably, this is made more powerful through the medium of film, emancipated from the sometimes inappropriate satirical and humorous conventions of musical theatre. With more internalisation of the narrative, the 'conflict between content and context characterizes the moral ambiguity represented by the central characters' (Di Santo 2004).

Despite these radical advances, some critics persist in categorising Sondheim as 'the last survivor of a form that is all but extinct' (Brown 2010), and perhaps his desire to shake off that image explains his recent forays into film. When Hollywood came knocking again, the now septuagenarian Sondheim finally said yes. He understood the risks, he acknowledged that film musicals were 'a fascinating multi-media celebration constituting the world's most complex art form' (Altman 1989: 2), and he knew that the conventions of musical theatre were difficult to transfer successfully to the pseudo-realism of film; and yet he still chose to work with Burton and Marshall. By changing genres his preference for material that was unconventional could be turned to his advantage. As Collin states (2015), Sondheim 'leads you into the thorn bushes with a happy song, but once you're in there, all bets are off'. So his skill is that, despite the greed or the violence we witness, we still identify, or at least empathise, with his protagonists whilst simultaneously searching for the metaphorical or ethical justification for the carnage we have just witnessed, even if his protagonists are all authors of their own misfortune. Through these films Sondheim has surely thrown off the myth of monolithic auteuristic control and reasserted a commitment to the musical as a progressive and living art form that will continue to evolve 'in a dialogic process with its cultural frame, prior versions, and other contextual references (McGill 2014: 59–60).

Notes

1   With a combined global box office of almost half a billion dollars for both films one might assume both parties were happy with the outcome.
2   Burton could also deliver the perfect Todd, having worked with Johnny Depp on *Edward Scissorhands* (1990), *Ed Wood* (1994), *Sleepy Hollow* (1999), *Charlie and the Chocolate Factory* (2005) and *Corpse Bride* (2005), so the casting of the lead was no surprise. Thus Sondheim considered Burton 'a perfect fit … [as] you can see that he's telling a story he likes' (Sondheim in Levy 2007).
3   Including *Into the Woods* in 1990 by Brandman Productions, and *Putting It Together* in 2001 by Good Times Video.
4   On the recommendation of Sam Mendes.
5   Angela Lansbury was 53 when she created the role alongside the 39-year-old Len Cariou.
6   Another Burton, Depp and Bonham Carter film.

Bibliography

Altman, Rick (1989). *The American Film Musical*. Bloomington: Indiana University Press.
Banfield, Stephen (1993). *Sondheim's Broadway Musicals*. Ann Arbor: University of Michigan Press.
Banfield, Stephen (2014). 'Sondheim's Genius.' In R. Gordon (ed.), *The Oxford Handbook of Sondheim Studies*. Oxford: Oxford University Press, pp.11–24.
Brown, Mick (2010). 'Stephen Sondheim interview: Still cutting it at 80.' *Daily Telegraph*, 27 September. www.telegraph.co.uk/culture/music/8022755/Still-cutting-it-at-80-Stephen-Sondheim-interview.html.
Burlingame, Jon (2014). 'Rob Marshall Boldly Explores Disney's Take on Twisted Tale "Into the Woods".' *Variety Magazine*, 4 November. http://variety.com/2014/film/features/into-the-woods-rob-marshall-disney-1201346785/
Burns, Rachel (2009). 'Good Deeds: Sondheim Seduces Audiences.' *The Harvard Crimson*, 20 November. www.thecrimson.com/article/2009/11/20/sondheim-audience-todd-sweeney/

Collin, Robbie (2015). '*Into the Woods* review: Pure pleasure.' *Daily Telegraph*, 7 January. www.telegraph.co.uk/culture/film/filmreviews/11298668/Into-the-Woods-review-Meryl-Streep-Emily-Blunt-Anna-Kendrick.html.

Dabkowski, Colin (2014). 'Sondheim's "Into the Woods" comes out of the theater and onto the screen.' *Buffalo News*, 22 December. http://buffalonews.com/

Di Santo, Anthony (2004). 'Sweeney Todd: Some Ethical Perspectives.' Stephen Sondheim, www.sondheim.com/shows/essay/sweeney.html.

Ebert, Roger (2005). 'Review: *Rent.*' www.rogerebert.com/reviews/rent-2005.

Edwardes, Jane (2006). 'Stephen Sondheim: Interview.' *Timeout Magazine*, 9 May. www.timeout.com/london/theatre/stephen-sondheim-interview.

Flahaven, Sean (2008). 'The Sounds of *Sweeney.*' *The Sondheim Review* 14(4), pp. 16–17. www.sondheimreview.com/.

Frank, Leah (1990). 'A Morality Musical For the Modern Era.' *New York Times*, 17 June. www.nytimes.com/1990/06/17/nyregion/theater-review-a-morality-musical-for-the-modern-era.html.

Goodhart, Sandor (ed.) (2000). *Reading Stephen Sondheim.* New York: Garland Publishing.

Gordon, Joanne (1992). *Art Isn't Easy: The Theater of Stephen Sondheim.* New York: Da Capo Press.

Gordon, Joanne (ed.) (2014). *Stephen Sondheim: A Casebook.* London: Routledge.

Hutson, Nick (2007). 'Attend the Tale: "Sweeney Todd" Exclusive with Stephen Sondheim.' *Broadway World*, 20 December. www.broadwayworld.com/article/Attend-the-Tale-Sweeney-Todd-Exclusive-with-Stephen-Sondheim-20071220#.

Ilson, Carol (1992). *Harold Prince: From 'Pajama Game' to 'Phantom of the Opera'.* New York: Proscenium Publishers.

Ito, Ken (2008). *An Age of Melodrama: Family, Gender and Social Hierarchy.* Redwood: Stanford University Press.

Kakutani, Michiko (1987). 'Beyond Happily Ever After.' *New York Times*, 30 August. www.nytimes.com/books/98/07/19/specials/sondheim-happily.html.

Kirsch, Adam (2011). 'The Art of Making Art.' *Tablet Magazine.* www.tabletmag.com/jewish-arts-and-culture.

Knapp, Raymond (2016). 'Tem(ed)porality and Control in Sondheim's Middle Period: From Company to Sunday in the Park with George.' In Nancy van Deusen and Leonard Michael Koff (eds), *Time: Sense, Space, Structure.* Leiden, Netherlands: Brill Publishers.

Leavitt, Don (2015). *The Playwrights: Into the Woods.* Utah Shakespeare Festival. www.bard.org/study-guides/the-playwrights-into-the-woods.

Lebrecht, Norman (2015). *Stephen Sondheim: Into the Woods,* Sinfini Music. www.sinfinimusic.com/uk/features/guides/composer-guides/stephen-sondheim-disney-version-of-into-the-woods-musical-a-hit-in-hollywood.

Levy, Emanuel (2007). 'It's not a stage thing – it's a movie.' *Financial Times*, 22 December. www.ft.com/content/2e2c807a-ae00-11dc-97aa-0000779fd2ac.

Libresco, Leah (2014). 'It Only Angels Would Prevail: The Moral Tragedy. *Ethika Politika.* http://ethikapolitika.org/2014/03/03/angels-prevail-moral-tragedy-sweeney-todd/

Lipton, James (1997). 'Stephen Sondheim, The Art of the Musical.' *Paris Review* 142 (Spring 1997). www.theparisreview.org/interviews/1283/the-art-of-the-musical-stephen-sondheim.

McGill, Craig (2014). 'Sweeney Todd: Hypertextuality, intermediality and adaptation.' *Journal of Adaptation in Film and Performance* 7(1), pp. 41–63.

Menton, A. (2000). 'Maternity, Madness and Art in the Theatre of Stephen Sondheim.' In Sandor Goodhart (ed.), *Reading Stephen Sondheim*. New York: Garland Publishing, pp. 61–76.

Nogee, Rori (2015). 'Broadway in Movies: Musical Theatre for the Masses.' *New York Life*. www.tracysnewyorklife.com/2015/01/broadway-in-movies-musical-theater-for.html.

Peitzmen, Louis (2015). 'Why Stephen Sondheim Is A Genius.' *Buzzfeed News*. www.buzzfeed.com.

Philpotts, Kim (2008). 'Sweeney Todd: His Dark Material.' *The Sondheim Review* 14(4), p. 15. www.sondheimreview.com/.

Riley, Brian (2010). '"It's Man Devouring Man, My Dear": Adapting "Sweeney Todd" for the Screen.' *Literature & Film Quarterly* 38(3), pp. 205–216. http://connection.ebscohost.com/c/essays/52766628/man-devouring-man-my-dear-adapting-sweeney-todd-screen.

Sandhu, Sukhdey (2008). 'Sweeney Todd, demon barber, doesn't cut it.' *Daily Telegraph*, 25 January. www.telegraph.co.uk/culture/film/filmreviews/3670716.

Schiff, Stephen (1993). 'Deconstructing Sondheim.' *The New Yorker Magazine*, 8 March. http://archives.newyorker.com/?i=1993-03-08#folio=CV1.

Schulman, Michael (2014). 'Why "Into the Woods" Matters.' *The New Yorker Magazine*, 24 December. www.newyorker.com/culture/cultural-comment/why-into-the-woods-matters.

Shevchenko, Mila (2008). Melodramatic Scenarios and Modes of Marginality. PhD Thesis, University of Michigan. https://deepblue.lib.umich.edu/bitstream/handle/2027.42/61788/mshevche_1.pdf?sequence=1.

Sutcliffe, Thomas (1987). 'Sondheim and the Musical.' *The Musical Times*, 128 (September 1987). London: Musical Times Publications.

Taylor, Millie (2012). *Musical Theatre, Realism and Entertainment*. Farnham, Surrey: Ashgate Publishing.

Watts, James (2008). '"Woods" Goes Beyond Happily Ever After.' *Tulsa World*. www.tulsaworld.com/scene/woods-goes-beyond-happily-ever-after/article_ac9e01df-4ee1-530d-afed-f0ea9f3f46fa.html.

Wloszczyna, Susan (2007). '"Sweeney" showcases the artistic mayhem of Depp & Burton.' *USA Today*, 14 December. http://usatoday30.usatoday.com/life/movies/news/2007-12-13-burton-depp_N.h.

12

THE LAST FIVE YEARS

Medium, mode and the making of Cathy

Sarah Browne

Jason Robert Brown's musical, *The Last Five Years,* charts the tempestuous relationship between Cathy Hiatt, a struggling actress, and Jamie Wellerstein, aspiring novelist. It premiered in Chicago in 2001, transferring to the Minetta Lane Theatre, off-Broadway, in March of the following year. Although it only ran for a brief period of two months, it garnered a number of award nominations and won the 2002 Drama Desk Award for outstanding music and lyrics.[1] The original cast recording, featuring Norbert Leo Butz as Jamie and Sherie Rene Scott as Cathy, acquired cult status amongst musical theatre aficionados and the sung-through nature of the musical granted the listener an absolute knowledge of the intricacies and intimacies of the relationship at the heart of the story. Whilst Jamie's story runs in chronological order, Cathy's is told in reverse chronological order. The use of reverse chronology in storytelling prompts the audience to forensically examine unfolding events as they are already informed of the outcome of the narrative. The technique had previously been used in theatre in Kaufman and Hart's *Merrily We Roll Along* (1934) and Harold Pinter's play *Betrayal* (1978), later released as a film in 1983. This 'temporal gimmick' (Anderson 2013) undoubtedly contributed to the success of the cast recording; multiple listens revealed further secrets about the chronology of the story and Brown's use of the leitmotif throughout the score. The fractured temporality of the narrative was also reflected on-stage. The characters rarely sing to each other (with the exception of a brief overlap of their timelines in the central musical number 'The Next Ten Minutes') and director Daisy Prince chose to stage each song as a separate vignette, which invited the audience to view the material from two very different and distinct perspectives.

Whilst it can be argued that Prince's presentation of 'distinct set pieces of he said/she said' (Hofler 2002) and the use of reverse chronology force the audience to take sides, the material often prompts a more sympathetic reading of Cathy.

There is a suggestion throughout that Jamie has already moved on from his broken relationship; he is often propelled through the story, whilst Cathy seems stuck in both a dying relationship and a dead-end career. This sense of underlying pathos towards Cathy is aided by the staging of some of the musical numbers. Jamie's opening number, 'Shiksa Goddess', is performed alone on stage directly after his first date with Cathy has ended. The first verse is directed towards the space that Cathy occupied in the previous scene and when Jamie moves into the second verse the revolve of the stage begins to move, suggesting his walk home. With increasing speed, the revolve propels him on his journey as he internally recalls all the previous girls he has encountered throughout his dating years. Jamie's next song similarly suggests perpetual movement; the title alone ('Moving Too Fast') echoes the sense that the trajectory of his career, and the pace of the relationship, is not matched by Cathy. Her songs reinforce a sense of stasis; she tends to reflect on the moment ('Still Hurting', 'I'm a Part of That') and her 'failure to launch' is solidified later in the piece when she sings 'Climbing Uphill'. As a review of the stage production remarks, '*The Last Five Years* is actually her story; his is the next five' (Hofler 2002).

The set design, courtesy of Beowulf Boritt, also acted as a metaphor for Cathy and Jamie's dysfunctional relationship, featuring two circular stages, one standing on its side looming over both the players and the audience and suggesting 'gravity gone haywire … a matching sense of time out of joint' (Brantley in Boritt 2002). The upright circle, actually a scrim, is lit accordingly to suggest the changing seasons and at one point turns bright red following the marriage scene, which, as reviewers pointed out, suggests 'danger ahead' (Sommer 2002).

The complexities of transferring such a story to the screen are therefore multiple. Finding the right language to convey the intimacy of the narrative on screen fell to the director, Richard LaGravenese, who approached the musical as 'scenes from a marriage with music' (LaGravenese in Allen 2015). Working closely with Brown and filming the entire movie over a period of twenty-one days, LaGravenese placed the music at the centre of the shooting process, fitting dolly grips with headphones to ensure that the camera moved in synchronicity with the score. The director made several cinematic decisions that often disrupt and rupture the temporal framework and isolation of the characters portrayed in the stage production. With the exception of the opening number ('Still Hurting'), both characters often sing to each other and appear on screen together in every musical sequence. This is no small feat, particularly given that the musical features some exceptionally private, internal events in the relationship; even as Jamie attempts to hide his infidelity in 'Nobody Needs to Know', Cathy appears on the sofa occupying both his thoughts and the apartment space beyond the bedroom. 'A Summer in Ohio' is transformed into a dialogue between the couple through the inventive use of a Skype conversation, and Jamie recognises things are 'Moving Too Fast' whilst in bed with Cathy. Equally, the film is as much of a love story between the director and New York City as it is between Jamie and Cathy, and shots of the couple in various locations communicate the microscopic nature of the story set against a larger backdrop of continuous movement and change.

Through considering the medium of film, modes of filmmaking and the subsequent impact these decisions have on the position of the spectator, this chapter analyses the ways in which LaGravenese has approached transforming this material from stage to screen. The modes employed by LaGravenese allow the spectator to view the narrative from an entirely different perspective. The casting of the character, and the techniques and camera angles chosen by the director, present opportunities for an alternative reading of the character of Cathy.

The medium of film: signifiers and contexts

In transforming a musical from stage to the medium of film, it must be recognised that intertextuality may be present, that is, 'producers and consumers … may thus be in the position to compare and contrast a current film with a particular previous text' (Dunne 2004: 147). The genre of the film musical is inextricably linked to audience expectation and over time has developed to become more germane to contemporary audiences. *The Last Five Years* played Off Broadway during the post-9/11 winter; it belonged to a specific place and time and was adored by fans who listened to the cast recording on perpetual repeat. Indeed, as one theatre critic proposes:

> people who love stage musicals have learned to dread their movie adaptations; infidelity leading to disaster is pretty much in the contract. So those of us who treasure *The Last Five Years* … were just as happy that it seemed to belong only to us and was such an unlikely prospect for filming. What, after all, was filmic about it? … If we are honest with ourselves, we theater people want great musicals to be untranslatable.
>
> (Green 2015)

Altman (1987) proposes that there are three specific subgenres of the film musical: show (commonly referred to as 'the backstage musical'), fairytale, and folktale, which recalls an earlier time (ibid.: 127). Whilst he asserts that these categories are not exclusive, it is apparent that *The Last Five Years* does not neatly fit into any of them (essentially, to echo Green's words, it is potentially 'untranslatable'), nor can it be considered an overlap. It is therefore perhaps more appropriate to consider the film as a post-studio, auteurist musical, 'a place where directors accorded the status of authors have worked by deliberate choice' (Babington and Evans 1985: 226), which introduces the possibility of analysing the language and stylistic traits of the director.

As in theatre, the study of film as language can be justified through the use of semiotics. Part of the issue in undertaking such analysis is that, in film, 'the signifier and the signified are almost identical' (Monaco 2009: 127), thus resulting in a short-circuit sign. This is perhaps one of the main differences between theatre and screen. In viewing Boritt's set designs for the original production of *The Last Five Years,* we can interpret the up-ended circular stage lying on a vertical plane as representative of something about to topple over and collapse. The addition of folding guest chairs, laid out in the format for a wedding ceremony, further indicates to the audience that the remnants of marriage loom large over the action on stage. Film cannot suggest such signifiers in the same way; it can only state. It is capable of providing a precise depiction of reality and can communicate meaning in both denotative and connotative forms. Monaco argues that 'because film is a product of culture, it has resonances that go beyond its diegesis' (2009: 162). Furthermore, the spectator is aided in the analytic process by considering that the filmmaker has made certain choices, which also add to 'cinematic connotation' (ibid.): camera angles, lighting, soundtrack, movement within and timing of shot, and depth of field. These choices result in paradigmatic connotation.

LaGravenese's cinematic choices for the first few minutes of the film establish the locality of the story. While the credits appear on a black screen, a number of auditory signifiers are introduced; car horns, children playing and the sounds of traffic signify that the story will play out in an urban setting. However, the paradigmatic connotation becomes clearer when we hear car alarms and police sirens specific only to American cities. This is further cemented by the first visual image for the spectator: a New York brownstone apartment, the colour of the brick (almost porcelain against the other much darker apartments in the row) indicating that this is the focal point of the story. Somewhat unusually for film musicals, the narrative has been placed in a specifically local geographical setting. Historically, film musicals have generally used the medium to take advantage of the ability to use wider geographical locations and lavish scenery.[2] Later in the film we are introduced to a lake in Ohio but the vast majority of the story is set in New York. The apartment is held in shot for several seconds before the camera pans upwards to the top floor of the building. It then rests on the top floor window and we glimpse an elderly lady, framed in the light of her television, before zooming quickly down to the similarly lit second floor window, through which we see a pianist. Brown's haunting waltz melody is thus introduced as diegetic sound; the source is visible on the screen and the motif is coming from an instrument occupying the story space.[3] Rick Altman proposes that 'the movement from diegetic sound without music through diegetic music to non-diegetic music without diegetic sound' (1987: 67) forms part of the most common version of the audio dissolve. In this instance, the soundtrack will move from the sounds of the city, through the sequence of the pianist in the upstairs window, into Cathy singing 'Still Hurting'. The speed of camera movement throughout this scene thus far indicates that neither of these windows are the ones through which we will 'see' our story; the main protagonist has yet to be revealed, therefore delaying the introduction of non-diegetic music. The camera and music briefly pause as we reach the third window, shrouded in darkness, and the movement of the lens continues only when the strings are introduced, an example of how closely LaGravenese tracked the camera to the score. The sequence is an example of paradigmatic connotation, but it also illustrates what Monaco refers to as 'syntagmatic connotation' (2009: 163); the shot can be compared to other shots that either follow or, in this case, precede it. Both the movement and timing of the shot, coupled with the auditory signifiers indicate that we have reached the focal point of the story.

The shallow depth of field in this frame signals that the female character (soon to be revealed as Cathy, played by Anna Kendrick) is the most integral element of this scene. She remains in focus, drawing the spectator's attention to her portion of the frame, whilst the background of the apartment appears in soft focus. The looming circular stage of the Minetta Theatre in the original production has been similarly replaced by remnants of a marriage, here represented through various photographs of the happy couple lined up on a mantelpiece. The symbolic use of the mantelpiece is a technique often employed in film that allows the director to reference stories conveyed elsewhere in the narrative. As MacDonald proposes, the display of artefacts is seen as 'specific to the particular family, private, apolitical' (2009: 162). The technique was employed in other film musicals such as *An American in Paris* (1951) and *Moulin Rouge* (2001): 'the continuousness of the tracking of shots that register the varied objects suggests that all the events they represent are parts of a single, evolving set of … conditions that viewers can either pretend to ignore, or engage' (ibid.). The sequence becomes a voyeuristic glimpse into the anguish and pain Cathy is experiencing, further reinforced by the movement of the camera, which circles around her, according to the 180 degree rule, interrogating her from every angle; her stillness is set is sharp relief. Throughout the song, the camera pans around the apartment to provide us with further signifiers, mementoes of her marriage. 'Psychologically, the cut is the truer approximation of our natural perception. First one subject has our attention, then the other; we are seldom interested in the intervening space' (Monaco 2009: 196), therefore choosing to pan and linger, rather than cut to these items shows that the director intended our attention to be drawn to these objects, placing import on each and indicating they are integral to the narrative.

The camera pan and linger device is used at several points throughout the sequence, revealing signifiers that unlock clues to Cathy's current emotional state. Brown's lyrics to the final song in the musical ('I Could Never Rescue You' – the song based on the musical motif we have already heard from the pianist in the apartment) are shown in print on the letter left for Cathy; a screwed up, discarded piece of paper next to it indicates this was not something that was penned easily. When Cathy moves to the bedroom she removes her jewellery, including her bracelet, wedding ring and watch. She pauses briefly to survey the bare status of her hands and walks to the bed, whilst the camera lingers on the jewellery, signifying that these items were also mementoes, discarded reminders of a failed marriage and will be revisited at some point in the story.

The medium of film has also afforded the opportunity to insert moments of dance, previously non-existent in the stage production. Although these moments are fleeting, and only occur twice in the film, it is worth considering the ways in which LaGravenese has used such sequences to pay homage to the 'traditional' MGM studio musical. The first of these instances occurs in 'Moving Too Fast' and appears to reinforce Altman's proposition that often, in the film musical, 'dancing is just rhythmical walking' (1987: 68). In the bridge, or release, of the song, Jamie has twice stated that he keeps 'rolling on', so on the third and final statement of this phrase movement occurs in order to symbolise the climactic dramatic moment. As Jamie walks through the streets of New York, other pedestrians dressed in similar business attire circle him as he reaches this lyric, joining him to form a community; perhaps symbolic of the rat race into which he has now been initiated. The ensemble only moves together in unison at the next musical and lyrical cue and the 'normally dominant image track now keeps time to the music track, instead of simply being accompanied by it' (Altman 1987: 69). This type of relationship indicates how LaGravenese approached the material, stating 'it forced me to think in a visual language as opposed to dialogue' (Allen 2015). In discussing the relationship between non-diegetic music and the diegetic space, Heather Laing suggests that where this happens, 'the music becomes a powerful narrative force, displaying its emotionally-motivated control over the normally rationally-motivated sounds and actions' (Laing in Marshall and Stilwell 2000: 9). This same argument could be applied to the use of dance in Jamie's sequence; the dance becomes a powerful narrative force, displaying and reinforcing the character's heightened emotional response to his newly achieved success. The movement does not disrupt the realism of the scene but grows organically from the character's motivations and emotions.

The second instance of movement in this film musical appears in 'A Summer in Ohio' as diegetic dance. This occurs in a performative context where the dancers are aware they are dancing because it's a rehearsal scenario, prompted by the book of the musical. Of the two movement moments, the second is perhaps the more comfortable inclusion, largely because the relationship between dance and the film musical is a complex one where non-diegetic dance sequences are often placed in a non-realistic setting.

In an age when the lavish studio film musical is considered nothing more than a historical artefact, particularly in terms of its treatment of the dance break, Cohan suggests that the genre could be approached through 'heightening, disrupting, revising or multiplying the codes of cinematic realism ordinarily determining a film's diegesis' (2001: 2). In fact, the medium of the film musical has always been known for experimenting with techniques, 'technically, cinematically [and] choreographically' (Hansen in Grishakova and Ryan 2010: 147) and it is interesting to note how LaGravenese has revised the codes of cinematic realism during these choreographic moments to slightly alter the relationship between song, dance and its realistic context. In allowing dance to grow organically from the real-world realm, he has skilfully navigated perhaps the most complex element of the film musical: the inexplicable desire that prompts the on-screen character to move from song to dance. Both sequences have been integrated so carefully that the real-world contexts of the scenes remain intact.

Mode: film musical as documentary and observing the couple's decline

In terms of the primary modes of filmmaking, there has been a long-held binary opposition between realism and formalism. The Hollywood film has often found ways to balance these two extremes by employing various modes of filmmaking in the approach to the narrative, which can be arranged on the realist-formalist scale. Whereas realistic films are underpinned by an 'ethos of creating credible portrayals of daily life' (Etherington-Wright and Doughty 2011: 101), a formalist style will often displace a sense of reality, adopting a change in tone and style to do so. It can be argued that by their very nature of being utopian[4], film musicals are almost always formalist.

It is interesting to note that LaGravenese employs both methods in *The Last Five Years*. For this reason, the film stands apart from many film musicals, refusing to fit neatly into any single category. It is clear that the content of the musical has dictated these decisions and the intimacy of the story certainly accounts for the realist, documentary nature of the form. The main filming technique he employs throughout the musical appears to echo that of the documentary tradition. Bill Nichols, in his publication *Introduction to Documentary* (2010), proposes six modes of documentary: poetic, expository, participatory, reflexive, performative and observational. *The Last Five Years* fits neatly into the final category. This particular style of filming emerged as a result of advancements in technology,[5] allowing filmmakers to record events unfolding in a number of locations. More importantly, the filmmaker follows the action as a neutral observer, and the audience is left to determine their own conclusions. Although what appears on the screen is fiction and not a documentation of an actual lived experience of consenting participants, the observational documentary mode of filming is effective because it 'affirms a sense of commitment or engagement with the immediate, intimate, and personal as it occurs' (Nichols 2010: 113).

The realist observational documentary style is typified in the second scene of *The Last Five Years*, in which we are introduced to Jamie at the start of his relationship ('Shiksa Goddess'). Both Jamie and Cathy are in shot for the majority of the scene and the audience views the unfolding sexual encounter through the eyes of the filmmaker. This voyeuristic sequence is shot in almost uncomfortable close-up; the somewhat shaky, amateur-style footage (a pseudo-documentary filming technique) indicates we are following the action as it happens and at one point the camera appears to rest on the pillow, joining the young lovers in their most intimate of moments. Percussion and a drum kit now also feature in the newly re-orchestrated score and the bass line is high in the final mix, an auditory indication that we are now following a different timeline to the reverse chronology of Cathy's story. The realist nature of the filming throughout much of this sequence is evident in the naturalistic lighting – sunlight streaming through the window of the bedroom – and the movement of the camera. In sharp contrast to the revolve used in the stage production, the film sequence is set during the first date, thus eradicating the option of being privy to Jamie's private recollections on his return journey home. At this point, LaGravenese moves from the realistic style of filming and moves to formalism, more specifically a technique known as defamiliarization.

The sequence quickly shifts to Jamie opening a non-existent door in the bedroom to reveal his previous female encounters; 'the narrative takes an unexpected turn of events', a device that often serves to instigate a flashback (Etherington-Wright and Doughty 2011:57). This formalist tool rearranges the plot order, connecting both present and past and, as Turim proposes, implies the concepts of memory and history, 'understood either as a story-being-told or a subjective memory' (Turim 2013:1). The second verse of 'Shiksa Goddess' fulfils both criteria and cinematically this is a useful technique to employ at this point in the narrative; in the stage production we realise that these women do not constitute fond memories for Jamie, in the film version we understand exactly the reasons why. His interaction with these women in the flashback is an important source of information relating to the character, implying 'a psychoanalytic dimension of personality' (ibid.: 12).[6]

Similarly, Cathy is afforded her own flashback later in the film during the song 'I Can Do Better than That', which, when following both timelines in chronological order, occurs at the same point in the narrative as Jamie's. During a car journey, Cathy also remembers the events prior to their life together and the flashback features her move into an apartment in the city and a single previous sexual encounter. This is her subjective memory further signalled by the shallow depth of field used in the shot during the car journey: although Jamie is in the foreground of the shot, he remains in soft focus whilst selective focus draws the spectator's attention to Cathy. The flashback is equally as brief but the spectator is presented with two very different histories; Jamie's stream of women, coupled with the final sequence of his flashback showing his cheek being slapped by 'Janie Stein', juxtaposed against Cathy being dumped by her one sexual encounter, a guy from her class with 'some very well placed tattoos'. These flashbacks 'terminate at precisely the point at which they must be sealed off, in which the imperatives of fixing interpretations and reaching judgments in the present must be imposed' (Turim 2013:12), and in this case, the resultant effect is that the spectator is invited to reach further conclusions about where responsibility for the demise of the marriage lies.

In considering flashbacks as alternative worlds, Walters (2008) proposes that the skill in utilising such a device is the filmmaker's ability to 'handle a complex departure from the rudiments of everyday existence without fracturing the coherent relationships essential to our making sense of the events we witness as viewers' (Walters 2008: 214), which is exactly how LaGravenese has handled these complex moments of song. On stage, the audience is required to use their imagination in order to process the fleeting information provided regarding these previous relationships. On screen, the director has incorporated both realist (observational documentary mode) and formalist (flashback sequences) modes of filmmaking in such a way that ensures the world(s) of the story remain organised and coherent, providing additional contextual information and thus revealing a further dimension to the psychology of both characters.

Cathy and the camera lens: rethinking key characters.

Analysing the depiction of Cathy in the film version of *The Last Five Years* perhaps requires the spectator to adopt a feminist 'politics of vision' (Mulvey 1989: 77). In doing so, it must be acknowledged that the feminist film critic must explore the range of positions the text makes available, and in her chapter entitled 'Pleasurable Negotiations', Christine Gledhill proposes that she will be 'interested in some readings more than others' (Gledhill in Thornham 1999: 162). Therefore the reading of key moments offered in this chapter may also be subject to further negotiation.

Laura Mulvey's initial work in the field of feminist film theory helped to define spectatorship, highlighting how 'film reflects, reveals and even plays on the straight, socially established interpretation of sexual difference which controls images, erotic ways of looking and spectacle' (Mulvey in Thornham 1999: 58). She subsequently proposes that the gaze of the camera, the spectator and the characters within the visual images all occupy the masculine space. This therefore prompts the feminist film critic to read against the grain (by employing the oppositional gaze), seeking ways to consider the female spectator and subsequently leading to work in the field that highlights an emphasis 'not on the physical appearance of the women; rather … on their interiority' (Bolton 2011: 1). This interiority may, as Bolton proposes, be communicated by acknowledging the female character's history or through a 'feminization of the language and space of the film' (ibid.: 3). Revealing the inner thoughts, desires and fears of a female character allows the spectator to move beyond the exteriority and objectification of women on screen in the visual form, considering instead a female subjectivity. Drawing on the work of theorist Luce Irigaray, Bolton explores how a feminist politics of vision can be reconsidered in film.

Of course, the difficulty with applying this theoretical framework to *The Last Five Years* lies in the irreconcilable fact that the story is about a relationship between a man and a woman, thus suggesting binary differences from the outset. Therefore, Irigaray's proposition for self-expression and subjectivity of the female becomes somewhat problematic when there is the possibility of defining woman as male 'Other', instead of the preferred option of male and female as separate and different. In consequence,

> if relationships between men and women are to be represented in a way that accounts for the equally developed subjectivity of both individuals, then there needs to be evidence of the impact of the changing status of their subjectivity as they become more involved.
>
> (Bolton 2011: 58)

The Last Five Years ensures that this changing status is evidenced throughout, mainly as a result of the chronology of the narrative. Breaking tradition with the format of the Broadway musical, which frequently utilises the marriage trope to represent reconciliation, union and 'happy-ever-after', Jamie and Cathy's marriage scene occurs at the mid-point of the narrative arc, ensuring that the audience understands the changing status of these two individuals, before and after their union. Furthermore, Cathy's dramatic arc hurtles towards a much more optimistic finale; her perceived lack of strength in the opening number is eradicated with each musical moment. Despite the negative connotation of the title, Cathy's penultimate number ('Climbing Uphill') proves to be a powerful moment of interiority in which she voices her thoughts, fears and desires. This is further underscored by the filming techniques employed by LaGravenese, where the male gaze is exposed as artifice. In both audition sequences presented in the film, Cathy is placed centre stage in a theatre auditorium, scrutinised by a creative team of directors and producers. She notes later that they are 'always men', even though the first panel consists of two men and a female; the latter seems to react positively to Cathy's audition. She is alone on stage lit by a single spotlight, which draws further attention to the act of scrutiny; the male gaze is at play, the camera, the spectator and the characters on screen are all forced to simply 'look'. This scopophilic sequence is then repeated later in the song, with the spot acting as a backlight to Cathy as she prepares for the audition. This lighting state also signals to the spectator that the 'male gaze' is about to be activated once more. What then follows is a moment of interiority for the female character, and her internal thoughts are communicated even in the midst of this masculine space. These are complex thoughts, seemingly random, but they offer the female spectator a moment of identification and empathy with Cathy. Even in the midst of these thoughts, Cathy draws further attention to the male gaze, imploring the panel to 'stop looking at that, look at me'. The artificial male gaze is referred to one final time at the end of the verse as the camera cuts quickly to the male pianist who also, unusually, looks back.

Throughout the audition sequence, Cathy has highlighted a number of moments where she recognises other women in similar positions. In the stage version, Cathy makes fleeting reference to the other women waiting in line. This occurs in lyric time, with no accompanying visual reference and so the moment is brief, a mere mention-in-passing. The audience does not have time to reflect on how this might alter Cathy's self-esteem, or impact on her career. In fact, references to other women throughout the stage production usually fall into the domain of Jamie; he interacts with Elise in 'Nobody Needs to Know' (who is presented as a faceless being in the bed scene) and references her several times when charting the progress, and subsequent success, of his career. Being presented with these images on screen in the audition sequence – which are not afforded to the theatrical audience in the stage production – allows the female spectator to recognise the (patriarchal) constraints that have restrained and defined women, particularly in a male-dominated business that often has to make judgments about how a woman looks and sounds. Cathy uses these experiences to inform her final resolutions in the last verse of the song.

The cinematic version of this sequence is particularly powerful; her failed audition attempts are juxtaposed against Jamie's success, shown in a bookshop reading of his new bestseller. Cathy remains standing at the rear of the room, framed in shot by several other women. The score fades in as the camera slowly zooms in on her, and, as the moment grows in intensity we hear Jamie's words, reading from his novel: the internal voice of his fictional narrator describing the female heroine of the story, remarking that 'he did not recognise [her] fierceness'. When Cathy sings 'I will not be the girl stuck at home in the 'burbs', her resolve has clearly changed, indicated by her body language, which is in contrast to the other women standing in rapt attention around her. It is clear that Cathy has chosen to disengage herself from the moment and her interior thoughts become more important to her than listening to Jamie's reading. This is then further reinforced by the following sequence, which shifts to Cathy and Jamie's bedroom. Tension between the two characters has already been established in the bookshop, instigated only by Cathy's response to the reading, and the ensuing argument is therefore driven largely by her dissatisfaction and annoyance rather than Jamie's, something that is suggested in the stage production. For the first twenty seconds of the following sequence the camera is focused solely on Cathy in the right of the frame. More importantly, Jamie is nothing more than a disembodied voice and consequently, the song ('If I Didn't Believe in You') retains focus on her; she remains in shot throughout, often with Jamie in soft focus or completely out of frame. Employing these techniques aligns the spectator with Cathy's position, firstly through 'lingering, thoughtfully composed, motionless or near-motionless images; intense searching close-ups' (Kuhn 2008: 12) and later in the song, as the camera tracks Cathy's, rather than Jamie's, movements through the apartment.

The techniques employed to depict Cathy on-screen result in her story being both fully-rounded and, more importantly, concluded. Even in the final sequence, Cathy is present as Jamie leaves their apartment for the final time. This is achieved through the use of a crossfade, a transition that utilises a dip to white which often conveys a sense of passing time or location, thus allowing Cathy to be 'present' (albeit it perhaps in Jamie's memory) as he leaves. Her narrative arc is then concluded through the spectator being shown her return home to find the letter. The use of the filming techniques explored above present greater opportunities for the female spectator to align herself with the experiences and interiority of the character of Cathy. Situating Cathy's thoughts as the catalyst for these final few scenes allows the spectator to consider how the character's history and subjectivity continue to drive the narrative, providing evidence of the impact of her changing status, therefore demonstrating the equally developed subjectivity of both individuals.

Conclusions

Although this musical is a two-hander, the film version brings new dimensions to the character of Cathy; such dimensions are perhaps rather more nuanced in the stage production. Reviews of the film all testify to this through noting Kendrick's skill in portraying the character on-screen, declaring that she 'emerges to magnificent effect' (Romney 2015), 'makes it memorable' (Burr 2015) and 'qualifies as the movie's secret weapon' (Mondello 2015). The *New York Magazine* notes that 'the camera moves with heightened sensitivity, as if on currents of emotion, and Kendrick is infinitely winning' (Edelstein 2015). Indeed, the casting of Anna Kendrick in the role of Cathy indicates how LaGravenese perhaps wanted to re-balance the story. Kendrick, who achieved success and recognition largely as a result of her role in the musical comedy *Pitch Perfect* (2012), was considered the 'star-billing' for *The Last Five Years*. Cast alongside Jordan (a relative unknown on screen although not on stage), Kendrick appeared to be both the selling-point of the film and the focus of the majority of critical reviews; the casting alone reveals some of the intentions of the work on screen and perhaps prompts the spectator to pay more attention to Cathy.

Furthermore, through employing the techniques explored above, LaGravenese has not only acknowledged Cathy's specific individual histories but has reinforced the interiority of the character rather than how she looks on-screen, thus placing the spectator in alignment with Cathy's narrative. This is a remarkable achievement given the 'star-status' of Kendrick, but the documentary mode of filming and the ability of the medium of film to reorganise and present scenes in a wider context has allowed the spectator to experience a more rounded representation of the character of Cathy, often viewing her relationship to those around her and, more powerfully, allowing her to reveal her innermost thoughts during moments that, in the stage version, appeared to focus solely on Jamie. The documentary filming mode utilised here lends an authenticity to the work perhaps somewhat less apparent in the stage production. This sense of authenticity gains the spectator's trust and subsequently prompts them to analyse and draw conclusions from what is seen on screen, something which the liveness of musical theatre can often overwhelm.

In conclusion, *The Last Five Years* always appeared to be an unusual choice to make the transition from stage to screen. Historically, the film musical has always celebrated and relished the challenges presented in cinematically representing the 'genre's potential impossibility' (Cohan 2001: 2), nowhere better exemplified than in the artificiality of song, and spectacular dance numbers featuring endless chorus lines. Whilst the latter would not be a primary consideration in transferring *The Last Five Years* to the screen, the sung-through nature of the material, coupled with the intimacy of the story – rarely seen in the studio film musical – were unique challenges of their own. Whilst the form and structure of stage musicals had continued to progress, the film musical had not kept pace and the genre had subsequently lost its 'once important cultural function as the epitome of mass-produced, mass-consumed entertainment' (Cohan 2001: 1). Adapting a musical that featured only two lead actors and little to no dialogue would certainly require an experimental approach to the twenty-first century film musical.

Hansen asserts that the difficulty for the film musical lies in its inability to be categorised by a general model in terms of how it handles integration, proposing that either the diegesis' realism or the musical 'universe' is subordinated in favour of the other at any given moment. He notes that modern musicals (referring to those produced in the early years of the twenty-first century) 'more exclusively follow[s] only one of these strategies' and more importantly, that different audiences and periods have 'different means of fascination' (Hansen in Grishakova and Ryan 2010: 161). Contemporary audiences are acclimatised to the realist, documentary mode of film-making employed in narrative cinema of the twenty-first century. Although this is not a technique evident in other film musicals of this period, it was certainly employed widely in other genres, for example, Woody Allen's *Husbands and Wives* (1992), *28 Days Later* (2002) and *Black Swan* (2010), all of which lend a sense of realism and authenticity to the narrative. In his approach to filming Brown's musical, LaGravenese has recognised the merits of the documentary mode, which allow him to capitalise on the intimacy of the narrative to present the material in largely realist terms. As one reviewer astutely summarises; 'onstage, the perpetually elevated emotions of song are balanced by an equivalent suppression of visual information' (Green 2015), and this is perhaps why the documentary mode lends itself so well to the material; it provides authentic visual images for the spectator to 'fill in the gaps' of the stage production. Furthermore, the way in which the camera is so closely attuned to both the music and the actors allows the spectator to 'naturalize the singing … in relation to his or her real world model' (Hansen in Grishakova and Ryan 2010: 161). There are few musicals that could withstand such treatment but LaGravenese has modified the modes of the medium of film to combine techniques that highlight, authenticate and intensify the intimacy of *The Last Five Years*, and which position the spectator in a space that allows them to fully explore the subjectivities of both characters.

Notes

1   The Off-Broadway production received Drama Desk nominations in the following categories; Best Musical, Best Actor in a Musical, Best Actress in a Musical, Outstanding Orchestrations and Outstanding Set Design (Simonson 2002).
2   For example, the 1972 film musical of *Cabaret* was able to move the action away from the Kit Kat Club into the streets and surrounding areas of Berlin. Similarly, the 1979 film version of *Hair* widens its geographical focus from the East Village, instead moving from the plains of Oklahoma to Central Park to Nevada.
3   Other occasions where the director has used the score as diegetic sound include the introduction to 'A Summer in Ohio' (played by a member of Cathy's troupe, rehearsing in the theatre auditorium) and the introduction to 'A Miracle Would Happen'. Jason Robert Brown also makes an appearance as the pianist who 'hates' Cathy in the audition scene for 'When You Come Home to Me'.
4   Dyer (1992) proposes that the film musical does not present models of utopian worlds, 'rather the utopianism is contained in the feelings it embodies' (20). His study highlights the non-realist elements of the film musical, recognising that free-editing (switching between visual sequences) is often dictated by the music(al) rather than 'real-world logic' (54).

5   These include the introduction of lightweight 16mm, shoulder mounted cameras, portable sync-sound systems and multi-directional microphones.
6   Turim relates functions of the flashback to Roland Barthes's 1975 structural analysis, *S/Z*, in which he defines five codes of meaning; the process outlined above is categorised as the semic code.

Bibliography

Akande, Z. (2015). *Richard LaGravenese Dishes on 'The Last Five Years' and His Love of Theater.* www.indiewire.com/article/richard-lagravenese-dishes-on-the-last-five-years-and-his-love-of-theater-20150209. Accessed 26 March 2016.

Allen, N. (2015). *Richard LaGravenese on following the music of 'The Last Five Years'.* http://thefilmstage.com/features/richard-lagravenese-on-following-the-music-of-the-last-five-years/. Accessed 3 April 2016.

Altman, R. (1987). *The American Film Musical.* Bloomington: Indiana University Press.

Anderson, L. V. (2013). *Why Theater Nerds Love The Last Five Years.* www.slate.com/blogs/browbeat/2013/04/02/the_last_five_years_revival_is_jason_robert_brown_s_beloved_new_york_musical.html. Accessed 26 March 2016.

Babington, B. and P.W. Evans (1985). *Blue Skies and Silver Linings: Aspects of the Hollywood Musical.* Manchester: Manchester University Press.

Barthes, R. (1975). *S/Z. An Essay.* New York: Hill and Wang.

Bolton, L. (2011). *Film and Female Consciousness: Irigaray, Cinema and Thinking Women.* Basingstoke: Palgrave Macmillan.

Boritt, B. (2002). *Beowolf Boritt Design: The Last Five Years.* www.beowulfborittdesign.com/off-broadway/last-five-years. Accessed 26 March 2016.

Burr, T. (2015). 'Anna Kendrick makes "The Last Five Years" memorable.' *Boston Globe,* 19 February. www.bostonglobe.com/arts/movies/2015/02/19/movie-review-the-last-five-years/iQRsTTz0jj5FXFhVqHZiFL/story.html. Accessed 1 April 2016.

Cohan, S. (ed.) (2001). *Hollywood Musicals: The Film Reader.* London: Routledge.

Dunne, M. (2004). *American Film Musical Themes and Forms.* Jefferson: McFarland.

Dyer, R. (1992). *Only Entertainment.* London: Routledge.

Edelstein, D. (2015). 'Anna Kendrick is infinitely winning in the tastefully adapted *The Last Five Years.*' *New York Magazine,* 9 February. www.vulture.com/2015/02/movie-review-the-last-five-years.html# . Accessed 1 April 2016.

Etherington-Wright, C. and R. Doughty (2011). *Understanding Film Theory.* Basingstoke: Palgrave Macmillan.

Green, J. (2015). 'A Theater Critic's View of *The Last Five Years* Onscreen.' 13 February. www.vulture.com/2015/02/theater-critic-on-the-last-five-years-onscreen.html. Accessed 17 September 2016.

Gledhill, C. (1999). 'Pleasurable Negotiations.' In S. Thornham (ed.) (1999). *Feminist Film Theory.* Edinburgh: Edinburgh University Press.

Grishakova, M. and M.L. Ryan (eds) (2010). *Intermediality and Storytelling.* Boston: de Gruyter.

Hansen, P.K. (2010). 'All Talking! All Singing! All Dancing! Prolegomena: On Film Musicals and Narrative.' In M. Grishakova and M.L. Ryan (eds) (2010). *Intermediality and Storytelling.* Boston: de Gruyter.

Hofler, R. (2002). 'Review: *The Last Five Years.*' *Variety,* 3 March. http://variety.com/2002/legit/reviews/the-last-five-years-5-1200551060/. Accessed 17 September 2016.

Kuhn, A. (2008). *Ratcatcher.* Basingstoke: Palgrave Macmillan.

Laing, H. (2000). 'Emotion by Numbers: Music, Song and the Musical.' In B. Marshall and R. Stilwell (eds) (2000). *Musicals: Hollywood and Beyond.* Exeter: Intellect.

MacDonald, S. (2009). *Avant-Garde Film: Motion Studies.* Cambridge: Cambridge University Press.

Marshall, B. and R. Stilwell (eds) (2000). *Musicals: Hollywood and Beyond.* Exeter: Intellect.

Monaco, J. (2009). *How to Read a Film: Movies, Media and Beyond.* 4th edn. New York: Oxford University Press.

Mondello, B. (2015). 'Love from A to Z – and back again – in "The Last Five Years".' *NPR,* 13 February. www.npr.org/2015/02/13/385744743/love-from-a-to-z-and-back-again-in-the-last-five-years. Accessed 1 April 2016.

Mulvey, L. (1989). *Visual and Other Pleasures.* Basingstoke: Palgrave Macmillan.

Mulvey, L. (1999). 'Visual and Other Pleasures.' In S. Thornham (ed.) (1999). *Feminist Film Theory.* Edinburgh: Edinburgh University Press.

Nichols, B. (2010). *Introduction to Documentary.* Bloomington: Indiana University Press.

Romney, R. (2015). 'The Last Five Years Review: An engaging musical rom-com.' *The Guardian,* 19 April. www.theguardian.com/film/2015/apr/19/last-five-years-review-anna-kendrick-jordan-jamie. Accessed 1 April 2016.

Simonson, R. (2002). '*Millie, Success* Lead 2002 Drama Desk Nominations.' www.playbill.com/article/millie-success-lead-2002-drama-desk-nominations-com-105430. Accessed 26 March 2016.

Sommer, E. (2002). 'A Curtain Up Review: *The Last Five Years.*' 5 March. www.curtainup.com/last5years.html. Accessed 17 September 2016.

Thornham, S. (ed.) (1999). *Feminist Film Theory.* Edinburgh: Edinburgh University Press.

Turim, M. (2013). *Flashbacks in Film: Memory and History.* London: Routledge.

Walters, J. (2008). *Alternative Worlds in Hollywood Cinema.* Bristol: Intellect.

13

THE TROUBLE WITH 'LITTLE GIRLS'

Annie on the big (and small) screen

Olaf Jubin

In less than four decades, the 1977 Broadway musical *Annie* (music by Charles Strouse, lyrics by Martin Charnin and book by Thomas Meehan) has been filmed three times, twice for the cinema (in 1982 and 2014) and once for television (1999). Yet while the TV movie was a sizeable hit, the two film releases were despised by critics and turned into major box-office disappointments. The following chapter endeavours to answer the question of why exactly the story about the irrepressible little optimist has defied adaptation to the big screen.

On stage, *Annie* was one of the 'biggest musical-comedy hits of all time' (Mordden 2003: 223), running for 2,377 performances on Broadway, winning seven Tony Awards[1] and for a while – according to James M. Nederlander, one of its original producers – becoming 'the most profitable musical of all time' (quoted in Turan 1982). Since its original US production, the show has been revived twice in New York, in 1997 (239 performances) and 2012 (487 performances).[2] Nonetheless, the heart-warming story of the red-haired orphan and her loyal dog Sandy who win over the heart of billionaire businessman Oliver 'Daddy' Warbucks is not nowadays regarded as crucial in the development of the genre. Comprehensive historical overviews of Broadway musical theatre like *The Oxford Handbook of the American Musical* (Knapp *et al*. 2001: 291, 373) or Larry Stempel's *Showtime* (Stempel 2010: 500, 631) both refer to the show only in passing, while Raymond Knapp's groundbreaking two-volume sociocultural exploration of *The American Musical* (Knapp 2005 and 2006) doesn't mention it at all. More journalistic accounts, like those by Ethan Mordden and Denny Martin Flinn, vary wildly in their estimation of the show, with the former describing it as an 'inventively busy musical comedy', while conceding that it is not in the same league as true Broadway classics such as *Gypsy* or *My Fair Lady* (Mordden 2003: 227). Flinn is less generous, claiming that *Annie* would never have succeeded if it hadn't arrived at the 'tail end of a disastrous Broadway musical season' (Flinn 1997: 446). The misbegotten attempts by the authors to come up with a sequel, resulting in one outright disaster, *Annie 2: Miss Hannigan's Revenge* (1989), and one off-Broadway production which barely left a mark, *Annie Warbucks* (1993), may also retroactively have put a blemish on the original's reputation. Martin Gottfried's succinct verdict indicates how most theatre historians would situate the musical: '*Annie* is not great or significant, it is an old-fashioned book show built on the theater's corniest devices – children, Christmas, even a dog – but … it works' (Gottfried 1980: 160).

In spite of composer Strouse's claim that 'a comic strip is an ideal basis for a musical comedy because they are similar forms of popular American culture [as] both deal in broad strokes, telling simple stories in as few words as possible' (Strouse 2008: 210), there are only a handful of musicals based upon a cartoon,[3] of which *Annie* may be the most famous example. The source material for the 1977 Broadway smash, *Little Orphan Annie*, was created by Harold Gray (1894–1968) and took its name from James Whitcomp Riley's 1885 poem *Little Orphant* [*sic*] *Annie*. The daily comic strip was first published on 5 August 1924 in the *New York Daily News*. It soon became a bit hit with the public, topping a Fortune poll in 1937 of the most popular comic strips (Young and Young 2002: 268); at its peak, when it was syndicated in more than 500 US newspapers, it reached 47 million readers (Turan 1982). The comic even survived the death of its creator in the late 1960s: it was continued by other writers until its cancellation on 12 June 2010. At that time it ran in less than 20 publications (Wursthorn 2010).

How to deal with the 'New Deal' in family entertainment

Harold Gray was notorious for his extreme right-wing politics: he strongly believed in unregulated capitalism and thus abhorred liberals and especially Franklin D. Roosevelt. As a result, Annie and 'Daddy' Warbucks were constantly involved in the fight against organized labour, communists and the New Deal (Hill 2012: 90). The comic strip's radical political stance – in the late 1930s Gray even had Warbucks die from despair at the re-election of FDR[4] – didn't sit well with everyone, though, and the comic was attacked as early as 1935 by *The New Republic* as 'fascism in the funnies' (Hill 2012: 90).

Yet when Meehan, Charnin and Strouse began to musicalize the material in the crisis-ridden 1970s, their personal political convictions and the sociocultural mood after Watergate led them to drastically change Annie and what she stood for. In the words of Logan Hill, the creative team 'threw out everything but the rich man, the upbeat girl and the dog' (Hill 2012: 90). The three New Yorkers 'wanted to hearken back to a time when the White House was dedicated to the welfare of the American people' (Hill 2012: 90), and thus imbued the musical with a spirit of optimistic liberalism to the point where Roosevelt spontaneously conceives the New Deal after hearing Annie sing 'Tomorrow', her life-affirming ode to a better future.

In addition, the musical contains a song set among the destitute in a shantytown that sharply criticizes Roosevelt's predecessor, 'We Want to Thank You, Herbert

Hoover',[5] and also highlights the desperate situation faced by the rest of the country via an announcement on the radio: 'According to my latest figures, there are now fifteen million Americans out of work and nearly fifty million with no visible means of support' (Meehan *et al.* 1977: II–3–13). Ending with a cheerful production number called 'A New Deal for Christmas', the show was later celebrated – as Strouse proudly recalls – for 'helping to salve our post-Watergate wounds' (Strouse 2008: 239). Therefore the musical is far more blatantly political than many other family shows, which may explain why both of its US revivals were produced when a Democrat resided in the White House.

Not surprisingly, with President Ronald Reagan riding high on a wave of jingoistic conservatism, both 'We'd Like to Thank You, Herbert Hoover' and 'A New Deal for Christmas' were cut when the stage musical was filmed for the first time in 1982 (Hill 2012: 90). Neither the film studio nor executive producer Ray Stark wanted to offend a large segment of the American public, mainly because they couldn't afford to: they had too much riding on the project. Film critic Pauline Kael has claimed that the problems with the 1982 movie started when Columbia bought the screen rights for the record sum of $9.5 million: 'From that point on, the picture had to be thought of as a musical that would draw enormous audiences, and any chance for a film that might have a goofy, lyrical quality – might have floated – disappeared' (Kael 1984: 344).

1982: a mega-budget *Annie* – brash and bloated

Following the film industry's adage that one must spend big in order to win big, the movie wound up with production costs of around $50 million, making it one of the most expensive movies ever made (Kael 1984: 346), but then Hollywood insiders and other business analysts had high hopes for the adaptation, expecting grosses similar to those of *The Sound of Music*.[6] Consequently, the merchandise machinery was operating in high gear; there were tie-in deals with the Marriott hotel chain, Random House, Sears Roebuck & Company, Knickerbocker Toys, Procter & Gamble and other interested parties. As Kenneth Turan expounds: 'More than 50 companies [had] agreed to manufacture some 500 *Annie* products, everything from umbrellas, wigs, lunch boxes, dog accessories, a Parker Brothers board game and a line of Marvel comics to *Annie* ice cream, *Annie* cookies and *Annie* designer jeans' (Turan 1982). Inflated expectations are one explanation why everything in the movie is bloated, including its running time – with 126 minutes, the film version is nearly as long as the original stage production, which is 133 minutes without the interval.[7] Whereas the theatrical version succeeded partly because of its pared-down simplicity (Mordden 2003: 226), the film shows an 'unwieldy, top-heavy elephantitis' (Hirschhorn 1981: 420).

When assembling the creative team, Stark refused to hire Randall Kleiser (who had directed the hugely profitable film version of *Grease*, 1978) and rejected Thomas Meehan's draft for a screenplay without even reading it (Turan 1982). Instead he insisted on hiring John Huston, legendary for films such as *The Maltese*

Falcon (1941), *The Treasure of the Sierra Madre* (1948) and *African Queen* (1951), even though Huston had never worked extensively with children or directed a musical before.[8] The numbers themselves were entrusted to Tony Award-winning stage director Joe Layton (*Barnum*, 1981) and choreographer Arlene Phillips on the strength of her work for a Dr. Pepper commercial (Turan 1982). Stark organized a year-long, nationwide and widely publicized search for the right girl to play the red-haired orphan, auditioning 9,000 hopefuls (Turan 1982), the largest star-search since David O. Selznick went to similar lengths to find Scarlett O'Hara for *Gone with the Wind* (1939). In the end, ten-year old Aileen Quinn from Pennsylvania won the coveted role.

Screenwriting duties were taken over by Carol Sobieski, who according to Stark was instructed to 'put skin and complexion and flesh on what was the skeleton of a musical' (quoted in Turan 1982). Her attempts to 'make the characters more real', however, only led to a movie peopled with 'timeworn, adorable show-business types of real people' (Kael 1984: 344). Sobieski also introduced a new climax on the B & O Bridge on the Baltimore and Ohio Railroad that is both confusing and too suspenseful for little children. The plot changes necessitated additional musical numbers and as a result, the film cut six songs from the original Broadway score and added five new ones: 'Dumb Dog', 'Sandy', 'Sign', 'Let's Go to the Movies', and 'We Got Annie', with the last two intended to show off the impressive terpsichorean skills of Ann Reinking, who played Warbucks' secretary Grace.

Arlene Phillips later admitted that she 'was terrified when Ray approached me. All I'd ever done was these sexy dance things, how was I going to go from that to little girls?' (quoted in Turan 1982). To this author it seems that Phillips tries very hard to channel her Canadian colleague Onna White, who had staged the well-conceived if rather traditional dance numbers in the now classic family musicals *Oliver!* (1968) and *Pete's Dragon* (1978), and had shown particular affinity for incorporating children into large production numbers, without ever achieving White's aptitude or charm. Pauline Kael confirms Phillips' trepidation, arguing that the former dancer was 'not, perhaps the best choice for comic, folkloristic invention' and that every one of her dance sequences 'seems to be trying too hard to be upbeat and irresistible, and it's all ungainly' (Kael 1984: 344). Other critics were blunter, calling Phillips' work and the way it was edited 'completely incoherent' (Editors 1983: 148). With Ann Reinking, who had already lit up the screen in Bob Fosse's *All That Jazz* (1979), the English choreographer had one of the greatest of all Broadway dancers at her command, but failed to come up with any exciting steps for her to do. Unfortunately, the willowy triple threat isn't the only talent to be 'wasted' (Hirschhorn 1981: 420) in a thankless role, with Tim Curry and Bernadette Peters also struggling to make an impact in the small parts of Rooster and Lily (Kael 1984: 345).

The performer that fares best is Carol Burnett. The role of Miss Hannigan may have been 'fool-proof' (Hirschhorn 1981: 420), but Burnett's extraordinary talent for comedy (be it slapstick or delivering punch lines), honed to perfection through decades of show business experience, and her powerful singing voice make for a highly amusing antagonist. Advised by director John Huston to play the character 'soused' (quoted in Kael 1984: 343) when she had difficulties getting a handle on the role, she delivers a masterclass in cartoonish villainy that on occasion – as in her rendition of 'Little Girls' – transcends the surrounding mediocrity.

The shooting of *Annie* was beset by several major problems. The original set designer Dale Hennesy died of a heart attack; the movie went through four different cinematographers; and in the end had to scrap two major production numbers because they turned out unsuitable: 'Let's Go to the Movies' was originally conceived as a number in which Grace, during an outing to the cinema, chases Sandy onto the stage of Radio City Music Hall and then joins a group of dancers all wearing Ann Reinking masks.[9] Yet the footage shot by cinematographer Richard Moore was deemed too dark,[10] the bevy of chorus girls looked frightening rather than enticing, and some of them were also criticized by the studio for not being thin enough (Turan 1982). After long deliberations, the sequence now begins with Grace and Annie singing and dancing in the secretary's bedroom before they go out and watch the Rockettes at Radio City perform a movie-themed tap-dance (at one point forming the inside of a movie camera). That spectacle is then intercut with scenes from George Cukor's 1936 classic *Camille*, starring Greta Garbo.

Another number that had to be completely re-conceived was 'Easy Street'. For this elaborate showstopper, scheduled to run for six minutes on screen, Columbia built an entire street at the cost of $1million, but after shooting on it for a whole week, those in charge decided that the sequence 'looked overstuffed, and as a large-scale celebration of a plan to kidnap a little girl, ... sounded a surprisingly sour note' (Turan 1982). Therefore, nearly two months after the film had officially wrapped, Stark called back Huston and the number's three leads Burnett, Curry and Peters to reshoot the whole song on a studio set. Ironically, the finished number, which consists of Rooster, Lily and Hannigan dancing through the orphanage with the latter clumsily bumping into walls, arches and railings, is the sequence that was afterwards singled out by critics as one of the few to actually work, praised for being 'beautifully timed' (Editors 1983: 148).

Although *Annie* turned into the tenth biggest money-maker of 1982 with a domestic gross of $57 million ('Box-Office *Annie* [1982]'), and later did reasonably well on home video with US rentals of $37.5 million ('Box Office/Business for *Annie*' 1982), the film failed to recoup its enormous budget and was regarded as a major flop; it soon became clear that 'all the movie had going for it was hype' (Editors 1983: 147). *Annie* racked up two Oscar nominations in minor categories,[11] but the general apathy of the public and the overriding critical disdain were better reflected in the attention the movie got from the Golden Raspberry Awards, where it was nominated for 'Worst Picture of the Year', 'Worst Director', 'Worst Screenplay', and 'Worst New Star' (Aileen Quinn). The film also antagonized the show's creators; lyricist Charnin would later accuse the filmmakers of having 'destroyed the essence of *Annie*' (quoted in Rizzo 1996) when they re-rigged the relationships between the characters.

1999: A Disney *Annie* – cost-conscious and charming

In the late 1990s, Craig Zadan and Neil Meron decided to produce a television version of the material for ABC – a channel owned by the Disney Company – and they were adamant not to repeat the mistakes made by the earlier adaptation. The two producers had already successfully charted the waters of the television musical with *Gypsy* (1993), another stage classic whose original screen version (1962) had been botched, and the second remake of Rodgers and Hammerstein's *Cinderella* (1997). Both TV movies had been rating smashes and later went on to secure multiple Emmy Award nominations. This time around, they entrusted Tony Award nominee Rob Marshall not just with the dance numbers,[12] but with directing the whole movie. Once again, a newcomer, Alicia Morton, was hired for the title character.

The story is reset in winter, and although the more overtly political songs are still missing – this is a 'Disney presentation' after all – Marshall includes several succinct visual references to the hardships of the Depression. Both as a concession to political correctness and as a continuation of the successful casting strategy of *Cinderella* (which incorporated actors of varied racial backgrounds), the group of orphan girls is now ethnically diverse. Where everything about the 1982 version vied for your attention by being grandiose and brash, the 1999 remake is clearly budget-conscious and thus rather small-scale, especially in its design elements. There are no excesses here; the TV adaptation keeps its running time to a lean 90 minutes. Quality for a price also seems to have been the *modus operandi* when it came to casting, as the roster of actors consists of one Oscar winner (Kathy Bates as Miss Hannigan) and several performers (Victor Garber, Audra McDonald, Alan Cumming, Kristin Chenoweth) who had made a name for themselves on Broadway but were not (yet) widely known. They provided ample talent but, just like the director, came in rather cheap when compared to TV or movie veterans.

All of this actually works to the remake's advantage: instead of being fanciful, it is direct and, like its 12-year-old lead, pleasantly subdued – we care for this Annie as she has an affecting vulnerability, in marked contrast to Aileen Quinn's 1982 little trouper; the latter who, like Andrea McArdle in the stage production, seemingly had brass lungs, was 'too professional a Broadway babe, there [was] nothing spontaneous or touching about her' (Kael 1984: 344). Marshall's handling of 'Easy Street' is proof – if proof was needed – that a musical number does not have to be extravagant to work; the staging is simple, but fun, and Marshall knows that he can trust his fine cast to deliver the goods.

In production terms, the most elaborate sequence is 'NYC', re-inserted from the theatrical version, which also offers those viewers nostalgic for the 1977 Broadway staging as chance to have a look at original Annie Andrea McArdle, now all grown-up, in the small but noteworthy role of 'Star-to-Be'.[13] Unfortunately, this ode to the 'Big Apple' is one of the show's least accomplished numbers, with uninspired, pedestrian lyrics,[14] a fact that no amount of clever choreography and skillful singing can disguise.

Broadcast on a Sunday night during the sweeps period[15] of November 1999, the production was a major hit for ABC, attracting more than 26 million viewers (Huff 1999), which amounts to an audience share of 24 percent (Windeler 1999). Out of twelve Emmy nominations (including one for 'Best TV Movie'), it took home two of the prestigious awards, for 'Best Choreography' and 'Best Music Direction'; when it was released on home video, it sold more than a million copies (Anon. 2000: 49). It also satisfied the musical's creators,[16] and remains the adaptation which found the most favour with audiences.[17]

A few months before the TV *Annie* went into production, the score received renewed attention from a rather unexpected quarter. Rapper Jay-Z sampled one of the show's signature songs for his second album, and the single 'Hard-Knock Life (Ghetto Anthem)' became a global success; it was nominated for a Grammy in the category 'Best Rap Solo Performance' and was certified by the US Recording Industry Association of America (RIAA) as a gold single in March 1999, finally reaching platinum status 17 years after its initial release, on 15 July 2015 ('Gold + Platinum'). In Britain it reached No. 2 on the charts; additionally, the 12 inch single also peaked in the Top Ten of various other countries, including Canada, Germany, and Sweden.[18]

2014: A (post)modern *Annie* – unconventional and unconvincing

Proving beyond doubt that a more modern treatment of the famous songs would find an appreciative audience, Jay-Z's 'Ghetto Anthem' also provides the link to the latest screen incarnation of *Annie*. In 2010, the rapper's record label Roc Nation released a highly successful single, 'Whip My Hair', by then ten-year-old Willow Smith, daughter of actors Will Smith and Jada Pinkett-Smith. Shortly afterwards, plans were announced for a remake of *Annie* as a showcase for Willow, that would be produced by her parents and Jay-Z and would also include new songs by the latter (Anon. 2011). Yet coming up with a suitable script[19] and pre-production took much longer than anticipated, and by the time cameras started to roll on 19 September 2013, Willow Smith had become too old. Therefore the title character was recast with then 10-year-old Oscar-nominee Quvenzhané Wallis. But replacing the red-haired, freckled orphan with an African American foster kid was just the beginning of what is less a traditional remake than a radical re-imagining (Haun 2014: 22).

'Daddy' Warbucks has been turned from a war profiteer into cell phone billionaire Will Stacks,[20] with telecommunication considered a less offensive and more modern means of having accrued an enormous fortune, while Miss Hannigan is now a disillusioned former background singer who still dreams of having a career in showbusiness. Annie herself was abandoned by her parents in a restaurant called 'Domani' when she was four; she returns regularly to the Italian eatery hoping that her father and mother may show up again.

Unfortunately, these new spins on old material trigger questions that the film does not answer: would a single woman without children of her own, without a

FIGURE 13.1 Quvenzhané Wallis as Annie in *Annie*.

Credit: Village Roadshow Pictures/Sony Pictures/DR/Collection Christophel/ArenaPAL.

regular job or any other qualifications ever be selected as a foster mother by the authorities? We learn that Hannigan gets paid $157 a week per child to look after the five girls in her care, but even with $785 a week, how can she afford that spacious an apartment in New York? And how is it possible for parents to abandon their young daughter in a crowded restaurant without anyone noticing or the girl making a noise?

The set-up of how Annie became a foster kid is also undermined by the basic premise of the 2014 movie, since most of its plot hinges on modern phone technology: everything that happens is immediately filmed and uploaded onto the Internet. Thus Annie encounters her surrogate father when Stack saves the little girl from being run over by a truck, a good deed that immediately finds its way online and drastically improves the billionaire's chances of becoming mayor of the city. After Annie is abducted by the couple posing as her parents, their attempt to flee New York is thwarted by young fans of Internet celebrity Annie.[21] The kids constantly message about their idol on Twitter or take images of her and upload them onto Instagram, which allows Stack and the police to track her every move. Yet when everyone and everything is recorded around the clock, why is there no trace or visual record of Annie's parents? The emphasis on the importance of 'staying connected' via smartphones and the fact that in the end the permanent surveillance saves Annie's life, effectively undercuts the movie's half-hearted attempt at drawing attention to the potential invasion of privacy that our constant reliance on telecommunications technology represents. When Stack's chauffeur Nash at one point remarks to Annie: 'People shouldn't be scared of governments, they should be afraid of phone companies,' he proffers a critical stance the movie afterwards all too willingly abandons. That film studio Columbia is a subsidiary of Sony Corporations, which through another business branch has become one of the world's leading sellers of telecommunication equipment including smartphones, must surely be a coincidence – *honi soit qui mal y pense...*

The film is full of details that either fail to make sense or feel like cursory attempts to reference the original stage musical. Since the plan of having Annie live with the billionaire for a few weeks is a strict business arrangement on both sides and is only meant to secure positive PR by manipulating the media, why do they discuss the scheme in front of two dozen photographers? There is also the unnecessary revelation that Stacks has no hair and wears a toupee – why would Stack be afraid to expose his baldness in a society where shaving your head is a popular fashion choice for men? The social worker Mrs. Kovacevic inexplicably has a heavy Eastern European accent and – a particularly nasty detail – casually steals items wherever she goes. Just as puzzling is the moment that triggers Hannigan's change of heart: when she is told that Annie likes her voice because it 'made her feel good about herself', the audience – having been assaulted by Cameron Diaz's atrocious singing throughout – may be tempted to attribute Annie's comment to Stockholm syndrome.

Yet it is not just the story that has been updated; the score has undergone a comparable transformation to make it more accessible for modern, especially younger, audiences. As director Will Gluck explains: 'There are a couple of the old songs that we didn't touch... . But a fair number, we did change the melody and lyric a little bit' (quoted in Haun 2014: 23). 'We' in this case also included Grammy-nominated songwriters Sia Furler and Greg Kurstin, like the director both novices in the field of musicals, who were hired to rearrange the classic stage hits and to compose additional numbers. 'I Think I'm Gonna Like It Here', 'You're Never Fully Dressed', 'Little Girls' and 'Easy Street' have all been re-mixed, i.e. they have popped-up orchestrations, usually courtesy of an incessant synthesizer drum beat, and added bridges/verses. In addition, the film has four new songs, with one of them ('Moonquake Lake') only used on the soundtrack and another – 'Opportunity' – clearly inserted as Oscar-bait.

In praise of consumerism or from liberal to neo-liberal

The opening scene not only pits a stereotypical red-haired, tapdancing Annie against her fresh-faced updated counterpart, it also suggests that the movie will be outspokenly political as its young protagonist delivers a presentation on Franklin Delano Roosevelt, the Depression and the New Deal in the form of a performance piece, complete with stomps and hand claps: 'Everybody was poor. So pretty much like now, but without the Internet.' Even without pointing out that Annie's summary of FDR's economic policies is decidedly simplistic, as she reduces them to 'work hard and you get rich', one soon realizes that the film's intriguing premise of drawing a parallel between the Great Depression and the current social inequalities in modern America is a red herring, since it is quickly replaced by a glorification of unbridled consumerism. The film's uncritical endorsement of the craving for possessions includes scenes of Annie and her friends enjoying brand new smartphones – a gift from Will Stack – and gorging on free goods at the after party of a movie premiere. These foster kids do not really yearn for finding a loving home; before they even hit puberty, the girls know that what really counts in life is material possessions. As one of them advises the others: 'Save your dreams for good stuff: like shopping with an unlimited credit card.'

Two of the new songs emphasize that all that is needed to succeed in New York is ambition and stamina as exemplified by Annie's 'can do' attitude – as she insists: 'Luck's for suckers.' When Stack takes his young ward on a helicopter tour of his business assets, he explains to her that his success is all down to hard work and drive:

> Stack: The harder I work, the more opportunities I get. See, you gotta play
>   the cards that you've been dealt, no matter how bad the cards are.
> Annie: What if you don't have any cards?
> Stack: Then you bluff.

Apart from the fact that Stack's final retort does not make any sense, it also negates the need for outside interference, when the stacks are unfairly loaded against the player. Annie adumbrates that there are people who not only have none of the aces, but have not even been invited to the table. Isn't it all about 'Opportunity', as her new song underlines? Although that number is awkwardly placed as well as badly integrated, the song's very title emphasizes that what the New Deal provided through government regulation of free enterprise were opportunities for those Americans who were unable to help themselves. Considering the film's initial proposition that the USA faces similar economic hardships today, Stack's subsequent claims that 'anyone can make their dreams come true' is both inconsistent and illogical; furthermore, it is insulting to those millions of American citizens living in poverty. But then this is a film which plays the following scene for laughs: during a photo opportunity Stack tries the food he serves to the destitute and then disgustedly spits the mush into a homeless man's face. Nobody shows any concern for the impoverished man's humiliation.

That Stack finally quits the race to become mayor, thereby effectively rejecting the chance to better the fate of his fellow New Yorkers via politics, is thus only logical for a movie that starts out praising a strong government and then retracts completely, replacing calls for political intervention with the shopworn adage beloved by all neo-liberals, that if you want to succeed '[y]ou gotta want it hard enough and work hard'.[22]

'Realism' and the musical, or undermining the genre

The cast is filled with well-known actors who – with the exception of Jamie Foxx[23] – are not known for their musical skills. Just like Quvenzhané Wallis, Cameron Diaz, Rose Byrne and Bobby Cannavale are not trained singers or dancers. With the whole cast therefore adopting a style of performing that resembles warbling more than proper singing, the filmmakers rely on technical assistance and employ 'slimy AutoTune' (Lapin 2014) for every number, making even Foxx sound neutered.

Nevertheless, there is something more afoot here than a rather peculiar casting strategy, as is confirmed by the remake's approach to choreography. Zacharay Woodlee, who as resident choreographer of TV-series *Glee* has had plenty of experience devising movement for non-dancers, expounds: 'We didn't want any … Broadway-choreography for the movie… . We wanted the movement to be real for every song and every situation' (quoted in Haun: 23). This statement goes right to the heart of the problem with the 2014 movie: the creative team led by director Gluck attempted to make their film more 'realistic', which seems particularly dubious in a genre as artificial as the film musical.[24]

So why then choose this approach for a Hollywood musical? Throughout the film, the viewer becomes more and more convinced that the people behind (and in front) of the camera are embarrassed by the very fact that they are doing a musical. Thus they decided to adopt a self-protective postmodern stance that is supposed to erase the assumed 'silliness' of traditional song-and-dance movies. This becomes evident, for instance, in the incessant insistence on 'motivating' the film's numbers. In the opening scenes a jackhammer, van doors slamming shut, as well as car horns honking in traffic are perfectly in synch with the 'Overture', while regular citizens (sitting on stoops or creating street art) sing snippets of the score. At first this conceit seems like a charming attempt to apprise audiences that the urban sounds of New York City form the soundtrack of our heroine's life, but then it gets more and more desperate and unconvincing with the squishing and scrubbing noises of cleaning house 'initiating' 'It's the Hard-Knock Life' and a chord heard on television triggering 'Little Girls'.

Most telling is the handling of 'Easy Street': PR expert Guy Danilly takes Hannigan to a restaurant where he explains to her his plan of presenting false parents to Annie. On the one hand, his justification for this ruse – to quote from the script, he expects a lot of 'ka-ching' for both of them – lacks persuasiveness as Danilly is clearly both highly successful in his profession and very wealthy; by his own admission, he sleeps in 'silk sheets'. On the other hand, the staging and filming of this number is highly revealing: when Guy breaks into song, Hannigan asks him incredulously: 'Are you singing to me?', before seeking confirmation from the woman sitting at the next table: 'Is this really happening?' The woman nods, and the two actors then get up and execute some simple dance moves. But as their dancing is intercut three times with dialogue snippets that show them sitting back at the table, the audience is allowed to draw the conclusion that all of this takes place only in Hannigan's imagination. Whatever choreography was conceived for 'Easy Street' is further undermined by the camera work and the editing; the former opts mostly for medium shots and close-ups which don't allow the audience to see the performers' feet, and the second exposes the extras in the background as incapable of moving in rhythm with the song. Here and elsewhere the film takes confounding sideswipes at the genre it belongs to: at one moment, Hannigan lectures Guy that 'People love musicals. Bursting into song for no apparent reason. It's magic.' Then she proceeds to give an example by starting to screech to ironically highlight the unreality of 'All Singing! All Dancing' movies. But all genre conventions are silly when looked at from the perspective of 'realism': why do the villains always miss, while James Bond always hits? Why does nobody realize Clark Kent is just Superman wearing glasses, especially when both look like top models?

The last of these desperately hip attempts to undermine musicals as a genre arrives just before the end credits start to roll: because Annie's rescue and the subsequent reunion with Stack and Grace (including the number 'Together at Last') are broadcast on live television, Gluck cuts to a man sitting in a bar who looks at the TV screen and then comments to the fellow sitting next to him: 'Keeps singing and dancing like that, there's no way [Stack] was ever gonna win [the mayoral race].' Thus Stack is basically deemed unelectable because he behaves like a character in a musical. But on that account, neither would anyone ever elect Batman for public office, when he behaves like a character in a comic book adaptation and dresses head-to-toe in black rubber to fight crime. This line may be intended as an ironic postmodern deconstruction of the genre, but comes across as simply another snide comment on the Hollywood musical.

Conclusion or Why some film musicals are bound to fail

Is it really necessary to point out that the magic of musicals lies in the talent on display? Of course nobody admires untalented people who make a spectacle of themselves, but when a great singer or dancer demonstrates her/his craft, it *is* transporting, especially when it is framed by artists behind the camera who know how to ensure that the performance achieves its full impact. Unfortunately, this is not the case with the 2014 *Annie*, as is proven irrefutably by 'Together at Last', a prime example of movie-making incompetence that exposes the people involved as hopeless amateurs: throughout the whole sequence the camera is practically never in the right place, often leaving the right third of the screen as empty space, or cutting off the dancers' feet. The editing, which randomly employs helicopter, long or medium shots, clearly hasn't been planned in advance,[25] so the images not only do not connect in any meaningful way, they also fail to flow. The lead actors and the extras all seem to be moving to different rhythms, with the latter rather embarrassed by their futile attempts to shake their shoulders and hips in synch with the music; as a result the scene stutters along in fits and starts, constituting the exact opposite of a great musical number.

When the 2014 *Annie* came into cinemas, critical reaction was overwhelmingly negative;[26] it later won a Razzie for 'Worst Prequel, Remake, Rip-Off or Sequel'. The film was also a financial disappointment, barely making its money back with global earnings of $133.8 million, most of which ($85.9 million) came from North American cinemas ('Box-office *Annie* [2014]'). The remake thus confirms what the *Consumer Guide* concluded after reviewing the 1982 version: 'Musicals cannot be sloppy' (Editors 1983: 15). Still, even the earlier movie has found an appreciative audience on home video and DVD over the last three decades,[27] and it is to be feared that in the coming years a non-discerning audience of little girls and their parents will resign themselves to this latest abominable incarnation of *Annie* as suitable 'family entertainment', and that it will someday also come to be regarded as a 'classic'.

If the three retellings of *Annie* teach us anything, it is that musicals on both the big and the small screen are doomed to fail when they are made by people who have no trust in the material and are not passionate practitioners or ardent fans of the genre: the only director who managed to pull off the transfer from stage to screen was Rob Marshall, a real 'Broadway Baby', whereas the lack of enthusiasm for musicals is visible in practically every frame of the Huston and Gluck versions. And as all musicals remind us, you cannot create or experience something magical, if you don't believe.

Notes

1   For 'Best Musical', 'Best Book', 'Best Songs', 'Best Choreography', 'Best Sets', 'Best Costumes' and 'Best Actress in a Musical' (Dorothy Loudon).

2   In London, the show, although a sizeable hit, wasn't quite as popular. With Sheila Hancock in the role of Miss Hannigan, the 1981 West End production closed after 1,485 performances, while a 1998 revival, starring Lily Savage (Paul O'Grady's alter ego), lasted for five months.

3   Others examples include *L'il Abner* (1956), *You're a Good Man, Charlie Brown* (1967), *Andy Capp* (1982) and *Spider-Man: Turn off the Dark* (2011).

4   That storyline was later adjusted: it turned out that Warbucks had only faked his own demise and he returned to the living in 1945 – after the death of Gray's *bête noire*, FDR.

5   'We'd like to thank you: Herbert Hoover/For really showing us the way/We'd like to thank you, Herbert Hoover/You made us what we are today' (Meehan *et al.* 1977: I–3–17).

6   Columbia's president Frank Price was hoping for box-office receipts of $200 million (Turan 1982).

7   Act One lasts approximately 75 minutes, while Act Two clocks in at 58 minutes (Gottfried 1980: 155, 157).

8   Charles Strouse observed on the set that Huston seemingly had no 'emotional connection' whatsoever with the little girls he directed (Strouse 2008: 243).

9   This conceit is taken from *Shall We Dance* (1937), in which Fred Astaire, looking for his beloved in the film's final number, is faced with countless chorus girls all wearing a mask of Ginger Rogers's face.

10 Moore was subsequently fired and replaced with Richard Kline.
11 'Best Art Direction – Set Decoration' and 'Best Music, Original Song Score and Its Adaptation or Best Adaptation Score'.
12 Marshall had been Emmy-nominated for his choreography in *Cinderella.*
13 McArdle's cameo got great notices from many US critics (Windeler 1999: 54), but I personally find her hyper-charged performance crude and charmless.
14 'NYC/What is it about you/You're big/You're loud/You're tough/.../Too busy, too crazy/Too hot/Too cold/Too late/I'm sold/Again/On NYC' (Meehan *et al.* 1977: I–6–40).
15 The sweeps period is the time each fall, winter, and spring when television ratings are accrued and studied and advertising rates are reset.
16 In the words of Charles Strouse: '[It] made all the authors and millions of viewers very happy' (Strouse 2008: 243).
17 Its average rating on the Internet Movie Data Base is 6.7 ('Annie [1999]'), slightly above the 6.5 rating for the 1982 film ('Annie [1982]') and much higher than the 5.2 rating for the 2014 remake ('Annie [2014]').
18 For a detailed listing see the song's Wikipedia entry ('Hard Knock Life [Ghetto Anthem]').
19 The first draft for the remake was written by two-time Oscar-winner Emma Thompson, but later revisions by director Will Gluck and Aline Brosh McKenna proved so extensive that Thompson is no longer credited in the finished film (Haun 2014: 23).
20 It's also likely that the name change was intended to prevent any associations with a company which nowadays is one of the most famous in the world, but wasn't yet a global brand in 1977, Starbucks.
21 A Twitter account set up in her name immediately attracts 1.3 million followers.
22 After discovering that Annie has never learned to read (a fact that is never properly explained), Stack starts a campaign against illiteracy; once more, the movie propagandizes private initiative over government intervention.
23 Foxx has cut five studio albums, with two of them (*Unpredictable*, 2005; *Intuition*, 2008) going platinum in the USA.
24 Before even asking the question why the filmmakers felt that this was the right style for their re-imagining, it should be highlighted that a similar angle to shooting a picture seems inconceivable for any other genre: an action film where the stunts are supposed to look like real-life car accidents and the fist-fights looks like schoolyard fisticuffs? A Western where the showdown depicts two fumbling unfit men unable to hit a target that stands right in front of them? A comedy where the performers have the comic timing and the punch lines of untrained actors?
25 Surprising for a film with editing as haphazard as this one, the end credits list a storyboard artist, Grant Shaner.
26 Its Rotten Tomatoes score is a dismal 27 percent ('*Annie* [2014]' [b]).
27 The average rating for the movie on amazon.com, based on 2,770 votes, is an astonishing 4.5 out of 5 stars, with more than three quarters of the consumers (76 per cent) giving it the highest rating of 5 stars ('Annie [Special Anniversary Edition]').

Filmography

Annie (1982). Directed by John Huston. Special Edition. DVD, Sony Pictures Home Entertainment 2004, ASIN: B0000WSTKQ.
Annie (1999). Directed by Rob Marshall. DVD, Walt Disney Home Entertainment 2004, ASIN: B0001IM99G.
Annie (2014). Directed by Will Gluck. DVD, Sony Pictures Home Entertainment 2015, ASIN: B00M0GMAKK.

Bibliography

'1982 Domestic Grosses'. www.boxofficemojo.com/yearly/chart/?yr=1982. Accessed 16 April 2016.
'*Annie* (1982)'. www.imdb.com/title/tt0083564/?ref_=tt_rec_tt. Accessed 9 April 2016.
'*Annie* (1982) Special Anniversary Edition'. www.amazon.com/Annie-Special-Anniversary-Aileen-Quinn/dp/B0000VCZKM/ref=sr_1_1?ie=UTF8&qid=1460884112&sr=8-1&keywords=annie+dvd+1982. Accessed 16 April 2016.
'*Annie* (1999)'. www.imdb.com/title/tt0207972/?ref_=fn_al_tt_4. Accessed 9 April 2016.
'*Annie* (2014a)'. www.imdb.com/title/tt1823664/?ref_=tt_rec_tti. Accessed 9 April 2016.
'*Annie* (2014b)' www.rottentomatoes.com/m/annie_2012/?search=Annie. Accessed 12 August 2015.
Anon. (2000). 'DGA Nom to Marshall', *Back Stage* 41(6), p. 49.
Anon. (2011). 'Will Smith Planning *Annie* Remake with Jay-Z', *Screen Rant*, 20 January. http://screenrant.com/will-smith-annie-jay-z-sandy-97354/. Accessed 16 April 2016.
'Box-Office *Annie* (1982)'. www.boxofficemojo.com/yearly/chart/?yr=1982. Accessed 15 April 2016.
'Box-Office *Annie* (2014)'. www.boxofficemojo.com/movies/?id=annie2014.htm. Accessed 12 April 2016.
'Box-Office/Business for *Annie* (1982). www.imdb.com/title/tt0083564/business?ref_=tt_dt_bus. Accessed 15 April 2016.
Editors of *Consumer Guide* with Phillip J. Kaplan (1983). *The Best, Worst & Most Unusual: Hollywood Musicals*. Skokie: Publications International Ltd.
Flinn, Denny Martin (1997). *Musical! A Grand Tour. The Rise, Glory, and Fall of an American Institution*. New York: Schirmer Books.
'Gold + Platinum: Jay Z, Hard-Knock Life (Ghetto Anthem)'. www.riaa.com/gold-platinum/?tab_active=default-award&ar=Jay+Z&ti=Hard+Knock+Life+%28Ghetto+Anthem%29. Accessed 16 April 2016.
'Hard Knock Life (Ghetto Anthem)'. https://en.wikipedia.org/wiki/Hard_Knock_Life_(Ghetto_Anthem). Accessed 12 April 2016.
Gottfried, Martin (1980). *Broadway Musicals*. New York: Harry N. Abrams, Inc.
Haun, Harry (2014). '*Annie* Reanimated,' *Film Journal International* 117(12), pp. 22–24.
Hill, Logan (2012). 'All in the Family. How *Little Orphan Annie* Went from a Conservative Icon to a Mouthpiece for Hope and Change', *Business Week* 4307, p. 90.
Hirschhorn, Clive (1981). *The Hollywood Musical*. London: Octopus Books.
Huff, Richard (1999). '*Annie* Helps Seal Total Victory for ABC Family Viewers, Pro-vide Net with Nielsen Edge', *New York Daily News*, 10 November. www.nydailynews.com/archives/entertainment/annie-helps-seal-total-victory-abc-family-viewers-provide-net-nielsen-edge-article-1.855227. Accessed 9 April 2016.
Kael, Pauline (1984). *Taking It All In*. New York: Holt, Rinehart and Winston.

Knapp, Raymond (2005). *The American Musical and the Formation of National Identity*. Princeton/Oxford: Princeton University Press.

Knapp, Raymond (2006). *The American Musical and the Performance of Personal Identity*. Princeton/Oxford: Princeton University Press.

Knapp, Raymond, Mitchell Morris and Stacy Wolf (eds) (2001). *The Oxford Handbook of the American Musical*. New York: Oxford University Press.

Lapin, Andrew (2014). '21st-century Musical Still Haven't Found a Way Out of the Woods,' *The Dissolve*, https://thedissolve.com/features/expositions/876-2014s-musicals.-might-just-save-us.-all/. Accessed 8 March 2016.

Meehan, Thomas, Charles Strouse and Martin Charnin (1977). *Annie. Libretto/Vocal Book*. New York: Musical Theatre International.

Mordden, Ethan (2003). *One More Kiss. The Broadway Musical in the 1970s*. New York: Palgrave Macmillan.

Rizzo, Frank (1996). 'Another Tomorrow for *Annie*, Goodspeed's Guardian Angel', *The Courant*, 29 September, http://articles.courant.com/1996-09-29/entertainment/9609270030_1_charnin-first-goodspeed-opera-house-broadway-annie/2. Accessed 9 April 2016.

Stempel, Larry (2010). *Showtime. A History of the Broadway Musical Theater*. New York/London: W. W. Norton & Company.

Strouse, Charles (2008). *Put on a Happy Face. A Broadway Memoir*. New York/London: Union Square Press.

Turan, Kenneth (1982). 'Hollywood Puts Its Money on *Annie*', *The New York Times*, 2 May. www.nytimes.com/1982/05/02/magazine/Hollywood-puts-its-money-on-annie.html. Accessed 9 April 2016.

Windeler, Robert (1999). 'TV *Annie* Wins Big', *Back Stage* 40(50), p. 54.

Wursthorn, Michael (2010). '*Little Orphan Annie* Won't Be Singing "Tomorrow" Anymore, Tribune Ends Comic Strip after 86 Years', *New York Daily News*, 12 June. www.nydailynews.com/entertainment/orphan-annie-won-singing-tomorrow-anymore-tribune-ends-comic-strip-86-years-article-1.184746. Accessed 13 April 2016.

Young, William H. and Nancy K. Young (2002). *The 1930s. American Popular Culture through History*. Westport: Greenwood Press.

14

LONDON ROAD

The 'irruption of the real' and haunting utopias in the verbatim musical

Demetris Zavros

The use of documentary material appeared in musical theatre at least as far back as Joan Littlewood's *Oh! What a Lovely War* (1963), but it was not until *London Road* (2011) when the potential for a more experimental approach to the 'setting' of verbatim material was used in musical theatre. *London Road* began as an experiment, part of a scheme at the National Theatre Studio in 2007 where composers and writers were brought together to workshop ideas and exchange practices; among them were Alecky Blythe and Adam Cork. Based on Blythe's purist approach to verbatim theatre practice, all the text was directly transcribed from a lengthy series of interviews she conducted in Ipswich between December 2006 and July 2008, after the community of Suffolk became the epicentre of the events surrounding the tragic serial killings of five female prostitutes. First performed in the Cottesloe auditorium on 14 April 2011, the stage performance transferred to the Olivier on 28 July 2012 and was adapted into its cinematic version and released in 2015 (Live Film Premiere and Q&A, 9 June; general release 12 June).[1] Both the spoken text and song lyrics were derived from the interviews as recorded (including all the 'ums and errs'), with the metre, pitch and rhythm of the music following the patterns of the original recorded speech as closely as possible (Original cast recording CD inlay, 3–4). This practice can arguably be viewed alongside a long tradition of exploration into the relationship between music and language that has been at the centre of some more experimental music theatre work (e.g. Berberian, Berio, Stockhausen, Ligeti, Wishart, Maxwell Davies, Gaburo, etc.). The 'verbatim' aspect, however, offers new possibilities of examining this relationship through a different prism of critical and practical engagement, especially within the context of musical theatre. The initial jarring between 'verbatim' and 'musical', and the reconciliation between the hyper-naturalistic approach of verbatim and the heightened language of musical theatre aesthetics (Young 2012: 101–102), introduces only one in a series of initial binaries that this performance dismantles.

In doing so, I believe, *London Road* offers a very fertile space of research into how we can re-evaluate avenues of exploring not only aesthetic practices but also political potential through this hybrid genre.

In his thought-provoking *The Musical as Drama* (2006) Scott McMillin suggests a conceptualisation of the aesthetics of musical theatre based on 'disjunction' rather than the more traditional idea of integration. The primary instigator of this disjunction is the existence of two distinct 'orders of time' embedded in the form: book time and lyric time. Book time is concerned with the linearity of the story to be told; lyric time with a different mode of expression that suspends linear time in favour of elaboration and extension through repetition and difference. Lyrical moments/songs/numbers break away from the cause-and-effect logic of the dramatic plot (and its connection to Aristotelean action, recognition, reversal, etc.) encapsulated in the book, and it is this insertion/disjunction between the two different orders of time that gives the genre its distinct aesthetic as well as its political potential. McMillin explains that 'the resistance that occurs between book and number wants to rule out simple answers to questions of identity' as well as invite the subversive and the 'multiple' (McMillin 2006: 191). Richard Dyer also proposes that the 'deeply contradictory nature of entertainment forms' (Dyer 2002: 27) is what provides them with their political potential and situates this contradiction in musicals between the narrative and the numbers. The contradiction, he explains, is analogous to 'the heavily representational and verisimilitudinous (pointing to the way the world is, drawing on the audience's concrete experience of the world) and the heavily non-representational and "unreal" (pointing to how things could be better)' (ibid.: 27). He supports that in order to 'fit with prevailing norms', the genre has a tendency to resolve 'contradictions at all levels in such a way as to "manage" them, to make them disappear' (ibid.). At the same time, the film musical creates a utopian sensibility which lies at the core of its escapist aesthetics in a way that allows the 'latent' possibility (Dyer 2002: 35) that solutions to the problems are not always normalised through the capitalist system that produced them in the first place.[2] The temporal distinction made by McMillin between lyric/number and book, as well as Dyer's distinction between narrative and number, seem to become problematized in *London Road* initially because the division between spoken and sung material is almost obliterated (in a near absolute integration), but I would argue that the result of this particular occupying of the 'troubled space between song and spoken dialogue' (Whitfield 2011: 310) is a lot more profound than it may originally appear.

Lib Taylor's illuminating article (2013) examines *London Road* alongside other performances of contemporary documentary theatre that have introduced a critical frame (in this instance, the music) in their re-presentation of the primary source material to 'provide a dynamic strategy for the destabilisation of the real to promote critical insight' (Taylor 2013: 370). Taylor suggests that while Blythe has constantly striven for the transmission of 'truth' and 'authenticity' through the exact replication of every vocal detail in the original utterance, in *London Road* 'the use of song becomes the mechanism for a reflexivity that Blythe had not envisioned' (ibid.: 373).

I will initially be expanding on this discussion in the context of the postdramatic,[3] which Taylor alludes to in her article, in an effort to rethink her assertion that 'voice in *London Road* both claims and defers authenticity and authority, in as much as the voice signifies presence and the embodiment of identity but the reworking of speech into sung tunes signals the absence of the real' (Taylor 2013: 379). I will offer a slightly alternative perspective into the performance based on my belief that 'the reworking of speech into sung tunes' does not signal an absence as much as an 'irruption of the real' as discussed by Lehmann (2006). I will consequently compare the stage and film versions of the musical in relation to their contiguity to the 'real' vs a utopian sensibility that accompanies the more traditionally escapist approaches to the film musical.

The re-composition of 'the everyday' into the aesthetic form; performing community through (a special type of musical) song

London Road focuses on the coming together of a community 'to heal itself' (according to Blythe 2012: vii, Introduction to *London Road*) during and after the events surrounding the murders of the five female sex-workers. This is what becomes the central dramaturgical axis; not the events of the murders/the murderer or the victims as such. What we are presented with as the performance unfolds on stage is *the reactions* to the events; and this creates an interesting 'peripheral' focus of a near-postdramatic effect.[4] The 'thematic centre' supersedes the more traditional concerns with 'plot' as it focuses on exposing the multifarious ways we express ourselves as we per-form communities.

While the building of a community can be found at the core of a huge selection of performances throughout the history of musical theatre, and it becomes an essential component of the utopian sensibility proposed by Dyer, the difference here is that the coming together of the community, and the variety of ways of performing that coming together, are not offered as an 'unreal', utopian escapist vision. Rather, it is presented as a process under a magnifying glass: a musicotheatrical forensic examination that uses style and abstraction in a way that it unveils (and reveals in an exceptionally unique – if not unprecedented – way) aspects of the 'real' that partake in that performative situation. In this way, *London Road*, resists the utopian as well as the uniformly constructed community often inscribed in escapist forms of entertainment. Instead of creating a shared space of shared wants, needs and opinions, and proposing through song and dance utopic alternatives 'as solutions to real needs and lacks like scarcity or the lack of community' (Nichols 1985: 221), *London Road* carefully presents the formation of community as the residents come together to overcome the trauma of the murders, not as a uniformly constituted ensemble/chorus but as a community that partakes in the 'multiplicity' of decent. As the audience witnesses this 'coming together', the reality of per-forming community surfaces as a real political and ethical dilemma.

Cork describes *London Road* as a choric theatre, where 'the choral presentation of this story in particular seems to underline the ritual aspect of human communal experience' (Blythe and Cork 2012: x). In discussing his process of setting the source material to music, he explains that it progressed from a 'slightly freer hand' to a more 'faithful' approach to the verbatim ideals and a forensic detail in the transcription of the original speech material. The resulting melodic lines are composed together into musical structures which 'are often built out of key elements of the transcribed voice, translated into harmonic progressions, or rhythms in the accompaniment' (ibid.: ix). Consequently, the 'poetic' transformation of the source material (the reframing of the prosaic and quotidian form of the linguistic document through a heightened aesthetic level) happens on a continuum of levels/ degrees between the essentially unaltered, absolute forensic transcription (austere replication of rhythm/pause, prosody and all other paralinguistic attributes) and the heightened moments of harmonisation, polyphony and counterpoint in choral numbers.[5]

In between these extremities, the composition retains several degrees of poetic relationship to the original document. But in their artifice, these variously heightened moments retain the connection to the source material in such a way that they don't only critically frame it (and I am not suggesting that this layer of signification is entirely dissolved), but crucially always point towards it: not so much as an 'absent' authentic original, but as a stylised repetition in itself. This musical recomposition is not *imposed* as a critical frame only to reveal the artifice and constructed nature of (the) performance. It is a poetic accentuation of the musical attributes that *already exist* in the language, which comments on the artificiality of the source material itself: the performativity inherent in what we might usually assume to be (expressions of the) 'real/authentic/personal' in the everyday – in 'real talk'.

The nature and structure of the sung sections always point to the musical structural components as inseparably connected with not only the linguistic, but crucially the paralinguistic, aspects of the prosaic text: 'how' it was spoken. As early as his 1987 article on verbatim theatre, Dereck Paget almost prophetically instigates that 'there is something almost musical in these idiosyncratic rhythms. Whereas "ordinary" speech requires the actor to learn, interpret and "play" them through his/her vocal physical skills, here it is a case, indeed, of "the actor as instrument"' (Paget 1987: 331). In interview with Paget, Salt, Robinson and Thacker discuss the idiomatic everyday speech and the 'repetitiveness, the stumbling, the oddity' and the 'extraordinary juxtapositions, loops and circumlocutions' as a trademark of 'real talk in verbatim theatre as opposed to other highly stylised dramatic language' (ibid.: 330).

While 'repetition' is usually one of those attributes that pertain to the 'lyric time' domain and the 'unreal' that McMillin associates with musical numbers, here the 'songs' supersede the traditional popular song function of representing a clearly delineated 'emotional, physical and formal excess' which occurs as a temporary disruption of the narrative (Laing 2000: 10). Repetition, a notion par excellence musical[6] but also inextricably part of the nature of 'real talk', becomes thematised on a variety of levels that are specifically illuminated in *London Road* because of the continuum opened up between spoken and sung vocal utterance in the compositional process.

> STEPHANIE: But – ye know. (Pause.) Cuz I fink, if yer gonna dies, yer– gonna die – so… (Beat, laughs.) Thass that'ss **my** – point of view. (Beat.) Yeah.
>
> (Blythe and Cork 2012: 12, emphasis in the text)

Even when the words are spoken (as in the example above), the performative aspect of the prosaic utterance is magnified as a result of our becoming attuned to and aware of the musicality inscribed in 'how' the text was voiced. In this instance the musical intonation is what underlines the irony behind the statement that follows the trite truism: 'that's *my* point of view'. Repetition exists here on at least two levels: on the one hand, as part of the idiomatic quotidian utterance, and on the other, as we become specifically attuned to the citational nature of the 'apothegm' both in terms of content and expression (intonation, accent, etc.). So, contrary to more conventional uses of musical repetition, here repetition does not create a temporal stasis that contradicts 'putative diegetic time' in a way that it makes the song enter the unreal, as much as it invites a different reflection upon every utterance;[7] a different kind of listening perception. In consequence, not only does (the abstraction in) repetition not absolve the utterance from its cultural baggage, but it is in fact signalled as a process that produces it. The musical treatment of the utterance exposes the culturally performative nature of repetition qua (musical) repetition. And this reflexivity is produced exactly as the musical component flirts with, but constantly resists, the full-blown entering into the unreal/utopian space of 'lyric time'.

Stage: 'treading the borderline' between reality and construct in actu

The potential inscribed in the treatment of the verbatim utterance is capitalised upon through the aesthetic opportunities of the theatrical medium (and the related notions of liveness and presence). In the stage versions, we are welcomed and invited to participate in this coming together and sharing of the community (in its performance). The experience is intimate and palpable (especially on the Cottesloe stage) at the same time as the theatrical/presentational frame is explicitly evident. Some of us handshake with the actor (Nick Holder) who 'welcomes' us into the theatre, at the same time as Ron – the character – 'welcomes' us into the starkly minimalistic representation of the 'church hall just off London Road'. We hear the original audio recording of Ron's actual speech over the PA, which slowly fades as Holder repeats and extends the speech into the first live utterance in the performance; *sung* (?):

'Song: 'Neighbourhood Watch AGM'
RON. *Good evening. (Beat.) Welcome. (Beat.)*

The characters address the audience in a bewildering hybrid *Sprechgesang* without the clear signification of a different time order. The performance of the vocal hybrid happens in a quasi-'lyric time' order, which always retains a clear connection to a concrete reality that supersedes the 'book'. In the theatre space we come in direct 'encounter' with the performance, which reasserts its rights to multiplicity and subversion through a multi-layered experience of temporality as it immediately 'forces us to realise "that there is no firm boundary between the aesthetic and the extra-aesthetic realm"' (Lehmann 2006: 101). It is exactly in the 'indecidability' of 'whether one is dealing with reality or fiction' that the 'irruption of the real' resides (ibid.: 101). Here, the theatrical situation invites us to be immersed in its diegetic universe at the same time as it signals its connections to the past event and the liveness of the present.

In both the stage versions, the 'hyper-realist' approach of Blythe's transcription and performance of the words is to a certain extent coupled with the ostensibly stark (though expressly imaginative) theatrical staging of the interviews in different settings, always somehow incorporating a clear framing,[8] almost constantly presenting the spoken lines in quotation marks. The theatrical presentation indicates how the residents perform their community as it is in the process of becoming, but in essence also how all the different communities (residents/reporters/and sex-workers) are performed through repetition, stylisation and citation.[9] Due to the multi-roling in the stage version (as opposed to the film), the same actors are constantly seen interchangeably performing different communities, exposing the 'act of performing community' as a stylistic repetition, a performative aspect of our culturally shaped realities. It is because of the continuum opened up through the musical treatment of the documented text that the stage performance exposes the theatrical sign as 'always a "sign of a sign"' (Fischer-Lichte 1992). But, in extension, the stage performance invites an 'irruption of the real' by creating, through the performance idiom itself , 'an awareness of the semiotic character' of the material products it borrows from the specific culture and 'consequently identify[ing] the respective culture in turn as a set of heterogeneous systems of making meaning' (to slightly paraphrase Erica Fischer-Lichte in Lehmann: 102).

Because the characters essentially never 'break into song', in the replication of the original utterance we hear/witness the labour (even as it is stylised) in finding the 'right words' to communicate and express opinions and ideas.[10] It is almost as if we witness the 'sign' in the process of becoming. And it is a sign that completely disorientates us when we first come in contact with it, it's not one that we can immediately recognise, categorise and ascribe meaning to, but one we have to work for, to figure out. This disorientation in the initial encounter with the sign pierces the fictional frame by making us aware of our reception process.

The theatre audience role becomes unstable (at once participant/observer/witness) as we become aware of the sense of unattainability of the limit of an absolute/exact performance of the immensely complicated vocal score.[11] By constantly witnessing the possibility of the 'accident', we begin to strongly invest in our participation in the event. We want the performers to get it right (as much as we – originally at least – like the characters who invite us into their 'space') and in an extension of that, we join into the experience of the community in a strongly visceral way.[12] And it is a rather visceral shock that results from our buying and investing into the frame of the community in the here and now of the theatrical event, simultaneously with being aware of the usual contract which expects us to 'willingly suspend our disbelief' when, indeed in disbelief, we hear Kate Fleetwood/Julie utter:

> What's happened's happened but I' m not sad. (*Beat.*) Ya know (*Beat.*) I'd still shake his hand. I'd love to just shake his hand an' say 'Thank you very much for getting rid of them.'
>
> (Blythe and Cork 2012: 65)

The 'now of the drama' and the 'now of the theatre' (Robert Edmond Jones in Power 2008: 43) fuse in the climactic moment of the stage version; the 'real' violently irrupts as three performers (clearly representing sex-workers who survived the events) creep onto the stage from darkness and stare at the audience for a chilling 80 seconds of 'un-organised' (un-stylised, non-categorised) time that opposes itself to both the musical, the fictive and even the theatrical. The threatening and unnerving silence that ensues floods the theatre along with our experience of their 'intrusion'[13] in the space (among the dimly-lit sofas representing the 'living rooms' of the community). We come face to face with the process of perception (as again we are thrown into a crisis of non-recognition) in this liminal, multi-temporal state, but through that we also become aware of our implication in the political and ethical dilemma; we are not involved in an act of 'reception' but we've become active participants in an 'encounter' (Boenisch 2010: 171). The spectatorial distance that we normally assume is shaken as we are forced in the long chiasmic caesura to experience the break from a closed off (but already porous) diegetic universe and 'to wonder whether [we] should react to the events on stage as fiction (i.e. aesthetically) or as reality (for example morally)' (Lehmann 2006: 104).

This moment not only provides the climax but also frames the rest of the performance and our experience of it in the theatrical now that already always lies underneath and threatens the surface of the 're-presentation'. The political inscribed in this 'poetic' reframing of the 'document' supersedes the didactic tone of the Brechtian estrangement techniques and does not propose specific solutions/answers.[14] It makes us co-responsible not only in the production of meaning, but ethically implicated in the questions that are unearthed from the source material. We become aware of how the 'treading of the borderline of the real unsettles this crucial predisposition of the spectators: the unreflected certainty and security by which they experience being spectators as an unproblematic social behaviour' (Lehmann 2006: 104). At its core the performance is asking us to consider how *we* 'per-form community' without excluding 'the other'. And this happens not as we enter the un-real and utopian, but as we become fully aware of our reception process while we 'tread the borderline' between 'real' and 'construct'.

While I am not suggesting that *London Road* is a postdramatic performance per se, I think that it exposes some of those mechanisms behind the reality of theatre that Lehmann bestows on the postdramatic. The film differentiates – while not entirely separating itself from the original theatrical aesthetics – in ways that mean that the 'irruption of the real' as discussed here is marred in the transplantation into the new medium, as I will argue in the following section. And this happens in a variety of ways as the film re-establishes connections with 'the dramatic' at the same time as it reconnects with the non-realistic/spectacular and more utopian aesthetics of the film musical.

Number and narrative in the film: expanding and demarcating

The aesthetics of the film allow the creative team to play with an expansive pallet of interpretative possibilities, and 'expansion' indeed lies at the core of this film adaptation. While retaining a sense of 'theatricality', the film departs from the minimalist theatrical settings and staging solutions and takes advantage of camera travelling sequences, scale, editing and movement in a 'cinematic treatment' that clearly lies outside a realist orientation/approach. The multi-roling which pervaded the small ensemble aesthetics of the stage version is now replaced by a substantially expanded cast that includes celebrity actors (Olivia Coleman in the role of Julie; Tom Hardy and Anita Dobson). Chorus/ensemble sequences and choreography become a lot more elaborate to fill the more expanded filmic space mirrored in the musical space of the orchestrations. The film also departs from the original dramaturgical structure as it follows the linear chronological succession of the events. The result is the creation of dramatic suspense (and the expectation of a cause-and-effect logic) that begets a stronger sense of a 'book time', or at least the constant illusion of one, as well as a distance from the in-between temporality inscribed in the choric/ritual quality which was so crucial in the stage performance. As all these (expansive) changes happen, the rift between narrative/book and number/lyric broadens and we move from the 'irruption of the real' towards the utopian ideal, as I will be discussing in the following section.

Expanding: ghosting celebrity and the cinematic 'tracing' of the speech/song continuum

Actors with star quality change the audience perception of the relationship between actor and character. Marvin Carlson discusses celebrity status (in his celebrated *The Haunted Stage*, 2003) and the 'aura of expectations' (Carlson 2003: 67) that ghost the actor based on role types in which they have appeared, but also expectations of their particular approach (ibid.: 67). This often is seen to collide with the 'role' as Michael Quinn describes it (in his 1990 essay 'Celebrity and the Semiotics of Acting') because it 'exceeds the needs of fiction, and keeps them from disappearing entirely into the acting figure or the drama' (Quinn in Carlson 2003: 86). The celebrity status of the star cast members here, and the different types of 'haunting' related to that, create an 'overdetermined quality' that I believe potentially collides not so much with the role and the fictive dramatic universe, but with exactly the potential disruption of that dramatic cosmos and the emanating politics of the 'encounter'.

Olivia Coleman, who plays the role of Julie in the screen adaptation, is an extremely popular and likeable actress. However, the fact that we can recognise Olivia Coleman's 'voice' in the role of Julie because we all 'know' Coleman's style of acting through a series of roles on TV and film (e.g. *Peep Show*, *Twenty Twelve*, *Broadchurch*, and BBC's *Fleabag*) adds an extra layer of complexity to the dynamics of perception and the notion of 'authenticity'. The ghosting of the actress's voice becomes disruptive of the process that Blythe was so categorically insistent on. Most importantly, however, it is perhaps not the ability to re-enact the vocal utterance exactly as much as the audience's belief that the actor does – 'as an instrument'– that allows the critical reflection back onto the 'how' these utterances are signs of a community in performance. Because Coleman's voice is inadvertently haunted by her celebrity status, that belief is slightly unfulfilled.

At the same time Tom Hardy's celebrity status haunts his role in an additional way. In the film, the 'Shaving scratch' song is transplanted from the County of Suffolk pub (stage version) to the claustrophobic atmosphere of a taxi and re-composed. Hardy's casting as the taxi driver who seems a rather plausible potential murderer,[15] lends the film more of the quality of an 'addictive forensic thriller set to music' (Bradshaw 2015, *The Guardian* review of the film). The

FIGURE 14.1 Tom Hardy as Taxi Driver Mark in *London Road*.

Credit: Collection Christophel/ArenaPAL.

audience almost expects that the star will have a central role in the 'action' of the film: 'Is it him, is it him?'[16] Here Hardy's celebrity status and 'remnants' of previous roles[17] (States in Carlson 2003: 67) haunts our experience of the film and introduces the sense of a stronger narrative drive, dramatic suspense and linearity that becomes a lot more central to our experience of the film. The separation between book and lyric times becomes more prominent; as a sense of a teleologic linear ('dramatic') narrative is introduced, the 'how' of the performative utterance becomes almost of secondary importance and consequently enters the domain of the abstracted, the 'lyric' and un-real.

The difference in approach and a stronger separation between 'lyric' and 'book' time is signalled from the beginning of the film. The first few bits of interview material appear completely unaccompanied and 'in preparation';[18] the musicality of the words is not at all pronounced. The indicative/indexical 'ask away then' by one of the characters/residents establishes the connection with 'the interview', ends the introduction and signals the beginning of 'the journey' as the music enters in true suspense-full filmic fashion. Words and music are initially entirely separate. This first instance of music originally appears as non-diegetic (accompanying the first view of 'the Road') as the orchestra is allowed to take on the usual allusion of omniscience (with the use of leitmotifs from pieces that will appear later in the film). However, as the camera moves from the street into the first house (in a rather oneiric fashion), we realise that the musical accompaniment could very well be diegetic, accompanying the newscast about the murders (the sound design supports this assumption). The play between diegetic/non-diegetic continues as the music transposes in time with the camera travelling movement into the subsequent living rooms we visit, in a markedly filmic, non-diegetic fashion. The reports only gradually begin to take on a more musical tone, eventually clearly in tune and in time with the musical accompaniment; and the collapse of diegetic and non-diegetic music happens at the same time as the lines between song and speech are obliterated. The reportage of the news stories/bulletins is composed into a contrapuntal chorus that enters the musical domain while also retaining connections to the dramatic situation, no less through the use of TV monitors and accompanying localisation of sound. This smooth transition and play with the conventions of music and song in film is indeed ingeniously constructed. However, it already heralds a big difference between the stage and film versions and their connection to 'the document'.

Even as this opening sequence exemplifies/traces the poetic continuum from speech to song, the 'transitory' manifestation is arguably *demonstrating* rather than allowing us to experience the in-between straight away (as the stage opening did) and, at the same time, is critically subsumed within a more linear dramatic framework. This initial separation of music and words in the opening of the film signals a different approach to the connection between the two that will persist throughout the film in its use of musical underscoring.[19]

After the climax of the contrapuntal news reports (at the end of the introductory sequence), the camera follows Coleman/Julie outside, where she performs the first slightly more musicalized utterance by a resident: 'Everyone is very, very nervous.'

As she leaves the camera frame, we remain on the road to seal the filmic establishing of place, all complete with the orchestral eerie and ominous cadence/modulation (from F minor to A flat minor) –and the accompanying driving ostinato – with the close-up on the 'London Road' sign. The use of leitmotifs in the original stage music, which is mainly comprised of the songs, is rather minimal. As Cork explains:

> I didn't foresee much cross-pollination of musical motifs from one song to another, although I did want the identity of each individual song to be clear; I felt this was the only way I could create musical meaning from this un-versified, spontaneously spoken text.
>
> (Blythe and Cork 2012: viii)

In the film version, however, the (admittedly masterful) fragmentation of some of the original songs (as in the case of 'Everyone is very, very nervous') and the underscoring required to accompany the expanded cinematic sequences results in the use of leitmotif material as usual 'to guide the listener through the performance, providing atmospheric associations with characters, and reminding the audience of earlier moments in the story' (Taylor 2009: 83). While this was essentially obsolete in the stage version, through these changes the film creates a sense of a plot driving the action which, again, triggers a clearer separation between lyric and book times. There is, however, a special type of the use of leitmotif in the underscoring in this film musical that almost has the potential to reverse the more usual function of the orchestra. When the melodies utilised in the orchestral underscoring are directly related to the rhythms and intonations of the original utterance (one that we have already heard), and especially in a way that it escapes a clearly discernible or easily surveyable melodic structure, the orchestral underscoring itself seems to be 'haunted' by the original words uttered; the paralinguistic 'how' of the utterance becomes a ghost that hovers inside the orchestral music. This type of ghosting is almost constantly in competition with the sequential dramatic linearity produced as the orchestra is confined to more conventional devices of dramatic underscoring (such as the suspense-full cadence mentioned above).

Expanding further: 'refrain' and performative reality vs the ominously unreal

The intimate reportage-like setting of the residents' interviews in their homes is clearly demarcated from the more expansive space (mall/market, bus, courthouse, etc.) of the ensemble numbers, which are choreographed and filmed in a dream-like manner (even as both movement and set are using some form of the 'pedestrian' or 'real'). The residents come together for the first time in the choral repetition of (Coleman's) 'Everyone is very, very nervous and very unsure of everything' set at the Christmas market. The nervousness of the dramatic situation is coupled with the peculiarly eerie Christmas spirit (through the use of the juxtaposed, ironic 'It's the most wonderful time of the year' and the monstrously oversized[20] and nauseatingly gyrating Santa statue among other Christmas paraphernalia that take on a grim air of a (capitalist) dystopia). This 'nervousness' overflows the narrative situation and enters the un-real (via the 'supernatural' or 'unearthly') by clearly self-reflexively signalling the first synchronised ensemble movement/choreographed sequence almost as a 'miracle'. This 'un-real' coming together into an ensemble, as well as a 'breaking into (choral) song' moment, marks the first coming together of the people as they start to form a community (in fear). But the separation between the 'real' (as that which is consistent with everyday life experience) of the 'book' time order and the 'lyric time' of the number is not only clearly demarcated, but unmistakeably underlined.

This demarcation has a pervasive effect in the way that repetition is perceived in the film version as part of the unreal 'lyric time'. The film is using substantial 'realistic' continuity editing in an effort to achieve the unity with diegetic time, but also engages with a more 'oneiric logic of time' (Dyer 2012: 24) in the more extensively choreographed numbers through a variety of cuts and shots ranging from space-expansive overheads to extreme close-ups. However, these possibilities of editing mar the performative function of repetition as it had surfaced both in the 'musicalisation' of the 'real talk' utterance and its exploration on stage. Every repetition of the song choruses in the film is accompanied by a completely different sequence of camera shots, either in the interests of driving the plot or, more usually, enveloped within the 'lyric time' of the ensuing numbers.

In the stage version the possibilities are far fewer within the reality of the theatrical time frame, but every time the performers repeat the 'refrain', there is an explicit and intelligible indication that they are repeating it. While this is partly subsumed within the characteristics of lyric time, in other cases, in the absence of a clear distinction between lyric and book times in the stage performance (coupled with the special peculiarity of the musicalised verbatim material as discussed earlier), the repetition takes on another role. Because time and space are shared between auditorium and stage even when, through song, time is expected to be elongated or suspended, every re-iteration of the 'refrain' makes testament to the fact that exact repetition is impossible. There is always a degree of slippage, or what Foucault calls the sudden illumination of multiplicity' within the similarity that exists in repetition (Foucault 1970: 232) and Deleuze ascribes to a secondary type of repetition; not a 'naked' or 'bare' repetition, which simply reproduces its original, but a dynamic repetition, evolving through time (Deleuze 2004: 27).

In the stage version of the 'Shaving scratch' song[21] there is a rather unconventional chorus/'refrain'.

> MARK. *I uhm. I I I've studied serial killers since in my mid-teens. It doesn't mean I am one but err…*
> GRAHAME…*Ooh I don't know. Ha, ha,ha*
> MARK. *I just er, find it interesting. But as I say just to emphasise that doesn't make me a serial killer so…*
> GRAHAME. *Oh that'll get you off the hook/after all that you've just said!*
> MARK. *That's alright then*

The performers make an effort (to the actual labour of which we are witnesses) to repeat the words/lyrics in the exact same way (if they are to be 'true' to the document[22]), while the rest of the elements of the *mise-en-scène* change with every repetition.[23] This exposes 'repetition' as a stylised simulation at the same time as it thematises the notion of 'slippage' in every reiteration in real time. The effort to repeat the original as closely as possible is what makes the slippage even more evident in the staged version. Not only do we become aware of our own reception process as this effort to repeat is always (by definition) failing, but we become witnesses to the event of slippage. The repetition of the musical 'refrain' in performance evades the unreal/utopian space of 'lyric time' to which it is usually ascribed.

The film tries to capture the 'reality of the moment' and its transient quality by recording the voices live on the set and not resorting to the more traditional dubbing of the singing (avoiding what Dyer calls (2012: 16) 'severing the body from the voice' by cinematic technology in the presentation of songs). At the same time, the ensemble numbers sung by the chorus are occasionally treated through rather intimate sound localisations (effectively, extreme sound 'close-ups' coupled with their visual counterparts) as we focus down to a particular performer's voice within the ensemble sound. This last technique produces an illusion of a (hyper)'realistic' approach and also acts as a faint reminder of performing these pieces live.[24] However, it is indeed marked by the artifice of the medium, which at the same time allows a microscopic look into its source as well as producing a mediated distance from it, highlighting its reception as the result of a careful post-production mix. Perhaps more importantly, this localisation also interrupts our ability to experience the 'slippage' in the repetition of the (choral) refrain, which was so intrinsic to the process of reception in the stage performance. To experience the specifically transitory nature of the event of its utterance (through a difference in repetition in time) is essential to the connection between the performative nature of the theatrical and the everyday. The film audience becomes less able to viscerally and experientially appreciate the connection between the original and the aesthetic reconstitution (or the 'real' and the 'performed') that Lehmann so profoundly connects to the 'irruption of the real' in performance (Lehmann 2006: 99–104).

The promise of utopia: happy endings?

The spatial expansion in the film finds its apogee in the climactic final sequence, which includes the imposing structure of a water tower; space, 'distance' (and separation) become thematised in this enlarged frame/space. The film ends on an incredibly colourful[25] 'London Road in Bloom' party that essentially mixes and overlays a multiplicity of realities , including the representation of real events, a real space (but not the real London Road), as well as performers and creative team members joining the celebration alongside original residents and local ones. This mixing of 'realities' relates to the in-between achieved on stage, but, here, it is obviously of a different order.

In the stage version the 'sex-workers' claimed a very 'real' space in a very real time (as discussed earlier), one that makes clear the porosity of the real/performed binary and introduces the irruption of the real. They do, in fact, appear in the film a lot more frequently than the stage version. However, throughout the film the 'claiming of space' happens in an abundantly voiceless/silent, ghost-like manner,[26] supported in the end by their placement higher up – at a distance from the street (which almost creates a conflation between the living and the murdered).

Kate Fleetwood, representing one of the sex-workers in the film, walks through the street party and is offered a balloon by one of the girls before she climbs the steps up the tank tower to watch the party from a distance. Another girl waves at her and they both release their balloons to the sky. This inclusive time-space allows the co-existence of reality and performance, but at the same time proposes an oneiric (complete with slow-motion sequences), unattainable, utopian vision of a new generation that reaches out to the ghostly presences of the sex-workers (nobody else seems to acknowledge them) into their world. This utopic world does fall within the aesthetic that was opened up by the filmic re-imagination, which separated the 'real', book time and the lyric time of the 'spectacular' numbers. The spectral claiming of space within the utopia is the filmic equivalent to the sex-workers' staged-but-real, uncomfortable, silent, long stare into the audience. The disparity between the two experiences, I believe, exemplifies the rift between the stage and the film; the 'irruption of the real' vs the proposed utopia as a form of political engagement with the source material.

The stage performance ends with a reprise of the 'London Road in Bloom' song. The peculiarly nostalgic quasi-waltz-like music at the end creates a very hybrid form of song, one which at first glance seems to partake both in lyric time and utopian escapism. We are almost invited to participate in the utopian sensibility inscribed in the nostalgia of the music as well as the endless list of flowers (coupled with the actual smell of flowers on stage).[27] Yet the song also provides us with a feeling of uncertainty, both in terms of the constantly changing metre irregularly alternating between 3/4 and 2/4 around the more regular refrain and in the uncertainty of the residents' sketchy gardening/floricultural knowledge. This apprehensive quality dislocates the end away from the usual utopian 'happy ending' as it points to another convention of musical theatre song-writing. This 'list-song' inescapably mirrors another list we were presented with in the performance: 'The Five Counts of Murder' – Tania Nichol, Gemma Adams, Anneli Alderton, Paula Clennell, Annette Nichols. The stage version does not allow for a complete entrance into an unproblematised utopian space. Ending the stage version with the song creates a very distinct feeling of unease, which in the film is replaced with a hopeful vision of utopia in the bittersweet yet hopeful 'happy ending'.[28]

Even as the film tries to imbue the ensemble numbers with the 'multiple' and the 'real/pedestrian' by entering into a clearer separation between book and number, it veers towards the utopic and the unreal and – as the community comes together in synchronised movement sequences – perhaps closer to the limit of the conformity associated with such understandings of utopia (even if more usually than not those moments are presented as dystopic). So while it does not entirely abdicate the connection to the 'real' in favour of the 'utopian', the film tends towards the latter limit through its clearer separation between book and number; narrative and spectacle. The stage version, on the other hand, flirts with the utopian sensibilities of lyric time but rests closer to the former limit; it capitalises upon the special peculiarity of the verbatim musicalized utterance and employs the transient nature of the theatrical event to expose the forming of community as a performative aspect of our culturally shaped realities. In so doing it opens up a space for critical reflection through the 'encounter' which compels us to deal with questions, but tries to avoid proposing utopian solutions.

The ontology of the verbatim musical allows for a significant new reconceptualization of the possibilities engendered in the form, not only in terms of a shift in aesthetics, but also the resulting political engagement. It has the potential to utilise its connection to the 'document' to captivate the audience beyond the aesthetic, political and ideological implications of the 'utopian', by drawing on its relationship with the multiplicity inscribed within the 'real'. *London Road* demonstrates how we inextricably perform our identity as part of the communities we build, not by tapping into the escapist politics of entertainment (and the utopian sensibility inscribed in the non-representational aspects of the musical idiom), but through the 'politics of perception' that surface from the exploration of the continuum between music and language; the 'real' and the 'performed'.

Notes

1 All stage and film versions were directed by Rufus Norris.
2 In musicals Dyer supports that this contradiction can also be found 'within numbers, between the representational and the non-representational, and within the non-representational due to the differing sources of production inscribed in the signs' (Dyer 2002: 27).
3 In *Postdramatic Theatre* (2006), Lehmann refers to 'documentary theatre' as a genre in the geneology of the postdramatic. He notes the documentary post-dramatic tendency in that 'suspense is not located in the process of events but is an objective intellectual, mostly ethical one: it is not a matter of a dramatically narrated, 'discussed' world' (55). In conjunction to this he notices that documentary theatre 'demonstrated a tendency toward oratorio-like forms, towards *rituals* (56). Interestingly, the discussion follows a section on lyrical drama/'poetic theatre' and the example of Tardieu's *Conversation-Sinfonietta* (1960), which 'builds a musical composition out of fragments of everyday language' (54).
4 In as much that at least it does not concern itself with 'narrative in its linear organisation around conflict', but a 'reporting' on the events in a variety of ways (Harvie and Lavender 2010: 12).
5 Cork also discusses those instances where the approach of building the song out of the musicality of the words themselves 'led towards the wrong sort of song', which led to the composition of a musical '"container" unconnected with the musical surface of the

words, but inspired by their literal content, or the tone in which they are spoken, or the mood of the situation in which they are uttered, or that of the situation which they describe' (Blythe and Cork 2012: x). Even in this instance, however, the resulting container makes a clear statement on the artificiality of the original utterances, especially as they connect to specific professional jargon and etiquette (e.g. the reporters' fugue-like contrapuntal ensemble outside Ipswich Crown Court – 'The Five Counts of Murder').

6 Deleuze and Guattari's notion of the 'refrain' as the 'content proper' of music (2007).

7 Cork also suggests that 'hearing the natural speech patterns sung in this way can have an effect of distancing the audience from the "character", and even the "story", but in a positive way that alters the quality of listening. Making spontaneously spoken words formal, through musical accompaniment and repetition, has the potential to explode the thought of a moment into slow motion, and can allow us more deeply to contemplate what's being expressed. This seems particularly interesting when many different people speak about the same thought or feeling' (Blythe and Cork 2012: x).

8 Often by directly addressing the audience even in dialogic parts, e.g. at the market place – between the Orange girl and the Radio DJ.

9 I will return and expand on the use of repetition on stage in the comparison with the film.

10 Expressed by Ron in the opening 'AGM' as: 'An' they always say "it's not the right choice a words". Yeah' (p. 8).

11 Michael Schaeffer is one of the cast members (stage and film versions) who have testified that the process of rehearsal and learning the material was rather challenging: 'It was incredibly difficult. There's some amazing musicians in our company. The girls were known to go off to the toilet for a little cry; I think some of boys were as well' (Film, Live Premiere Q&A).

12 There is actually a song entitled 'Cellular Material' (Blythe and Cork 2012: 49) that thematises the notion of 'getting it wrong' in a musical dramatisation of the impossibility of reporting the newscast (by reporter Simon Newton) because of the complexity of the reportage language/phraseology while trying to avoid using the word semen. Interestingly, repetition is used here as part not only of the musical number (which works as a 'refrain' in development) but also of the dramatic situation. The song, however, points directly to a very real possibility as it arises from the stage performance itself: getting it wrong (but, in this case, not being able to do a 'retake'). In addition, implicitly this variation on every repetition musically indexes the inherent performative side of real-life language and the slippage involved in 'every repetition' of utterance, which I will return to later.

13 This sense is indeed a result of their markedly noticeable absence from the performance (due to its 'peripheral' focus), one that has been criticized by a number of reviewers. However, (the politics of) their absence is indeed *also* presented in quotation marks on stage; an absence that is imperative for this moment of 'encounter' that erupts in their 'intrusion' and 'disruption' of our spectatorial gaze.

14 For a very illuminating discussion of postdramatic 'Reality theatre' performances and a political engagement that supersedes the Brechtian in favour of the 'encounter', see Garde and Mumford (2013).

15 An expectation also supported by recent castings.

16 The question in the film acquires a double meaning. As the two girls on the bus look down into the taxi, we see him for the first time, like they do. 'Is it him?' connects both to the inquiry regarding the murderer simultaneously with the question about the star actor. One of the girls in the bus answers a twofold 'Yeah' in evident elation.

17 E.g. Bronson in *Bronson* and the Kray Brothers in *Legend.*

18 Almost as the equivalent to the sounds of the tuning band instruments in the pre-show of the stage version.

19 In addition, the residents' prosaic text does not undergo any poetic heightening/ re-composition in this opening sequence; it is only the journalist reports that appear to be musically performed at the beginning of the film. The performative aspects of the journalistic utterances will, in fact, become a lot more central in the film, accentuating the critical comment on their stylised and formal performances as they perform *their* community, with all its ritualised (and vacuous) etiquette.

20 Achieved through the use of close-ups on facial features and low angle camera shots.

21 This is the song that gets transplanted into the 'taxi' sequence in the film.

22 After all, as Blythe explains 'with both the songs and the spoken text the audio has remained intrinsic to the process, so that the original delivery as well as the words are learned' (Blythe and Cork 2012: vi).

23 On a first level, this shows something essentially reflexive (and honest) about the stage performance: while the words are repeated verbatim, the *re-framing* can change the meaning substantially; e.g. from 'real concern/nervousness' to 'ironic comment', etc.

24 Arguably this also exemplifies the notion of the 'chorus in descent' mentioned earlier: a community comprised of individual voices (metaphorically and literally through the help of technology).

25 The film also uses gradual colour saturation and intensity in a metaphoric reflection of the community's journey.

26 In the taxi sequence 'It doesn't make me a serial killer', which is overlaid with 'Silent Night', they appear in 'blurry' slow motion shots (almost David Lynch-like surreal images) as we see them from inside the moving taxi.

27 I am indebted to Sarah Whitfield for this note.

28 'London Road in Bloom' will not be reprised until after the end of the film, well into the titles sequence.

Bibliography

Blythe, A. and Cork, A. (2012). *London Road.* London: Nick Hern Books.

Boenisch, P. (2010). 'Towards a Theatre of Encounter and Experience: Reflexive Dramaturgies and Classic Texts.' *Contemporary Theatre Review* 20(2), pp. 162–172.

Bradshaw, P. (2015). '*London Road* Review: Gripping, macabre verbatim musical about real-life serial murders.' *The Guardian,* 11 June. www.theguardian.com/film/2015/ jun/11/london-road-film-review-gripping-macabre-verbatim-musical. Accessed 20 November 2016.

Carlson, M. (2003). *The Haunted Stage: The Theatre as Memory Machine.* Ann Arbor: University of Michigan Press.

Deleuze, G. (2004). *Difference and Repetition.* London: Continuum.

Deleuze, G. and Guattari, F. (2007). *A Thousand Plateaus: Capitalism and Schizophrenia.* London: Continuum.

Dyer, R. (2002). *Only Entertainment.* London: Routledge.

Dyer, R. (2012). *In the Space of a Song: The Uses of Song in Film.* London and New York: Routledge.

Fischer-Lichte, E. (1992). *The Semiotics of Theatre.* Trans. J. Gaines. and D.L. Jones. Bloomington: Indiana University Press.

Fisher, A.S. (2011). 'Trauma, Authenticity and the Limits of Verbatim.' *Performance Research* 16(1), pp. 112–122.

Foucault, M. (1970). 'Theatre Philosophical.' In T. Murray (ed.) (1997), *Mimesis, Masochism and Mime: The Politics of Theatricality in Contemporary French Thought.* Ann Arbor: University of Michigan Press.

Garde, U. and Mumford, M. (2013). 'Postdramatic Reality Theatre and Productive Insecurity: Destabilising Encounters with the Unfamiliar in Theatre from Sydney and Berlin.' In Jurs-Munby, K, Carroll, J. and Giles, S. (eds) (2013), *Postdramatic Theatre and the Political.* London: Bloomsbury Methuen Drama.

Harvie, J. and Lavender A. (2010). *Making Contemporary Theatre: International Rehearsal Processes.* Manchester: Manchester University Press.

Julien, M. (2015). 'From There to Here: Canadian Stage's Production of *London Road.*' *TDR: The Drama Review* 59(3), pp. 161–168.

Laing, H. (2000). 'Emotion by Numbers: Music, Song and the Musical.' In B. Marshall and R. Stilwell (eds), *Musicals Hollywood and Beyond.* Exeter: Intellect, pp. 5–13.

Lehmann, H-T. (2006). *Postdramatic Theatre.* Oxon: Routledge.

McMillin, S. (2006). *The Musical as Drama.* Princeton: Princeton University Press.

Nichols, B. (ed.) (1985). *Movies and Methods.* Vol. II. Berkeley, Los Angeles, London: University of California Press.

Paget, D. (1987). '"Verbatim Theatre": Oral History and Documentary Techniques.' *New Theatre Quarterly* 3, pp. 317–336.

Power, C. (2008). *Presence in Play: A Critique of Theories of Presence in the Theatre.* Amsterdam, New York: Rodopi.

Radosavljevic, D. (2013). *Theatre-Making: Interplay Between Text and Performance in the 21st Century.* Basingstoke: Palgrave.

Taylor, L. (2013). 'Voice, Body and the Transmission of the Real in Documentary Theatre.' *Contemporary Theatre Review* 23(3), pp. 368–379.

Taylor, M. (2009). 'Integration and Distance in Musical Theatre: The Case of *Sweeney Todd.*' *Contemporary Theatre Review* 19(1), pp. 74–86.

Whitfield, S. (2011). 'Two Different Roads to New Musicals in 2011 London: *London Road* and *Road Show.*' *Studies in Musical Theatre* 5(3), pp. 305–313.

Young, S. (2012). 'London Road (review).' *Theatre Journal* 64(1), pp. 101–102.

CONCLUSIONS

George Rodosthenous

At the time of publication of this book, the musical film *La La Land* (2016) has caused a sensation among musical theatre and non-musical theatre lovers. *La La Land* became the talk of the 2017 Oscar ceremony (for many reasons) and surprisingly it won, amongst others, seven Golden Globes awards (in all seven categories it was nominated for, including Best Motion Picture), six Oscars (including Best Achievement in Directing, Best Achievement in Music Written for Motion Pictures and Best Achievement in Music Written for Motion Pictures – Original Song) and five BAFTA awards (including Best Film and Best Director)[1]. This highlights a renewed interest in the film musical, but it is crucial that we view this success within its social-contextual framework because

> the escapist tone of the film has been commented on as a contributing factor for its overall success. Musical comedy films have a long history of lifting America and the rest of the world out of depressing political and social times and it seems that once again this light-hearted yet substantial film has certainly ticked a lot of boxes even amongst non-traditional musical theatre fans.
>
> (O'Hanlon 2017)

In a way, this verifies once again that audiences are *still* viewing musicals as a form of escapism. However, the increasing richness and complexity of the film musical is now unparalleled. *La La Land* unfolds on two levels of enjoyment: for the audience members who encounter musicals for the first time, it works as a bittersweet film full of nostalgia and an ambivalent (non-)happy ending; for the experts, it functions as a puzzle of intertextual references and a homage to the MGM post-war golden era. And there is plenty there for both camps to enjoy.

But then, there are musicals such as *Dancer in the Dark* and *London Road* that have entirely revolutionised the film musical genre. The twenty-first century musical 'interrogates, parodies and subverts its own status' (Roesner 2016: 652) and as audience members we are becoming more alert to these underlying qualities. Musicals are all around us, part of us and responsible for billions spent within the cultural industries where film companies such as Universal Pictures and Disney are increasingly backing and developing stage musical theatre work. The stage version of *Wicked* has already brought in more than $4 billion[2], and this implies that the forthcoming film musical (December 2019) is expected to have substantial financial returns.

Increasingly, there is a need to reconsider the 'political' in musical theatre, in a way that resists the utopian and critically engages with the performative, and in so doing we can seek for a deeper understanding of how musicals work. How do musicals use music in a way that circumvents the stasis usually inscribed in the 'oneiric' conceptualisation of the popular song 'refrain' (Zavros this volume: 222–224)? The recent trends of singing live on camera, non-musical celebrity casting, raising audience expectations (because of the excellence of the stage original), deviations from the canon norm and the introduction of performance of 'the self' have shaped contemporary appreciation and experience of film musicals. In this way, the music exposes the performative in the real, and how the way the music is performed relates to our performative construction of identity. We belong to certain social/national/cultural classifications because we perform according to the rules. We cut and repeat them and thus we perform our belonging to them.

The Twenty-First Century Musical: From Stage to Screen offers new readings, insights and provocations on how those codes, behaviours and strategies are now changing the way in which we construct and view new musical theatre on film. 'Musicals are often, wrongly, regarded as a globalized art form of effortless innocence that is designed to bring simple pleasures to its audiences. What musicals truly offer their audiences are complex interdisciplinary creations that allow their creators to articulate the audience's deepest fantasies, fears, and anxieties through a subversive presentation of song and dance' (Rodosthenous 2014: 52). Film musicals stay with us, in our collective memory, console us and offer repeated excitement; by being reliable, precise and inexhaustible, they sustain and promote their political status and impact.

Notes

1   For all the awards please check here: www.imdb.com/title/tt3783958/awards. Accessed 1 May 2017.

2   See   www.hollywoodreporter.com/news/universals-wicked-movie-adaptation-gets-903598   and   www.forbes.com/sites/hughmcintyre/2016/03/16/wicked-has-now-made-over-1-billion-on-broadway/#76862292134c. Accessed 1 May 2017.

Bibliography

O'Hanlon, Dom (2017). 'La La Land – a Movie Musical for the Modern Age.' www.londontheatre.co.uk/theatre-news/west-end-features/la-la-land-a-movie-musical-for-the-modern-age. Accessed 13 March 2017.

Rodosthenous, George (2014). 'Relocating the Song: Julie Taymor's *Jukebox Musical Across the Universe* (2007).' In D. Symonds and M. Taylor (eds), *Gestures of Music Theater: The Performativity of Song and Dance*. New York: Oxford University Press, pp. 41–53.

Roesner, David (2016). 'Genre Counterpoints: Challenges to the Mainstream Musical.' In Robert Gordon and Olaf Jubin (eds), *The Oxford Handbook of the British Musical*. Oxford, New York: Oxford University Press.

INDEX

Note: "n" denotes a footnote (e.g. 113n6 refers to note 6 on page 113). References to images are italicised.